THROUGH
THE
CORRIDORS
OF
POWER

'Alexander is a mature civil servant who had carried out several assignments, national and international, with exemplary competence. I saw him at his best when he was Principal Secretary to Indira Gandhi during her second term as Prime Minister. Always sober, objective, clear and concise, he used to guide Indira Gandhi against any precipitate action. He was no "yes man", and courageously put forth his views even if unpalatable at the moment, but always meticulously carried out decisions even if he disagreed with them.'

R. Venkataraman (former president of India in
My Presidential Years, 1994)

✧

'In ancient times advice to those involved in statecraft came from the *Rajguru*. Dr Alexander is not only a *Rajyapal* [Governor] but also a *Rajguru*.'

Atal Behari Vajpayee (former prime minister of India,
while releasing Dr Alexander's book,
India in the New Millennium, on 29 April 2001)

✧

'I cannot tell you how much I appreciated your talk on Gandhiji.... I have heard a number of talks at the Bhavan, but I have not heard one to equal your performance.

I was not scheduled to speak [on that occasion]. But after hearing you, I could not help getting up and telling the audience that they have heard the greatest talk ever delivered in that auditorium [at Bharatiya Vidya Bhavan, Mumbai].'

Nani Palkhivala (eminent advocate and writer,
in a letter dated 1 February 1999 to the author)

THROUGH THE CORRIDORS OF POWER

AN INSIDER'S STORY

P.C. ALEXANDER

HarperCollins *Publishers* India
a joint venture with

New Delhi

HarperCollins *Publishers* **India**
a joint venture with
The India Today Group

First published in India in 2004

Third impression 2004

HarperCollins *Publishers*
1A Hamilton House, Connaught Place, New Delhi 110 001, India
77-85 Fulham Palace Road, London W6 8JB, United Kingdom
Hazelton Lanes, 55 Avenue Road, Suite 2900, Toronto, Ontario M5R 3L2
and 1995 Markham Road, Scarborough, Ontario M1B 5M8, Canada
25 Ryde Road, Pymble, Sydney, NSW 2073, Australia
31 View Road, Glenfield, Auckland 10, New Zealand
10 East 53rd Street, New York NY 10022, USA

Typeset in 11/14.3 Sabon
Atelier Typecraft

Printed and bound at
Thomson Press (India) Ltd.

Contents

Preface

DURING MY LONG PUBLIC SERVICE CAREER, SPANNING OVER FIVE AND A half decades, the most memorable and satisfying period was my tenure as Prime Minister Indira Gandhi's principal secretary. Even though she had not known me closely before I started working with her in 1981, I realized within a short period after joining the Prime Minister's Office (PMO) that she was dealing with me as an individual whom she implicitly trusted. She had stated, in unambiguous terms, that she wanted me to get involved not only in government matters but also in political and party matters. In other words, she was keen that I handle *all* issues with which she was concerned. Since I had opted for retirement from the Indian Administrative Service (IAS) a few years before I joined the PMO, I was not constrained by any service regulations in undertaking such a multifunctional role. Some of my friends and well-wishers had cautioned me that if I expressed my opinions frankly about issues on which she had strong views of her own, she would not relish my candour; however, my experience, to put it mildly, was quite different. I found that she not only welcomed my forthright expression of views but also respected me more because of my firm stand. I was a ringside witness to all the major events of this period and privy to all the relevant information:

both classified and non-classified. I have tried to give a full account of these events (except where I feel national interest is involved) without holding back any important facts as I feel I owe it to posterity to do so.

✧

I had known Rajiv Gandhi closely ever since I joined the PMO in 1981. When he became the prime minister (after the assassination of Indira Gandhi on 31 October 1984) he continued the tradition set by his mother in bestowing great trust in me and not treating me merely as a civil servant for assisting him in government work. My relations with another prime minister, P.V. Narasimha Rao (1991–96), were equally close though I did not occupy any official position in the PMO. Rao and I had developed mutual respect for each other during the period when he was a minister in Indira Gandhi's and later in Rajiv Gandhi's cabinet. We had maintained our cordial relationship whether in office or not. I have recounted my experiences with both these prime ministers in as objective a manner as possible.

While I was fortunate in developing and sustaining excellent relationships, apart from confidence and esteem, with three prime ministers in my journey through the corridors of power, I hit a roadblock during the term of office of some other occupants of this post. I had had the unpleasant experience of incurring the wrath of Prime Minister Morarji Desai (1977–79) when I was secretary in the Ministry of Commerce. On certain issues, I stuck to my guns despite intense pressure being exerted on me by the Prime Minister's Office. I opted for retirement from service to preserve my self-respect; I refused to make any compromise as far as my integrity and commitment to duty were concerned. Again, I felt hurt when V.P. Singh (prime minister during 1989–90), who had known me well during his tenure as the Union commerce minister, arbitrarily sacked me when I was governor of Tamil Nadu, along with some other governors, on the ground that I was a political appointee of the previous Congress Government and therefore could not be trusted to be impartial and fair in the new dispensation. I have narrated my experiences with both these prime ministers.

The most surprising and distressing experience of my career was when, in mid-2002, the Congress leadership vehemently opposed the proposal made by Prime Minister Atal Behari Vajpayee and other leaders of the National Democratic Alliance (NDA) seeking its support for fielding me as a candidate for the post of president of India. What saddened me the most was the campaign of personal vilification launched by certain Congress leaders in an attempt to justify their obstinate opposition to my candidature. Equally hurting was the fact that the Congress leadership had instructed its party Members of the Legislative Assembly (MLAs) in Maharashtra to cast their votes for my opponent in the election to the Rajya Sabha, for which I was a candidate (after my resignation from the post of governor of Maharashtra). Despite such stiff opposition I was elected by a three-fourths majority. However, the fact that the Congress leadership could go to this extent to jeopardize my chances really amazed me. I felt I should share with the people at large the full facts relating to my candidature for presidentship, which I have attempted to do in the first chapter itself.

This book sums up the story of my life right from my childhood years to the present. I have been fortunate enough to occupy some senior positions that are not in the normal reach of a civil servant. I did not possess the advantages bestowed by factors such as birth, caste or community; nor did I seek political backing for reaching these positions. I do admit that luck plays its role in everyone's life and I had perhaps a larger share of it than many others. However, I have also had to face frustrations and disappointments in my career. My intention in narrating the experiences of my life, both pleasant and bitter, is to convey to the readers in general and to the younger generation in particular the very important lesson I had learnt in life, namely, that if one is firmly committed to certain lofty values and remains determined not to compromise with one's self-respect, integrity and sense of duty in order to gain short-term advantages, one would not have any cause for regret in the long run.

I belong to a generation that grew up in the colonial years and witnessed the transition from foreign rule to freedom. As one born and brought up in the former state of Travancore, I had witnessed the obdurate resistance of the princely order to the winds of change sweeping across the country and its ultimate capitulation to people's power.

As one of the earliest entrants to the IAS, I was a witness to, as well as a participant in, the transition from the colonial to the democratic system of administration. I have dwelt upon some of my experiences during my early years in the IAS in Tamil Nadu and in Travancore-Cochin. My years in Central Government service were marked by professional advancement, out-of-turn promotions and due recognition. Though I had to end my service in the IAS in the most unexpected and unpleasant circumstances, what seemed as an end to my career fortunately turned out to be the beginning of several more challenging assignments both at the national and international levels. I had also the privilege of serving as governor of two major states in the country, Tamil Nadu and Maharashtra, for a total period of about twelve years.

Most autobiographies tend to be exercises in self-indulgence, if not self-aggrandizement; or else, they seek to exonerate the writers from all blame and culpability. In this volume, I have tried to avoid these pitfalls, but it is for the readers to judge for themselves the veracity or otherwise of my statements.

My publishers have done an excellent job in bringing out my book. I am particularly grateful to them for their valuable suggestions for editorial changes. I also acknowledge with thanks the secretarial assistance received by me from Parvathy Venkitachalam, K.S. Malik and G.P. Khare, private secretaries, in the making of this book.

New Delhi   **P. C. Alexander**
31 March 2004

ONE

From Raj Bhavan to Rajya Sabha

We deem it as an outstanding positive achievement to get Alexander out.

We won't say yes to anybody without consulting him [President K.R. Narayanan] since we have used his name to keep Alexander out.

IT MAY APPEAR STRANGE THAT I AM BEGINNING THE STORY OF MY LIFE by recounting the events that took place a few months before my leaving the Raj Bhavan, Mumbai, for the Rajya Sabha, Delhi, though logically, they should have found a place towards the end, if one were to follow a chronological sequence. But so much of misinformation and malicious propaganda had been unleashed against me by a few individuals operating from Delhi in pursuance of their one-point agenda of eliminating me as a candidate for the presidential election of July 2002 that I feel it necessary and appropriate to share with the public the full facts about my candidature in the first chapter itself.

Let me start with the two epigraphs to this chapter. They are taken from a statement that Jaipal Reddy, the chief spokesman of the Congress Party, made during the course of an interview to Harish Khare, a senior journalist with *The Hindu*, on 11 June 2002.

Reddy's observations, to say the least, were in bad taste by any standards; however, they were important as they reflected the attitude of a group of individuals in the Congress Party who were determined to ensure that I be kept out of the contest. His observations probably displayed the overebullience of a recent returnee to the Congress fold after a long sojourn in other pastures, though, unlike a few other colleagues of his in the party, he did not have any malice or ill-will against me personally. In a mood marked by glee and exultation at the fact that I was out of the race, he went to the extent of claiming it as 'an outstanding positive achievement' of his party. This observation was bad enough, but to add that the Congress Party had used the name of President K.R. Narayanan to keep me out made the situation worse because it revealed the astonishing fact that some Congress leaders had no inhibitions in using even the president's name in their efforts to prevent me from becoming a candidate for the presidential election. Reddy did not reveal whether Narayanan had knowingly allowed the Congress leaders to use his name for this purpose, or whether he was kept in the dark regarding their true intentions while persuading him to stay on in the race. Such a stand would have given Narayanan the impression that they would be able to garner enough votes to ensure his victory. Either way, it was a most astounding statement for the chief spokesman of the Congress to make.

Now to the inside story of 'off with Alexander'.

It all started with my acceptance of the offer of a second term as governor of Maharashtra by the new National Democratic Alliance (NDA) Government (of which the Bharatiya Janata Party was the chief constituent), which had come to power at the Centre on 19 March 1998. In the normal course, I would have completed my five-year tenure as governor on 12 January 1998 and I had begun well in advance all preparations to leave the state. To my pleasant surprise the Shiv Sena–Bharatiya Janata Party (SS–BJP) leaders in the state conveyed to me their wish that I should stay on for one more term as governor and that their respective party high commands would gladly offer me a second term if I would indicate my willingness to accept such an offer. I felt happy and even flattered that a person with my background of close association with three Congress prime ministers in the past (Indira Gandhi, Rajiv Gandhi and P.V. Narasimha Rao) was being asked to continue for another term as governor by the SS–BJP Government in power both at the Centre and the state. I took this offer as a tribute to the impartial and non-partisan stand I had always taken in my dealings with all political parties in my five years as governor.

Within three weeks after the new NDA Government was sworn in at the Centre, the Union home minister, L.K. Advani, telephoned me on 11 April 1998 offering a second term and expressing the hope that I would accept it. I did. I was sworn in again on 21 April 1998, thus becoming the first governor of Maharashtra to have had the honour of being appointed for a second term.

The entire media in Maharashtra and all parties, including the Congress, welcomed the decision. I felt, without any shadow of doubt in my mind, that the Congress leaders in Delhi would also gladly accept this decision, as it was a vindication of the stand taken by the Congress prime ministers in the past in that they had entrusted me with several highly responsible positions in the government one after the other. But my feelings were misplaced. I was way off target in what I expected from the top Congress leadership in Delhi, though I came to know about it several months later.

The Congress president, Sonia Gandhi, as a member of the Indira Gandhi household, was personally well aware of the esteem and regard that both her husband and her mother-in-law had for me even though she had no role in politics those days. My duties first as principal secretary to Indira Gandhi and later Rajiv involved frequent visits to their official residence and Sonia Gandhi had seen how closely I was associated with the decision-making process at the prime minister's level. She had always treated me with great courtesy and regard whenever we met at the PM's house or at social functions. Even after the tragic assassination of Rajiv (on 21 May 1991), I had maintained contacts with her by calling on her during my visits to Delhi. However, towards the end of August 1998, Sharad Pawar, then a senior leader of the Congress Party in Maharashtra and personally known to me for several years, informed me that Natwar Singh, who by now had come to be known as one of Sonia's important advisers, had told him that she was not happy at my accepting the SS–BJP Government offer for a second term as governor. Natwar Singh, it appears, had told her that I had 'wangled' a second term and thus become an ally of the SS–BJP group in the state. A few other senior Congress leaders from Kerala (my home state) also informed me of similar 'revelations' that Natwar Singh and some other Congress leaders had made to them. Naturally, I was astonished to hear such stories. What surprised me most was that Natwar could convey such stories and, worse, that Sonia Gandhi, who had known me well enough not to need a certificate about my conduct, could believe them. I never had imagined till then that Natwar Singh, who had always been close to me and highly respectful in his attitude, would spread such stories. I had treated him as a trustworthy junior colleague in government service and as a well-wisher of mine. For my part, I could not recall even a single instance of my having said or done anything to harm his interests. On the other hand, I had only tried to be helpful to him whenever he needed my support or assistance.

An important instance of one such intervention on his behalf towards the end of 1984, when I was principal secretary to Rajiv Gandhi, comes to my mind. I was aware of the fact that Natwar was very keen to enter politics and had obtained Indira Gandhi's approval informally to resign from government service and contest the elections to the Lok Sabha from Rajasthan. However, Indira Gandhi's assassination on 31 October 1984 threatened to alter the situation for him. Arun Nehru and a few other influential aides of Rajiv Gandhi, working close to him from the prime minister's house, were totally opposed to Natwar entering politics and had almost succeeded in frustrating his ambitions for a political career. They had convinced Rajiv that the best thing was to appoint him as lieutenant governor of Delhi. Natwar was quite upset when he heard this news and came to me in a highly agitated mood, seeking my good offices to prevent this appointment.

Rajiv was personally well aware of the extremely difficult law and order situation in the capital after the outbreak of violence against members of the Sikh community and had already transferred the lieutenant governor. As a trusted principal aide of Rajiv, I told him that Natwar Singh, by training, temperament and past experience, was hardly a suitable choice for a highly demanding executive post like that of the lieutenant governor. And, also that I was personally aware of the fact that Indira Gandhi had accepted Natwar's request to be fielded as a candidate for election to the Lok Sabha. My arguments clicked and Rajiv promptly put Natwar Singh's name on the list of approved candidates for election from Rajasthan. Natwar personally expressed his gratitude for my timely intervention. On the social plane also, my relations with him were very good. He, his wife and children had been our guests in the high commissioner's residence at London during their private visits and my wife and I had also attended parties at his New Delhi residence on a few occasions. I had always counted on him as a friend.

I also recall how strong his opposition was to the candidature of his former senior colleague in the Indian Foreign Service, K.R. Narayanan, for the post of vice-president in 1992. P.V. Narasimha Rao, soon after his assumption of office as prime minister (in mid-1991), had told me that he was seriously considering me as the Congress Party's candidate for the office of vice-president in the election of 1992. However, the candidature of Narayanan and his special claim for consideration on the ground of his being a politician from the socially oppressed community of Dalits suddenly gained strength because of the support of leaders such as former prime minister V.P. Singh. Even though I had done nothing to push my candidature, Natwar Singh had become one of the ardent champions of my claims for this office and had expressed himself very strongly against V.P. Singh and others for bringing in caste considerations into the election to the high office of vice-president. He even kept me informed of the views of different groups of Members of Parliament (MPs) and of the campaign, which had been launched by the newly formed Dalit Forum of Parliamentarians in favour of Narayanan's candidature. Hence, it seemed ironical that ten years later Natwar had become a strong supporter of the proposal of a second term for Narayanan as president and a bitter opponent to my candidature.

The reports about Natwar Singh's campaign in Delhi against me not only amazed me but also caused me a lot of sadness. When I enquired into the veracity of these reports, more surprises were in store for me. According to some reliable sources Natwar had even told Sonia Gandhi that President Narayanan had also expressed to him his unhappiness in my accepting a second term as governor of Maharashtra and that I appeared to have worked for it. I do not believe that Narayanan could have talked in this manner about me to Natwar Singh. However, my sources emphatically asserted that Natwar had, in fact, used Narayanan's alleged views about me to support his version.

At this stage, I decided to talk to Sonia Gandhi and I got the opportunity to do so on 23 September 1998 at her residence in New Delhi immediately after the meeting of the Advisory Committee for the Indira Gandhi Award for National Integration, of which I was a member. I was burning with righteous indignation at the fact that my having been fair and just to all political parties was being interpreted as partiality to the BJP and the Shiv Sena. I felt insulted at the canard that I had moved closer to these parties in order to get a second term. Therefore, I was in a rather agitated mood when I took up this subject with Sonia Gandhi. I informed her about the campaign that had been unleashed against me by Natwar Singh and a few other Congress leaders in Delhi. I felt that I needed no testimonials from him or anyone else about my conduct and that no one in my long career as a public servant had ever even hinted that I would seek any personal favour at the cost of my self-respect and integrity. The fact that the new government had offered me a second term as governor knowing fully well about my close association with Indira Gandhi and Rajiv Gandhi should have been rightly taken by her as a tribute to the political wisdom and sagacity of these leaders who had appointed me to several politically important and sensitive assignments in the past. I expressed my unhappiness at the fact that anyone could carry such stories about me to a person like her who had known me and my work for long years.

Sonia Gandhi did not question the sincerity of my feelings or even the veracity of my statement about who had conveyed such a story to her. Of course, I did not tell her what I had heard about the views alleged to have been expressed by K.R. Narayanan about me as I did not wish to drag the president's name into this matter. She affirmed that she did not allow any individual or group to influence her opinion about me. Also, she was frank enough to admit that she had indeed felt unhappy when she heard about my acceptance of a second term as governor. However, she reiterated two or three times in the course of our conversation that I should forget this episode of misunderstanding and should consider it as a matter of the past. The meeting ended on a happy note and there was no trace at all of any misunderstanding or unhappiness on her part whenever I met her on subsequent occasions. I also thought that people in Delhi who were carrying on a campaign of vilification against me would now desist from doing so. But I was wrong.

Natwar Singh came to know of my conversation with Sonia Gandhi and my rather strong comments on his conduct and became even more resentful. This situation, however, did not prevent him from asking a favour from me for getting admission in a private engineering college in Maharashtra for the son of a person in whom he was personally interested. I frankly told him that as governor I had never interfered in admissions to educational institutions and therefore I could not do anything about his request. I used this opportunity to tell him what I had known about his role in spreading stories about the extension of my tenure as governor and conveyed my strong displeasure about it. I did not forget to remind him that I had not done any wrong to him at any time, but, on the other hand, had tried to be only helpful to him. He obviously did not like this strong expression of resentment from me and from then on turned against me as if I were his bitter personal enemy.

Natwar got the best chance to settle scores with me when reports started appearing in the media that the NDA leaders, Atal Behari Vajpayee and L.K. Advani, were seriously considering my name as a candidate of the NDA for the presidential election. What else could be further proof for his charge that I had already been sold to the BJP? The fact that it was the responsibility of the ruling party to field a candidate for the post of president did not bother him or the few other leaders of the Congress who supported him in the campaign against me. What mattered to them was that the BJP had taken the initiative to propose my name and this step, according to Natwar Singh, proved what he had told Sonia earlier about me when I accepted the offer of a second term as governor. A splendid opportunity had landed in the lap of the small group of the new 'senior Congress leaders' for teaching me a lesson.

Their next attempt was to convert their personal agenda into the Congress Party's agenda and they succeeded easily in this task as all that they needed to do was to make Congressmen believe that if I were to be elected president, it would block Sonia Gandhi's chances of becoming prime minister as the people might not favour both the president and the prime minister from the Christian community. They knew that once my candidature was presented as a likely threat to Sonia's chances of becoming prime minister, all Congressmen would faithfully rally around her. This group of leaders did not wish to take any risk about Sonia Gandhi's chances of becoming the prime minister as their own political future depended on this factor. In other words, they wanted to play the role of the protectors of Sonia Gandhi's political interests. And this is how the strategy for 'getting Alexander out' was evolved and allowed to gather momentum in subsequent weeks.

Speculations about my emerging as a candidate for presidentship started with an article 'The Alexander Ace' in the *Times of India* (6 May 2001) written by Dilip Padgaonkar. A week earlier, my book, *India in the New Millennium*, had been released by Prime Minister Vajpayee in the new conference hall at the prime minister's house in New Delhi. A large gathering was present on this occasion. Vajpayee in his speech had paid very generous compliments to me and had remarked, *'Dr Alexander is not only a Rajyapal but also a Rajguru'*. Commenting on Vajpayee's speech, Padgaonkar had made the following observations in his article:

At the book release function, however, uppermost in the minds of the assembled guests was the unstated significance of the proceedings. A single comment by Vajpayee (*Dr Alexander is not only a Rajyapal but also a Rajguru*) generated much speculation about Alexander's future. Age doubtless does not favour him. But his track record, not to mention his Christian faith, which goes well beyond the ecumenical, would indeed make him a strong candidate for a high constitutional office. Vajpayee's hand in the current game of political poker appears to be somewhat weak. Alexander could well turn out to be his ace.

Close on the heels of this article, speculation started in the media, particularly in the Marathi press, which had always been extremely generous in its support for me, that I might well be under consideration for the presidentship. Several articles continued to appear in the Marathi newspapers describing my contributions as governor in highly laudatory terms and creating an atmosphere of great goodwill and support for me for being considered for the office of the president.

Some time in the middle of 2001, I received information from a person who had been maintaining very close contact with the organizational wing of the BJP and the RSS (Rashtriya Swayamsevak Sangh, a pro-Hindu organization) leadership, that my name was indeed under consideration as a probable candidate of the NDA for the post of president. However, I had not been sounded by the prime minister or the home minister or any other senior leader of the NDA. Nor had I ever broached this subject with them though I had met them on several occasions both in Delhi and in Maharashtra.

Given the background of the misunderstanding that had been created in the mind of Sonia Gandhi, I thought that it would be advisable for me to apprise her of the reports I had been receiving.

Apart from my desire not to give room for any more misunderstanding between Sonia and myself, I had sincerely believed that if I was ever to be nominated as a candidate for the post of president, it should also be with the cooperation and support of the main opposition parties in the country, particularly of the Congress, because of my very close association with Indira Gandhi and Rajiv. Under these circumstances, I decided to meet Sonia Gandhi and take her into full confidence.

I met her at her New Delhi residence at 10.30 a.m. on 25 August 2001 and informed her of the reports about the BJP and its NDA partners considering my name for the presidential election. I told her clearly that I had *not* been approached by anyone, nor had I ever mentioned my interest to anyone. I also made it very clear that I did not propose to meet any leader of the NDA or of the opposition parties at any time to seek support. I told her that I considered it my duty to inform her about what I had heard from others taking into account my close association with her late mother-in-law and husband and expressed the hope that if the NDA eventually decided to sponsor my name, I would have the backing of all the main opposition parties, particularly of the Congress.

Sonia Gandhi expressed her appreciation of the fact that I had chosen to inform her of the reports. She mentioned that some senior Congress leaders had already approached her expressing their wish to be considered as candidates for the post of president or vice-president but that she had made no promises to anyone. In this context she mentioned the name of Dr Karan Singh (former head of the state of Jammu and Kashmir) as a candidate interested in the post of president and of Dr Najma Heptullah (deputy chairperson of the Rajya Sabha) as one interested in the post of vice-president. She said that it was then too early to take a decision on the candidates for these posts and that she would get back to me after a few weeks, by which time she would have also had the opportunity to talk to some of her senior colleagues in the party. I got the impression that she was happy at the fact that I had taken the earliest opportunity to inform her of the reports I had received. In fact, I even got the impression that if these reports turned out to be true she might be willing to support my candidature, though I did not ask for an assurance, nor had she offered any. This was of course long before the Christian–Christian factor had been invented by a few Congressmen who wanted to be seen as more loyal than the king and for whom eliminating my candidature had become a single point agenda.

There were no major developments on the issue of the NDA candidate for the presidential election till 30 November 2001, when Pramod Mahajan, Union minister for parliamentary affairs, met me at the Raj Bhavan, Mumbai, by prior appointment at 7 p.m. and spent over an hour with me. He had been deputed by Prime Minister Vajpayee and Home Minister Advani specifically to ascertain whether I would be willing to be a candidate of the NDA if the alliance decided to field me. Mahajan told me that the NDA leaders were very keen to avoid any unpleasant campaign for the presidential elections. They were hopeful that if the NDA Government supported me, there would even be a unanimous election because they expected that the Congress would gladly endorse my candidature having known me well in the past. I told Mahajan that I felt honoured and grateful to receive such an enquiry and that I would indeed be happy to be a candidate if the NDA made such an offer to me. However, I pointed out to him that since I did not belong to any political party, I would very much appreciate if I was projected as a candidate of the NDA as well as of the main opposition parties. I told him that I also did not anticipate any objection from the Congress Party for my candidature if the NDA were to make a proposal to it, but I would not be able to canvass support from any political party for my candidature if an election became unavoidable. Mahajan assured me that the NDA would take care of canvassing votes for me from the parties outside the alliance if a contest was found necessary and I would not be asked to undertake any such exercise. He said that I should keep the discussions he had with me as confidential for the present. I kept my word. However, *The Asian Age*, on 1 December 2001, splashed a seven-column spread on its front page with the heading: BJP WANTS ALEXANDER TO BE PRESIDENT. This news was later reported in several newspapers all over the country and, from then on, my name remained prominently in all media speculation as the most likely choice of the NDA for the presidential election.

✧

The results of the elections in Uttar Pradesh, Punjab and Uttaranchal came to be known by the last week of February 2002. These results revealed a major setback for the BJP in all these states. Immediately after the reverses, the NDA Government was caught up in the Ayodhya Ram temple controversy and very soon in the outbreak of communal riots in Gujarat. The NDA Government in general and the BJP in particular suffered a serious blow to their prestige as a result of these developments and there were speculations in the press that the NDA might face problems in getting its candidate elected in the presidential elections, which were to be held later that year.

It was around this time that some Congress leaders, who were till then content with masterminding a whispering campaign against me, came out openly to spread the canard that if I was elected the president in 2002, that would make it impossible for Sonia Gandhi to become the prime minister in 2004 because the people would not like the idea of both the top posts in the country being held by Christians. Further, they also put forward the theory that the BJP leadership had deliberately chosen me, a Christian, as a candidate for the presidentship to achieve their larger political objective of eliminating Sonia Gandhi as a contender for the post of prime minister. I was informed by several Congressmen, who had been visiting Delhi, that a few of their party colleagues had indeed talked to them on these lines. Most Congressmen at that time were unconvinced about the logic of this argument and had felt very uncomfortable at the thought that I would have to be opposed by them if a contest became inevitable.

No one in India had really considered Sonia Gandhi to be a Christian till the Congressmen themselves had brought forward the issue of her original religion. If some people had raised objections to Sonia becoming prime minister, it was never on the ground of the religion into which she was born, but was on the basis of her foreign origin or on the issue of her competence to hold such a position in a highly complex society like India. In fact, people in India had generally accepted her as a convert to Hinduism and no one had ever thought that she herself wished to be acknowledged as a Christian. But by raising this Christian versus Christian factor, these ardent supporters of Sonia Gandhi were asserting her Christian identity, which virtually the entire country had ignored so far. Some Congressmen, in fact, argued with these leaders that I, being a person known for fairness, would never manoeuvre to frustrate Sonia Gandhi's chances of becoming prime minister if her party secured the majority and she herself was elected as leader of the Congress Party in Parliament. These arguments had little effect on them, and they became increasingly aggressive as the days went by in intensifying this unfair campaign against me. They had taken on themselves the role of the most loyal and zealous protectors of the political future of Sonia Gandhi. In assuming this role they probably believed that they could ingratiate themselves further; they exploited the opportunity presented by the forthcoming presidential election to strengthen their own leadership status in the Congress Party.

I was totally unaware of the intensity of the campaign against me till I received reports from several important Congress leaders who had personally felt unhappy at the charge that I was being used by the BJP for fighting its battles against Sonia. However, they did not or could not do anything to stop this campaign. When the Congressmen were being asked to choose between Alexander becoming president or Sonia becoming prime minister, their choice was obvious. In an either/or situation, all Congressmen would naturally like to be seen as strong supporters of the president of their party and, in this sense, the strategy devised by the clique of Congressmen proved very successful.

✧

When Pramod Mahajan conveyed to me the messages of Vajpayee and Advani on 30 November 2001, he had also explained the main reasons why the NDA leaders wished to project me as the candidate for the presidential election. Apart from the obvious reason that they believed that the Congress would wholeheartedly welcome my nomination and thus near unanimity of support for my candidature could be ensured, Mahajan had spelt out four additional reasons. First, the BJP leaders were convinced that the candidate for the presidential post, in order to be acceptable to all the members of the NDA and their allies, had to be a non-party individual, but at the same time, had to be someone with adequate experience and background in political management and administration. They thought that I satisfied these criteria. Second, the candidate had to possess a sound reputation for impartiality and fairness in order to make it easy for the NDA leaders to secure a consensus and they believed that my record on this criterion also was very good. Third, given my fairly long experience in senior positions in the UN and also given my background in representing India in bilateral and international negotiations and my experience as India's high commissioner in London, I would be specially suitable for projecting our country's concerns and interests to the leaders of various foreign nations. Fourth, no one from the Christian community in India had ever been elected as president or vice-president, though others belonging to minority communities like Muslims, Sikhs and Dalits had occupied such positions. The Christians had a genuine complaint of having been overlooked even though in the election to these positions in the past, the community factor had always been a consideration. Mahajan declared that now that they had found in me an eligible candidate on the basis of merits also, the fact that I belonged to a hitherto unrepresented community would be a plus factor. The thought that my selection would in any way affect the prospects of Sonia Gandhi becoming prime minister did not even enter our discussion. The irony of the situation as it developed was that instead of the Congress welcoming me wholeheartedly, this party considered me highly unacceptable, not on the criteria of merit and suitability but on the most untenable ground that I might in future prove to be a hindrance to Sonia's chances of becoming prime minister. At any rate, this was the argument that was used with telling effect. The two motivations converged most conveniently for those who wanted to pursue their single point policy of 'anyone but Alexander'.

The Congress leaders, who had taken on the task of ensuring the elimination of my candidature, soon found that the Christian versus

Christian campaign was not cutting much ice and was, in fact, becoming counterproductive because several sections of the media started criticizing the Congress for introducing a religious element into the presidential election. They then launched a campaign of personal vilification against me and started spreading several stories unashamedly to throw dirt on my impeccable record of honesty and integrity in public service in order to create misgivings and doubts in the minds of the senior leaders of the NDA and its allies.

They resorted to propagating the most shameful lie that my name had also been tarnished in a spy case that had attracted a lot of public attention in the country in the mid-1980s and that I had to resign from my office as principal secretary to Rajiv Gandhi in disgrace. The true facts of the spy case were not known to the people in power in government now and these Congress leaders probably thought that by raising a cloud of doubt they could get away with impunity without having to bear responsibility for their allegations. They cleverly hid the fact that the then prime minister, Rajiv Gandhi, had made a statement in Parliament paying a handsome tribute to me for very promptly submitting my resignation for the lapses on the part of some clerks working in the Prime Minister's Office and had described it as an 'act in the finest tradition of the civil service, though Dr. Alexander was in no way involved in this affair'. They had also hidden the fact that almost all the newspapers at that time had lavishly praised me for such an act on my part. While some clerks and junior functionaries in certain other ministries such as defence, finance and commerce, and in institutions such as the Rashtrapati Bhavan, had also been accused of passing information to outsiders, I was the only secretary to the government who had resigned as a gesture of moral responsibility for the criminal acts of others. They knew very well that within four months of my resignation as principal secretary, Prime Minister Rajiv Gandhi, who was in possession of the full facts about the spy episode, had appointed me to a very sensitive and politically important post as high commissioner of India in the UK. They also knew that Rajiv Gandhi had later specially selected me to take over as the governor of Tamil Nadu when the state was placed under president's rule. But what these Congressmen aimed to achieve by bringing up the spy scandal was only to create some nagging doubts in the minds of the top leaders in the government about the advisability of selecting me as a candidate for the post of president.

The 'dirty tricks' campaign launched against me by this clique continued unabashedly. Some newspapers, with the help of some obliging journalists, carried negative reports about me. This time it was through a totally false allegation that I had, as governor of Maharashtra, deliberately desisted from taking any action against the BJP–SS cadre who had been charged by Justice B.N. Srikrishna with complicity in unleashing violence against Muslims in Mumbai city in the communal riots of 1992–93. The accusation against me was that I had prevented the prosecution of Shiv Sena chief Balasaheb Thackeray and others indicted by the Srikrishna Commission in order to please the BJP–SS Governments in the state and in the Centre. This was a malicious lie because anyone familiar with the Business Rules and the provisions of the Commission of Inquiry Act would have known that the governor *has no role at all* in such matters. His permission is not necessary for appointing such commissions of inquiry or for taking action on the basis of their reports. In spite of this legal position, I had, on my own initiative, called for a copy of the commission's report immediately after it was submitted to the government and after studying it thoroughly, had visited Delhi and briefed President Narayanan, Prime Minister Vajpayee and Home Minister Advani on the findings and recommendations in the report and on their probable repercussions on the state. However, the blame for the BJP–SS Government in Maharashtra for not taking action on some of the important recommendations of the report was placed on me by these Congress leaders as it suited their objective of maligning me. They, however, failed to realize the contradiction in their accusation. If I was to be blamed for the BJP–SS Government's decision not to take action on the main recommendations of the report, I should have also been praised for the decision taken by the subsequent Congress–NCP* Government in the state when it later ordered the prosecution of all those charged by the Srikrishna Commission. The truth is that

---

* Nationalist Congress Party.

the governor deserved neither blame nor praise, as he had no role at all in such matters. Nevertheless, those who were playing the game of vilifying me planted these stories in the media with the sole objective of tarnishing my reputation for impartiality and fairness and depicting me as a partisan of the BJP–SS group.

Finding that the vilification campaign against me was not finding many takers, this clique in the Congress resorted to the ultimate in character assassination and that was to invent utter falsehoods about me like, for instance, that I had been suspected of having links with the CIA or that I had been leaking secrets about India's nuclear weapons programme. Many such atrocious stories were fabricated by them to create serious doubts in the minds of the top leaders in the government. These doubts related to whether my candidature would lead to embarrassment for them if such stories were to break out during the election campaign. I have been told that the prime minister and the home minister were even informed by them that the leaders had with them reliable 'evidence' to substantiate their charges and that they would make the 'evidence' public if they persisted with their decision to announce my name as the NDA's candidate.

I was deeply hurt when I heard about these machinations and wondered at the ruthlessness of some so-called senior leaders in trying to ensure my exit from the presidential race. Those familiar with my five and a half decades of public service knew that I had a record marked by unimpeachable personal integrity without a speck of blemish on it. Still these people were trying to hurl some vile allegations against me hoping that they would create some doubts at least for a short period in the minds of the leaders who were backing my candidature for presidentship. They, of course, did not have the courage to make any such statement about me publicly.

Deeply anguished at the reports I received about the insidiousness of some Congressmen, I wrote to the prime minister and the home minister exposing the utter hollowness and maliciousness of these stories. Fortunately, the two top leaders were in no way influenced by the antics of these men. In fact, Advani was pained at this campaign of vilification against me. In his letter of 2 June 2002 he wrote: 'The campaign unleashed against you is really distressing. It only reveals the depths to which some political elements can descend to subserve their narrow objectives.'

By this time, developments relating to the presidential election were quickly moving towards their final stage. The NDA realized that it could no longer postpone the formal announcement of my name as its candidate for the election. During the last several months newspapers had been highlighting my name as the 'frontrunner' (because of the reported support I was getting from the NDA) along with the names of a few others like Vice-President Krishan Kant, Dr L.M. Singhvi (former high commissioner to the UK), Dr Karan Singh, Dr Farooq Abdullah (the chief minister of Jammu and Kashmir) and Dr Najma Heptullah. The names of Dr Farooq Abdullah and Dr Najma Heptullah were being projected mostly for the post of vice-president, which was due to fall vacant in August 2002, while the president's post was due to fall vacant in July 2002.

A special feature of the forthcoming election was that President K.R. Narayanan continued to remain in the race almost till the very last stage, though he kept insisting that he would agree to a second term *only* if he had the backing of all parties. The very fact that the NDA had made it known that other names were being considered for this post should have been enough to convey the message that the alliance was not in favour of a second term for him. But he was being repeatedly assured by the Congress leaders that they would try their best for his eventual emergence as a consensus candidate and, if a contest became necessary, it would be possible for them to garner the required support for him.

There were several reasons why the Congress strategists insisted on projecting Narayanan as the party's nominee. They probably believed that the person with the best chance of victory in a contest against me would be Narayanan. He had developed the image of being a person with a leftist ideology and therefore was the darling of the various left parties right from the time of his election as vice-president. The Congress leaders obviously felt that with the assured support of the left parties, they would be able to secure further support for his candidature from a few other like-minded parties outside the NDA such as the Samajwadi Party (SP), the Telugu Desam Party (TDP) and the Bahujan Samaj Party (BSP). However, the formation of the BSP–BJP Government in Uttar Pradesh in May 2002 and the assurance given by the BSP that it would support the BJP's candidates for the presidential and vice-presidential elections upset the calculations of the Congress leaders, who now realized that Narayanan's victory would not be that easy any more. It was well known to all who had been observing Narayanan's state of health during the past few months that he might not be in a position to function effectively as president for another period of five years if he were to win the election. For health reasons he had to cancel several public engagements. Even during the few unavoidable public engagements in which he had to participate, such as the opening of the joint session of Parliament, his poor physical condition had been clearly projected through live TV. Everyone expected that he himself would publicly declare that he would not run for the presidential election, not only for reasons of health but also because of the fact that there had been an established convention, after Dr Rajendra Prasad's second innings, that no president should be given a second term. Even after the NDA leadership had sent informal messages through some friends of Narayanan that the alliance was averse to the idea of a second term for him, he appeared to be willing to wait for the odd chance of an eventual consensus emerging in his favour or even to contest the election if he was assured of the required numbers.

Meanwhile, some Congress leaders like Buta Singh (himself a Dalit MP) were making Herculean efforts to trump up support for Narayanan from other MPs belonging to the Dalit community irrespective of their party affiliations or even party directives. The Dalit card had been very successfully played in favour of Narayanan at the time of his selection as the candidate for vice-presidentship in 1992. In fact, a few Dalit MPs like Buta Singh kept assuring Narayanan that there would be adequate numbers of Dalit MPs from even the NDA parties willing to vote for him because he belonged to that caste. Those persons who wanted to use the caste card in the election to the highest office in the country appeared to be the least worried about its ethical aspects. While always speaking about high principles of national integration and secularism, they appeared to think that there was nothing wrong if the Dalits used the caste argument in support of another Dalit. However, this time the Dalit card proved to be not so very helpful for Narayanan as it was on the previous occasion. Some important MPs of this community made it known that it was only appropriate that Narayanan, who already had put in ten years as both vice-president and president, should step down in order to allow some other eligible Dalit to make a bid for one of these posts. However, the Congress strategists would not so easily accept the emerging scenario because they believed that Narayanan had to remain in the race so that 'his name could be used' by them to 'get Alexander out'. Hoping that the situation would change in his favour, Narayanan continued to remain a candidate, though taking care always to add a rider to his public statements that he would be in the reckoning *only* if consensus was arrived at with respect to his candidature.

It was under these circumstances that the prime minister convened a meeting of the NDA on 11 May 2002 to formally ascertain the views of its members on the candidate to be fielded on behalf of the alliance for presidentship even though their views had been informally ascertained earlier. Though it was agreed in advance that no names should be discussed at the meeting, the members who spoke at the meeting made it amply clear that they were against a second term for Narayanan and that their preferred candidate among all the names under consideration was Alexander. The NDA, at the end of the discussions, authorized the prime minister to continue consultations, as he considered necessary, and to announce a final decision on the NDA candidate. It was clear to all those who attended the meeting that the NDA was solid in its support to me as its presidential candidate. The newspapers published the news with bold headlines on 12 May that I was the candidate agreed upon by the NDA.

Even at this stage the Congress clique would not give up its efforts to gather support for Narayanan. He had to leave for about a fortnight's stay at a place near Ooty (a hill station in Tamil Nadu) for Ayurvedic treatment for his ailments. His enthusiastic supporters in the left parties and the Congress came out with lavish praise for what they described as his 'brilliant record in defending the Constitution' and hailed him as having been an 'exceptionally good president'.

For the small group in the Congress Party masterminding the strategy for the election, the concern was not so much to project Narayanan as president for another five years, but to ensure that he did not quit the race, thereby denying them the opportunity to 'use his name to keep Alexander out'. They had no compunctions to jettison him and pledge support for Krishan Kant within a few days after discovering that he could not be a winner as they expected him to be. But more on this topic later.

Let me continue with the account of the developments that took place during the last few days before the Congress finally declared its support for Dr A.P.J. Abdul Kalam, the new NDA candidate who emerged after my exit from the contest. The Congress kept up the posture that it had only one candidate to propose and that was Narayanan whatever be the opinion of the NDA regarding his candidature. When Sonia Gandhi was sounded by the prime minister about her party's preferred candidate for the presidentship, she had made it unequivocally clear to him that it was Narayanan. Meanwhile, a very ingenious argument had also been advanced through statements in the press by Narayanan's supporters in the Congress and the left parties. Their contention was that in view of the growing tension prevailing on the Indo–Pakistan border and the amassing of troops on both sides, there was a likelihood of war breaking out between the two countries and, therefore, this would not be an opportune time to expose divisions of opinion on the choice of the country's president. In their view, the right approach in order to demonstrate the unity of the nation was for all parties to agree to the unanimous choice of Narayanan as president. Even the tension along the Indo–Pakistan border thus became a device to back Narayanan's claim for a second term as president. Also, the argument of making an exception in favour of a Dalit president getting a second term was put forth as a very logical and natural course to follow.

The prime minister held a meeting with Sonia Gandhi at his residence on 19 May essentially to brief her about the security situation in the country at that point of time. He used that opportunity to again bring up the issue of the candidate for the presidential election. Sonia Gandhi, as on earlier occasions, had no hesitation in reiterating that she preferred Narayanan being given a second term. The prime minister then told her plainly that the NDA was against such a stand. Even when faced with this important statement from the prime minister, Sonia Gandhi was not prepared to lend support to the idea of forming a consensus in favour of the NDA candidate. She knew that the combined strength of the Congress and its allies in the electoral college was far below that of the NDA, but she insisted on a consensus on the candidate proposed by her and not by the NDA.

✧

President Narayanan returned to Delhi from Ooty on 22 May. Most people thought that he would at least at this stage announce his withdrawal as a candidate since he had been informed that the NDA would not be backing him for the post. The Congress Working Committee (CWC) met on 22 May 2002 to discuss the question of its candidate for the presidential election for the first time and authorized its president to take a decision in the matter. Meanwhile, the Samajwadi Party took the stand that either Dr Abdul Kalam or Jyoti Basu (a former chief minister of West Bengal) would be acceptable for the president's post, thereby raising serious doubts in the ranks of the opposition parties about the actual number of voters who would support Narayanan.

In the midst of these speculations, Sonia Gandhi called on President Narayanan at the Rashtrapati Bhavan on 28 May 2002 and renewed her party's support for his candidature. According to media reports, she advised him to remain in the race and expressed her confidence that enough support would be forthcoming in his favour. Though Rashtrapati Bhavan kept silent about this important meeting, news was discreetly let out by the Congress Party that Narayanan had an 'open mind' on the subject and that he would be willing to offer himself as a candidate for a second term if all parties agreed to it. The Congress Party went to the extent of informing the media that Narayanan might even be prepared for a contest if a consensus was not possible. This part of the news was attributed to 'a member of the Congress Working Committee'.

This news was flashed by the media, but Rashtrapati Bhavan remained silent without contradicting even that part of the statement which referred to Narayanan's willingness to contest if it became necessary. It was rather unusual for Rashtrapati Bhavan to remain silent when the statement attributed to the president by the Congress Party involved a major departure from the stand he had been taking publicly till then. The media started speculating that Narayanan must have been regularly assessing the strength of his support in the event of a contest and had always been willing to fight an election if he was satisfied that the arithmetic was in his favour.

Next, it was the turn of Prime Minister Vajpayee himself to make the NDA's position formally known to the president if he was still in doubt as to where the alliance stood on this issue. Vajpayee called on Narayanan at 5 p.m. on 30 May and, after briefing him on the Indo–Pak border situation, told him clearly that the NDA was *not* in favour of a second term for him. This news, which confirmed the NDA's position, was also leaked to the press.

Having conveyed the NDA's views to Narayanan in unequivocal terms, its top leadership started contacting its allies from outside the government for their support for my candidature. At this stage a totally unforeseen development took place, which contained all the ingredients of a palace plot – the sudden projection of Vice-President Krishan Kant as a candidate for the presidential election. The principal characters behind this new move were Natwar Singh and, most unexpectedly, Brajesh Mishra, principal secretary to the prime minister.

On 6 June 2002, Chandrababu Naidu, president of the Telugu Desam Party and also the chief minister of Andhra Pradesh, had been invited by the prime minister for discussing the issue of his party's support for my candidature. Naidu's party was a vital constituent of the NDA, although its members were *not* ministers in the Central Government. According to Naidu's version of his meeting with the prime minister, he had told Vajpayee that he had no reservation regarding my candidature, but the PM should try to obtain a consensus on my name. In such an eventuality, he would be quite willing to support me as the presidential candidate. His main objective was that he

should be involved in the *finalization* of the candidate. After his meeting with the prime minister, Naidu told the media that he had authorized the PM to take the final decision on the choice of candidate. Everyone interpreted this statement as his giving a blank cheque to the prime minister to go ahead with his announcement of the candidate for the presidentship. However, subsequent developments showed that Naidu had been left very confused and unhappy by the sudden declaration of support extended to Krishan Kant's candidature and its equally sudden withdrawal, all as a result of the move made overnight by two former bureaucrats who had neither the official authority nor the political standing to take such decisions on their own, thereby upsetting the firm decision taken by the core group of top NDA leaders, which included Vajpayee, Advani, Jaswant Singh (foreign minister), George Fernandes (defence minister) and Pramod Mahajan.

Events suddenly took a new turn when a delegation made up of the senior leaders of the left parties, the Congress and the Samajwadi Party called on President Narayanan at the Rashtrapati Bhavan and pledged their support to his getting a second term. After meeting the president these leaders spoke to the media assembled in the forecourt of the Rashtrapati Bhavan and clarified their position. For Narayanan this was a most welcome development because, till then, the Samajwadi Party had been opposing the idea of a second term for him. With Amar Singh, general secretary of the Samajwadi Party joining the delegation of the Congress and the left parties, the chances of Narayanan winning the contest, if it became necessary, appeared somewhat better than before. Consequently, the Congress supporters of Narayanan were convinced that they could secure similar support from some other parties as well, which, till then, had not publicly made their stand known on this issue. However, the promise of support by the Samajwadi Party to Narayanan's candidature lasted only for a very brief period; soon it became clear that the party was considering other options.

Now let me go back to the sudden propping up of Vice-President Krishan Kant as a candidate for presidentship. Krishan Kant would have been the natural contender for the high post if the major political parties in the country had proposed his name seriously in the early stages. As it turned out, neither the Congress nor the NDA ever thought of sponsoring his name. The NDA, by opting to field me, had ruled out Krishan Kant's candidature from the very beginning. Similarly, the Congress, by supporting K.R. Narayanan for a second term, had made it clear that it was not in favour of elevating Krishan Kant. Even Chandrababu Naidu, who had once strongly backed Krishan Kant for the post of vice-president, had not chosen to come out in his support for the post of president. When the Congress realized that there would be very little support for a second term for Narayanan, it was desperate in its search for a candidate who could block my chance because, at that stage, the only objective of the Congress was to get me eliminated from the race. It was against this background that Natwar Singh and Brajesh Mishra came up with the last-minute proposal of Krishan Kant.

This proposal would have had two advantages for those who wished to see me out. It would drive a wedge between Naidu and the NDA leaders on the choice of the presidential candidate. Naidu would feel happy if the person whom he helped to get elected as vice-president would now get elected as president because of his support. After confabulations between Natwar Singh and Mishra, Krishan Kant was informed that his candidature would have the support of both the NDA and the Congress. The second advantage, which they calculated upon, according to *India Today* (quoted later in this chapter), was that if Kant could become the agreed-upon candidate of the Congress and the NDA, Natwar Singh could emerge as the agreed-upon candidate for vice-presidentship. No one in the NDA had ever considered Natwar Singh for the post of vice-president at any stage but those who managed to put forward Krishan Kant's name for the presidentship probably believed that they could succeed in this move as well. At any rate, this was the version that a responsible journal like *India Today* gave in its report of 24 June 2002. How such major decisions could be taken independently by Mishra and Natwar and then be hurriedly communicated to Kant and through him to Naidu, without consulting the top leaders of the NDA, baffles one's imagination. Equally baffling was the fact that Natwar Singh could convey such a major decision without the concurrence of the other members of the CWC. The CWC in the past had never even considered Kant as a candidate for this post. In the case of the Congress Party, perhaps there was nothing unusual in this type of decision making, because the entire decision to keep Alexander out had been made by just four or five individuals long before this subject was even placed for discussion in the CWC. Of course, no one in the Congress, including senior members of the Working Committee or the senior chief ministers, would have expressed their views to the president of the party when they knew her personal views in this matter. But how the principal secretary to the prime minister could go to the extent of giving the nod without taking the PM's explicit orders, as it turned out later, was just unthinkable for a person like me who has some knowledge and experience with regard to the conventions and procedures for decision making at the highest levels in administration. But this is what actually happened. As far as I am concerned, I cannot think of any reason why Mishra should have taken so much interest in 'keeping Alexander out' as some others in the Congress Party had. I can only say that his role in the whole episode has pained me and remained a riddle to me.

The core group of senior NDA leaders were horrified when they came to know of this move and quickly put their foot down to bring to an end this unauthorized move on the part of Brajesh Mishra and Natwar Singh. This group met at noon on 8 June 2002 at the prime minister's residence and emphatically rejected the plan to support Kant for the president's post. This rejection, of course, also nipped in the bud Natwar's ambitions of emerging as a consensus candidate for the post of vice-president. But while this development prevented Kant from becoming president and thwarted the vice-presidential hopes of Natwar Singh, it served one important purpose, namely, creating a rift between Naidu and the NDA leadership on the issue of my emerging as the agreed candidate for the presidential election.

I had been getting reports from very reliable sources that Mishra had been repeatedly expressing his concerns to Vajpayee that he was taking a big risk in continuing to back me in the presidential election and that if the TDP backed Krishan Kant, the chances of my victory might be in doubt. It appears Mishra had been expressing the view that if I were to be defeated, Vajpayee would be forced to resign and that it was too big a risk for the prime minister to take. Vajpayee never endorsed Mishra's views and he and his senior colleagues were quite determined to back me till the very end. However, the damage had been done by creating a misunderstanding between Naidu and the NDA leadership by dragging in Krishan Kant's name at the last minute and the NDA leaders found that it was too late to repair the damage.

It would be appropriate to reproduce here the report in the *India Today* (24 June 2002) on these developments. (Since this story has not been repudiated by any of the principal participants in this strange drama, I cannot question the correctness of the account regarding the sudden emergence of Krishan Kant as the so-called consensus candidate.)

8 June [2002]: The NDA and Opposition scripts, which had been running on separate lines, suddenly intersected and dramatically impacted on the next round of events. At 11.30 a.m., Brajesh Mishra, the prime minister's principal secretary, played host to senior Congress leader Natwar Singh. Mishra gave Singh the impression that Kant was the NDA's choice. The suggestion that Mishra was executing Vajpayee's brief is only partly correct. As the prime minister was quite aware of the strong reservations within the NDA over Kant, it is unlikely that he would have authorized Mishra to convey a definitive impression. As things turned out Vajpayee had to give up his quest for a consensus in the face of sustained opposition of his senior colleagues.

But Mishra's solo run was the reason why Naidu spurned NDA overtures on Alexander. Natwar Singh lost little time in informing his leadership of what Mishra had to say. Kant called up Naidu to thank him for his support. By this time, however, George Fernandes had reported to the NDA core group that no major partner viewed Kant with anything but disfavour.

Mishra's lack of finesse also created a politically delicate situation for the NDA.

A cabinet minister admitted that if the Oppositon had grabbed Kant as its candidate on Sunday [2 June 2002], it would have ensured a break between the NDA and Naidu. The People's Front and Congress then called upon [President] Narayanan who indicated that he would "consider" contesting.

Congress sources feel that the Mishra episode was part of a kerbside deal that the PMO was keen to work out with the Congress. This meant that while the NDA would support Kant, and thereby keep Alexander out, Natwar Singh could then be considered for vice-president.

It is indeed strange and disturbing that a very important decision taken by the NDA consisting of twenty-three political parties from all over the country could be sought to be reversed in so casual a manner by two persons acting on their own and for reasons of their own. Of course, those who believe in the principles of democratic administration can draw some comfort from the fact that this unauthorized interference was rejected outright by the leaders who had the political credentials to do so. However, this most unexpected development eventually led to choosing an altogether new candidate, Dr Abdul Kalam, as the NDA nominee.

To resume the narration of the events that finally resulted in the selection of Dr Abdul Kalam as the NDA candidate, let me go back to the developments that took place on 8 June, when the move for sponsoring Krishan Kant came out in the open. At the meeting of the core group of the NDA leadership held in the prime minister's house on that day (attended by Vajpayee, Advani, Jaswant Singh, Fernandes and Mahajan), it was decided that the formal announcement of my name as the candidate of the NDA should not be postponed any further.

Vajpayee spoke to Naidu over the telephone and requested him to come over to Delhi to attend the meeting of the NDA, where he was due to make the formal announcement. Vajpayee believed that Naidu had indicated his readiness to support my candidature during their talk on the phone, though later Naidu maintained that he had not been properly understood by Vajpayee. Under the bona fide belief that Naidu was fully supportive of my candidature, Vajpayee conveyed the NDA's decision to field me as the NDA's candidate for presidentship to me over the phone at 2.30 p.m. on 8 June and congratulated me warmly. This was followed by congratulations over the phone from Advani and Mahajan. Mahajan told me that he would be leaving on a foreign tour within two days and probably the date of filing my nomination could be fixed after his return in three to four days time. I was naturally very happy at hearing this important and gratifying news.

Later in the afternoon of 8 June, Mahajan telephoned me from his house to inform me that the news about my nomination as candidate would be formally announced by the prime minister at a meeting of the NDA and till then he requested me not to meet the media in Mumbai. He also told me that it would be advisable for me to resign as governor even before 13 June, which had been the date fixed by me for the discussion on the confidence motion to be moved by Vilasrao Deshmukh, the chief minister of Maharashtra, in the State Assembly. Mahajan added that Advani also felt that whatever be the correctness of my decision after the confidence vote, it was likely to be opposed by the losing group and it would be better that my name was not dragged into any controversy soon after the formal announcement of my candidature for the post of president. I replied that I would not have any difficulty in resigning as governor in the next two or three days if an acting governor could also be appointed by then.

However, within two days, the whole situation changed dramatically as far as my candidature was concerned due to a fallout of the failed plot to project Krishan Kant at the last minute as the joint candidate of the NDA and the Congress.

The news of the NDA's decision to field me as its candidate for the presidential election was flashed all over India by the evening of 8 June 2002. Chandrababu Naidu – who had been informed by Krishan Kant that he had been accepted by both the NDA and the Congress as their agreed candidate and had been profusely thanked for his valuable help – became very upset at the news that the NDA was, in fact, backing me and not Krishan Kant. The NDA leaders were expecting Naidu to come to Delhi on 9 June morning to be present when the prime minister was planning to make a formal announcement of my name, but Naidu suddenly started playing difficult to get. He took the stand of a person who had been badly let down by the NDA leaders on the issue of dropping Kant. He considered their attitude as 'taking him for granted', and stubbornly refused to go along with the NDA on this issue. Vajpayee and other senior members of the NDA core group requested him to come to Delhi to attend the special meeting of the alliance but he remained adamant in his refusal. Even though the prime minister thought that he had obtained Naidu's clearance on the phone for announcing my name, apparently there was a lack of proper communication and the NDA leaders found it impossible to convince Naidu of the correctness of their position. This state of affairs created real panic in the core leadership of the NDA. They did not want Narayanan to be the president at any cost. In fact, the prime minister had told Narayanan in no uncertain terms that he was not acceptable as a candidate. Nor did they want Krishan Kant as they had always maintained that he would not be acceptable to all the members of the NDA. Further, supporting him at this stage would have been seen as capitulating and accepting a candidate thrust on them by Naidu and the Congress. At the same time, they appeared to be hesitant to formally announce my name without ensuring the unequivocal support of Naidu who controlled about 5 per cent of the votes in the electoral college for the presidential poll. They probably thought that if Naidu threw in his lot either with Narayanan or with Krishan Kant, such a step might even lead to a new alignment of political forces in the country. The NDA had always been banking on Naidu's support for me, but now, at the proverbial eleventh hour, they found their calculations going awry. The intervention of the Natwar–Brajesh duo had done real damage to the whole plan of the NDA, leaving little time or room for NDA leaders to manoeuvre. One can only describe this intervention as unprecedented in nations with democratic traditions. But very soon it had altogether changed the course of events and given it an unexpected turn.

Caught up in a state of confusion, doubt and uncertainty, NDA leaders considered another alternative: that Naidu be asked whether he would agree to my being the candidate for presidentship with Krishan Kant continuing as vice-president for a second term. If Naidu could not be persuaded to accept this formula, the NDA had decided on a fallback position and that was to propose Dr Abdul Kalam, whose name had appeared in the media off and on as a candidate who had the support of the Samajwadi Party. They decided to make one more effort to persuade Naidu to change his stand in my favour and deputed Pramod Mahajan to rush to Hyderabad on the morning of 10 June. The Mahajan mission to Hyderabad to get Naidu's support for me failed. Faced with this situation the NDA leaders apparently did not want to take any risk and finally decided to drop me and to secure Naidu's concurrence for fielding Dr Kalam as the presidential candidate in my place. Naidu enthusiastically seized this offer as it also gave him an opportunity to claim that Dr Kalam had always been his favoured candidate for the post. Such a turn of events also gave Mulayam Singh the opportunity to claim that Dr Kalam had been his first choice and he asserted that what the NDA had done now was only to belatedly accept his suggestion. The NDA, for its part, drew satisfaction from the fact that Dr Kalam was its preferred nominee after the fiasco created by the projection of Kant as the agreed candidate of the NDA and the Congress. The NDA, the TDP and the SP could all claim to be the sponsors of Dr Kalam and the prime minister now felt confident in projecting him as the NDA's candidate for presidentship.

Mahajan came to Mumbai direct from Hyderabad to inform me of this sudden turn in the developments regarding the presidential election. In his meeting with me at 2 p.m. at the Raj Bhavan on 10 June, he explained to me how much effort the NDA leaders had put in to get Naidu's support for my candidature and how things went out of their hands because of the unexpected developments of the last two days. He expressed his great disappointment and sorrow at this development and tried to assure me that things had taken this unexpected turn in spite of the earnest attempt of the NDA leaders to stand by their earlier decision to back me.

I was naturally quite upset and unhappy at receiving this unexpected message. The NDA leaders had conveyed their decision to field me as a candidate as early as seven months ago. When they encountered the Congress Party's stubborn opposition to my candidature, I had naturally expected that they would tie up all loose ends with their principal allies well in advance and ensure that I could win the elections in spite of the hostility of the Congress leadership to my candidature. When the NDA, which controlled the government at the Centre, had conveyed its decision at the highest level that my name would be formally announced in a few hours time, I had no reason to doubt that I would have the necessary support for a clear win. However, Mahajan's message to me revealed that the last-minute support promised to Krishan Kant had created an altogether new situation beyond the control of the NDA leaders. What could I tell Mahajan except what any gentleman in that position could have said? I had not asked to be chosen as a candidate, nor had I expressed any interest in this position till I was sounded about my willingness to be a candidate. Now when I was presented with an altogether new situation, I had only one honest option left and that was to inform the prime minister, through Mahajan, that I accepted the decision of the NDA leadership. Thus ended the prospects of my candidature for presidentship.

✧

The news was out that Naidu would be coming to Delhi to attend the meeting of the NDA and the announcement about Dr Kalam's nomination by the alliance would be made in his presence. Before such an announcement was made in the presence of Naidu and several other allies of the NDA by the prime minister, Vajpayee telephoned me at 8 a.m. on 11 June and expressed his sentiments at this sudden turn of events. *Words fail me to express my sadness at this [development]'*, said Vajpayee. For my part, I told him: 'It would be dishonest on my part if I say that I am not upset.' I added: 'But I accept the decision as something which I have to in the present circumstances'. The prime minister then told me that Mahajan had reported to him how gracefully I had accepted the decision and he thanked me specially for this attitude on my part. Advani also called me up and expressed his sadness and disappointment in having to drop the proposal at this very last stage.

Now let me come back to where I started this story, namely, the observations made by Jaipal Reddy, the chief spokesman of the Congress about 'getting Alexander out' and having used Narayanan's name for this purpose. During one of his TV appearances I had heard Reddy putting forward a rather strange explanation about the Congress party's attitude to my candidature. When asked why the Congress was so vehemently opposing my candidature for presidentship, Reddy replied that his party did not approve of a person going straight from the level of a governor to that of the president. The implication was that I should have put in a period of apprenticeship as vice-president also, as the Congress Party's favourite candidate Narayanan had done. Probably in Reddy's assessment my twelve years' experience as governor of two of the most important states of India, Maharashtra and Tamil Nadu, and my long experience in top positions in national and international civil service were not adequate to be considered as an eligible candidate for the post of president. I am glad that at least in the case of the eminent scientist, Dr Kalam, Reddy did not find lack of experience as vice-president a disqualification for being supported by his party for the presidentship. One can only hope that the forty-eight hours' delay in endorsing Dr Kalam's candidature was not caused by doubts about lack of experience, as he had not served a term as vice-president!

However, a legitimate question that arises from Reddy's observations is how the Congress can claim that by opposing my candidature so bitterly, it had achieved something 'positive' and 'outstanding'. The fact remains that the Congress found itself as the only party with egg on its face after the presidential election. The NDA could claim with some satisfaction that it was its nominee, though not its first choice, who was finally accepted by most parties. The TDP and the SP could claim that their preferred candidate was Dr Kalam and he had eventually won the endorsement of the NDA. The left parties could claim that they had taken a 'principled' stand to oppose Dr Kalam, though few people outside these parties can understand what 'principle' they were referring to. The Congress, which persistently supported Narayanan and even went to the extent of supporting Kant as its next choice, finally found that it had to give up both its candidates. In the end, it was forced to endorse the candidature of a person sponsored by the NDA and that too after a delay of two days vacillating from 'yes' to 'no' to 'yes'. In fact, because of the intrigues of a few self-appointed guardians of the political interests of Sonia Gandhi, the Congress was left with no other option but to accept Dr Kalam. The Congress had constantly been blaming the NDA for not consulting it adequately in the choice of a candidate though, on all occasions, when its leader was consulted, she had opposed my candidature, thereby leaving little room for a consensus. Several impartial observers have pointed out that having raised the Christian–Christian issue at the time of my candidature, the question of having both the president and prime minister from the minority communities cannot be easily wished away. Probably this was the question that worried the Congress leaders for two days when they delayed their approval of Dr Kalam's candidature.

Another point about the Congress Party's role in this election needs mention here. If the Congress had not persisted with its uncompromising opposition to me, it was possible that there could have been an honourable agreement with the NDA by which a suitable nominee of the Congress could have received the support of the alliance for the post of vice-president. Now for the first time in the history of the elections to the posts of president and vice-president, the Congress Party found itself having had no say in the selection of the candidates for either of the posts. This may have been an 'outstanding positive achievement' for some of the new leaders of the Congress, but history will record that it was the personal spite and ambitions of a few persons that landed the Congress Party in a situation like this.

Now a word about the Congress using Narayanan's name to keep me out. I have already referred to the meeting that the senior leaders of four political parties, the Congress, the Communist Party of India (Marxist) [CPI(M)], the Communist Party of India (CPI) and the SP, had with Narayanan at Rashtrapati Bhavan to pledge support to him in a possible contest against me. Narayanan's response to this request was not reported in the papers. The *Times of India*, in its issue of 10 June 2002, reported that 'although the opposition is still to finally announce that Mr Narayanan will contest, it seems unlikely that the leaders (of the four opposition parties) would have gone this far without getting Mr Narayanan's nod'. During the half an hour meeting of the opposition leaders with Narayanan, they explained to him, according to the *Times of India*, 'the distinct possibility of his success'; Narayanan, according to this report, agreed to consider their plea but added that he would convey his decision later. Even as Natwar Singh and Brajesh Mishra had been confabulating with each other on projecting Krishan Kant as the candidate of both the NDA and the Congress, the latter was proclaiming that it was absolutely confident of Narayanan's victory in an election.

It was only when it became very clear to the Congress that I was no longer the candidate of the NDA and, that Dr Kalam might be the NDA's new candidate, that the Congress abandoned the idea of continuing its support for its 'only candidate' Narayanan, and switched support to Kant. When it found that the Kant candidature collapsed as quickly as it was propped up, it switched its support to Dr Kalam though after two days of hesitation. Finally, Narayanan did what he could have gracefully done at the very beginning when speculation started about the presidential election eight months ago, namely, declaring that he was not a candidate. A press statement from Rashtrapati Bhavan finally made Narayanan's position clear: 'There have been recent media reports suggesting that President K.R. Narayanan may be the candidate for the presidential election 2002. This is to clarify that K.R. Narayanan is not a candidate.'

The Congress had used Narayanan's name against me with very little concern about how it would affect the dignity of the office he was holding. What is important to note is that he himself did not do anything to prevent his name from being used. This resulted in his having to leave the Rashtrapati Bhavan with 'a reputation substantially lower than when he entered it' according to the *Statesman*'s editorial of 14 June 2002. No departing president would have received so sharp a rebuke from so respectable a national daily as the *Statesman* as Narayanan had. The title itself, 'Unceremonious Exit – Yet Not Undeserved', was pungent enough. The contents were severe and sharp in their impact. The editorial pointed out with brutal frankness that he 'awaited the eviction order rather than say clearly that he would be leaving when his time was up' and described his conduct as 'unbecoming of a person occupying the highest office in the land'. It further criticized Narayanan for remaining silent when his supporters were using the Dalit card to strengthen his claim to the post. It went on to say 'silence however is not new to Narayanan: he raised nary a whimper when his elevation to that office was trumpeted as a victory for the Dalits – surely the president must rise above caste or creed and castigate those who reduce his election to the lowest of levels'.

I do not endorse what the *Statesman* has described as Narayanan's unceremonious exit, but by his conduct in the last few months of the presidency, he allowed his critics to affirm that he badly wished to run for a second term, but desisted finally from a contest only when he found the numbers not favouring him. In the process he had allowed himself to be used by a few leaders of the Congress to fight their battle against me.

Even though I had taken the sudden developments that led to my exit from the presidential contest rather coolly for about a week, the thought that my continued stay as governor in Maharashtra might not be that happy as it had always been in the past started nagging me. One of the important factors that gave me full satisfaction in my service as governor was the unstinted support I had received from all the chief ministers who had worked with me – Sudhakar Rao Naik, Sharad Pawar, Manohar Joshi, Narayan Rane and Vilasrao Deshmukh. They had treated me with great courtesy and respect and there has not been a single instance of any serious difference of opinion between the chief ministers and me during the entire period of my service as governor even though I was exercising certain special powers unlike the governors of the other states. They had sought my advice on controversial and difficult problems when they felt the need for it and I myself on certain occasions had offered my suggestions without waiting for their requests. I worked in an atmosphere of perfect trust and understanding and the chief ministers and their cabinet colleagues had considered me as a totally impartial head of state on whose judgement and advice they could always rely. However, with the very unfriendly attitude that the Congress in Delhi had taken towards me in the presidential contest, I felt that the chief minister (Deshmukh)

might find it difficult to work with me with full trust and confidence as before. I noticed a sudden change in his attitude towards me after the presidential election. I am not blaming him for this attitude as I know how helpless chief ministers are when they are asked to carry out the diktats of the powerful high command. However, the sudden coolness on the part of Deshmukh, who had always been very cordial and respectful to me, came somewhat as a surprise. I had nine and a half months more to serve as governor in my extended term, but I began to think that it might be better that I quit at that stage if I were to preserve my honour and self-respect.

I also suddenly started feeling disgusted at the unexpected turn of events relating to my candidature for the post of president and the conviction for quitting my post grew stronger within me. I mentioned my thoughts to a few of my close friends and well-wishers who had been calling on me regularly during this period. Meanwhile, the rumour about my impending resignation was getting strong and some newspapers also had reported about its possibility.

It was in these circumstances that I received a most unexpected offer from Sharad Pawar, the leader of the Nationalist Congress Party (NCP) and a person whom I had known well long before I had become governor of Maharashtra. He had been out of the country for a few days and, immediately after his return, he called on me at the Raj Bhavan on 22 June. After referring to the rumours about my resignation from the post of governor, he told me that the country should not lose the benefit of my long experience in public service and therefore I should not think of going into a life of retirement at this stage. He pointed out there was a lot I could contribute to the nation without having to hold a post under the government. He further observed that Maharashtra state could benefit from my services if I continued to be in public life. He then straightaway offered me the Rajya Sabha seat that had just fallen vacant and for which his party had the right to nominate a candidate according to its unwritten understanding with the Congress, its partner in the state government. Mukesh Patel, an NCP member of the Rajya Sabha, had passed away within three months of his election and Pawar said that I could be elected to that vacancy as an independent. He clarified that the NCP would never expect any support for, or involvement in, that party's activities, but would fully respect my independent status. He also added that the Congress would accept the right of his party to nominate a person to fill the vacancy. He said that the BJP–SS combine could also be expected to support me and therefore I could be unanimously elected to the Rajya Sabha. Pawar volunteered to ascertain the BJP's views on this matter and let me know its reaction in a few days. The prospects of being elected unanimously as an independent candidate appealed to me. We both agreed that this proposal should be kept confidential till he had consulted the senior members of his party and had also ascertained the reaction of the BJP.

Events moved very quickly thereafter. On 2 July Sharad Pawar called on me at the Raj Bhavan to confirm that Pramod Mahajan had informed him that the BJP would be very happy to support my election to the Rajya Sabha. Mahajan had a talk with Balasaheb Thackeray (the Shiv Sena chief) the same night about this proposal and he promptly promised his party's support. Sharad Pawar told me that the senior colleagues of the NCP whom he had consulted had enthusiastically welcomed the proposal. The elections were scheduled to be held on 25 July and the last date of nomination was 15 July. This meant my sending in my letter of resignation and the acceptance of it by the president before 14 July.

The expectation that I would be elected unopposed, however, was soon proved wrong. The Congress leaders who had succeeded in frustrating my nomination as the candidate for presidentship wished to see a repeat performance happen in the election to the Rajya Sabha also. For the record the Congress announced that it was not fielding any official candidate for the Rajya Sabha election, but the Maharashtra chief minister and the senior state Congress Party functionaries were instructed by the party high command that they should make sure that *all* Congress MLAs (Members of the Legislative Assembly) and the independents supporting it in the Assembly cast their votes for Suresh Keswani, a businessman from Mumbai who had filed his nomination after due consultations in Delhi. They probably believed that Keswani might succeed in getting an adequate number of votes from other parties and independents to notch up a win against me. This state of affairs put the senior Congress leaders in Maharashtra in the embarrassing position of having to oppose my candidature even for the election to the Rajya Sabha and to canvass support for Keswani against me. After the experience I had to go through in the presidential election, no decision of the Congress leadership would have caused me surprise. But this one act revealed the limits to which some people could go in pursuit of their personal interests or just to be spiteful.

I knew I would get elected to the Rajya Sabha with a comfortable majority in spite of the instructions from Delhi to the chief minister to ensure that I did not get the votes of the Congress Party and its allies. Some of my well-wishers in the state Congress suggested that I should issue an appeal to all MLAs to vote for me as such an appeal would make some Congress members respond favourably, but I politely refused to issue any such appeal. I told them that the MLAs of Maharashtra who had known me well for nine and a half years did not require any appeal from me and it was up to them to decide how they should exercise their vote. I did not ask any MLA from any party for his vote and I left it to the MLAs' own discretion as to whom they should vote for. Eventually, when the votes were counted on the evening of 25 July I had secured a three-fourth majority, which clearly showed that I had received the votes of some members of the Congress Party also, besides the votes of all other political parties represented in the Legislative Assembly. Naturally, those who sent the instructions to the Congress leaders in the state to do all they could to get Keswani elected to the Rajya Sabha were not very pleased with the results of the election.

I took the oath as a member of the Rajya Sabha on 30 July 2002 and thus an altogether new chapter opened up in my public life in the most unexpected circumstances.

Several persons, who had been closely following the unexpected twists and turns the presidential election process took, have asked me why some senior members of the Congress Working Committee like A.K. Antony, who had known me closely for long years, chose to remain silent when a few of their party colleagues, who had so vehemently opposed my candidature, unleashed a campaign of personal vilification against me and even ensured that the Congress oppose my candidature for election to the Rajya Sabha. Yes, Antony had known me well for long years as will be seen from some of the accounts in this book itself. Besides, he was the chief minister of Kerala, my home state. I can only say in answer to such questions that I have been as much pained and surprised as the questioners themselves.

TWO

The Early Years

SOME OF THE EARLIEST MEMORIES OF MY CHILDHOOD YEARS ARE ABOUT the festivals in the Bhagawathi temple and in the St Mary's Church at Puthiacavu in Mavelikara, my home town in Travancore, one of the former Princely States in South India. The temple was situated about 150 metres west of my ancestral house and the church about 250 metres east. In an otherwise small sleepy town in those days, the temple and church festivals were the most exciting events, eagerly looked forward to, and actively supported by, the people of all communities in Mavelikara.

According to the strongly held traditions in our family, my ancestors who were said to have been members of a ruling family in a small principality in the northern part of Kerala, had moved over a thousand years ago displaced from power by a neighbouring ruling prince, a common event in the history of those unsettled days. They are believed to have moved to Mavelikara carrying with them their gold and silver treasures in search of a fertile place for pursuing farming activities and they first settled down at a place called Modiyil in the Akkanattukara region of Mavelikara. They were warmly welcomed by the Hindu chieftains of the place with offers of land for cultivation and for building their new houses. The new settlers in Modiyil acquired extensive agricultural land in Mavelikara and in due course moved to Puthiacavu where land for building a house was sold to the head of the family by the Edassefril Thangals, hereditary managers of the properties of the Bhagawathi temple there. The site for the house was at the western head of the northern side of the street stretching from the compound of the Bhagawathi temple at Puthiacavu towards the east and the name of the family therefore became 'Padinjarethalakal' or 'western head'.

This property is described in the land revenue records as 'Puthiacavu Bhagawathi Vaka thettam Survey 139/10 Tharakan ayyathu Puraidam', that is, Tharakan's land which originally belonged to the Puthiacavu Bhagawathi. Tharakan was a hereditary title conferred by the rulers of Travancore on rich and influential members of the St Thomas Christian community and it is still part of the names of several Christians in Kerala whose ancestors had received the title. In the Padinjarethalakal family also this title was in use till a generation ago. My father and his elder brother dispensed with the practice of adding this title to their names and today there is no one in the family using the title of Tharakan. After the establishment of the St Mary's Church at the eastern end of the street, more or less at the same time, several other Christian families moved over to Puthiacavu from other parts of Mavelikara and settled themselves on either side of this street. Puthiacavu and the neighbouring areas to the west and the east of it soon became a flourishing settlement of the Nazranis or St Thomas Christians, as the community was known in those days.

The Christians living in Puthiacavu were mainly engaged in trading activities and the location of their houses on either side of the road connecting Mavelikara with other towns in central Travancore suited the requirements of their occupation. Further, the Achankoil river, a branch of the Pampa river, skirted Mavelikara to the north and this facilitated transport of goods by large country boats to and from other trading centres in central Travancore. Our family was one of the few among the Christians in Puthiacavu which also owned agricultural properties.

The Nairs, the dominant community among the Hindus, lived near their agricultural properties, some distance away, but Puthiacavu remained their ancestral home since the Bhagawathi temple was situated there. Wherever they lived they considered the ancient Bhagawathi temple at Puthiacavu as their ancestral place and for them therefore the festivals of this temple were very important occasions to demonstrate their continued loyalty to their ancestral place of worship. The Christian community living in close proximity to the temple also participated in, and celebrated, the festivals of the temple with enthusiasm and bonhomie.

The most important festival at the Bhagawathi temple was the Kettu Kalcha, or the chariot festival, celebrated on the day marked for the Bharani star in the Malayalam month of Meenum (corresponding to March–April of the modern calendar). A similar festival is also held on the day marked for the Bharani star in the Malayalam month of Kumbham corresponding to February–March at another Bhagawathi temple at Chettikulangara (about 8 km south-west of Mavelikara). Many historians believe that these festivals were a continuation or a close imitation of the Buddhist car festivals common in Kerala in the early centuries of the Christian era, when Buddhism was widely prevalent in Kerala. Many Buddhist images have been discovered in places close to the temples at Puthiacavu and Chettikulangara, lending weight to the theory that Buddhism was once popular in this region.

The day of the Bharani star of Kumbham was also an occasion for great celebrations at the Puthiacavu temple. This day was observed by taking out the deity in a solemn procession during the night along the road to the accompaniment of music, fireworks and brilliantly lit torches. A replica of the idol was carried in an artistically decorated small carriage mounted on a pair of strong wooden rods resting on the shoulders of two temple priests, the senior one in the front and the other in the back. By deft movements of the shoulder muscles, the priests carrying the decorated carriage would make the carriage swing from side to side without their having to hold the rods with their hands to the great wonder and excitement of the huge crowds watching the procession from either side of the road. While observing the swinging of the carriage as a child, I used to believe along with rest of the crowd that the Puthiacavu Bhagawathi or the deity of the temple was expressing her happiness at the devotion of the people. On certain occasions, the priests would go into a state of ecstasy and perform a brisk dance to the beat of the drums with artistic movements of their feet without using their hands to hold the rods of the carriage.

Cultural shows, mainly Kathakali and Ottam Thullal, were the other interesting events of this festival. Ottam Thullal was a one-man show depicting certain events from the Hindu epics to the accompaniment of *chenda* or drum and cymbals. Kathakali or dance drama had dancers for each part, but unlike the Thullal, the dancers never sang their verses, which was left solely to the background singer. Even though I had witnessed several Kathakali performances later in my life, the images of this dance drama performed under the open sky in the compound of the Puthiacavu Bhagawathi temple in the dim light of the traditional brass lamps are still deeply etched in my memory.

Equally vivid in my mind are the memories of the festival of the St Mary's Church at Puthiacavu which were held on two days in the first week of the Malayalam month of Makaram corresponding to January–February of the modern calendar. Normally, one would expect a festival in the church to be one to honour the memory of the saint in whose name it is dedicated. But for some unknown reasons the St Mary's Church conducts the festival to honour the memory of a Metropolitan named Mar Ahathulla from West Asia who had arrived at the Kochi port in a ship in the mid-seventeenth century but was not allowed to meet the St Thomas Christians by the Portuguese, who had, by then, gained complete control of the port. The Portuguese, who were fanatic in their attempts to propagate the Roman Catholic faith, are believed to have tied the hands and feet of the visiting Metropolitan and drowned him in the sea. Such cruel treatment had caused great anguish and anger among the St Thomas Christian community in Kerala and it is believed that the festival in Puthiacavu church was instituted to honour the martyrdom of this Metropolitan.

The main events connected with the festival were two processions, one on the night of the first day and the other in the afternoon of the second day. If anyone from outside Kerala were to watch these processions, it would have been difficult for him or her to know whether these were processions taken out by the Christians or the Hindus. The only difference was that in the church processions large sized crosses in wood or silver would be carried along with the usual festoons and silken umbrellas to the accompaniment of the beating of drums and playing of a band and other musical instruments as well as the display of fireworks, which were common to all religious festivals in Kerala. The festival days were great opportunities for us children to buy and relish delicacies like dates and sugarcane, which were rarely seen in Mavelikara on other days.

The culture of religious tolerance and communal harmony prevalent in the society in which I grew up as a child at Mavelikara had greatly influenced my outlook about other religions and helped me unconsciously to develop an attitude of understanding and respect for all religions, particularly the Hindu religion.

I was born in a family of Christians in Kerala bearing the denominational title, the Malankara Orthodox Syrian Church. The Christians of Kerala, who claim the St Thomas heritage, were known by different names from the early years of the church in Kerala.

What is the St Thomas heritage? Very briefly, it is the belief strongly held by the Malankara Nazranis as irrefutable historical truth that their ancestors were converted from the upper castes of the Hindus to the Christian faith by St Thomas, one of the twelve apostles of Jesus who visited Kerala about 2000 years ago. According to the apocryphal book, *Acts of Thomas*, written in the third century A.D., a conclave of apostles was held in Jerusalem after the Crucifixion of Jesus Christ. The purpose was to decide, by drawing of lots, the territory to be allotted to each apostle for spreading the gospel of Jesus and India fell to the lot of St Thomas. He is believed to have landed at a place called Maliankara (near the ancient port of Kodungalloor) in A.D. 52. Some writers believe that the name Malankara is derived from Maliankara. Regular trade existed between the west coast of Kerala and the middle-eastern countries from ancient times, and merchants used to be particularly attracted towards Kerala for its valuable products such as ivory, pepper and teakwood. These trade routes also brought non-trading visitors to Kerala, and

St Thomas' journey to Kodungalloor, therefore, was considered a normal event in the long history of cultural and commercial contacts between Kerala and the middle-eastern countries. After completing his mission in Kerala, St Thomas left for China essentially to carry on with his missionary activities there. On completion of his mission in China he returned to India, this time to the east coast town of Mylapore (now a locality in modern-day Chennai), to continue his missionary work. He was martyred at Mylapore and buried in the church there. This place of martyrdom has since become a centre of pilgrimage for Christians not only from Kerala but also from all parts of India and the Afro-Asian continent.

The Orthodox Church of India, which, as already stated, has a history of around 2000 years, is one of the oldest churches in the world. But during the last five centuries its history has got entangled in conflicts, splits and internecine quarrels.

Till the rise of the Portuguese power in Kerala in the sixteenth century, the Christians there had never experienced political or social tensions or oppression of any type. They lived a life of close integration with the rest of the population, feeling secure and safe in view of the high status they enjoyed in Kerala's caste hierarchy and the special rights and privileges granted to them through royal charters. Till about the middle of the nineteenth century, they were in no way different from the higher castes of the Hindu society in dress and observance of social customs. Their menfolk grew their hair long, wore earrings and smeared their foreheads with sandal paste as the upper caste Hindus did and they observed most of the rituals followed by the Hindus on occasions like birth of children, weddings and death. They had very little contacts with Christian churches outside India and the few Christian dignitaries who had visited them in the pre-Portuguese period, mainly from the East Syrian Churches of Persia, had never tried to interfere in their internal affairs. They continued to enjoy their privileged position as members of a highly respected indigenous church, following their own customs and forms of worship.

The Syrian Christian community in Kerala has always been economically and socially one of the most advanced communities in the state. Since its members were mostly converts from the landowing castes, they had prospered well through farming operations. Many of them had taken to trading activities and have done well in this field as well. Educationally too, they are quite advanced compared with the rest of the population in India. On the whole, this community could be described as middle class in terms of social and economic progress and in many places has provided distinguished leaders to society.

When the Portuguese held sway in Kerala, they had converted several influential families from the Syrian community to the Roman Catholic Church, but they preferred to retain the caste name 'Syrian' to distinguish themselves from the new converts who were called Latin Catholics. In later centuries when the British had become rulers of India, they had also indulged in conversion activities among the Syrian Christians, though on a much smaller scale than what the Portuguese had done. The new converts also continued to call themselves Syrian Protestants to distinguish themselves from other new converts. The Syrian Church went through another major split when a group of families influenced by the Protestant missionaries in the nineteenth century formed a new Reformed Church called Mar Thoma Church, but they also kept using the caste name 'Syrian' to mark their distinct identity from other converts to Christianity. The Orthodox Church, which had maintained close relations with the Orthodox Church in Syria under the Patriarch of Antioch, suffered another split in the early years of the twentieth century when one group remained loyal to the Patriarch in Syria, whereas the other asserted its independence from Antiochan control by establishing the institution of the Catholicate with its headquarters in Kottayam (in Kerala), and claiming to be the direct legatees of the St Thomas heritage. This church adopted a new constitution, which, for all practical purposes, made it independent of the control of the Patriarch of Antioch. The followers of this church are now one of the most economically advanced communities among the entire family of St Thomas churches in Kerala.

Mavelikara, my home town, is one of the most important centres of this group of the Orthodox Church. I was born in an upper middle-class family owing allegiance to this church. I was the fifth among the eight children of my parents, Jacob Cherian and Mariama, who had three daughters and five sons. My three sisters, Thankamma,

Elimma and Kunjamma and one brother, Jacob, were elder to me. The three brothers younger to me were Thomas, Kurien and Cherian. According to the traditions of the Syrian Christian community in Travancore, in my generation, girls were married when they were about fifteen to eighteen years of age and boys when they were about eighteen to twenty-two years. Almost all marriages in the community were arranged.

My father's mother had died when he was only a one-year-old infant and his father, when he was just thirteen. He grew up under the parental care of his elder brother, Jacob Kurien, who was a prominent leader of the Christian community in central Travancore and a member of the Legislative Assembly of the state. Jacob Kurien was a highly talented speaker and the editor of a weekly published from Mavelikara. My father was highly respectful towards his elder brother so much so that in all family matters such as marriages or celebrations of family functions (say, baptism), he was quite willing to follow the latter's advice and guidance.

My mother Mariama came from an entirely different family background. She was the eldest child of her parents who belonged to the Mar Thoma Church, which, as I have stated earlier, was established as a result of a Protestant reform movement in the Orthodox Church. My mother's family, Meenathethil, had settled at Chettikulangara, a place about 8 km south of Mavelikara town several generations ago and had accorded special importance to providing higher education to its members. My mother's father, K.U. Alexander, was one of the earliest graduates from the Syrian Christian community of Travancore and it was his earnest wish that his children also should get the benefit of higher education. Incidentally, my name Alexander is derived from him. According to the customs of the Syrian Christians, the eldest male child is given the name of the paternal grandfather and the eldest female child the name of the paternal grandmother, while the second male child and second female child are given the names of the maternal grandfather and the maternal grandmother, respectively. The letter 'P' in my initials stands for my family name Padinjarethalakal and 'C' for my father's name Cherian. The customs regarding names and initials have changed very much in recent years.

The decision regarding the marriage of my mother to my father was taken by K.U. Alexander's uncle, who made the formal proposal to my father's elder brother Jacob Kurien without bothering to even ascertain the wishes of the girl's father. My mother, at that time was hardly thirteen years old and was a middle-school student at the Miss Baker School, Kottayam, where she was a boarder. K.U. Alexander was working as a subregistrar in the service of the Travancore Government at Shertalai a place over 60 km away from Chettikulangara. He was only informed of the settlement of the marriage after the date and place of the marriage had been fixed. However, K.U. Alexander did not question the decision taken by his uncle though he is reported to have expressed his unhappiness at sending his thirteen-year-old daughter to a landowning family where she would not have even the guidance of other older women.

In spite of the fact that my mother did not have the benefit of even a high-school education, she understood well the value of higher education and was determined that her sons should take to studies instead of the traditional agricultural occupation of our family. She used to tell us, repeatedly, that the days of landowning as an occupation were over and the future was only for those with high educational qualifications. It was this valuable advice and wise guidance of a mother, who herself had to stop her studies at the middle-school level, which made me and my brothers take to education with all earnestness and eagerness right from our young age. Personally, it was my mother's strong will and perseverance that created in me an intense interest in higher education and the determination to avail of every opportunity to pursue higher studies even after completing my normal college course. When my mother passed away at the age of sixty-three in 1958, she had achieved the great satisfaction of having seen all her sons well educated and settled in various occupations totally unrelated to agriculture. I joined the Indian Administrative Service (IAS), my elder brother Jacob joined the Cooperative Department in the Kerala State Government service, my younger brothers, Thomas, Kurien and Cherian, chose medicine, engineering and business, respectively.

A very beneficial influence on my life, besides my mother, was my eldest sister Thankamma. She was ten years older than I and had taken on the full responsibilities of guiding me and my immediate younger brother Thomas to achieve success in our studies. She also ensured that we developed good conduct and a strong character. In a large agricultural family like ours, she became the 'assistant mother' for me and my brother. She was a person who would insist on our reading the Bible and saying our prayers and doing the homework before going to sleep. She would also tell us stories or parables every day about the importance of simple virtues like honesty, obedience, respect to elders and compassion. She would reprimand and even punish us if we misbehaved.

A brief account of the system of education in the state of Travancore during my younger days may prove interesting to the present generation. Even though Travancore was well known as an educationally advanced state, the fact remained that the facilities for education during that period were availed of mainly by the well-to-do families, belonging to the upper castes among the Hindus and the Syrian Christians. Fees had to be paid for all courses above the primary level and scholarships or concessions in fees were very few and inadequate, if and when available. Further, facilities for high-school education existed only in a few urban centres of the state. College education was beyond the reach of the economically underprivileged castes and classes, as the students had to bear the expenditure for boarding and lodging in college hostels or other privately managed residences, besides having to pay the tuition fees, which were considered rather high by the standards of those days. In the entire state of Travancore there were only four first-grade colleges in arts and science and three intermediate colleges. For those parents living in places other than where the colleges were located, sending their children for studies imposed a huge financial burden. Acquiring high-school education was an arduous experience for the young boys and girls who had no such schools in or near their own places of residence. Some of the students in the high school with me at Mavelikara had to walk 6 to 10 km one way. Transport facilities to reach the places where high schools were located were nonexistent and walking the whole distance to the school and back to their homes every day was the only option open to them. A few high schools offered hostel facilities, but the Bishop Hodges High School, where

I studied, was not one of them. Fortunately for me, my school was just 300 metres from my house and this made acquiring school education quite convenient for me.

It was very common in those days for parents to send their children to pre-schools known as *asan pallikudam* or schools run by an *asan* or teacher. These pre-schools provided opportunities for little children in the age group three to five to learn the Malayalam alphabet. There was one such school very near my house and I recall vividly the experiences of my early introduction to learning in this institution. It was a small thatched shed with a stool as the only item of furniture for the *asan* to sit on. The young pupils sat in rows on the little mats they brought with them on the ground and they wrote with their pointer fingers, on the sand, the Malayalam letters starting with the vowels. The *asan* would shout out the letter to be written and the pupils would collectively repeat the letter after him while writing it on the sand. The *asan* would then go round to see whether the letter had been correctly written by everyone and give guidance to those who needed it and then proceed to shout out the next letter to be written. The *asan* provided each student a palm leaf on which the vowels were written and the pupil could look at the palm leaf if he desired to do so, while writing the letter on the sand. After a few weeks the *asan* would provide the second leaf starting with the first consonant of the Malayalam alphabet and, in due course, the young pupil would get a full bundle of palm leaves covering all the letters of the alphabet neatly tied together with a string. Simultaneously, the pupil was introduced to the numerals and by the time he acquired the knowledge of the alphabets, he also got trained to count up to 100.

The *asan's* monthly remuneration was very little, but he considered it his right and privilege to invite himself to a noon meal in the houses of the pupils by rotation every day. However, he chose his hosts very carefully. Some of his pupils came from poor families and the *asan* would therefore skip such families. My house was one of those frequented by him. He was considerate to the hosts in remembering to send a communication on a small piece of palm leaf that the *asan* would be having his noon meal the next day in their house. I recall that my *asan* was not particularly popular with the servants in our house because they considered him to be too generous with his invitations to himself.

After learning the alphabets, the child was ready to go to the first standard of the four-year primary school where he would come to possess a slate, a slate pencil and a regular textbook instead of the palm leaves. Above all, he would sit on a bench instead of on the ground. The primary school where I was a student for four years was situated within 50 metres from my house. This is a school in which all my brothers and sisters had also studied and is still functioning. By the age of eight, I had passed the primary school examination and was ready to be admitted to the English medium high school.

The Bishop Hodges High School managed by the Church Missionary Society had then enjoyed a well-deserved reputation as one of the best educational institutions in Central Travancore. It had a long tradition of giving equal attention to instruction in the classroom and to the all-round development of the personality of the student through extracurricular activities. The staff consisted of a devoted band of teachers who had considered teaching as not just a profession but a calling.

The two most important influences on me as a student in the Bishop Hodges High School, where I spent seven years, were the Boy Scout movement and the Balajana Sakhyam. The Boy Scout movement was very popular in Travancore state those days and the fact that the young maharaja of the state was himself the chief Scout of the state had given it a special importance. I joined the Cubs' Wing of the Scout movement in the school while I was in the first standard and remained active till I reached the high-school classes. The assistant headmaster of the school, P.M. Thomas, in charge of the Cubs' Wing, took personal interest in organizing various activities like picnics and cleanliness drives in the colonies in which the Scheduled Caste families lived.

Thomas frequently stressed the importance of certain values and qualities in life like selflessness, courage, service for the poor, and uprightness. He made us believe that we as Cubs should be models for other students.

The Balajana Sakhyam was a students' movement started by the illustrious editor of the *Malayala Manorama*, K.C. Mammen Mappilai with the main objective of developing leadership qualities in the youth and instilling in them proper values and ideals. An additional objective of the Balajana Sakhyam was to encourage talents in young persons in literary and cultural fields, especially with respect to activities such as writing, speech making and singing. The *Manorama* reserved two or three columns of space every week for publishing short stories, poems, essays or articles contributed by the young members of the Balajana Sakhyam and for reporting about the activities of its various branches. I felt thrilled whenever I saw my name in print and used to keep cuttings of those papers in which my name appeared.

The first occasion for me to discover that I had some talent in speech making was when I won the first prize in an elocution competition organized by the branch of the Balajana Sakhyam in my home town when I was a boy of nine. The subject given to the competitors five minutes before each was called upon to speak was *kshama*, which means both patience and forgiveness in Malayalam. I don't think there was any worthwhile content in my five minutes performance from the platform. Even if I had been given ten or fifteen minutes to prepare the speech I couldn't have added to the content because at that age I had little knowledge of any subject outside my textbooks. But I recall that I spoke without any stage fright and words flowed without any break. In short, I displayed some evidence that I had eloquence bereft of substance and I was awarded the first prize even though my fellow competitors were from higher classes and more knowledgeable on the subject. This first prize became the launching pad for my ambition to win a name as a speaker and I started entering elocution competitions wherever there were opportunities for doing so in Mavelikara or in neighbouring towns.

I should here acknowledge the great support and encouragement I received from my father in this field. He encouraged me to enter interschool elocution competitions organized by the YMCAs in towns like Chengannoor and Alapuzha and also by the Balajana Sakhyam and the Syrian Students' Conference at their annual conferences held in different places in the state. I was a regular winner not only in my school competitions but also in those outside my home town.

My father felt very proud and happy when I returned with medals and certificates and this was a source of special encouragement to me. Though he was himself a shy and reserved person unlike his elder brother Jacob Kurien, who was acknowledged as a silver-tongued orator all over Travancore, my father found great satisfaction in seeing me emerge as a good speaker.

A close rival of mine in my school years for the elocution competitions was my friend and classmate, C.M. Stephen, who later distinguished himself as a great leader of the Congress Party. In competitions in which both Stephen and I participated, I used to invariably win the first prize in English and the second prize in Malayalam while Stephen won the first prize in Malayalam and the second prize in English. For Stephen these experiences proved to be great assets in his career as a parliamentarian and a Congress leader, while for me such experiences had little importance in my career as a civil servant.

THREE

The Unforgettable College Years

THE CHOICE OF COLLEGE ON PASSING THE HIGH SCHOOL EXAMINATION in 1936 was fairly easy for me: it was the Union Christian College at Aluva a place about 110 km north of my home town. This college was established in 1920 by a group of four eminent old students of the Madras Christian College, K.C. Chacko, A.M. Varkey, C.P. Mathew and V.M. Ittiarah. The first two belonged to the Orthodox Church and the latter two to the Mar Thoma Church. Chacko was a saintly person, highly respected in the Christian community of Travancore. He was deeply committed to Christian ideals and to the use of education for instilling in the youth the noble values of life. It was his leadership and inspiration that prompted the other three to take up the task of building up a residential college with practically no capital except their own faith in divine guidance and commitment to a cause. Ittiarah had, a few months before I joined the college, married my mother's younger sister the former Annama Alexander, head-mistress of the Nicholson High School for girls at Thiruvalla and the Ittiarahs were thus my local guardians. In my days, the college was exclusively for boys; later, girls also were admitted.

At the age of fifteen, life away from home in a hostel was altogether a new experience for me. There were a few other students also from my home town in the same college and hostel along with me, the notable among them being P.M. Mathew (who later joined the IAS) and C.M. Stephen. The younger students among the freshers were put up in the Tagore Hostel during their first year in the intermediate class and Mathew, Stephen and I thus found ourselves as fellow residents. Some of the students with us in the Tagore Hostel had lived in boarding homes during their school days and were not therefore new to hostel life like me. I felt very homesick in the first few months in the hostel and this was reflected in the frequent letters I wrote to my parents from my hostel in 1936.

I was not very clear in my mind as to what subjects I should take as my optionals and I had put down a combination of physics, chemistry and logic in my application to the college. My uncle, V.M. Ittiarah, discussed with me my plans for the future after completing my university studies. I had then told him that I would like to take the Indian Civil Service (ICS) examination after obtaining my postgraduate degree and he advised me to opt for a group of three subjects, ancient history, modern history and logic. He felt these subjects were ideal for me. I had no hesitation in following his advice.

It is interesting to note that when I was a student in the intermediate class with history as the main subject, ancient history meant that of Greece in the first year and of Rome in the second year and modern history meant the history of Britain. There was no provision for the study of Indian history in the college as the Madras University, to which my college was affiliated then, had been strictly following the syllabus and courses of instructions of the colleges in Britain. Thus, I had to complete my study of history in the intermediate classes without any instruction in the history of my own country.

✧

Political life in the state of Travancore was relatively placid with few agitations or demonstrations by political parties. The dominant political party in British India – as the provinces outside the Princely States were then called – was the Indian National Congress. Its influence in the Princely States was negligible and the people in these states had not yet become active in demanding responsible government or a share for the people's representatives in running the government.

However, there were active socio-political movements in Travancore seeking increased representation for the backward communities in the legislature and in public services. These movements eventually led to the demand for responsible government in the state. Travancore had a bicameral legislature whose members were elected on a highly restricted qualification of payment of land revenue or possession of a university degree. This electoral system benefited only the upper castes among the Hindus as they were the main landholders in the state. This inequitable electoral system led to a strong movement by the Christians, the Ezhavas and the Muslims for radical electoral reforms ensuring representation according to the strength of the population. There were also persistent demands from these communities for representation in the civil services of the state according to population. These demands gained considerable momentum when the three communities – Christians, Muslims and Ezhavas – founded a new political organization called the Joint Political Party or the Samyukta Party. At a large public meeting held at Kozhencheny on 13 March 1935 under the presidentship of the charismatic Ezhava leader C. Kesavan, these demands were reiterated and a new demand was also forcefully raised for the dismissal of the legal and constitutional adviser of the maharaja, Sir C.P. Ramaswamy Iyer, who had been seen by the people as the real power behind the throne. This demand led to very strong repressive action by the government and Kesavan was arrested on charges of sedition and sentenced to two years' imprisonment.

Kesavan's arrest and imprisonment marked a turning point in Travancore's political history. The Joint Political Party transformed itself into the Travancore State Congress in 1938 and was considerably strengthened in its representative capacity with the inclusion of the Nairs and other upper castes of the Hindu community. The Travancore State Congress adopted responsible government as its principal goal, and a new era of open confrontation between the people and the government started in 1938. Sir CP was considered by the common people of Travancore as the 'brain' masterminding the repressive measures against the Congress and, naturally, he became the target of criticism, if not hatred, of the people. Even though he was faithfully carrying out the wishes of the maharaja (Shri Chittira Thirunal) and his mother (Sethu Parvatibai), the people believed that the maharaja was only a puppet in CP's hands and that he and the maharani were keeping the ruler in ignorance of the real sentiments of the people. The rift between the people and the ruler widened as the Travancore State Congress stepped up the agitation for responsible government and the government, in turn, unleashed a reign of repression and terror on all those who were seen as supporters of the Congress. Sir C.P. Ramaswamy Iyer had brought into the state a large number of persons from Madras Presidency to head the important departments of administration including the judiciary and the police. This move also created great resentment among the people who saw it as his lack of confidence in the Travancoreans and part of a plan to run the state with the help of his trusted supporters from Madras.

Even though the political climate of the state started hotting up, the educational institutions remained practically untouched by these developments. Till the middle of 1938 the student community had not been drawn into the agitation for responsible government and therefore perfect calm and discipline prevailed in the college campus at Aluva during the two years I was a student there. However, the whole situation changed radically in the latter half of 1938 with the launching of a statewide agitation against the government and the student community found itself drawn into the vortex of this great struggle. Thiruvananthapuram, the capital city and the seat of the new Travancore University and several government colleges, became the centre of the agitation for responsible government from mid-1938 onwards. By this time, I had joined the Maharaja's College of Arts and was in the first year of the three-year BA Honours course in history, economics and political science.

Thiruvananthapuram those days was a relatively quiet city unlike the capital cities of other states and provinces in the south like Madras (now Chennai) or Kochi. There were no industries worth mentioning in Thiruvananthapuram unlike in Chennai; nor was it a prominent trading centre, like Kochi. The one institution that had been dominating life in the city for several years was the palace where the maharaja lived as the head of the ruling family along with his mother, his sister (Princess Karthika Thirunal) and his brother (Prince Uttradom Thirunal Marthanda Varma).

Ramaswamy Iyer had the reputation of being an autocrat and, in the eyes of the common people, he was the originator and perpetrator of a repressive regime, the likes of which the state had never seen till then. After the formation of the Travancore State Congress, the people had lent support to the demand for responsible government, but the very idea of transfer of power to the elected representatives of the people was unthinkable to the maharaja and his *dewan*. The British authorities were watching with great concern how the movement for freedom from foreign rule was influencing the people in the Princely States to demand transfer of the substance of power. They were determined to do everything in their power to stop the spread of this 'seditious' movement in the Princely States and had informed Ramaswamy Iyer that the British Government would stand firmly behind the state government as far as any measure taken by the latter for suppressing such movements was concerned. Fortified by the assurances from the British Government, the ruler and his *dewan* went ahead with implementing a ruthless programme of suppression. Even the most inoffensive expression of dissent was not tolerated.

A strange feature in this scenario was that the common man believed that the maharaja was not being kept fully informed by the *dewan* about what the state machinery was doing to put down the struggle and that the *dewan* had been resorting to such harsh measures on his own, acting only with the support of the maharaja's mother Parvatibai. However, the recent publication of some state papers – relating to this period and containing the notes sent by the *dewan* to the ruler almost on a daily basis about the former's briefing of the latter and the latter's unambiguous approval of the measures adopted by the government to deal with the state Congress agitation – clears all doubts about the fiction of innocence on the part of the ruler. Every decision was taken by the *dewan* with the approval of the ruler and, in some cases, the ruler wanted to go even beyond the levels of severity proposed by the *dewan*. Ramaswamy Iyer's total loyalty to the ruler had clouded his own judgement and he carried out every wish and whim of the ruler and his mother in ruthlessly suppressing the people's movement for responsible government.

A harsh but very important step taken by the palace and the *dewan* as part of the programme to suppress the movement for responsible government was the forceful closure of the Travancore National and Quilon Bank, the biggest private bank in the state formed by the amalgamation of two flourishing banks, the Travancore National Bank and the Quilon Bank. K.C. Mammen Mappilai, the founder of the former bank, and C.P. Mathen, the founder of the latter, had been strong supporters of the state Congress and after the two banks had been amalgamated in 1937, the power and influence of the bank as a provider of employment and loans for business and industry had increased manifold. The largest number of beneficiaries of the bank in terms of employment and financial assistance were the Syrian Christians who, as a community, had been active in the struggle for responsible government. From a careful scrutiny of the notes and minutes of the meetings between the maharaja and the *dewan* during 1937 and 1938, now available to the public, it is very clear that the decision to bring about the collapse and eventual closure of the bank was undertaken on the basis of a joint decision by the palace and the *dewan*. This move was primarily intended to convey a clear message to the people of Travancore in general and the Christian community in particular that any support to the state Congress movement would be mercilessly dealt with. CP's loyalty to the ruler and his mother was so high that he had taken good care to keep the palace out of any controversies and criticisms by himself owning up responsibility for all acts against the bank.

It was into this environment of confrontation between the people and the government surcharged with intense anti-CP sentiments that I stepped in as a student in Thiruvananthapuram. When I arrived there in the early months of 1938, my life pattern underwent a big change from the secluded and disciplined atmosphere in a residential college like the Union Christian College, Aluva, which was unaffected by political activities such as agitations, strikes, hartals and processions.

During most of 1938, our studies were seriously disturbed because of strikes and hartals that were being frequently called by the

Travancore State Congress. Out of the six of us in the first year of the history and economics honours group, three were always regular in their attendance, strike or no strike. One of the three was the first cousin of the maharaja and the other two belonged to families very loyal to the government. As a result, classes went on uninterrupted in our Honours group and the three of us who boycotted the classes during the period of strike suffered heavily in coping with the missed lectures.

Life outside the college, however, was quite exciting because of the happenings on the political front. The year 1938 witnessed some of the most disgusting acts of repression by the state government. A shocking incident that year was the burglary committed, under the orders of senior government officials, in the house of Anne Mascarene, a firebrand leader of the Congress, who was very popular with the people because of her unflinching courage and powerful oratory. The newspapers reported that every item of furniture and household articles, except the ladle for salt, had been taken away from the lady advocate's house in an act of intimidation and punishment for her fiery speeches criticizing the state government. Equally shocking was the physical assault on two highly respected editors, M.R. Madhava Warrier, editor of the *Malayali*, and Thomas Mathew Muthalali, editor of the *Malabar Advocate*, by *goondas* (hired hoodlums) in broad daylight in a public road in Thiruvananthapuram on instructions from the district magistrate and the chief of the police force for their alleged anti-government writings. Warrier was one of the top leaders of the press and Muthalali was a frail and saintly looking gentleman held in great esteem for his commitment to high principles and values in life. The fact that such eminent and respected editors could be physically assaulted by rowdies under orders of the government officials made people wonder at the depths to which the administration could sink in its attempt to intimidate its critics.

Newspapers were carrying daily reports of similar acts of rowdyism organized by the government to disturb state Congress meetings and to physically attack the state Congress leaders participating in such functions. In June 1938 a senior Congress leader and advocate, K.P. Nilakanta Pillai, was badly beaten up by the *goondas* of the government at the Pattom junction in Thiruvananthapuram and he had to be hospitalized. This incident enraged the people, particularly the student community, which started organizing demonstrations against the government, boycotting the classes.

✧

By the middle of 1938, the student community was on a confrontation course with the government. The government had issued strict instructions to all its employees that they should not allow their wards to participate in the agitation against the government, but the students had been so greatly enraged by the government's high-handed actions that their guardians could not, even if they tried very hard, control them. The students were in no mood to attend classes and could not remain unaffected by the hurricane of protests sweeping across the length and breadth of the state.

The political situation in Travancore took a turn for the worse when the state Congress leaders submitted a memorandum to the maharaja on 31 May 1938. They demanded the replacement of the *dewan* by a council of ministers responsible to the legislature. What offended the *dewan* and the palace most was that the memorandum contained a detailed account of the misdeeds on the part of the *dewan*, including several acts that ostensibly involved corruption. The *dewan* considered the action as a personal attack on him and was so enraged that he insisted on the unconditional withdrawal of the memorandum before the government could agree to holding any talks. The Indian National Congress leadership too did not agree with the levelling of personal allegations against the *dewan*. Mahatma Gandhi in particular was unhappy and considered it an unethical act. He advised them to withdraw the allegations in the memorandum. The younger elements in the Congress, represented by the Youth League, were strongly against withdrawing the allegations and it looked as if a serious rift had developed in the Congress on this issue. CP became more rigid in his stand. Apart from insisting on the withdrawal of allegations, he also wanted an apology. The government resorted to even harsher measures of repression against the Congress and in August 1938 banned the Travancore State Congress and the Youth League as unlawful organizations. This step led to the launching of a massive civil disobedience movement by the state Congress leaders. Consequently, top Congress leaders such as Pattom Thanu Pillai and T.M. Verghese were arrested. The Congress leaders gave a call for disobeying the prohibitory orders, which led to police firing and *lathi*-charges in several places in the state. Large numbers of Congress leaders and workers courted arrest by violating prohibitory orders and when one Congress president was arrested, the successor nominated by him or her took charge as acting president and continued the agitation in defiance of the ban.

A novel method of violating prohibitory orders was resorted to by Elizabeth Kuruvilla, the fifth acting president of the Congress, when she travelled by a special train accompanied by hundreds of Congress workers from Kollam to Thiruvananthapuram on 28 September 1938. Since railway properties were outside the jurisdiction of the state government at that time, it could not prevent large crowds from assembling at various railway stations enroute to welcome Elizabeth Kuruvilla. A huge crowd, including hundreds of students, had assembled at the railway station and the adjacent maidan at Thampanoor to welcome her. Even though she was later arrested by the state government, her novel method of displaying the public resentment against the government provided a great impetus to the civil disobedience movement.

The twelfth president of the Congress, Ackamma Cherian, organized a more defiant form of protest in Thiruvananthapuram on 23 October 1938, which was the birthday of the maharaja. She had given a call to Congress workers all over the state to come to Thiruvananthapuram a day in advance for holding a massive demonstration at the Fort area. The maharaja too would visit the area on that day to worship at the Padmanabha Swamy temple. Thousands of Congress workers and students had assembled on either side of the main road, leading from the Kawdiyar Palace, the residence of the maharaja, to the temple in the Fort area. As the pilot car of the maharaja rolled down the main road, the crowd became very restive and the demonstration turned more aggressive and noisy. The maharaja, sitting with folded hands in the back seat of his car, appeared calm and unruffled, as was his usual style on all occasions when he took a car ride through the city roads. It was a time-honoured practice on the part of the ruler to visit the Padmanabha

Swamy temple every morning for worship and, on all such occasions, he used to be greeted very reverentially by the people on either side of the road. Vehicles would pull up to the sides of the road and come to a stop. Those on bicycles would dismount and bow respectfully till his car passed by and even pedestrians would move to the sides and greet him with folded hands and bowed heads. But his experience on this day was quite different all along the route. Thousands of people from all over the state had gathered in that area, occupying every inch of space. Their mood was definitely hostile. The Congress workers were preparing for a grand march to the Kawdiyar Palace to stage a demonstration before the maharaja on his return from the temple. If the government had used force to disperse the crowds, there would have been a blood bath in the city. Fortunately, better counsel prevailed and the maharaja and the *dewan* decided to handle the delicate situation with restraint and conciliatory gestures. The maharaja announced, through a proclamation, the lifting of the ban on the Travancore State Congress and the Youth League and the granting of general amnesty to all those arrested for violating prohibitory orders. The Congress leaders responded by calling off the proposed march to the Kawdiyar Palace.

The period 1939–40, the second year of my BA Honours course in Thiruvananthapuram, was particularly satisfying and rewarding for me. It was only at Thiruvananthapuram that I could get opportunities to participate in intercollegiate elocution competitions and win several prizes. I also won the contest for the post of secretary of the Arts College Union for the year 1939–40, where my main duty was to organize talks and debates by college students on topics of special interest to them and to arrange for special lectures by distinguished guests from outside.

My contemporaries in the Arts College included some eminent writers and poets who had already earned a reputation for their valuable contributions to Malayalam literature. The famous poet of Kerala, Changampuzha Krishna Pillai, was a student of the first year of the MA class in Malayalam literature. His was a household name in Kerala because of the distinctive lyrical attractive style of his poetry. I used to meet him with requests for his participation in various functions. However, I found him very reserved and wanting his privacy to be respected without being embarrassed by the adulation of his fellow students or seeking to be treated as anyone deserving special attention. Of the other distinguished writers and poets, the persons I remember best are S. Guptan Nair, T.N. Gopinathan Nair, Edayaranmula K.M. Daniel and K.M. George. The presence of these distinguished writers made the student community of that period a star-studded one.

Another important event during this year was my winning the gold medal at the intercollegiate debate organized by the Travancore University at the Law College Hall at Thiruvananthapuram. The subject was: 'The World Is Fast Degenerating into Chaos'. The cheers I received from the large crowd when my name was announced as the winner are still etched in memory as one of the proudest experiences of my student years. This success gave me the courage and confidence to compete for the post of president of the Travancore University Union, which was being set up by the university authorities during 1940–41, when I was in the final year of the BA Honours class. I won with a big margin.

The high-water mark in my life as a student at the Travancore University during the years 1938–41 was reached when I was nominated as leader of a four-member team to participate in inter-university debates in Madras, Bangalore and Mysore. We spent about ten days visiting these places. My involvement in the university union activities as its president and my visits to universities outside the state seriously impeded my preparations for my final examinations. But such involvement helped me a great deal in acquiring leadership training and personality development. I recall the very friendly paternal advice given to me by my lecturer, Pappu Pillai, who taught us constitutional history. A few months before the examinations, in an open class he declared: 'Alexander, winning medals and prizes in elocutions and debates is all right but if you win all medals but fail to do justice to your studies you may regret it all your life.' It was a well-meant piece of advice by a genuine well-wisher of mine, but I was lucky I did not have to regret on either count as he feared.

FOUR

Academic Research and Beyond

W HEN THE RESULTS OF MY UNIVERSITY EXAMINATIONS WERE ANNOUNCED, I was confronted with the question as to what I should do next. C.V. Chandrashekaran, pro-vice-chancellor, Travancore University, was gracious enough to inform me that the university would offer me a research fellowship if I was interested. I was keen on doing research, but the stipend was quite small and I would have needed extra financial support to maintain myself in Thiruvananthapuram. The more serious reason for my not feeling enthusiastic about doing research in the Travancore University was that there was no one in the history and political science department who had any research experience and therefore could have guided me.

One day I received a telegram from my mother's brother, K.A. Thomas, who was then a senior manager in a European-owned group of tea estates in the Nilgiris asking me to reach Coonoor immediately. He had arranged for an assistant manager's job in one of the tea estates in the Nilgiris, which entitled me to good facilities like a bungalow, a few servants and a horse, apart from a fairly comfortable salary. However, I was unenthusiastic about taking up such a profession as all my dreams of a great career with opportunities for further development of my intellectual interests and tastes would collapse. I was so fresh from my university, with all the inflated importance I had enjoyed in Thiruvananthapuram, that it was unthinkable for me to spend even a few months in an estate job and that too in a lonely place like the Nilgiris. I felt I would be trapped in a job like this, which would have effectively put paid to a worthwhile future career. Those were the years when the Second World War was raging. Opportunities for employment for a young postgraduate were practically limited to certain civilian jobs in the defence services. Vacancies for jobs in colleges or universities were very few and, even when they were advertised, previous experience was always a precondition. After a week's stay in Coonoor with my uncle, I left for Madras, telling him that I needed more time to think about the offer he had made.

Then I saw an advertisement in *The Hindu* for the post of assistant lecturer in Annamalai University located at Chidambaram, a renowned temple town (now in Tamil Nadu). The salary was relatively low, but I knew I would gain good opportunities to fulfil my ambitions for carrying out research in that university. I knew that the chances of getting the job for an outsider like me, with no teaching experience to my credit, were slim. Nevertheless, I sent in my application and much to my surprise, I received the call for an interview. Vice-chancellor of the university, Sir K.V. Reddy, was very much an old-world gentleman. He had served as a member of the Governor's Executive Council and also as the acting governor of Madras for some time. I was only twenty when I appeared before the selection board. I was greeted with K.V. Reddy's repeated question in a tone of great disbelief: 'How old are you?' 'How old are you?' The particulars of my age and other qualifications were there in my application form before him but he probably had not noticed my date of birth given in it. When I replied I was twenty, he asked me even before telling me to take a seat whether I knew that most of the students in the university were older than I and how I thought I could manage the classes. I thought I had lost the job even before the interview began, but very soon I found that he had overcome his initial adverse reaction to my age and was getting into a mood of sympathetic interest in my candidature. He seemed quite pleased with some of my answers to his quick-fire questions and the confidence with which I claimed that I would be able to manage the classes well. I got the job. My record of extracurricular activities had obviously compensated for the lack of experience in teaching.

The Annamalai University job was doubly satisfying as, apart from the intellectual stimulation I was looking for, it provided an excellent opportunity for me to revive my hopes for research. As a residential university Annamalai offered full facilities to the students for extracurricular activities, particularly in areas such as music, debates and theatre. When I joined the History and Politics Department of the university, as an assistant lecturer in July 1941, it had two well-known scholars in history, Dewan Bahadur C.S. Srinivasachari as head of the department and Professor R. Sathianathaier, both acknowledged authorities on Indian history with rich experience in research. I wanted to register for a Ph.D. degree while doing my lecturing work but Professor Srinivasachari thought that I should take an M. Litt. first before thinking of a doctorate. The Annamalai University had not registered anyone for doctorate in any discipline in the Arts Faculty before, though the university had been established in 1929, and the professor belonging to the old school was not very enthusiastic about registering a twenty-year-old for the first Ph.D. of the university in history. I accepted his suggestion and started my research for M.Litt. on a subject suggested by him: 'The Dutch in Malabar'. I took my M.Litt. degree within two years and then requested the professor to allow me to register for D.Litt. instead of Ph.D. as the university rules permitted a person with either M.Litt. or Ph.D. to register for D.Litt. This time Professor Srinivasachari did not raise any objection on the ground of my age and I was able to get my D.Litt. degree within three and a half years of my getting my M.Litt. thus becoming the first person to get a doctorate from the Arts Faculty of the university. I had the good fortune of getting valuable guidance from both Professor Srinivasachari and Professor Sathianathaier for my research on 'Buddhism in Kerala', a subject suggested to me by the latter. It was during my service in the Annamalai University that my marriage took place. My bride, Ackama, hailed from a planter's family in Kottayam and was then doing her

BA (Honours) in English literature at the Arts College, Thiruvananth-apuram. She was two years my junior at the Arts College. I was aged twenty-one and Ackama nineteen, both considered normal age for marriage in the Christian community in Travancore.

My services as assistant lecturer in the university ended in 1944 when I accepted the post of head of the History and Politics Department at the Venkatagiri Raja's College at Nellore (now in Andhra Pradesh), which had been upgraded to a first-grade college that year. The college was looking for someone with experience in teaching undergraduate and postgraduate students and also in conducting research. I was conscious of the fact that working in a college would be a great disadvantage for my research work, but I had serious problems in making both ends meet on the salary of an assistant lecturer. Therefore, financial considerations weighed heavily with me in deciding to accept the offer and I moved to Nellore. Throughout my stay in Nellore I continued my close association with the Annamalai University as I had been elected to the Senate and Academic Council of the university.

My stint at Nellore was memorable because of the historic developments in India during that period. For instance: the release of Gandhiji and other national leaders who had been detained after the All-India Congress Committee (AICC) passed the Quit India Resolution in August 1942; the Simla Conference of 1945; the formation of the interim government in Delhi; the 'direct action' launched by the Muslim League and the ghastly Calcutta killings of 1946; and the Cabinet Mission's plan and its failure. Moreover, the various fast-paced developments culminating in the partition of India and the declaration of independence on 15 August 1947 were momentous events of this period, which changed the whole course of India's history. The people of Nellore, as in most other parts of the Telugu districts at that time, were politically highly conscious and alert and took keen interest in the unfolding political drama. The Venkatagiri Raja's College had become an important centre of political activities because most of the students were members of one political party or the other. The college had a large group of Muslim students and, with a few exceptions, they were all ardent supporters of the Muslim League. The majority of other students were active members of the Congress, but there was also a hard core of Rashtriyaswayam Sewak Sangh (RSS) members among the students. The RSS was a markedly pro-Hindu organization. This state of affairs broadly reflected the political complexion of the people of the district. The debates, which were a common feature of the college's extracurricular activities, amply showed up the sharp division of political opinion among the students.

The debate under the auspices of the College Union held on the evening of 30 January 1948 was an unforgettable event in my life. The topic for debate, initiated by a student who was an enthusiastic supporter of the RSS, was: 'Gandhi's Leadership Has Done More Harm Than Good for India'. The pro-RSS student made a very forceful speech sharply attacking Gandhiji. Several speakers who followed him were also severely critical of Gandhiji's leadership. Those who spoke opposing the topic were not as good as those who had spoken in its support. One of the lecturers of the college had also spoken in support of the topic and it looked as if the vote would go in favour of the motion. At this stage, I asked for the floor and was invited to speak. I could demolish all the arguments presented by the anti-Gandhi group. The motion, when finally put to vote, was defeated by a huge majority. As I left the college gate, I saw some students running towards me shouting that Mahatma Gandhi had been shot dead a few minutes ago at a prayer meeting in Delhi. All of us ran to a hotel located near the college where the radio was announcing the tragic news. At an interval of every two minutes the announcement came over the radio that Mahatma Gandhi had been shot dead and that the assassin was a *Hindu*. The latter part of the announcement was intended to prevent any misunderstanding among the people that the assassin could have been a Muslim. Indeed, the announcement of the religious identity of the assassin was a very thoughtful one, as the country would have been plunged into serious communal riots without it. Everyone at the hotel broke into uncontrollable tears. For me the tragedy appeared particularly poignant because only a few minutes earlier I had been speaking very spiritedly about the Mahatma's great contributions to the nation. I went back to my house and from then on till the cremation was over we were all glued to the radio – there was no TV those days – plunged in great anguish and depression.

Within a few months I changed my place of work. I was on vacation in my home town when I received a message from R. Shankar the founder of the Sree Narayana College at Quilon (now in Kerala) enquiring whether I could meet him for a friendly talk. Within a few minutes of our meeting, he offered me the post of professor and head of the Department of History and Economics. The college had just been started and the management had appointed a dedicated team of experienced teachers; most of them retired professors from various first-grade colleges in Travancore, as heads of departments. Sree Narayana College was started by the Ezhavas, at that time an economically backward community, by voluntary contributions from the ordinary people of the community and Shankar, one of the senior leaders of the community, had been in charge of the arduous task of raising the funds for this venture and setting it up on solid foundations. I was quite impressed by his charismatic personality and his deep commitment to the cause of making higher education accessible to the economically backward sections of the state. I accepted the offer, but while doing so, I told him that I was expecting the Indian Administrative Service (IAS) results in a few months time and, if selected, the college should not stand in the way of my joining the service. Shankar readily accepted my condition.

My tenure at the Sree Narayana College was the shortest, lasting just five months, but very rewarding. The IAS results came much earlier than I expected and Shankar, true to his word, released me within a week of my getting the orders.

The news of my selection to the IAS came to me in a most unexpected manner. One morning when I reached my office in the college, I found a sheaf of telegrams from my old friends from outside the state congratulating me. Very strangely no telegram had mentioned the fact that it was for my selection to the IAS. Telephone facilities were practically nonexistent in Quilon and I therefore could not talk to any of these friends. The evening dailies in Madras had published the results of the IAS selection in their edition of the previous day and that was how my friends knew about my selection before I could! As the day progressed I received more telegrams and only then did the thought occur to me that the congratulations could be for my selection to the IAS. The train from Madras carrying the dailies of the previous evening was expected to reach the Quilon railway station by 5 p.m. and I proceeded to there to check whether the papers carried the news. I bought a copy of the *Madras Mail* and much to my delight (and excitement), I saw my name in the list of selected candidates on the front page. I rushed home to inform my wife about the happy news. By evening, more congratulatory telegrams poured in. When I went to the college next day, I found that the whole college community had known the news as the morning papers in Kerala had carried it along with my photograph. Thus an altogether new chapter in my life opened up by mid-1949.

FIVE

IAS and Beyond

THE TRAINING FOR THE NEW RECRUITS TO THE INDIAN ADMINISTRATIVE Service was conducted at the Metcalfe House in Old Delhi till 1959, when it was shifted to the present academy at Mussourie. The experiences that about forty persons underwent while living together in a campus, eating meals at the same place and time, and attending classes together evoked memories of my hostel days as a college student. S.M. Bapat, the establishment officer of the Government of India was our principal and J.D. Shukla of the UP cadre of the former ICS was the vice-principal. Classes were held for subjects such as law, economics and Hindi by special lecturers. The classes for public administration were taken by the principal and for district administration by the vice-principal. Special lectures by distinguished persons from public life and senior ICS officers were a regular feature of the training course. Activities such as rifle and revolver practice and horse riding were compulsory for all.

Since our training took place in the months immediately after independence the experience that our principal and vice-principal had gained in the working of the democratic system of administration was rather limited. Consequently, there was very little that we as probationers could learn from them about the type of problems that we were to encounter later while dealing with ministers and other elected representatives of the people or while tackling the press. The culture of administration was still very colonial and the training course originally designed for the ICS officers had not undergone much change. It was a period of transition from the colonial era, whose main focus was on revenue collection and maintenance of law and order, to an altogether new era of government *by the people* with emphasis on development. Therefore, one cannot claim that the training we acquired in Metcalfe House was of much relevance for shouldering the responsibilities we were to undertake in the new democratic system. However, as a course in getting an orientation for a new career, it was certainly helpful.

Two unforgettable memories of my Metcalfe House days were our calling on C. Rajagopalachari, independent India's first governor-general, at Rashtrapati Bhavan and on Sardar Vallabhbhai Patel, the Union home minister, at his residence on Aurangzeb Road, New Delhi. As Rajaji walked into the hall where we had all assembled, formally escorted by his military secretary and a complement of ADCs, we were greatly impressed by the simplicity of his dress and demeanour in an otherwise very formal and 'imperial' atmosphere. He put us at ease straightaway by his relaxed and informal manner of talking to us. He spoke about the changed role of the civil servants in independent India and emphasized the importance of getting fully familiarized with the problems of the ordinary people particularly those in rural India.

Sardar Patel was already in very poor health when we called on him. He talked to us in a very low voice and stressed the importance of the fact that the civil servants had been given constitutional protection against any arbitrary action in the bona-fide discharge of their duties. We were quite aware of the crucial role he had played in creating a new All-India Civil Service in spite of the fact that several state chief ministers and senior politicians were against the continuation of the old ICS pattern of administration and giving the benefits of constitutional guarantees to civil servants. I vividly recall his advice, as he was about to leave the room. He observed: 'We have done our duty by creating the frame in which you can work with freedom and impartiality and from now on it is your duty to do your best to your country.'

At the time of my recruitment to the civil service, the IAS scheme had not yet been extended to the Part B states, as the former Princely States were then known. Therefore, I, as one belonging to the Travancore-Cochin state, was initially posted to the then Madras state on completion of my training in Metcalfe House. Under the scheme of training for the IAS probationers they had to undergo a short period of orientation in the state secretariat and about a year in the district before they were given charge of their respective subdivisions. The secretariat training helped us to get a very rough idea of how the administrative system functioned at the top but it was too general to introduce us to the process of decision making at various levels of the secretariat hierarchy.

The most lasting impression this training left in my mind relates to the advice given to us by Sir K. Ramunni Menon, chief secretary to the Government of Madras, on the 'do's and don't's' to be borne in mind in our relations with ministers, MPs and MLAs. He told us in clear terms that it would be very wrong if a civil servant sought the help or recommendation of any politician on any matter concerning his career. He pointed out that we might find some decisions of the government unpleasant to us but, in all such circumstances, we should approach only the chief secretary, if we wished, for a redressal of our grievances and never any MLA or minister. If we felt aggrieved about postings, promotions and other aspects, he affirmed that we had the freedom to write demi-officially to him and he would deal with such letters promptly and sympathetically.

At the end of the secretariat training, each probationer departed for the district to which he was posted for field training. In my case my district training was to be in Tirunelveli, one of the largest districts of the then Madras state.

The district training mainly meant spending a few weeks, first at the collector's office to become familiar with the work of the different sections there, followed by interaction with the different functionaries of the Revenue Department. The process started with the lowest step of the ladder, namely, the village accountant or *karanam* and the village headman or *munsif* as they were called in the Madras state at that time. The training then continued with the revenue inspector who was in charge of a group of villages. Next, the training continued with the deputy *tahsildar* who was in charge of a sub*taluk*, and the *tahsildar*, in charge of a *taluk* and finally with the revenue divisional officer, in charge of a subdivision. The training also included a few days of familiarization course in various departments such as police, forests, public works and labour at the district level. As there were no forests in Tirunelveli district, I was deputed to the Coimbatore district for this part of the training. Towards the end of my training in the district came the district treasury training and a period when I had to hold independent charge of the district treasury. Simultaneously, I was trained in magisterial work also. I was first invested with the powers of a third-class magistrate and then with the powers of the second-class magistrate. By the time I was almost finishing my training course, I was invested with the powers of a first-class magistrate. At each level a few criminal cases appropriate to my powers were transferred to me for my hearing and disposal and my judgments in such cases were being sent to the superior officers for their review.

Among all the different types and levels of training, I found the training with the village accountant or *karanam* most interesting and useful. I had to go to the *karanam's* office-cum-residence at a village called Tiruvannadapuram, about 8 km from the district headquarters. This *karanam* knew a few words in English, just sufficient to communicate with the officers who were new to the Tamil language. However, since I knew Tamil, I faced no problem in understanding him. He had the reputation of being the best village accountant in the district and he had maintained all the prescribed registers and statements relating to his village in an updated manner, which very few village accountants were capable of doing. This *karanam* had trained several assistant collectors, mostly Englishmen, in the past and was very proud of the fact that his 'trainees' had risen to high positions in the state administration. He took me through the various registers and statistics and proved to be a great help in understanding the basics of revenue administration at the grass-roots level.

The scheme of district training for the probationer was exactly the same as was followed during the British administration and the key element in it was the role of the collector in giving the right orientation to the young officer. In fact, the collector was expected to be a model for the probationer to emulate. During the colonial years many probationers were young Englishmen fresh from their universities with little knowledge of India and its people and totally unfamiliar with the culture of district administration. Most of them then used to live in the collector's bungalow during the early months of their training. They accompanied the collector in his tours within the district and thus had ample opportunities of watching him at work, handling different problems in different situations.

A probationer could consider himself lucky if he had the opportunity of being trained by a good collector. Unfortunately, I cannot claim that I had this luck. My collector, R. Subbayya Pillai, was very thorough in his revenue work, but he had the tendency to get involved too much in the trivial matters of administration. He tried to do everything himself, and not knowing the value of delegation of responsibility, he tried to interfere with the work of every senior officer working with him. Very soon I found that he could not be a role model for a new entrant to the civil service like me.

On completion of training, I was posted as subcollector of Tuticorin, which today is a full district. I was also the ex officio chairman of the Tuticorin Port Trust. Tuticorin was a well-developed town by the standards of those days and a subdivision with some good irrigated areas as well as a few dry and famine-stricken regions providing a wide variety of work at the subcollector's level. The people were generally peace loving and law abiding though there were a few areas where law and order problems and serious crimes like dacoity and robbery were creating problems for the administration.

I would like to narrate two experiences of mine, both not very pleasant, as subcollector in the Madras state. The general elections in 1951 under the new Constitution of independent India provided a totally new experience for the entire administration in the country. Apart from my role as subcollector, I also doubled as the returning officer endowed with additional responsibilities for conducting elections in all the three constituencies in my subdivision and also for holding training courses for the presiding officers and various other categories of election personnel. As this was the first election based on adult franchise and use of election symbols, there were no precedents for us to go by. We were receiving detailed instructions from Delhi and the chief election officer in Madras almost every day and we had to be very thorough in interpreting and applying them to our constituencies. I had to allot a symbol to a Scheduled Caste candidate in a double member constituency and I did that according to my interpretation of the instructions. Five days later Subbayya Pillai, the collector, arrived at Tuticorin and, after going through the papers, expressed great surprise and concern at the decision I had taken on the allotment of the symbol. He told me that I was quite wrong in my decision and therefore I should cancel my orders and allot a different symbol to the Scheduled Caste candidate. The collector, of course, had no authority to overrule the decision of a returning officer on a subject like this but he told me that I had committed a grave mistake that might result in the cancellation of the election in that constituency and advised me that any delay on my part to change my decision would lead to serious consequences. I tried my best to convince him about the correctness of my interpretation of the instructions on the subject, but his reply was that I should indeed be grateful to him that he had discovered the mistake in time. I finally yielded to his pressure and revised my earlier allotment of the symbol.

Two days later, the chief election officer, S. Venkateswaran, a very senior ICS officer of the Madras cadre, arrived at Tuticorin as part of his tour of the southern districts to review the election arrangements. He visited my office along with the collector and saw the order that I had passed on the symbol under pressure from the collector. He told me in the collector's presence that my order was wrong and explained to me what the instructions on the subject really meant. His interpretation was exactly the same as mine when I issued my original order. At this stage I expected Subbayya Pillai to inform Venkateswaran what had actually happened but he kept quiet without uttering a word on this subject. I felt badly let down by the collector. However, I kept quiet as I thought it would be wrong on my part to expose the mistake committed by him just to prove that I had been right.

Fortunately, for me the story did not end here. The election deputy *tahsildar* who was working with me happened to be one who had worked as the camp clerk of Venkateswaran several years earlier. Using his old connections he met Venkateswaran at the travellers' bungalow the same evening and told him the truth about Subbayya Pillai's unnecessary and wrong intervention in my decision. Next morning, I received an invitation from Venkateswaran for breakfast with him. He expressed great happiness not merely at the fact that I had interpreted the instructions correctly but more so because I had not tried to defend myself by blaming the collector for changing my decision though he expected the collector himself to come out with what actually happened. The collector received a good dressing down from Venkateswaran later, particularly for letting down a young officer for no fault of his.

Another equally unpleasant experience relating to elections was when I had to oversee a parliamentary by-election a few months later in a very undeveloped sub*taluk* called Vlathikulam in the Koilpatty *taluk*, which formed part of the constituency. There were very few motorable roads in Vlathikulam and the communication facilities were equally primitive. Presiding officers and other election personnel who were new to the places where polling booths were located had been instructed to be present at their respective places well in advance on the previous day so that elections could start on time. I had personally inspected three-fourths of all the polling stations to ensure that all arrangements had been made satisfactorily and had assigned to my *tahsildar* the responsibility for inspecting the remaining polling stations in the sub*taluk*. On the eve of the election day, I had received a report from the *tahsildar* that all arrangements had been checked by him and that elections would start on time in the area allotted to him. I returned to the travellers' bungalow at Koilpatty at about 10 p.m. and was about to take a well-deserved rest when Subbayya Pillai unexpectedly arrived there. He reviewed the arrangements with me and suddenly created a panic about the fact that I had left out a few polling stations from my schedule to be inspected by the *tahsildar*. He told me that I should have inspected all the polling stations myself and the failure to do so was a grave omission on my part, even though there were no instructions from any quarter that the returning officer himself had to inspect every polling station before the election. He held the opinion that I should immediately go to these polling stations and personally ensure that everything was right. When I persisted with my stand that there was no need for my rechecking the work of the *tahsildar* and that I was convinced that all arrangements were satisfactory, he responded that if I did not go to these places he himself would do so. I quietly went back to my room allowing, him some time to cool down. At that time K. Subrahmanyam, an officer of the 1951 batch of the IAS, now a well-known defence analyst in Delhi, undergoing training with me, had been camping at Koilpatty along with me. He had accompanied me in my inspection visits of the polling stations and was present when the conversation between Subbayya Pilla and myself took place. He rushed to my room and told me that Subbayya Pillai was preparing to visit these places and if I did not offer to go in deference to his suggestion, he would surely 'discover' many 'defects' in my arrangements, even though there would be none, just to establish that, but for his visit and corrective action, the election arrangements would have gone out of control. Subrahmanyam pointed out that Subbayya Pillai was quite capable of projecting me in a bad light and that I should not give him such an opportunity. I saw the practical wisdom in my young colleague's advice, though I was quite convinced that the visit was a totally unnecessary exercise. Consequently, I told the collector that I would carry out the second inspection myself. Subrahmanyam accompanied me and we returned to the travellers' bungalow only at the break of dawn. I had to again go out into the nooks and corners of the constituency in a couple of hours to see how polling was going on in different polling stations.

I have mentioned these two experiences to highlight how some people in senior positions try to put others in the wrong to prove themselves right and how petty minded they can be in letting down their own officers even when they realize that they had committed a mistake. I am sure that after gaining more experience in election management, Subbayya Pillai would have learnt that physically inspecting *every* polling station, despite the best efforts put in by the returning officer, was an impossible task and also that it was not necessasry for any returning officer himself to go to such lengths.

✧

By 1952, the Travancore-Cochin region had opted for the IAS scheme and I was transferred to this region's cadre along with four officers – two from the former ICS and two from the IAS – belonging to the Madras cadre. We constituted the first group of the All-India Civil Service in the state. Very soon, practically all the officers who had been selected to the then Travancore Civil Service had also been promoted to the IAS. I was very happy working in the relatively large Madras state and not particularly keen to go to a small state like Travancore-Cochin, which did not have a tradition of an all-India service. However, there was no alternative but to accept my transfer to the new cadre. I took over as subcollector and subdivisional magistrate at Alleppey, in central Travancore, in 1952.

I soon found that the work as subcollector at Alleppey was quite different from the work in Tuticorn. The bulk of my job here was devoted to hearing and disposal of criminal cases and those under the Rent Control Act that was in operation in the Alleppey municipal town. (This was because the judiciary was not separated from the executive in Travancore-Cochin.) The workload imposed by such cases was very heavy and there was little scope for any revenue or development work. The Subdivisional Magistrate's Court in Alleppey was notorious for its huge backlog and nobody appeared to have been bothered much to rectify this state of affairs. Alleppey subdivision at that time consisted of half a dozen *taluks* and was one of the largest subdivisions of the state. (It has since been raised to the level of a district.) No magistrate, however, hard working he may have been, could possibly dispose of even a small percentage of the cases filed in his court and therefore heavy arrears had accumulated over the years. In my youthful enthusiasm to clear the arrears expeditiously, I used to attend the court from early morning till late in the evening. Even back home I spent quite a few hours every night for writing orders and judgments. Since there was no resident second-class magistrate in the town, I was also frequently being disturbed for performing other duties such as taking down dying declarations in the hospitals. The heavy schedule of court work continued unabated for nearly two years and had started putting a serious strain on my health. Doctors advised that a change of work would do good for my health. So, I decided to act on the advice of Ramunni Menon, chief secretary of Madras state, about approaching him directly if we had any personal representations to make and sought a meeting with the chief secretary of Travancore-Cochin to place before him my request for a change of work. A change of work at that stage of my career would have meant a posting to the Secretariat at Thiruvananthapuram, and I considered such a request quite reasonable. However, my experience in this simple matter was surprisingly an unpleasant one. Chief Secretary V.N. Rajan, an ICS officer from the Madras cadre on deputation to Travancore-Cochin, was well known as a highly self-opinionated and pompous person. When I met him at Thiruvananthapuram and made my request for a Secretariat posting on bona-fide reasons of health, he reacted with great annoyance and stated that I should never have approached him with such a request. I asked him as to whom should I have approached if I had a legitimate personal reason for requesting a change. I also told him about Ramunni Menon's advice to us about such matters; this statement only increased his anger. I knew I was also losing my calm and therefore I left his room abruptly, saying that this was not the treatment I had expected when I had a legitimate reason for asking for a transfer.

The news about my unpleasant experience with the chief secretary soon came to be known to my colleagues in the service and also to some persons in the political establishment, even though I had not uttered a word to any politician. One prominent leader, E. John Philipose, a senior and influential member of the ruling Congress Party and a resident of Thiruvananthapuram, was quite outraged when he heard about this incident and came to see me at my house in Alleppey as soon as I returned after my meeting with Rajan. Philipose had known me closely from my student days and had great regard and affection for me. He felt that a great injustice had been done to me and considered it his duty to take up the matter with the chief minister, who was his close personal friend. Philipose was a great idealist among politicians, enjoying a very high reputation for integrity and efficiency as a minsiter. He had resigned from the state cabinet when a colleague of his in the Congress Party had levelled some thoroughly baseless charges of corruption against him. He had filed a suit of defamation and had won the case, but had not yet rejoined the cabinet. I pleaded with him not to do anything about a change of workplace for me, as I was strongly opposed to the intervention of political leaders in such matters. After a long argument, Philipose left my house expressing his unhappiness at my attitude on this issue.

Rajan displayed his petulance by transferring me in the same post to a subdivision worse than Alleppey from the point of view of convenience of work and living, namely, to Devikulam, in the high ranges of Travancore. I contented myself with the thought that, in due course, Rajan would realize on his own that he had been unfair to me. However, I doubt whether he ever felt that way because it was his nature to be rude in dealing with junior officers while being overly obsequious to his seniors, a defect not uncommon in some civil servants. Rajan obviously meant this step as a lesson for me, though I can never imagine that any other chief secretary would have reacted the way he did.

Rajan himself did not rise high in the civil service. He left the Travancore-Cochin Service soon and was sent on deputation to the Central Government, where he did not have much luck in getting promoted to senior positions, in spite of his seniority in service.

An important event that I had organized during my tenure at Alleppey has now become one of the major events of the state – the Nehru Trophy boat race. Travancore is well known for the boat races conducted in different parts of the state, particularly in the central Travancore region. The 'snake boats' of Kerala, which are very narrow in width, but very long, could accommodate 50 to 150 rowers well trained in the use of oars. These boats are owned by individuals, societies or institutions in various villages. They participate in races on special occasions such as Onam, the famous festival celebrated by the Malayalees, or during festivals in certain ancient temples. Attractive prizes and trophies are offered to the winners and the events generate tremendous excitement and enthusiasm among the thousands of spectators who watch them. The Travancore-Cochin state government decided to stage a boat race on the occasion of Pandit Jawaharlal Nehru's visit in 1953. I was asked by the state government to take on the responsibility for organizing the race in the backwaters near Alleppey town. A small committee consisting of some senior officers working in Alleppey and a few prominent citizens who had gained long experience in organizing such races was formed. Along with the members of the committee I visited several sites in the backwaters and finally selected a venue that provided a straight course for the race and also facilities for large crowds to watch the event. A sturdy platform for the prime minister and his retinue to watch the race was erected in the middle of the backwaters near the finishing point. Nehru and his entourage, which included his daughter Indira Gandhi and her two sons (Rajiv and Sanjay), arrived at the site by a speed boat from Alleppey town. I had met the prime minister on a few occasions when he had come on election campaigns to the state, but this was the first time that I welcomed him personally and also met Indira Gandhi. (Little did I know at that time that I was destined to work closely with her as principal secretary.) Nehru appeared very excited at the sight of several competing boats racing at great speed. After presenting the trophies, he jumped onto one of the boats and asked the men to row for some distance, much to the anxiety and concern of his security personnel. The boat race has continued to be an event of great importance to the people of the state all these fifty years; its golden jubilee was celebrated with great enthusiasm in 2003, though the organizers did not remember to invite me, the man who had laboured hard to get it started.

My period of service in Devikulam, though intended by V.N. Rajan as a punishment, fortunately, turned out to be an important one in my career. When I was posted there, there was a change of government in the state and also a change in the post of the chief secretary. Pattom Thanu Pillai, who after resigning from the Congress, had formed a government with the support of that party. More importantly, B.V.K. Menon, a senior IAS officer, had replaced Rajan as the chief secretary. The new government decided to launch a massive programme of allotment of land in Devikulam *taluk* to landless farmers. Entrusted with the responsibility of implementing it, I had to identify suitable surplus land in Devikulam for establishing self-contained colonies of farmers. I was given the powers of a collector for the allotment of land. This experience was very satisfying in that I finalized many allotments.

A dicey situation that I had to handle in Devikulam almost immediately after my posting there was created by the agitation launched by the Travancore Tamil Nadu Congress, an influential political party in south Travancore. The main objective of this agitation was to get the Tamil-majority *taluks* of Travancore merged with the neighbouring Madras state. The Tamil-speaking population in Devikulam and Peermade *taluks* consisted predominantly of tea plantations workers who were members of one of the two rival labour unions. One union owed allegiance to the Congress Party of Travancore-Cochin and the other to the Tamil Nadu Congress. Rivalries between the two unions were sharp, often leading to violent clashes and disturbance of law and order. The agitation for merger of the Tamil-speaking *taluks* in south Travancore and Devikulam and Peermade *taluks* with the Madras state had gained great momentum by 1953. The rival parties had started organizing massive demonstrations to prove their respective strengths. In certain places in south Travancore, the situation had deteriorated to the extent that the police had to resort to *lathi*-charges and even firing, resulting in the death of some Tamil demonstrators. Such a state of affairs created a good deal of unrest and anger among the people, particularly among the members of the Tamil Nadu Congress in the state.

Such were the circumstances when I received information about the proposed visit of three senior leaders of the Travancore Tamil Nadu Congress to Munnar town in Devikulam district to stage a demonstration in support of the demand for merger of Devikulam and Peermade *taluks* with Madras state. I was convinced that the visit of these leaders would provoke counter-demonstrations by the Travancore State Congress and the labour union affiliated to it, which could lead to violent clashes between the two groups. Under these circumstances, I felt that the best course of action could be to ban all public meetings and demonstrations for a period of fifteen days in Devikulam under Section 144 of the Indian Criminal Procedure Code. I did not consider it necessary to consult the chief minister or anyone else in Thiruvananthapuram for this step as I had dealt with such situations in Tamil Nadu before without having to seek clearance from any political authorities. I promptly received a letter from the Tamil Nadu Congress leaders in Devikulam to the effect that their senior leaders would be visiting Munnar despite the prohibitory orders, as already planned by them.

On the eve of the proposed meeting, three top leaders of the Tamil Nadu Congress, A. Nesamony, and two MPs, Abdul Razak, and Chidambara Nadar, met me at my residence and affirmed that they were determined to hold the meeting at Munnar the next morning and I would be held responsible for any outbreak of violence at the meeting if I did not withdraw my orders prohibiting gatherings. I emphasized the importance of maintaining peace in Devikulam and warned that if they violated the prohibitory orders, I would be constrained to deal with them strictly under the law. They were in a defiant mood, but I left them in no doubt about my intention to enforce the prohibitory orders.

The police made all necessary arrangements during the night itself to cordon off the town centre in Munnar, which was to be the venue of the meeting. En route to Munnar early in the morning, I saw large group of plantation labourers (supporting the Tamil Nadu Congress) assembled at the hills around the Munnar town ready to come down to the site of the meeting when their leaders were due to address them. Nesamony, Razak and Nadar arrived by car at 10 a.m., which was the time fixed for the meeting to begin. Upon alighting from the car I informed them again about the orders banning meetings and were requested to desist from holding any meeting. When they declared that they had come to break the prohibitory orders, they were promptly arrested and, within a span of two or three minutes, they were whisked away from the scene in a police vehicle. The crowds watched these activities from a distance, but did not get an opportunity to plan the next move. Nesamony, Razak and Nadar were produced before the magistrate and sentenced to short periods of imprisonment.

The prompt arrest of the leaders and the tactful handling of the crowds received warm appreciation from all sections of the media. They drew the contrast between the police *lathi*-charge and firing against the demonstrators in south Travancore and the smooth handling of the situation in Munnar. Consequently, I was complimented by almost all political leaders.

The Tamil Nadu Congress Party leaders, however, were sharply critical of my action in issuing prohibitory orders under Section 144, resulting in the arrest of their senior leaders. They alleged that I was performing my duties under the orders of the chief minister and they moved an adjournment motion in the State Assembly, which was in session at that time to condemn my action and the alleged instructions given to me by the chief minister. Moving the motion Chattanatha Karayalar, leader of the Tamil Nadu Congress in the Assembly, severely criticized me for the alleged hasty action taken and attacked the chief minister for 'instructing' me to issue the prohibitory orders. The chief minister, Pattom Thanu Pillai, one of the top leaders of Travancore-Cochin at that time, made a very spirited reply defending my action. The following extracts from the proceedings of the state Legislative Assembly of 13 July 1954 will show the powerful support the chief minister gave me while emphatically denying that he had any prior knowledge about my action in issuing the prohibitory orders under Section 144:

> I may in all honesty, declare to this House that this order was passed by the Magistrate without any reference to the Government. It was passed in the normal course of his duty as a Magistrate who was courageous and at the same time convinced of the necessities of the situation. A man endowed with a sense of duty, on his own accord, promulgated the order...
>
> I do not blame him. Certainly, he was right. I understand that very often such orders are passed at the instance of the Government, after reference and after obtaining the consent of Government. But this Magistrate had the grit to act on his own...

Pattom Thanu Pillai's statement in the Assembly greatly boosted my morale apart from serving as a source of encouragement for me. The chief minister did not stop at just commending my action in the legislature; within five days he came over to Munnar along with the chief secretary, B.V.K. Menon, and at a meeting he had convened (of the senior revenue and police officers of the district), congratulated me warmly for the manner in which I had handled the potentially explosive situation. He affirmed that he had full confidence in me and that no one would interfere with my discretion in dealing with the agitation organized by the Tamil Nadu Congress or any other such group.

SIX

In Central Government Service

TOWARDS THE LAST QUARTER OF 1954, I RECEIVED AN ENQUIRY FROM the state government whether I would be interested in being sponsored for deputation to the Central Government. Under the IAS scheme, every state has an allotted quota for the deputation of officers to the Centre for various periods. For example, the deputation period for an undersecretary-level officer was three years; for a deputy secretary, four years and for a joint secretary, five years. I promptly replied that I would definitely be interested and by mid-January 1955, I had been posted to the Ministry of Commerce and Industry at Delhi.

Apart from commerce and industry, this ministry at that time dealt with a wide range of subjects such as steel, mines, chemicals and fertilizers, which are presently handled by individual ministries. T.T. Krishnamachari, himself a very successful businessman in his early years, was the cabinet minister, and he had a formidable reputation as an expert in the fields of trade and industry. He also had a reputation of being a hard taskmaster, who was intolerant of mediocrity, but appreciative of ability and hard work on the part of the officers. At the Secretariat level, the Ministry of Commerce and Industry was then studded with some of the most brilliant officers of the former ICS who were manning its senior posts. H.V.R. Iyengar was secretary, S. Boothalingam was special secretary, and L.K. Jha, K.B. Lall and P. Govindan Nair were joint secretaries. Officers of the IAS had not yet attained sufficient seniority to be posted as joint secretary or to higher levels. Three of the eight posts of deputy secretary in the ministry were held by IAS officers, among whom was my friend M.K.K. Nayar who had an impressive record as a dynamic and competent officer.

I felt happy when I found that I had been assigned the work of deputy chief controller of imports and exports, although the subject was totally new to me. In the districts I had worked earlier, opportunities for gaining any exposure to this type of work were nonexistent. To make matters more difficult for a newcomer, I was appointed to a division dealing with those items of import for which no specific policies had been laid down by the government. At that point of time, there were very tight controls on imports and every item was governed by a specific policy stipulated in the *Import Control Book*, known as the *Red Book*, which was revised every six months. Applications for imports of items not covered by the relevant policy in the *Red Book* were to be dealt with ad hoc and all such cases had to be brought to the minister's attention for further action. My immediate senior officer was an Englishman, who had opted to stay back in the service of the Government of India after independence. He was near retirement age and used to fall ill very often. Nevertheless, he had instructed me that files should *not* be held up for him to see and that I should send them direct to the ministry with my own comments and recommendations. Since every ad hoc case had to be decided by the cabinet minister, my work came to the personal notice of Krishnamachari. My comments and recommendations generally received his approval, which gave me a good deal of confidence. Within six months I was appointed deputy secretary in charge of imports in the ministry, with an additional new charge of the small-scale industries, for which the government had just announced its new comprehensive development policy and had established a fairly large organization under the development commissioner for small-scale industries (DCSSI).

During this tenure I was selected for the prestigious Nuffield Foundation Fellowship for Indian civil servants, which involved a six-month course of study in the United Kingdom on a subject relevant to one's work. This fellowship had just been instituted and, two officers, one from the ICS and one from the IAS, were selected for the first batch. The ICS officer selected was N.N. Kidwai from the Assam cadre. I was assigned to the Board of Trade which was the UK counterpart of the Indian Ministry of Commerce and Industry. The fellowship provided for extensive travel throughout the United Kingdom for the selected candidate and his spouse. This provision gave me a useful opportunity to make an in-depth study of the working of industrial estates in the United Kingdom. The Government of India had just decided to launch a programme for setting up industrial estates in various parts of the country. In this context, my report on industrial estates and industrial areas in the United Kingdom became specially relevant in formulating policies with regard to this area.

While working as deputy secretary, I was selected to the Central Pool of the civil services, which meant that I did not have to revert to my parent cadre. In the pre-independence period the British Government had created the Central Pool, consisting of a few officers, mostly from the ICS, to man the senior posts in the economic ministries of the Government of India. The objective was to ensure that the Central Government had the advantage of procuring and retaining the services of some officers who would have gained good expertise in economic administration. This pool scheme had been revived to include some posts in administrative ministries too. Moreover, the strength of the pool was raised to one hundred, of which twenty-five were allotted to ICS officers.

I held the post of deputy secretary for about five years, after which I was promoted, rather unexpectedly, to the post of DCSSI, though I was three years junior to be considered eligible for such a position at that time. There had been a quick turnover of development commissioners in this period for a variety of reasons. The new commerce and industry minister, Lal Bahadur Shastri, was not favourably disposed to the then DCSSI, A.S.E. Iyer. In fact, Shastri was not happy with Iyer's style of working and had conveyed his displeasure to the secretary, S. Ranganathan. Ranganathan, who had succeeded H.V.R. Iyengar, was told by the minister that he should be on the lookout for another officer for this post. Though I had been dealing with the small-scale industries sector for a fairly long period and both Ranganathan and Shastri had been happy with my work, I thought I would not be considered for a promotion for another three years because of the IAS rules. However, much to my surprise, suddenly one day Shastri informed the secretary that Iyer should be asked to go on leave immediately and that I should be appointed in his place. Ranganathan pointed out to the minister that though he was quite confident about my suitability for this post, I was still too junior to be appointed to it. But Shastri told Ranganathan in no uncertain terms that for a post like the DCSSI, seniority in the IAS should not be an important criterion. Ranganathan quickly arranged to get the necessary clearance from the Appointment Committee of the cabinet. I took over my new post on 1 July 1960.

My appointment as development commissioner created in me a great urge to justify my out-of-turn selection. The Small-scale Industry Organization (SSIO) was a fairly large one comprising more than fifty subordinate offices. This organization was endowed with the responsibility for maintaining a close liaison with various state governments at senior levels and also ensuring very close interaction with thousands of small industrialists all over the country. Apart from the heavy administrative work involved in managing a large department, the DCSSI had to be continuously on tour to ensure a high standard of efficiency in the extension services provided by the various institutes and extension centres under his charge and to assess the impact of the different programmes in the field.

During the early part of my three-year stint as DCSSI, I had to experience some tension, mainly as a fallout of the strained relationship between Shastri and his minister of state, Manubai Sha. Sha was a dynamic and hardworking minister and was quite knowledgeable on matters relating to trade and industry, but he had the habit of trying to ignore the jurisdiction and powers of his senior while dealing with the cases submitted to him. Very often, he would write down final orders on the relevant file, overlooking the fact that the file had been marked to the cabinet minister through him. When Shastri came to know about what was happening, he asked the secretary to ensure that *all* files that had to be seen by him were actually sent to him again even if the minister of state had returned them to the officer concerned. The secretary, in turn, had instructed me and the other senior officers to ensure that Shastri's orders be strictly followed.

Since it was not in Shastri's nature to ignore or sideline his minister of state, he did not take away the subject of small-scale industries from the list already allotted to his deputy, but made sure that the rules regarding the levels at which orders were to be issued were strictly observed by all concerned.

During my tenure as DCSSI, the Ford Foundation of the USA awarded a fellowship for a short-term assignment at the Stanford Research Institute, California, for a research study on the working of the programmes for industrial estates and small industries in different countries. This institute had a wealth of information on the small industries development programmes under implementation in various parts of the world. Several senior members of the institute's staff had worked as advisers in the Small-scale Industry Organization in India and other developing countries. Therefore, the close interactions I had with them through events such as workshops and seminars organized by the institute were quite useful to me. I had also utilized this opportunity to write my book on *Industrial Estates in India*, which was published in 1962, with a Foreword by Professor Eugene Staley of the Stanford Research Institute, a world-renowned expert on small industries development.

Looking back to my tenure as DCSSI, I would like to state that I enjoyed the work thoroughly and derived great job satisfaction. Those were the early days of the development programmes for small-scale industries in India and I consider it my good fortune that I could be closely associated with both policy formulation and programme implementation in this formative period. Perhaps the fact that I was elevated to the position of DCSSI quite ahead of my entitlement on the basis of seniority in service was an important factor that contributed to my job satisfaction.

In October 1963, unexpectedly, I received an offer of appointment as senior adviser on small-scale industries and industrial estates at the UN headquarters in New York.

My tour of duty involved visiting developing countries interested in introducing schemes for promoting small industries and establishing industrial estates and advising them on the proper policies and programmes they should adopt after a careful study of the problems of industrial development in these countries.

During the three years I worked as senior adviser at the Centre for Industrial Development, I had undertaken technical assistance missions to over fifteen centres in Latin America, the Caribbean region and the Anglophone countries of Africa. However, the long delays involved in implementing the recommendations of our missions by some countries led to a marked degree of frustration in me. As a result, I began wondering after a couple of years of service with the UN whether it was worthwhile for me to continue in this type of work. In India, on the other hand, the direct responsibility for implementing time-bound programmes was solely mine. I missed the job satisfaction that I valued very highly in my own country. In spite of the very attractive financial rewards as a senior UN adviser, the feeling within me that I should return to the service of my own country early grew steadily as I could not enjoy any work unless it also provided job satisfaction.

This was the period when the UN had taken a firm decision to upgrade the UN Centre for Industrial Development to the status of a full-fledged agency to be called the United Nations Industrial Development Organization (UNIDO) based in Vienna. Those working at the centre at that time were getting quite excited at the prospects of working in the new organization. However, I did not feel very enthusiastic about a UN service career. I felt that if I moved to the UNIDO, I might find it more difficult to leave the UN as I might get used to the high salary and perks and to the relatively easier lifestyle of a senior international civil servant.

When I was in this frame of mind, K.B. Lall came over to New York from Brussels where he had been working as India's ambassador to the European Community. (Lall was an old colleague from the Ministry of Commerce and Industry.) He told me that he was being posted as secretary in the Ministry of Commerce in Delhi. (The Ministry of Commerce and Industry, had, meanwhile, been split into two separate ministries – one for commerce and one for industry.) He added that he was keen to put in place a good team of senior officers to work with him and that he would be happy if I could join his team as joint secretary. I had enjoyed working with Lall. He had great personal regard and affection for me and I thought that working with him could be very fruitful and satisfying for me. Lall's offer set at rest the doubts in my mind about continuing for a longer period in UN service and I readily accepted it. I returned to Government of India service as a joint secretary in the Ministry of Commerce in October 1966 after having completed three years in UN service.

As joint secretary in the Ministry of Commerce, I was assigned the section responsible for handling trade with the Soviet Union and the East European countries. I also had to deal with the two big corporations under the Ministry of Commerce – the State Trading Corporation (STC) and the Minerals and Metals Trading Corporation (MMTC). I paid several visits to these countries for various matters related to trade negotiations. There was plenty of scope for personal initiative in this type of work and I enjoyed it thoroughly.

An interesting innovation that Lall had introduced with the support of Dinesh Singh (the cabinet minister) was the appointment of Prakash Tandon, chairman of Hindustan Lever, as chairman of STC. This was the first time a top-level executive from a private sector company had been appointed to head a government corporation. I was in charge of negotiating the terms of contract with Tandon, but he made my task easy by not making any extravagant demand. However, my role was more difficult in breaking in Tandon to the culture of government administration. H.N. Ray, a senior ICS officer from the Finance Ministry, was a member of the Board of Directors of the STC along with me. Tandon, who was quite new to government procedures, used to get quite frustrated and sometimes very annoyed by what he thought was the rigid attitude of Ray at the meetings of the Board of Directors. Often, I had to step in to soften Ray's opposition to some of the new proposals that Tandon had put forward before the board for its approval. At the same time, I had to point out to Tandon the importance and practical wisdom in following some of the well-established practices of the government with regard to decision making.

In his book *Return to Punjab 1961–1975*, Tandon has described my role as one of inducting him to the STC and of 'keeping an eye on his private-sector ways'. Elsewhere in this book he has stated with his tongue wedged firmly in his cheek: 'K.B. Lall kept a close eye on me and made Alexander my wet nurse. Alexander was to see that with my private-sector training I did not leave my decisions unrecorded and unguarded so that years later they might be questioned.' I should, however, acknowledge that Tandon, though a reluctant beginner, soon became a convinced practitioner of the conventions and procedures in the working of the government system. I must also acknowledge that he had succeeded in infusing into the STC a new culture of management, which proved very beneficial to its functioning, as a trading company. On the whole, my four-year tenure as joint secretary in the Ministry of Commerce was very satisfying.

Even though I thought that I had left the UN service for good, the UN had not left me. Within four years of my return from UN service, I had to take up again a long-term UN assignment, this time to Iran, much against my own wishes. The offer for this assignment came to me under very special circumstances. During the period I was working at the UN Centre for Industrial Development in New York, I had visited Iran on a technical assistance mission to prepare a project for the restructuring of a large industrial estate complex at Ahwaz in the southern part of the country set up by the Government of Iran, but which had not really taken off. The Government of Iran took four years to reach the final decision to accept my recommendations, but when it decided to implement them, it laid down a stipulation. It informed the UN that it would do so only if that body could secure my services as the head of the UN team in executing the project. The Iranian Government was insistent that I, who had formulated the project, should also be given the responsibility for overseeing its implementation. These were the early years of closer Indo-Iranian economic cooperation and the Government of India was very keen to honour any request from the Government of Iran for assistance in its industrial development programmes. Very soon, pressure on the Government of India from both the Government of Iran and the UN for securing my services for this project became strong. In January 1970, I joined my new post in the Ministry of

Economy of the Government of Iran as chief of the UN project and chief adviser to the government on development of small industries and industrial estates.

My assignment in Iran was expected to last five years. My UN team consisted of half a dozen international advisers who were experts on different subjects such as marketing, extension services and feasibility studies. During the early 1970s the Shah's government in Iran had introduced several new projects with the help of the UN for the promotion of both large- and small-scale industries. The UN's expectation was that the government would remain committed to a comprehensive industrial development programme that would help the country to diversify its oil-based economy. A variety of several teams of UN experts were working in the Iranian Ministry of Economy on different sectors of industrial development, but very soon we realized that most Iranian officials working with us had little enthusiasm for, or faith in, these programmes. I noticed that the mood of the senior government officers about the programme was one of cynicism. Some were not even qualified to do such work. Most of them were using government service as an address of convenience and were engaged in their own private jobs. Even though the Iranian revolution under the leadership of Ayatollah Khomeini, which overthrew the Shah's regime and dynasty, was still a few years away I could sense the rumblings even during 1970–74. Most of the Iranians occupying senior positions in the ministry where I worked were very critical of the Shah and his ministers and particularly about the widespread corruption at the highest levels of state administration. Every government office had a few agents from the much-feared and notorious secret service of the Shah, known as SAVAK, to spy on the officers. Still, such a state of affairs did not prevent them from expressing their cynical views and making critical comments to us foreigners and even predicting very optimistically that the Shah's regime would collapse very soon. The upshot of it all was that we (the UN experts), who were expected to be only advisers, had to shoulder the main responsibility for actually doing the work towards which the Iranian officers had virtually no commitment.

By the end of the fourth year of my assignment, my colleagues and I had succeeded in placing the industrial estate project on a sound basis. We had introduced a workable programme for the promotion of new industries and for training our counterparts for carrying on the work on their own. It was at this stage that I received an enquiry from the Government of India whether I would be willing to return to its fold as development commissioner, small-scale industries, and additional secretary in the Ministry of Industry. In fact, I had become eligible, by virtue of my seniority, for promotion to these posts. I decided to accept this offer though, had I put one more year in UN service in Iran, I would have become eligible for a handsome pension. I was fully conscious of the financial loss I would be incurring, but again, I felt the compelling urge to return to my own government's service, which alone could provide the job satisfaction I was missing badly. By the end of 1973 I returned to Delhi to take up the new assignments.

My return to the post of DCSSI was homecoming for me. The SSIO had not changed much since I had left it a decade earlier, though it had grown much larger. As additional secretary in the ministry I looked after the entire range of small-scale industries including khadi and village industries and the coir sector.

I had been in my new position for hardly a year and a half when I was promoted as secretary, although there were a few officers senior to me (in various ministries) in my own year of allotment in the IAS, i.e., 1948, still at the additional secretary level. One of them, R. Tirumalai was additional secretary in my ministry itself. I came to know later that when Prime Minister Indira Gandhi selected me from the panel submitted to her, the cabinet secretary, B.D. Pande, had specifically pointed out to her the fact that my appointment as secretary would cause embarrassment to Tirumalai. However, the prime minister had overruled this objection. She informed Pande that Tirumalai could be transferred to another ministry as additional secretary if he wished to leave. Tirumalai got his promotion a few months after I joined and was posted to another ministry as secretary. I took over as secretary in the Commerce Ministry in June 1975, when D.P. Chattopadhyaya was the minister of state with independent charge and V.P. Singh was the deputy minister. Later, Chattopadhyaya was elevated to the cabinet rank and V.P. Singh to the minister of state rank.

Within a few days of my joining as secretary, a series of major political events were set in motion, which shook the whole nation. The decision of the Allahabad High Court (on 12 June 1975) setting aside the election of Indira Gandhi on a technical charge of electoral law violation and the declaration of Emergency (on 25 June 1975) brought about stupendous changes not only in the political system but also in the entire bureaucracy.

The period of the Emergency imposed great stress and strain on civil servants. It was a truly testing time for them. Some ministers and political leaders constituted themselves into a new power centre in Delhi and started interfering in the work of the civil servants both in the Delhi Administration and the Central Government. They seemed to believe that Emergency meant dispensing with normal laws and regulations and that they had the right to decide what the bureaucrats should or should not do. Often, such interference was on the pretext of getting the grievances of the people redressed but, in reality, they were using the Emergency for their own benefit or to favour their friends and followers. An atmosphere of fear prevailed among the civil servants as those who did not comply with the demands and dictates of the new power centres were quickly transferred from their posts to less important ones or even punished through suspension or police investigations on flimsy or frivolous grounds. Unfortunately, there were several officers 'willing to crawl when asked only to bend' as was stated candidly by a senior opposition leader.

Even though I worked as secretary in the highly sensitive Ministry of Commerce for the entire duration of the Emergency, I was never pressurized by the new power centres to do anything wrong or violative of rules and regulations. Some attempts were made to ascertain whether I could be made to bend the rules to favour some people, but when they found that I did not comply, they left me alone without trying to put any pressure on me. I would like to mention two such cases.

The first case related to Colonel J.S. Anand, father-in-law of Sanjay Gandhi (Indira Gandhi's second son). As secretary in charge of foreign trade, I was responsible for the administration of the policies for imports and exports, a sensitive field in the heydays of the licence and permit quota Raj. The government had imposed a ban on the export of chrome ore in order to conserve it for indigenous requirements, except by those who had exported this ore prior to the date the order banning exports came into force. This commodity fetched very high profits in the export market and businessmen were interested in getting the ban order relaxed in their favour. Buta Singh, who was the deputy minister in the Ministry of Railways, informed me that Colonel Anand wished to see me with respect to an urgent business matter and requested me to grant him an early appointment. When Colonel Anand met me, I found that he had come with a request for a relaxation on the ban on the export of chrome ore on behalf of a party. I told him that if a relaxation was made in one case, it would have to be made in a number of other similar cases as well and that would nullify the purpose of the ban. Much to my surprise, he then told me that *he* was the real beneficiary in this case, though his name had not been given in the application. He obviously thought that this vital piece of information would compel me to relax the order in his favour but I firmly told him that several such applications for exports had been rejected and that there was no justification in making an exception in his case. He felt very unhappy at my negative reaction to his request and promptly suggested that I should bring the case to the attention of the cabinet minister, D.P. Chattopadhyaya, instead of turning down his request at my level. I told him very politely that this was not a case that needed to go to the cabinet minsiter as the policy of banning export of this material had the approval of the minister himself. In any case, I pointed out that the minister had the right to call for the file if he so wished, but I was certainly not going to put up the file to him for his order. He left my office very abruptly and later complained to Buta Singh and others in the political establishment about my 'unhelpful' attitude in his case. I understood later that Sanjay Gandhi, when he came to know of Colonel Anand's meeting with me, told him that he should never have made such a request to me and advised him not to approach me with any such requests in future. I never heard about this case after that.

Another case of attempting to exert pressure on me during Emergency related to my firm stand in refusing a high-value import licence to the Chamanlal group of firms against the exports of *zari* goods that this party claimed it had made several years ago when a scheme of giving import licences linked to certain exports was in force. The request of this party had been rejected by the chief controller of imports & exports (CCI&E) on the ground that the party had not repatriated to the country the foreign exchange said to have been earned by its exports. Further, the Enforcement Directorate, under the Ministry of Finance, had started proceedings against the firm for the violation of foreign exchange regulations in this case. The party obviously believed that political pressures could help it to procure the import licence, which had been rightly rejected at the level of the officers. The party was trying to present itself as one which had been wronged by the officers and was seeking the intervention of the minister to do 'justice'. I had taken the stand that the Ministry of Commerce could not consider this group's request till the investigations by the Enforcement Directorate had been completed and it had been cleared of the charges. I had recorded this view on the file. However, some prominent political leaders had put great pressure on Chattopadhyaya for a review of this decision.

Early in 1977, just a few days before the general elections, I received a message from the minister's office that I should send the Chamanlal group's file to him at his residence in Calcutta where the minister had been staying during election campaigns. I sent the file to him with a note that the case should first be referred to the Department of Economic Affairs for its advice regarding the eligibility of this party to receive a licence. The miniser's office had asked me to send only the file to him, but I thought I should reiterate the stand I had already taken in this case and added these comments on the file for the minister to see before taking his decision.

I understood later that Chattopadhyaya had first written an order on the file directing that the licence should be issued to the party. But it appears on going through all the facts recorded on the file, he himself changed his order and simply endorsed my recommendation by signing below my note. When the file came back to me, it clearly showed that his earlier order had been pasted over with a piece of paper before the minister put signature below mine. He obviously felt that my stand was correct and overruling me would not be proper.

When the file was referred to the Department of Economic Affairs, the DEA returned it with a rather non-committal note to the effect that the Commerce Ministry should first consult the Enforcement Directorate. The director of enforcement, to whom the case was then sent for advice by the CCI&E, observed that issue of a customs clearance permit to the Chamanlal group would prejudice the case initiated against it by the directorate. The directorate further advised that the party be asked to repatriate the export proceeds first without prejudice to the proceedings already started against it. Fortunately, there was no further pressure from any political authority for accepting the claims of the Chamanlal group.

By this time Indira Gandhi and the Congress had been voted out in the general elections of 1977 and a new Janata Party Government with Morarji Desai, as prime minister, had taken charge at Delhi. The experiences of many civil servants during the Janata Government were as bad as they were during the Emergency, if not worse. A massive witch-hunt started from the day the new Janata ministers were sworn in. Almost the very first act after occupying their ministerial chairs was to order the transfer of the officers whom they had perceived as having close links with the power centres during the Emergency period. The ministers carried readymade lists of officers who were to be transferred or against whom more serious action was to be launched and they did not wait for even a few days to hear what these officers would have liked to say. Very soon a plethora of commissions had been appointed to deal with the alleged crimes committed by Indira Gandhi and some of her cabinet colleagues. Several civil servants too had to face such commissions of enquiry and police investigations. One of the most high-handed actions taken against civil servants pertained to the arrest of B.B. Vohra, a highly respected secretary in the Central Government reputed for both integrity and efficiency. This arrest sent shock waves throughout the bureaucratic ranks and most civil servants felt their effects. Some senior secretaries (including myself) decided to meet Nirmal Mukherji, the cabinet secretary, and apprise him of the reaction in the senior ranks of the civil service to Vohra's arrest. Accordingly a small group of secretaries consisting of Praxy Fernandez, Vishnu Ahuja, Mantosh Sondhi and myself called on Mukherji and conveyed to him how distressed and demoralized the civil servants felt at the treatment meted out to Vohra. We requested his urgent intervention in this matter. Mukherji expressed his inability to act in this area as the decision had been taken at the highest political levels of the Janata Government.

With the change of government I thought that the licence case relating to the Chamanlal group would be allowed to take its own course and would be dealt with on its merits, but I was mistaken. In fact, I was to experience internal pressure to carry out a thoroughly dishonest act and when I firmly resisted, I was to lose my job as commerce secretary. I feel I should narrate the details of this episode after Chattopadhyaya rightly decided not to interfere with my decision in this case.

The Chamanlal group renewed its attempts to secure the import licence with redoubled vigour and submitted a petition to the new prime minister, Morarji Desai, complaining against alleged delay and injustice on the part of the Commerce Ministry in dealing with this case and seeking his intervention to get 'justice'. I was truly surprised when I was sent for by V. Shankar, principal secretary to the prime minister, and asked to review the stand I had taken in this case. I explained to Shankar the full facts of the case, thinking that the prime minister or he may not know the details about the Chamanlal group's efforts to pressurize me during the Emergency period to grant a licence. I pointed out that the Commerce Ministry would be committing a serious blunder if it were to issue the licence without waiting for the report of the Enforcement Directorate. However, Shankar knew all these facts, but he was still trying to twist my arm to make me take a thoroughly improper decision in this case. He mentioned, on several occasions over the phone, how keen the prime minister was to see that 'justice' was done to the party. I had known from my long experience of dealing with such issues in the Commerce Ministry that whenever anyone tried to make recommendations on behalf of an undeserving party, it was always in the name of 'justice'. I continued to resist Shankar's repeated attempts at pressurizing me on behalf of the Chamanlal group.

A rather curious development took place on 10 May 1977. The director of the Enforcement Directorate wrote to the CCI&E reversing his earlier stand on the issue of licence to the Chamanlal group. He also stated that the directorate would have no objection if the CCI&E took a decision on the party's application in any manner it deemed fit. The directorate, however, added a proviso that if a licence were issued, it should be *without prejudice* to any action that may be taken by the directorate in the case pending before it against the party. Obviously, the pressures exerted on the director had made their impact and he was trying to chart a course that could be both right and wrong at the same time, but fixing the responsibility for taking a decision squarely on my ministry. Shankar promptly telephoned me to point out that the Enforcement Directorate had withdrawn its objection and the path was now clear for us to issue the licence as requested by the group. I explained to him the correct interpretation of the advice given by the director of the Enforcement Directorate. To my chagrin, Shankar then asked the director, who had already been summoned to his room, to speak to me directly on the phone. Consequently, in Shankar's presence, the director told me that the issue of the licence was *entirely a matter for the Commerce Ministry to decide.*

In view of the mounting pressure on me, I decided to place the facts of the case before the new commerce minister, Mohan Dharia, through a note. I also personally explained to him how ironical the situation was in that I found myself under pressure to issue a licence to this same party in the Emergency period and now in the Janata administration. Mohan Dharia wrote out an unambiguous order on the file that no licence should be issued to the party till its name was cleared by the Enforcement Directorate.

The Chamanlal group, however, continued to canvass its case through various highly placed sources. Shankar himself told me that the prime minister was getting very annoyed with my so-called rigid stand on this matter. He even hinted that if I persisted with my stand, my continuance in the Commerce Ministry or in the Central Government itself would be in doubt. As a member of the Central Pool, I was not liable for reversion to my parent cadre of the Kerala state. But there were rumours that the pool itself was about to be abolished and I might be sent back to my parent cadre. In spite of the intense pressure on me, I was not prepared to be an accomplice to a totally dishonest transaction involving about £400,000 worth of imports, a very large amount by the standards of those years, by a party which had absolutely no right to get such a licence.

After exhausting all methods of pressurizing me, Shankar one day asked me to see him in his office. Here, he told me that the prime minister would be writing to Mohan Dharia about this case and that the Commerce Ministry could, if it did not want to take a decision, refer the case to the prime minister for his advice. I could not believe that Morarji Desai, who enjoyed a great reputation for integrity in public life, would choose to intervene in a matter of this nature, but a letter promptly arrived from the prime minister to Mohan Dharia early in October 1977 stating that the case had been pending for over ten years and advising that it should be disposed off in a fair and equitable manner. However, Mohan Dharia stuck to his earlier stand that it would be improper to issue any licence to this party.

I knew that Mohan Dharia's reply would invite the wrath of the prime minister more severely on me and I was now mentally prepared for the worst. Mohan Dharia himself had told me that the prime minister had been very angry with me and had been asking him why I was still continuing as secretary in his ministry. For his part, the cabinet secretary also had told me that the prime minister had not liked the stand I had taken in this case in spite of his personal intervention through his letter to the commerce minister. I then decided to send, to the cabinet secretary, a note explaining the full facts of the case and why I considered the issue of a licence to this party as totally improper. In a detailed note dated 17 November 1977 I gave an account of the various attempts on the part of Shankar to armtwist me into committing a wrong act. I met the cabinet secretary and handed over my note with a request that it be brought to the prime minister's attention so that I would have the satisfaction of knowing that the PM was aware of the facts before taking any decision. Nirmal Mukherji told me that he would put up my note to the prime minister but also warned me that I should be prepared for the consequences. I affirmed that I was prepared to face the consequences of trying to be honest, and if I was to be penalized for it, such a step would certainly not bring any credit to our civil service system.

Mukherji told me a few days later about Morarji Desai's sharp reaction on reading my note. He felt outraged that I could so boldly write about the intervention made by his principal secretary and insisted that orders be issued for transferring me on that very day. Mukherji informed him that even according to the decision taken about abolishing the pool scheme, I could not be sent back to my state at that stage as I had less than two years of service left. This revelation infuriated Morarji Desai even more and he accused Mukherji of showing partiality to a fellow Christian. Mukherji was quite upset by this highly unfair allegation and he told Morarji Desai rather tersely that he was being accused of religious bias for the first time in his long civil service career. He felt that since the prime minister himself had accused him, he would take this accusation as an expression of lack of confidence in him. Consequently, in his opinion, it would not have been appropriate for him to continue in office. Mukherji offered his resignation orally and, on returning to his office, followed it by a formal letter of resignation. Morarji Desai was certainly not prepared for such an unexpected reaction on the part of his cabinet secretary. He sent one of his close aides to meet Mukherji, basically to assure him of the PM's continued confidence in him and ask him to withdraw his letter of resignation, which he later did. Meanwhile, I was asked to continue in my post as secretary.

During the latter part of 1977, I had been putting in a lot of effort as chairman of an important committee set up to recommend comprehensive changes in import–export policies and procedures. This committee, which came to be known as the 'Alexander Committee', comprised some eminent economists and economic administrators in the government at that time, such as P.K. Kaul, Bimal Jalan, K.V. Sheshadri, Vijay Kelkar, G.S. Sawney, Ram Malhotra and V.R. Panchmukhi (secretary). The business community had been eagerly looking forward to the recommendations to be made by this committee. In this context, Nirmal Mukherji had pointed out to the prime minister that were I to be relieved of my post as commerce secretary at that stage, the functioning of this committee would be considerably handicapped and that, in the government's own interest,

I should be allowed to complete the committee's agenda and prepare the final report. Mohan Dharia also insisted that I should fulfil the duties assigned to me and only then leave my post. I worked under tremendous mental strain, knowing pretty well that I had incurred the displeasure of the prime minister. Nevertheless, I submitted my report to the commerce minister on 31 January 1978. After that, I went on long leave.

The significance of the recommendations of the 'Alexander Committee' was validated by the fact that they laid the foundation for a new import–export regime, which, in due course led to a new policy of trade liberalization. One of the most important recommendations of this committee was that all items for which no specific policy had been laid down in the *Red Book* should be allowed to be imported under the open general licence (OGL). The committee also recommended a shift from controls to development in the import regime and, in order to bring about this change, it recommended that the chief controller of imports & exports be redesignated as director general of foreign trade. Most of the recommendations were warmly received by the business community and were eventually implemented by the government through a series of modifications in the policies over the following two to three years. My colleagues on the committee and I derived immense satisfaction from the fact that our recommendations had paved the way for the dawn of the new era of liberalization vis-à-vis the import–export policies and procedures.

Morarji Desai's hostility towards me did not end with my removal from the post of commerce secretary as some of his subsequent actions revealed. The post of secretary general of the International Sugar Organization (ISO), London, had fallen vacant and my name had been sponsored for this post by the Government of India as I fulfilled all the stipulations related to the qualifications and experience. The nomination of my candidature for this post was done in the routine course by the cabinet secretary after obtaining the approval of Charan Singh, who was the home minister in Morarji Desai's cabinet. The final selection for this post was to be made by a board representing the member countries of the ISO. India's high commissioner in London had reported to the Ministry of External Affairs that I stood a good chance of being selected and that support for my candidature could be secured from a few other member countries by offering a quid pro quo, i.e., India's support to their candidates for some other positions in the ISO, which were also to be filled along with the post of secretary general. (This is the normal practice followed in selections to posts in various international organizations.) Consequently, the Ministry of External Affairs sent out messages (through telegrams) to our ambassadors in the concerned countries asking them to enlist support for me in exchange for support for their candidates for other posts. Copies of such telegrams and their responses were sent to the Prime Minister's Office (PMO) as per the normal practice. When Morarji Desai came across these telegrams, he flew into a rage over the fact that the government was extending support to my candidature. He sent for Nirmal Mukherji and raised strong objections to my name having been sponsored without his permission and insisted that my nomination be immediately withdrawn. Mukherji pointed out that it was the home minister who was the competent authority to approve or disapprove the sponsorship of suitable candidates from the all-India services to such posts and that my name had been duly cleared by him. He also pointed out that it would be very embarrassing to the Government of India in general and to the home minister in particular if my nomination was abruptly withdrawn at that stage. This development occurred at a time when relations between Morarji Desai and Charan Singh had become rather strained and the former did not want to create a ruckus by overruling the latter's decision. Hence, he asked Mukherji to instruct the Ministry of External Affairs to neither extend any further support to my candidature nor enter into any understanding with other countries on the basis of reciprocal support as was being done at that time. These instructions were duly conveyed to the Ministry of External Affairs and strictly followed by its officials.

When I came to know about these new developments, I called on the cabinet secretary to ascertain the reasons for this sudden decision to withdraw support for my candidature. I asked him whether it was the prime minister's wish that he would rather let the post be bagged by a non-Indian than see me getting it. Since Mukherji felt very embarrassed by my questioning him thus, I did not pursue this matter any further. Nevertheless, I felt very bitter at the fact that an individual as eminent as the prime minister could carry his strong prejudices against me to this extent and began to wonder whether removing me from the post of commerce secretary was not enough punishment for the 'crime' of resisting pressures to commit a patently wrong act.

I knew I would not be able to obtain the post in the ISO without entering into reciprocal agreements with a few other countries. However, I went through the motions of appearing before the ISO Selection Board in London as my name was already on the panel. But, as I had anticipated, I did not get the job essentially because of lack of support from my own government.

From the incidents narrated above anyone can imagine the great mental anguish I was experiencing at that stage of my career. I was not worried about losing a job in the Central Government as I was confident that I would not remain unemployed and could find a suitable UN assignment if I chose to do so. The question that tormented me the most at that time was: why had I been punished so severely for no fault of mine? I could have easily sent the file through the commerce minister to the prime minister's office without offering any opinion on the merits of the case, leaving it to the prime minister to take a decision as was suggested to me by Shankar. However, I knew I would be acting dishonestly if I did not candidly express my views on the file in this case. It would indeed have been gross dereliction of duty and an act of connivance with a dishonest deed if I had not highlighted the blatant flaw in the case for the benefit of the prime minister. As I have stated earlier, several officers had been placed under suspension by the Janata Government for alleged wrong doings under pressure from powerful politicians or other higher-ups during the Emergency. Even though I had been occupying a very sensitive post during the entire period of the Emergency, there had been not even a whisper of a complaint against any of my actions during this period. What pained me most, therefore, was that the Janata Government, which had come to power with loud claims of fighting corruption and restoring high standards of cleanliness and honesty, should have chosen to punish a person like me for not being 'helpful' in issuing an undeserved high-value import licence to a party which was under investigation by the government itself for violation of foreign exchange regulations.

✧

When I submitted my application for long leave, I was very clear in my mind that I would not revert to the Kerala cadre. As the seniormost IAS officer in the Kerala cadre at that time, I would have been appointed chief secretary if I went back but I would have found the entire situation very embarrassing since I was being virtually thrown out of my post as secretary by the Central Government leadership. I decided that I would opt for a short assignment with the UN and resign from the IAS immediately after that.

I did not have to wait long. The UN International Trade Centre (ITC) at Geneva offered me an assignment for two months as senior adviser to the head of the organization. The main objective was to prepare a medium-term plan for the organization, which was mainly dealing with providing technical assistance to developing countries on matters relating to international trade. I promptly accepted the offer and was back in UN service in June 1978 for the third time in my career.

From the day of my taking up my new assignment in Geneva, I found that luck had started turning in my favour. When I was about to sign my formal contract for a two-month assignment with the ITC, I was informed that the UN had taken a decision that those with previous (UN) service could revalidate such service for purposes of pension if the total period including the duration of the new assignment could add up to five years. I had left the UN service in Tehran after completing four years and I was short by one year. The then head of the ITC told me that he would be happy to offer me a one-year assignment instead of the two months. Thus, I became eligible for a UN pension. Greater luck was soon to follow. Within a few months of my functioning as senior adviser to the head of the ITC, that post itself fell vacant and the authorities of the United Nations and the

GATT (General Agreement on Tariffs and Trade), which jointly controlled the ITC, decided to offer it to me and I took over as the head of the ITC in the senior director grade, which was soon upgraded to the level of assistant secretary general.

The post of the head of the ITC had remained at senior director's level ever since the organization was established fifteen years earlier. The director general of the GATT sent for me one day and told me that since I had been found to be a good choice for the post of the head of the ITC, the GATT and the UN would move for the upgradation of the post to the level of assistant secretary general. However, there was a ban on the upgradation of posts in the UN at that time and the proposal had to go through various stages before it could be finally approved by the Fifth Committee of the UN General Assembly, which meant practically a vote by all members of the General Assembly. Even though the Budget Committee of the UN and some of the important delegations like those of the USA and the UK had opposed the upgradation, the Fifth Committee approved the proposal by an overwhelming majority.

When the news of my promotion came out in the Indian media I received several letters and telegrams of congratulations and some of them specially emphasized the fact that a person who had been hounded out of the government had at last been rewarded for his courage and honesty. One telegram received from Dr S.K. Rao, my colleague in the IAS and a very close friend, was particularly interesting. He advised that I should put up a portrait of Morarji Desai in my house and offer flowers every day because if he had not sent me out of my commerce secretary's post in 1978 I would not have got the opportunity of earning a UN pension and being appointed as executive head of the ITC! I felt very gratified that what was intended to be a punishment eventually turned out to be a pleasant experience for me.

SEVEN

With Indira Gandhi: 1

DURING THE YEARS I WORKED WITH THE ITC IN GENEVA, I.E., 1978–81, epoch-making developments had been taking place in India. I kept myself fully informed of the rapidly changing political scenario not only through the Indian and foreign media but also through a large network of senior civil servants who had been visiting Geneva to attend various international conferences that were being held there frequently.

During the early part of the Janata Government's rule, Prime Minister Morarji Desai and his senior colleagues in the cabinet spent a lot of their time and energy in trying to punish Indira Gandhi, her son Sanjay and some of her former cabinet colleagues for what were described as 'Emergency excesses'. In fact, the only agenda on which senior leaders such as Morarji Desai, Charan Singh and Jagjivan Ram* could agree was the pursuit of their personal vendetta against Indira Gandhi and ensuring that she never returned to power. The

---

* Jagjivan Ram was once a trusted confidant of Indira Gandhi who had held many sensitive and crucial portfolios including the post of defence minister. He 'defected' to the Janata Party in February 1977.

Emergency period, of course, had witnessed numerous illegal and unconstitutional acts committed by top-level dignitaries and their minions who had wielded power and influence at that time. All these aberrations, no doubt, deserved to be investigated. But punishment of Indira Gandhi and her elimination from the political arena became an obsession with the new government even to the point of completely forgetting the promises of providing good governance on the basis of which the Janata leaders had been elected to power. A series of commissions were set up to enquire into various categories of Emergency excesses and the entire machinery of the government appeared to be devoted to these commissions. The Justice (J.C.) Shah Commission, the Justice (H.R.) Khanna Commission and the Justice (Jagmohan) Reddy Commission, for instance, continued to be in session during the major part of the Janata regime, while the government itself unleashed a programme whose basic objectives were to ensure (1) the arrest of former ministers; (2) the suspension of several senior civil servants; and (3) transfer of practically every officer suspected of having been close to the centres of power during the Emergency. The chief target was Indira Gandhi and the main objective was to deny her a chance to enter Parliament again.

However, much to the disappointment of the Janata leaders, Indira Gandhi succeeded in getting elected to the Lok Sabha in November 1978 from the rural constituency of Chikmaglur in Karnataka state. Her rival was Veerendra Patil, a highly respected political leader of Karnataka who had earned a well-deserved reputation for cleanliness and efficiency in administration when he had served as a minister and later as the chief minister. Most people expected him to win the by-election but he lost by a big margin of over 70,000 votes. Despite her huge victory, it was widely believed that she wouldn't be allowed to function as an MP for long and the Janata top brass would discover some loophole to terminate her membership of Parliament. When I heard the news about Indira Gandhi's election victory I felt very happy and sent her a letter of congratulations and good wishes to which she replied on 10 December 1978, observing that she had heard of the circumstances that had forced me to opt for retirement from government service. She added that 'it was a pity since the government is in dire need of honest and competent people like you'. Incidentally, she had sent this letter from 12, Willingdon Crescent, New Delhi, where she was staying during the period that she was out of power. By coincidence, as a Rajya Sabha MP, I became the occupant of this bungalow in 2003.

The rumours about Indira Gandhi's ouster from Parliament soon came true. The Privileges Committee of Parliament found her guilty of obstructing some officials who were investigating a criminal complaint relating to Sanjay Gandhi's Maruti (small-car) project set up at Gurgaon (Haryana) just to the south of Delhi. On 19 December 1978 a resolution was passed by the Lok Sabha expelling her from the membership of the House for breach of privilege and contempt and committing her to jail till the prorogation of the House. Consequently, Indira Gandhi was arrested and sent to Tihar Jail (New Delhi). After a week in jail she was released; when she came out of jail she had earned a good deal of sympathy and support from the common people of India who, only a few months earlier, had inflicted a humiliating defeat on her and her party. The person accused as the arch-villain of the Emergency by the people now became, in their eyes, a victim of persecution, thanks to the manner in which the top leaders of the Janata Party sought to deny her the seat in Parliament she had lawfully won in the by-election.

By mid-1979 the fissures within the Janata Party had become obvious. The general public was hugely dismayed at the manner in which the senior leaders were constantly quibbling with each other almost on every issue. The only issue on which they all could agree upon was punishing Indira Gandhi and very soon even this became a cause for mutual recrimination; blame was sought to be apportioned as to who was responsible for mishandling some of the attempts to arrest her. Meanwhile, the various commissions of inquiry had started finalizing the reports and courts had begun hearing the specific criminal cases pending against Sanjay Gandhi and some members of the Indira Gandhi cabinet. These moves seemed to be part of a witch-hunt to the common people of the country. They had been strongly opposed to the excesses of the Emergency in the past and had now started wondering whether or not the Janata leaders were capable of fulfilling their expectations of a fair, reliable and efficient administration. In fact, the very stability of the government was in serious doubt and the media started speculating as to when it would fall and who would be the next prime minister.

The Morarji Desai Government finally collapsed on 15 July 1979 when a no-confidence motion moved by Y.B. Chavan – who, like Jagjivan Ram, once held senior ministerial positions (including defence) in Indira Gandhi's cabinet, had joined Charan Singh as an ally – was passed by the Lok Sabha. Morarji Desai resigned as prime minister the same day and a new government was formed by Charan Singh with the support of the Congress MPs owing allegiance to Indira Gandhi. However, the Charan Singh Government did not survive for long and he resigned without facing Parliament for a vote of confidence as stipulated by President Sanjiva Reddy while inviting him to form the government. Consequently, Parliament was dissolved by the president on 22 August 1979 and fresh general elections were scheduled for the first week of January 1980. Charan Singh continued to be the caretaker prime minister during this period.

Indira Gandhi soon swung into action by launching a country-wide election campaign, the likes of which people had never seen before. She was reported to have covered over 40,000 miles, addressing some twenty meetings a day. Several thousands of people flocked to attend these meetings. Finally, the Congress Party won 351 of the 542 Lok Sabha seats and Indira Gandhi assumed office as prime minister on 14 January 1980.

I wrote to her again, congratulating her on her spectacular victory. Her reply (dated 13 February 1980) revealed how deeply worried she was about the grave law and order situation and the economic mess in the country she had inherited from the Janata Government.

Most people in India at that time sincerely hoped that Indira Gandhi would make a serious attempt at cleaning up the administration and imparting to it a new dynamism and a fresh spirit of fairness and justice. However, within a few months of Indira Gandhi taking over as prime minister, reports started appearing in newspapers in India and abroad about the rise of a new power centre in Delhi and its undisguised attempts to take over the entire business of government. Sanjay Gandhi emerged as the central point of power in the new dispensation and steadily but surely started gaining control over the government machinery, again sending shock waves of disappointment, if not disillusionment, among those who had become ardent admirers of Indira Gandhi when she was out of power. People at large started wondering why such an astute politician as Indira Gandhi, who had suffered much at the hands of the Janata leaders, should provide an opportunity to her critics to claim that the government was reverting to the style followed during the Emergency years. A majority of the population watched anxiously and helplessly how Sanjay and his small clique could, in so short a time, bring the levers of power under their control and become the dispensers of favours and wielders of power while remaining behind the throne. People viewed such a state of affairs as the exercise of power without accountability, as Sanjay Gandhi did not hold any ministerial post in the government. The line between the party organization and the government began to get blurred. Very soon the new government started losing the unstinted respect and cooperation that it had gained after the fall of the Janata regime. The Western media reports in particular, which I was following very closely in Geneva, were severely critical of the manner in which Sanjay Gandhi and his group were allowed by Indira Gandhi to acquire so much power and influence in the conduct of government business. Personally, I felt greatly disappointed and distressed that such a development could take place so soon after her triumphant return to power. From the media reports and from the feedback I was getting from some of my old colleagues in the service, I got the distinct impression that the administration was in danger of sliding back to the dark days of the Emergency.

When Indira Gandhi returned to power in January 1980 she had asked Krishnaswami Rao Saheb, an IAS officer of the Andhra Pradesh cadre who had been appointed as secretary to the prime minister by Charan Singh (during his brief tenure), to continue in the post till a new incumbent could be selected by her. Rao Saheb, who on the basis of seniority in service was expected to be appointed as cabinet secretary, was an exceptionally competent civil servant, highly respected by his colleagues for his efficiency and impartiality.

He knew his was a stopgap arrangement and therefore did not try to bring in any major changes in the PMO's (Prime Minister's Office) working culture as he saw it emerging under the new dispensation.

Upon resuming power, Indira Gandhi had asked the cabinet secretary to submit to her a panel of names for consideration for appointment as secretary in the PMO and he had sent her four names of senior officers along with their character rolls. In the list one was mine. I got this information one day in early 1980 from P. Shivshankar, the law minister in Indira Gandhi's cabinet, who visited Geneva to attend a UN conference there. Shivshankar was a trusted colleague of Indira Gandhi and she had asked him to meet me and discreetly ascertain whether or not I would be willing to accept the post of secretary to the PM if an offer was made. I was not personally acquainted with Shivshankar; in fact, it was only in Geneva that I met him for the first time. However, I had heard a good deal about him, particularly the fact that Indira Gandhi held him in high esteem and reposed a lot of confidence in him. He referred very guardedly to Indira Gandhi's interest in acquiring my services and how I could make a significant contribution to the functioning of the new government as the PM's secretary because of my long experience in administration both nationally and internationally.

When Shivshankar brought to my notice the fact that Indira Gandhi was seriously considering me for the post of secretary, I immediately recalled the unpleasant experience I had to undergo at the hands of Morarji Desai and his principal secretary for no fault of mine. I had gladly responded to the call to return to government service while I was serving in the UN on two occasions before and, on both these occasions, I could never have imagined that I was taking the risk of incurring the hostility of a prime minister. Those experiences had cured me of a lot of idealism; consequently, I was mentally unprepared for taking another risk. In fairness to Sanjay Gandhi, I should say that I personally never had any experience of being at the receiving end of pressures from him to commit any irregular or unethical act during the Emergency. However, the reports I had received about the working style of the government were rather discouraging and I was therefore not willing to jeopardize my career again by quitting a UN job. However, I didn't express any of my feelings to Shivshankar; I only pointed out that I was occupying a position that could enable me to serve the Government of India usefully even without having to join it. I also observed that if I left the UN post, it was highly unlikely that my successor would be another Indian. After hearing me out Shivshankar didn't put forward any further arguments to pressurize me except to say that 'it would be good for the government to have you back in the service'.

✧

I did not hear anything further about this job till 28 October 1980 when N.K. Singh (who later became a member of the Planning Commission), an official in the Commerce Ministry, brought up this topic at a dinner I had hosted at my residence in honour of P.K. Kaul, the new commerce secretary who was on a visit to Geneva. (N.K. Singh was one of the guests.) During this occasion, N.K. Singh told me that he understood from reliable sources that I was still under active consideration by the PM for the post of secretary in the PMO. I was somewhat surprised at hearing this news as I had believed that Indira Gandhi would have been informed by Shivshankar about my unenthusiastic response when I was sounded out by him earlier.

I later came to know that after the tragic death of Sanjay Gandhi in a plane crash in New Delhi on 23 June 1980, Indira Gandhi had decided to seriously renew her efforts to select an experienced and reliable person to head the PMO and had not taken my response to Shivshankar as negative. The officials of the Commerce Ministry knew that I planned to visit Delhi in November 1980 to attend a conference on small and medium entrepreneurs organized by the World Assembly of Medium and Small Entrepreneurs (WASME) in cooperation with the Government of India.

Within a few days of N.K. Singh's visit I received a call from a close friend of mine, Pupul Jayakar who was based in Delhi, also a personal friend of Indira Gandhi, asking me whether I was going to call on the prime minister during my forthcoming visit to Delhi. Pupul was aware of Shivshankar's meeting with me and the real reasons for my reservations about accepting the job in the PMO. Pupul briefly informed me that the entire system during Indira Gandhi's 'second innings' was undergoing a thorough change after Sanjay's demise. She emphasized the point that Indira Gandhi was very keen to bring in a person with useful administrative experience to help her in her efforts to improve the working of the PMO and that I should not have any misgivings about the conditions of work there. At any rate, she counselled me to the effect that a courtesy call on the prime minister by me, as an Indian heading a UN organization, would be in order and, therefore, I should request an appointment on a suitable date and at a suitable time. Consequently, I wrote to the PMO, seeking an appointment on any one of the days I was to be in Delhi (from 9 to 15 November 1980). I received a message from the PMO before leaving Geneva that the PM would be 'glad to see me at noon on 13 November at her office in South Block'.

A day before meeting Indira Gandhi, I had told K.B. Lall, my good friend and well-wisher, that I would be meeting her and the question of secretaryship in the PMO might crop up at the meeting. Lall, an experienced civilian well versed with Indira Gandhi's style of dealing with such subjects, informed me that Indira Gandhi would never ask anyone directly to work with her; instead she would lead the conversation to such a point that the person would feel obliged to offer his services to her. 'She is an empress', Lall put it. He added that 'she would never put herself in the position of having to hear a "no" from anyone.' Being forewarned, I was quite prepared for the conversation and the undercurrents that were inherent in it.

My meeting with Indira Gandhi lasted about twenty minutes. I found her in a relaxed mood. She started joking about her weakness for Swiss chocolates when I presented a box I had brought along with me. She then asked me about the nature of my work in the ITC, which I briefly explained to her. After a few questions with regard to the economic problems faced by developing countries in general and how people in the UN circle in Geneva were looking at the change of government in India, she came quickly to the point of ascertaining my interest in taking up the position of secretary in her office. 'I need good and competent men in the government now', she began. She then added: 'I have been looking for such persons for some time now but my problem is shortage of such persons. Several important posts have yet to be filled up. Take, for example, the position of secretary in the PMO. I am still on the lookout for suitable persons.' This statement was followed by a query as to when my present contract was to expire. I explained to her the finer points of my contract very briefly but did not follow it up by saying that I was ready to take up the post of secretary to the PM. She then repeated her earlier statement that she was badly in need of good and competent persons to work for her. 'We have many experienced and competent men in our country,' she declared, 'but when it comes to choosing the right person for certain key positions I find I have a problem.' I quickly realized that this was the nearest she would come in asking me to accept the post. I told her that I was on my way to Manila to spend three weeks of my holidays with my elder son Jawahar (who was working in the Asian Development Bank there) and that I would meet her again in Delhi on my return. The meeting ended on this note. I came to know later that she had taken my statement that 'I would meet her again' as an expression of my willingness to join the PMO as secretary. She had even joked, as I was taking leave, that the Government of India salaries were nowhere near the UN figures.

On 15 November 1980 I left for Bangkok en route to Manila. I returned to Delhi on 8 December 1980 to attend a symposium on oilseeds products, which had been organized jointly by the Government of India and the ITC. I called on Pupul Jayakar on 15 December at her residence and apprised her of my meeting with Indira Gandhi about a month earlier. Pupul told me that Indira Gandhi had informed her about the meeting and had found in me a suitable candidate for the post of secretary and only the terms of appointment between me and the government remained to be finalized.

On 16 December Pranab Mukherjee, the commerce minister, informed over the telephone that he would like to see me urgently to discuss certain matters related to my likely assignment in the PMO. When I met Mukherjee at his office in Parliament House, he told me that Indira Gandhi wished to make a formal offer of the job of secretary in the PMO to me even before I left India for Geneva. He also explained to me the constraints in offering any salary higher than that prescribed for the post. I told him that I was quite aware of the fact that the salary would be Rs 3500 per month and, in my case,

I pointed out that it would be further reduced by the pension I was drawing as I had already opted for retirement from government service. Therefore, I felt that there was very little to discuss about the salary aspect. Mukherjee then told me that the PM would like to meet me again before I returned to Geneva and that he would specify the date and the time very soon. I gave him my address in Cochin (now Kochi), which was my destination. I stayed at my brother's house there from 23 December 1980 to 2 January 1981, but, much to my surprise, I did not receive the expected message specifying the date of my meeting with Indira Gandhi from Pranab Mukherjee; nor did I check with him. I returned to Geneva without going via Delhi.

On 20 January 1981, Pupul Jayakar telephoned me at Geneva. She stated that Indira Gandhi had mentioned to her that she (the PM) was hoping to meet me at Delhi a second time when the formal offer of appointment was to be made to me personally by her and as to why I had not called on her. My response was that I had been waiting for a message from Pranab Mukherjee regarding the date for my meeting. The very next day I received a telephone call from Pranab Mukherjee at Geneva asking me why I did not come to Delhi to see the prime minister in spite of his sending a telegram to me. I told him categorically that I had not received any such telegram from him. I came to know later that some 'interested persons' in the government, who had come to know of my meeting with Indira Gandhi and the likelihood of my being appointed as secretary in PMO, had managed to ensure that the telegram from Pranab Mukherjee was *never actually sent*. People who are not aware as to how the government worked those days in Delhi may wonder how such a fairly important matter like arranging my meeting with the PM could be so casually handled. But this was what actually happened because those individuals, who wanted their own candidate to be chosen for the post, obviously thought that if I was prevented from meeting the PM, she would infer that I was reluctant to accept the post and would opt for another candidate. However, after this episode, she dealt with the matter of my appointment directly. Some people may also wonder why Pranab Mukherjee was brought into this affair by Indira Gandhi instead of the PM's secretary or the cabinet secretary or the home minister. All I can say is that this was her style of working. Indira Gandhi, as I soon discovered, used different ministers for different assignments, as she considered appropriate, though these ministers were not directly concerned with them.

Within an hour of Pranab Mukherjee's call, Krishnaswami Rao Saheb, secretary to the prime minister, telephoned me. The prime minister had asked him to ascertain from me the terms and conditions I had in mind. I told Rao Saheb that I did not have any special terms or conditions to be fulfilled for I knew the rules of the government very well. As regards the tenure, I clearly stated that it was for the prime minister to decide. By this time I had made up my mind to accept the offer and I told Rao Saheb to inform the prime minister accordingly. Rao Saheb called me again on 26 January 1981 to say that prime minister had formally appointed me as principal secretary. He also conveyed the message that I would serve under a contract without any fixed period but one which could be terminated on three months' notice from either side.

At this stage, I went in for some self-introspection. I had taken the plunge after overcoming all my initial misgivings. I began assuring myself that I would be able to do full justice to my job without having to face any serious problems from any quarter because I had been selected by the prime minister herself. I notified the authorities of the UN and the GATT about my intention to resign from my post as executive director of the ITC with effect from 1 May 1981. I returned to Government of India service exactly three years after having been abruptly removed from the post of secretary in the Ministry of Commerce.

✧

I went to the PMO at 1 p.m. on 2 May (one day after reaching India) and signed the relevant documents before officially taking over as principal secretary. Immediately thereafter, Rao Saheb and I together called on the prime minister for a few minutes. This was my first official act as her principal secretary. Rao Saheb had quit his post as secretary to the PM the previous day and had taken over as cabinet secretary.

There was very little time for the PM to brief me on 4 May as she had to make an unscheduled visit to Bihar on that day. (She returned only late in the night.) On 5 May, she was to begin an official visit to Switzerland, Kuwait and the United Arab Emirates and I was required to accompany her on these visits, within just three days of assuming my new responsibility in the PMO.

Within an hour of take-off from Delhi I was called to her cabin in the plane. She straightaway started prioritizing the problems that needed my immediate attention. The main thrust of her talk underlined the fact that I should get involved practically in every item of work she had to handle. For well over an hour she explained to me the main areas of concern to her at that time. She pointed out that the economy was in poor shape and she was hoping to give it a new direction by introducing a series of new policies and programmes. She emphasized that I should remain in close contact with L.K. Jha (who was her unofficial adviser on economic issues). Another major concern for her was national security. The Akali agitation in the Punjab was building up and gaining momentum day by day. She appeared to be quite concerned about the danger of the agitation being 'hijacked' by undesirable elements and posing a serious threat to national security. She observed that while she did not want to set up a formal committee to deal with national security, she expected that Rao Saheb, R.N. Kao, the chief of the Research and Analysis Wing (RAW)* and I should constitute ourselves into an informal core group responsible for all matters relevant to national security.

Indira Gandhi explained to me in great detail the weaknesses that she saw in her own party, the Indian National Congress. She affirmed that she would be spending quite a lot of her time in rebuilding her party as it had fallen into total disarray over the past few years. Several senior members of the party had deserted her after she lost power in 1977; in some states the Congress did not have even duly constituted state-level committees. She declared that her main effort would be to make the party an effective instrument in assisting the government in fulfilling the promises in the election manifesto.

---

* This agency is responsible for gathering and analysing intelligence from foreign sources.

She then turned her focus to giving me a candid assessment of the members of her own family. She explained the circumstances in which Sanjay Gandhi had come to play an important role in the party organization and how great a loss the party had sustained by his untimely death. I was quite surprised at the detached manner in which she spoke about Sanjay's death; it showed that she had completely overcome the grief she had experienced as a result of this intense personal tragedy in her life. She told me how very reluctant her elder son, Rajiv Gandhi, was to take up party work. Nevertheless, she stated that she was happy to find that Rajiv had accepted his new role with great enthusiasm.

All through her briefing I noticed that her main intention was to convey the message that she expected me not to be just a bureaucrat running the PMO and helping her in her administrative responsibilities as prime minister; very soon I found that I had to take on several duties and responsibilities far beyond the normal field of work allotted to a civil servant. Later, I shall refer to a few of the important confidential missions entrusted to me by her, missions that she did not want her political colleagues to handle or to know about.

This comprehensive briefing was extremely useful to me, as I came to know directly from Indira Gandhi herself what she was expecting from me.

An account of the PMO, from an historical perspective, would be in order. Jawaharlal Nehru, the first prime minister of India, was assisted by a senior officer, with the designation of principal private secretary (PPS), who was the head of the PM's Secretariat (as the PMO was then called). The role of the PPS during the Nehru era was quite different from that of his successors for obvious reasons. Nehru did not need the assistance of a secretariat to the extent that his successors did because the government then was still a small and compact institution. All the officers who worked with him as PPS were ICS officers at different levels of seniority. In those days the story was that Nehru briefed the bureaucrats instead of being briefed by them! Further, given his eminence as a national leader and the immense backing he enjoyed from his own party, the tasks of administration in the PM's Secretariat during his period were relatively simple.

However, the situation became very different when Lal Bahadur Shastri assumed office as prime minister after Nehru's demise in May 1964. The economic situation in the country had worsened considerably and the Congress Party itself had lost ground both at the Central and state levels. The prime minister needed a competent secretariat to support him in dealing with the enormous problems, both internal and external, which he had to face. He had wisely chosen L.K. Jha, a senior member of the former ICS with a formidable reputation as an economic administrator, as his secretary. (The designation changed from PPS to secretary during this period.) When Indira Gandhi succeeded Lal Bahadur Shastri as prime minister in 1966, she had retained Jha in the same post for a short period.

After the general elections of 1967, when the Congress was badly mauled and Indira Gandhi had to face serious challenges from within her own party, she chose P.N. Haksar, an eminent diplomat, whom she had personally known for some years. Unlike Jha, who was an orthodox bureaucrat, P.N. Haksar had strong political inclinations of his own and was deeply involved in the big political debate that was going on in India then as to whether India should opt for a left-oriented policy or a right-oriented one. Haksar was well known for his left-of-the-centre outlook, which was also in line with Indira Gandhi's own political convictions. He proved to be one of the most successful secretaries in the PMO and the valuable advice he rendered to Indira Gandhi during the split in the Congress Party in 1969 and with regard to major decisions like bank nationalization in the same year enhanced his reputation as a brilliant administrator.

Another illustrious individual, P.N. Dhar, had joined the PMO first as adviser (in the grade of secretary) in 1970. Haksar as the principal secretary and Dhar as secretary worked as a good team, each complementing the other. When Dhar succeeded Haksar, the designation reverted to 'secretary to the prime minister'. The designation of principal secretary was revived during Morarji Desai's time, when V. Shankar was appointed to this post. Again the designation was back to secretary when Krishnaswami Rao Saheb held the post for a year. The designation principal secretary was revived when I was appointed to the post in May 1981.

A popular misconception about the PMO was that it was a bloated institution with a large number of superfluous officers and staff. When Morarji Desai assumed office he had announced that he would trim the size of the PMO to the barest minimum and had criticized Indira Gandhi for having allowed the office to expand needlessly during her tenure. However, all that Morarji Desai did was to reduce the size of the staff from 229 to 211. When Indira Gandhi assumed office as prime minister in 1966 the strength of the PM's Secretariat (PMS) was 198 and it had increased by only 31 from 1966 to 1977. Indira Gandhi was very strict, to the point of being very parsimonious, in the matter of sanction of new posts, particularly for her own office. Whenever there was a need felt for creating a new post, we had often to suggest the abolition of an existing one to justify its creation.

It is a well-known fact that during the period of Indira Gandhi's stewardship as prime minister, the PMO grew tremendously as far as its importance, influence and power were concerned. This trend started in 1971, after India's spectacular victory in the Bangladesh war, when she emerged not only as the undisputed leader of her party, but also as a leader of the entire nation. Another factor that had contributed to the strengthening of the influence of the prime minister was the split in the Congress Party and the departure of many senior leaders who were strongly opposed to her policies and style of functioning. By the time Indira Gandhi returned to power in January 1980 with a massive majority in Parliament, she had become the unquestioned leader of her party. At the time of the general elections in 1980 many of the Congress 'old guard' had contested on the Janata Party ticket. In fact, several Congress candidates who were nominated to fight the elections had least expected that they would win, but the tide against the Janata Party was so strong that most of them, to their own surprise, got elected to Parliament. The prime minister is often described as *unus inter pares*, or at best, *primus inter pares*. But by the time Indira Gandhi formed her new government in January 1980, her position in her Council of Ministers was undoubtedly that of the supreme leader. Several members of her cabinet would not have been elected without her support and they knew that they had become ministers not as obvious natural choices based on their own qualifications or seniority but largely because of the fact that she had chosen them. During the last four years of her prime ministership (1980–84), she had received unqualified support from the entire party and her Council of Ministers. Such support, in turn, had served to enhance the prestige and importance of the prime minister. Naturally, the PMO also grew in importance and stature in the eyes of the people.

A clear division of functions existed between the PMO and the office in the Prime Minister's House (PMH). Indira Gandhi was very particular, specially after the demise of Sanjay Gandhi in June 1980, that the PMH should confine itself to assisting her in her *personal* work like movement of files, fixing appointments, arranging her tours and conveying important messages to senior party functionaries. The PMH was relatively a small one with R. K. Dhawan as private secretary and Usha Bhagat as social secretary with both holding the rank of 'director'. Two years later the post of private secretary was upgraded to the joint secretary level as a result of my initiative. The rest of the PMH consisted of a small corpus of assistants, personal assistants, stenographers and clerks. They had to deal with petitions from the people at large, which used to pour in their hundreds every week, mostly addressed to the PM. This office had to ensure that these petitions were promptly attended to by the concerned authorities in the government both at the Central and state levels. However, the PMH continued to have only a skeleton office under R. K. Dhawan who had known her style of working very well for several years and had also enjoyed her confidence.

In 1981 the PMO consisted of various officials, including myself. An information adviser (at secretary level) to assist in the area of public relations in general and specifically in drafting of speeches and messages for the prime minister was appointed. Also, an additional secretary to assist in economic matters was roped in. Finally, there was a small complement of half a dozen officers at director/joint secretary level in charge of different subjects such as external affairs, science and technology, environment, political affairs and administration. The post of information adviser was held with great distinction by H.Y. Sharda Prasad, who had worked with the PM earlier. The additional secretary's post, initially held by Arjun Sengupta, an eminent economist, was later upgraded to special secretary.

Within a few days of my joining the PMO, I introduced a proper system to streamline the movement of files from the officers of the PMO to the prime minister and back. The officers had the freedom to send most of the files direct to the prime minister without having to go through me. However, on their way back, the files were routed through me, enabling me to get to know their contents. These files were disposed of at their levels. I had told my colleagues that if they needed my guidance on any important matter, they could discuss the case with me before sending across the file to the PM or before routing the files through me to the PM. I had also introduced the practice of my meeting all PMO officers once a week. These meetings helped me in ascertaining the workload of every officer; they also presented a useful opportunity for my colleagues to interact with each other. I met my colleagues individually almost every day and kept myself fully acquainted with their work. Sometimes, if a file went directly to the prime minister from any of my colleagues and if she felt that my comments were also needed, she would send it to me. The PMO was made up of a team of efficient middle-level officers such as V.S. Tripathi, R. Rajamani, Arvind Pande and Chinmaya Garekhan who were totally committed to their work and were loyal to me as the head of the PMO. These factors greatly enhanced the usefulness of the PMO in its basic function of rendering timely and relevant advice to the PM. I used to explain to my senior colleagues during the weekly meetings my views and opinions on different issues handled by the PMO. Simultaneously, I used to invite their frank comments on certain issues, in case I felt they would prove helpful to me. This system worked very well and I did not have to seek any replacement of officers on grounds of indifferent work or lack of dedication to duty. Sharda Prasad, the most experienced hand in the PMO, was a source of great help to me. I used to consult him on some of the very sensitive issues I had to handle because I knew I could always rely on his sagacious and impartial advice. Salman Khurshid (a minister of state for external affairs in Narasimha Rao's cabinet and now an active member of the Congress Party) had joined the PMO for a few months during my time, but he probably was not interested in government service and switched over to the legal profession.

Indira Gandhi used to come to her office in South Block every day between 10 a.m. and 10.30 a.m. whenever she was in Delhi and stay on till about 1.30 or 2 p.m. She would return to office after lunch, usually between 3 p.m. and 3.30 p.m. and stay till 7 p.m. or 8.00 p.m., depending on the pressure of work. During Parliament sessions, she used to operate from her office in Parliament House, while officers in the PMO continued to work from South Block. On any working day the first engagement of the prime minister after reaching the office was to meet me. The files that I would have sent to her even very late on the previous day would be returned to me in the morning with clear-cut orders. In very rare cases, she would want a personal discussion with me. Such discussions usually took place during my morning meetings with her. If needed, during the course of the day, she would send for me for holding further discussions. I would always be present when important visitors like heads of foreign governments met her. Sometimes, I would be summoned to her office suddenly so that she could ascertain my views on a problem that would have just cropped up and then give instructions on the requisite action to be taken. Sometimes, after she would have returned home from the office or on holidays, I would be called to her house at 1, Safdarjang Road for focusing on problems that needed immediate resolution. I could reach her house within three to four minutes of receiving the call as my residence was located at 27, Safdarjang Road, quite close to the PM's residence.

She also used to bring to my attention some of the important letters she would have drafted herself, for my comments, if any, before they were dispatched. I had complete freedom to express my views on such letters.

With the passage of time, I gained the impression that she herself welcomed free and frank expression of views. Sometimes, she would very vigorously criticize, or vehemently disagree with, me. However, after listening to my counterarguments, she would invariably either agree with me or keep the file with her for further consideration. The file would be returned to me very soon, often the same day, with unambiguous orders. She often left it to me to record her final decision on the file without my having to send her the file again for confirmation of what I had recorded. Such a state of affairs helped a great deal in reducing decision-making time and the prime minister's decisions to the concerned authorities were conveyed promptly.

A special aspect of Indira Gandhi's working style was exchanging of notes. In the midst of a meeting or discussions, even if several people were present, she would pass on to me, on slips of papers, instructions or queries demanding immediate resolution. The queries on slips of papers would often have nothing to do with the discussions going on then. Invariably, they would be related to important matters that would have suddenly crossed her mind and on which quick action was called for. One had to be very alert and quick in responding to her queries or comments on these slips. Here are a few samples of the 'instant repartee' sessions.

The four samples given here are representative of the scraps of notes that the PM used to pass on to me while holding discussions with visiting dignitaries or engaged in talks with her senior cabinet colleagues. The first is a routine query on protocol when she was just about to begin talks with a visiting head of state. It also asks for further information on the number of parties in Parliament.

How do I address him?

Mr President.

How many parties do we have – parliament.

1. JP
2. BJP
3. Narpout
4. CPI
5. Akali Dal

6. DMK
7. AIDMK
8. D.S.P =(2)
9. Congress (s) (3)
10. National conference (2)

The second contains a query from me in the midst of the PM's conversation with a foreign dignitary, her reply to it and a question from her asking for my views on an issue raised by the visitor.

The third conveys to me her intention to appoint the law minister, Shivshankar, as a member of the important Cabinet Committee on Political Affairs (CCPA). The committee normally consists of the ministers of external affairs, home, defence and finance. However, the PM had been inviting Shivshankar to most of these meetings as she had found his views on political matters, particularly those involving legal issues, useful. Her intention in sending an informal note on as important a matter like this was to enable me to bring to her notice problems, if any, including procedural ones, in adding to the number of the CCPA members.

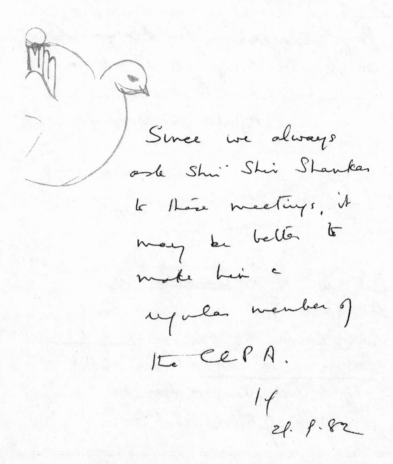

Since we always ask Shri Shiv Shankar to these meetings, it may be better to make him a regular member of the CCPA.

If

2*l*. *f*. 82

The fourth again is a decision conveyed to me while she was in the midst of a CCPA meeting. It then became my responsibility to give views on how to implement the decision, who should be the persons to take nodal responsibilities for these subjects and other related issues.

Readers may be amused to see Indira Gandhi's doodles on these slips of papers, but they did reflect a hidden talent in her to draw.

① We must have someone
to follow be continuously
following up muslim
affairs. This does not
interfere with the
3 monthly reviews

② The same for
pollution — air & water

EIGHT

With Indira Gandhi: 2

DURING THE PERIOD 1981–84 INDIRA GANDHI VISITED MORE THAN twenty-five foreign countries, and I accompanied her on all these visits. The year 1981 was an unusually busy one as she visited twelve countries from May to December, namely, Switzerland, Kuwait, the UAE, Kenya, Indonesia, Fiji, Tonga, Australia, the Philippines, Romania, Mexico and the UK. Some of the trips were made to attend international conferences such as the UN Conference on New and Renewable Sources of Energy (Nairobi, Kenya), the Conference of the Heads of Governments of Commonwealth countries (Melbourne, Australia) and the Summit Conference of twenty-two heads of governments (Cancun, Mexico). The other trips were essentially to carry out bilateral discussions. Her visits to five countries (Indonesia, Fiji, Tonga, Australia and the Philippines) in one month resulted in her absence from India for seventeen days. Indira Gandhi had felt the imperative need to meet various heads of government, most of whom she had known personally before, in order to revive her contacts with them. She was keenly aware of the fact that the Emergency had tarnished her image as a liberal and a democrat.

The author with Prime Minister Indira Gandhi just before a press conference.

The author with Prime Minister Indira Gandhi at a function in Delhi.

The author with HH the Catholicus of the East (the head of the Indian Orthodox Church) and Swami Ranganathananda at a function in Kerala.

The author with the former US president, Ronald Reagan, at the White House, Washington.

The author and his wife (among others) with Queen Elizabeth II
at the Buckingham Palace, London (1985).

The author calling on the British prime minister, Margaret Thatcher,
at 10 Downing Street, London (1985).

The author and his wife with Prime Minister
Rajiv Gandhi at the high commissioner's
residence in London.

The author with John Major, the former
British prime minister, at the Raj Bhavan, Mumbai.

The author with Dr Henry Kissinger, the former
US secretary of state, at the Raj Bhavan, Mumbai.

The author with the former president of the US,▶
George Bush (Sr.), at the Raj Bhavan, Mumbai.

Moreover, highly exaggerated accounts about the excesses during the Emergency period had been circulated in these countries during the period 1977–79, when she was out of power. Apart from renewing her personal contacts and trying the rebuild her image, she also wanted to use these visits to explore the possibilities of establishing closer economic cooperation between India and these countries.

Very often, the prime minister's entourage did not include the external affairs minister or any other senior minister. Consequently, the additional responsibility of explaining the new government's programmes and policies to the foreign interlocutors fell upon me. During almost all these visits Indira Gandhi interacted with the media and my duties were extended to assisting her, along with Sharda Prasad, during her various press conferences and other media-related events.

Although travelling with Indira Gandhi ensured a good deal of comfort and top-level accommodation, in my case, it involved a lot of work-related tensions as well. During the course of discussions with heads of foreign governments, she needed very little assistance on political issues from anyone accompanying her, but on topics such as bilateral economic relations or on international economic issues, she generally asked me to handle the situation. In all such meetings, whether in India or abroad, there was an unwritten rule that all officers accompanying the prime minister had to observe: none of them should intervene unless asked to while the PM was in conversation with foreign dignitaries. After participating in a few such discussions, I quickly grasped the nuances of her style and figured out precisely when to intervene with my comments. She also had her own way of signalling to me through gestures whenever she wanted me to pick up the thread and carry on with the discussion that she had set in motion. On many occasions, she would ask me to respond to a point raised by a foreign dignitary or to supplement her own statements. The junior officers present at such meetings were expected to merely record the details but not directly participate in the proceedings unless specifically asked by her.

Indira Gandhi visited Geneva in Switzerland to address the World Health Assembly on 6 May 1981. This event was organized by the World Health Organization (WHO). Since this was her first exposure to an international audience after her return to power in January 1980, her visit aroused considerable media attention.

On the return journey from Switzerland, Indira Gandhi visited a few Middle East countries such as Kuwait, Abu Dhabi, Dubai and Sharjah. In these places, wherever she went, she would come across large crowds carrying Indian flags and cheering loudly for her. In her meetings with the Arab heads of states she explained in great detail the efforts she had put in to establish friendly relations with Pakistan and how the 1971 war for the liberation of Bangladesh was thrust on India by the unexpected attack on Indian airfields by the Pakistani Air Force. She also explained how she had unilaterally announced a cease-fire after the surrender of the Pakistan Army in Dacca on 16 December 1971 and how she had released over 90,000 prisoners of war and returned the territories seized by the Indian Army during the war. From the warmth of the reception she received from all the heads of the states she visited in the Gulf region, she could discern that the anti-Indian propaganda unleashed by the Pakistanis in these countries had made very little impact on them.

✧

Only after my return from the trip to Switzerland, Kuwait and the UAE could I find the time to settle down in my new job and to properly organize and then streamline the systems and methods of work in the PMO. Among other duties, I had to formally call on President Sanjiva Reddy (whom I had the privilege of knowing from the time he was a minister in the Government of India). The meeting took place on 21 May 1981. He told me that I should make it a point to convey to the prime minister in case I found anything wrong or undesirable happening in various areas of administration. He felt that her own colleagues in the cabinet or people working close to her were not doing so. This was the first occasion for me to note that the relations between the president and Indira Gandhi were not quite cordial or relaxed.

After that events began to move rapidly. On 22 May 1981, I received a handwritten note from the prime minister marked 'top secret'. This note reflected her concern at the growing alienation between Sheikh Abdullah (the chief minister of Jammu and Kashmir) and the Government of India. (Such personal notes were intended to convey to me her own thinking on certain sensitive issues and to alert me about the seriousness of the recent developments. They were intended 'for my eyes only' and I would return such notes forthwith with my initials in a double-sealed cover as acknowledgement of having seen them.) Two days later B.K. Nehru, the governor of Jammu and Kashmir, spent an hour with me in Delhi. Bijju Bhai (as BK was affectionately called) a close friend of mine, conveyed to me his concern at the increasing estrangement between the Sheikh and Indira Gandhi. He tersely warned me that 'if the Sheikh was not with India, Kashmir was not'. He brought to my notice that a group of people close to the prime minister in Delhi were interested in ensuring that her relations with Sheikh Abdullah deteriorated and it was my duty to prevent that from happening. After my *tête-à-tête* with B.K. Nehru, I fully realized the significance of the 'top secret' note she had sent me.

On 30 May, early in the morning, I received the news of the brutal assassination of Zia-ur Rahman, the president of Bangladesh. Later, when I met the PM, I found that she had been quite shaken by this unexpected development. I had to meet the prime minister three or four times that day and, on all these occasions, she expressed her deep anxiety at the likelihood of Bangladesh getting enmeshed in a civil war. At about 1.30 p.m. that day there was quite a commotion in the corridor connecting Indira Gandhi's office room with mine, when the peons and security staff noticed her walking briskly towards my room, whereas she was expected to go straight from her office to her car. She told me to call a high-level security meeting immediately in the Defence Ministry. She wanted the heads of the three armed forces and other senior officers to urgently review the developments following the assassination of Zia-ur Rahman. The news about the situation in Bangladesh was not very clear at that point of time and everyone was wondering as to which military leader would seize power there. I attended the meetings in the Map Room of the Defence Ministry both on 30 May (Saturday) and 31 May (Sunday). I kept the PM informed of the views that emerged in our discussions. Very soon, the fears of a civil war breaking out in Bangaladesh were allayed and it looked as if stability had been restored.

Meanwhile, the relations between Sheikh Abdullah and Indira Gandhi were deteriorating almost day by day. Sheikh Abdullah's speeches were highly critical of the Congress leadership in Delhi and he accused Indira Gandhi of trying to oust him from power. News from the north-eastern state of Assam was also very disturbing and it looked as if the Centre would get deeply involved with fire-fighting operations both in Assam and J&K pretty soon.

On 26 June 1981, I received information that the Congress ministry under Chief Minister Anwara Taimur had lost its majority in Assam. Indira Gandhi was away from Delhi on tour. I received a call from Pranab Mukherjee to the effect that, in his view, Anwara Taimur should resign immediately without being voted out on the next working day of the Assam Legislative Assembly, which was 29 June. Anwara Taimur, accompanied by two or three members of her cabinet, came to see me in my office on 26 June itself and pressed me to inform the prime minister of her view that the Assembly should be dissolved and she should be allowed to continue as caretaker chief minister for six months. Before contacting the PM, I met N.D. Tewari (later chief minister of the newly formed Uttaranchal state) who told me that he held the same opinion as Pranab Mukherjee. The holding of elections in Assam after six months, as proposed by the chief minister, was impossible because the electoral rolls had not been prepared and in view of the large controversies with regard to the electoral roll issue, the possibility of publishing a revised list in such a short time was nonexistent. I contacted the prime minister (who was at Lucknow) over the telephone and apprised her of the situation in Assam. She instructed that a meeting be convened immediately on her return to Delhi. This meeting was held at the PM's residence at 9 p.m. on 27 June and was attended by senior cabinet minister P.V. Narasimha Rao (who later became prime minister in June 1991), N.D. Tewari and Pranab Mukherjee. I was also present. After listening to our views about what action should be taken in Assam, the PM called in Anwara Taimur who had been waiting in another section of the PM's residence to meet her. Anwara Taimur was very insistent in her stand. Indira Gandhi tried to convince her that that would be an unworkable solution and there was little point in creating further confusion by dissolving the Assembly. Anwara Taimur appeared to get quite agitated at Indira Gandhi's reaction to her suggestion and I could see that the PM was getting annoyed. At one stage of the proceedings, which were getting heated, Anwara Taimur said that it was she who had helped the flow of the oil from Assam to the rest of India. Indira Gandhi got even more annoyed at this statement and retorted that it was the Indian Army that was responsible for such a flow. When Anwara Taimur persisted with the suggestion of dissolving the Assembly, I found Indira Gandhi almost on the verge of losing her temper. She told Anwara Taimur with a degree of finality: 'You are being very stubborn. It is this type of stubbornness you have shown at this meeting that has created problems in Assam.' Anwara had no desire to test Indira Gandhi's patience any further and changed her stance to state that whatever the prime minister decided would be acceptable to her and left around 10.30 p.m.

These episodes show how I found myself drawn into the vortex of political exigencies and tensions and how unexpectedly and at very short notice I had to get prepared for assisting the PM in handling such crisis situations.

I could see that despite the magnitude of the tensions faced by Indira Gandhi almost every day, she looked very refreshed and relaxed when she came to office every morning. Sometimes, at the morning meetings, she would tease me jokingly on some topic or the other, which would have appeared in the newspapers. For instance, one such occasion was on 7 July 1981. As soon as I stepped into her office for my usual morning session, she greeted me with the question 'how do you find the PMO work compared with the work of the president of the General Motors' and started laughing (but discreetly). I could not quite decipher the point implicit in her question or the laughter that accompanied it. She immediately placed before me the copy of *India Today* (dated 1–15 July), wherein an article entitled 'A Well-knit Team' (written by the distinguished journalist Prabhu Chawla) had appeared. In his article, Prabhu Chawla had complimented me for setting up a 'well-knit office' and had also stated: 'The present team in the prime minister's Secretariat gives the impression of a well-oiled machine with very little evidence of the red tapism and back stabbing that goes on in most other bureaucratic offices. "It's one of the best teams the Secretariat has ever had", says a former aide, "and the captain, Alexander, with his talents, could easily be president of General Motors".' I blushed upon reading these sentences and told her that I had not read that particular article. I also admitted that I was lagging behind when it came to reading my morning newspapers. She laughed again at the joke she had hurled at me and soon settled down to tackle the normal business for the day.

✧

The first opportunity I got for a one-to-one session with Rajiv Gandhi was at a dinner that Indira Gandhi hosted at her house during the first week of July 1981. Besides the hostess and the members of her family, namely, Rajiv, his wife Sonia and Maneka, those invited for the dinner were Pupul Jayakar, Sir John Thompson, the UK high commissioner in India, Lady Thompson, my wife Ackama and myself. Before the dinner was served, Rajiv guided me to a corner of the room and started talking to me in an extremely warm and cordial manner. I was greatly impressed by his humility, courtesy and charming manners. Within a couple of minutes of our getting to know each other, he said: 'Dr Alexander your appointment has brought credibility and prestige to this office. It has helped a great deal in restoring the good name of the office.' I was quite taken aback by these unusually appreciative words from a person known for his reserved nature and shyness and that too at our very first meeting. Rajiv appeared to be quite keen in understanding and also keeping a tab on all the major problems facing the government at that time. This 'dinner session' marked the beginning of a series of interactions between us. We discussed in detail various issues and problems that the government had to tackle throughout the period of my service in his mother's office such as the formulation of the new 20-point programme, the Akali agitation, the situation in J&K and the Sri Lankan ethnic crisis.

Indira Gandhi was scheduled to leave on a visit to Nairobi, Kenya, on 9 August. A few days earlier she had asked me to submit a proposal for effecting major changes in the vital posts of secretaries in the Government of India. Several vacancies needed to be filled up and, in this context, I held close consultations with Krishnaswami Rao Saheb, the cabinet secretary. On 8 August, at about 9.30 p.m.,

I handed over to her an informal note that listed the names of over half a dozen officers with my recommendations as to which specific ministries they could be considered for. She went through the list and after asking a few probing questions about two or three names in the list, she granted her approval to the proposed names. I returned home and, within half an hour, sent (to the PM) the formal proposal recommending these names after consulting the cabinet secretary again. The formal proposal came back with her signature. The general impression among senior civil servants and also among the people at large at that time was that appointments to top-level posts were made on the basis of recommendations of politically influential persons and not necessarily on merit. Whatever may have been the veracity of such perceptions during the Emergency period, I can say without fear of any contradiction that throughout the period of my service in the PMO, there were hardly two or three cases wherein Indira Gandhi would have disagreed with the recommendations jointly made by me and the cabinet secretary on the postings of secretaries. I should also add that the ministers very rarely interfered with the process of selection and posting of secretaries. The new appointments made were P.K. Kaul for defence, T.N. Chaturvedi for home, Abid Hussain for commerce, Anna Malhotra for education, Sarala Grewal for social welfare, A.S. Gill for steel and D.V. Kapoor for heavy industries. The new list of secretaries helped in conveying the message to the rest of the civil servants that merit and suitability would be the only criteria for promotion to senior posts in the government.

The prime minister visited Kenya from 9 to 14 August to participate in the UN Conference on New and Renewable Sources of Energy. I had accompanied her as a member of her delegation. This time the prime minister's entourage included her daughter-in-law Maneka Gandhi and her young grandchildren Rahul and Priyanka (both offspring of Sonia and Rajiv Gandhi). I could see that from the day we arrived at Nairobi Indira Gandhi was feeling unhappy at the rather sulky behaviour of Maneka. She expected Maneka to take care of Rahul and Priyanka, but, much to her disappointment, Maneka remained reserved and aloof and Indira Gandhi had to personally attend to the children's needs such as their preference for food, choice of clothes and sightseeing programmes. No member from the High Commission had been specially deputed for this purpose. Indira Gandhi had to personally send for the protocol officials of the Kenyan Government and give them clear-cut instructions regarding the children's requirements and outings. It was obvious that relations between Indira Gandhi and Maneka were anything but cordial.

After our return from Kenya, a large part of my time was devoted to preparing for Indira Gandhi's forthcoming visit to Indonesia, Fiji, Tonga, Australia and the Philippines scheduled from 23 September to 9 October. During these trips, a noteworthy aspect that I must point out was her skill in time management. She had planned her visits with due attention to even the minutest detail. She had decided well in advance which sari she would wear on a particular occasion and her suitcases were packed keeping in view the exact sequence of her various engagements. She once told me during these visits, in a lighter vein, that men always complained about how long women took to get ready for an engagement but, in her case, while she could be ready in five minutes, some of the men accompanying her needed half an hour. Sometimes, she had to attend five engagements a day, including formal lunches and dinners, but she would never be late by even one minute. On a few occasions, when she found that some members of her party were not yet ready to join her motorcade, they would be left behind as she was very particular about arriving on the dot for her engagements.

Her journeys abroad also provided her opportunities to assess the performance of Indian envoys and to ascertain their suitability to the assignments they were entrusted with. Let me cite a case in point. Our high commissioner in Fiji was Soonu Kochar, a very smart and efficient Foreign Service officer. Indira Gandhi was toying with the idea of choosing her (Soonu) for her own office as joint secretary; she had mentioned this aspect to me before we left Delhi. I too knew Soonu Kochar and her husband Hari Kochar, who had been a colleague of mine as deputy secretary in the erstwhile Ministry of Commerce and Industry in the late 1950s. Consequently, I had responded positively to the PM's line of thinking. However, Indira Gandhi somehow got the impression that Soonu was overdoing her role (as high commissioner) and she was not very happy with her, though Soonu was only being zealous to the point of ensuring that nothing went amiss. Indira Gandhi always liked the ambassadors to be at hand, but did not like them to hover around her all the time. Unfortunately, Soonu's overenthusiasm for her work produced the opposite effect; Indira Gandhi dropped the idea of selecting her even before leaving Fiji.

It fell to my lot to solve a delicate diplomatic problem concerning Soonu's continuance in Fiji as high commissioner. A few hours before we were to leave that country, the secretary in the Foreign Ministry of Fiji, a person of Indian origin, came to see me at my hotel and informed me that Prime Minister Ratu Mara had been unhappy with Soonu and also with her husband as they both were, according to him, trying to interfere too much in Fiji's domestic affairs. He told me that his prime minister would like to make a formal request to Indira Gandhi for the immediate withdrawal of Soonu Kochar. I counselled against such a move as Indira Gandhi would not ordinarily approve of a senior diplomat to be withdrawn abruptly at the suggestion of the host government concerned. Nevertheless, I told him that she would be transferred when her term came to an end, which was rather close. I also assured him that the Indian Government did not intend to extend her term in Fiji. Consequently, I asserted that Ratu Mara should be advised not to make any formal request for her transfer to Indira Gandhi. Thankfully, he accepted my advice; Ratu Mara did not bring up this matter when he formally bade farewell to Indira Gandhi.

The next halt was Melbourne, Australia. The opportunity provided by the Commonwealth Conference from 29 September to 8 October 1981 was fully utilized by Indira Gandhi for renewing her links with a distinguished lot of old friends from various countries. During our stay in Melbourne, one night we received the news from Delhi that an Indian Airlines Corporation (IAC) plane had been hijacked to Islamabad by some Sikh militants. We were continuously kept informed of developments in the hijack drama over the 'hot line' by Delhi. I recall a particular moment in the course of this tension-ridden episode when Indira Gandhi's senior cabinet ministers in Delhi posed a delicate problem to her for a quick decision. The Pakistan

Government was unwilling to grant permission to India to send Indian commandos to undertake a swift operation to rescue the passengers. The Pakistanis were insisting that any such operation, if found necessary, should be carried out by their own men. I received a message from V.S. Tripathi, joint secretary in the (PMO), requesting me to obtain the PM's instructions on the stand our government should take. I rushed to her room and, within a minute of my explaining the problem to her, found that she was ready with her decision. Without even discussing the pros and cons of the issue with me, she declared emphatically: 'We should leave this decision completely to the Pakistanis. Let them take the credit if they succeed and also the blame if they fail.' I immediately conveyed the prime minister's decision to Delhi. I am mentioning this particular incident to show how, in crisis situations, Indira Gandhi could take decisions without any hesitation in a very short time.

Within nine days of Indira Gandhi's return from her five-country visit, she was off again on a foreign visit, this time to Romania, Mexico and the UK (from 18 to 27 October 1981). The main purpose of her visit to Mexico was to attend the conference (at Cancun) of twenty-two heads of government who were meeting to explore the possibility of reaching agreements on some of the major issues relating to peace and development.

As per a prearranged programme Indira Gandhi held a meeting with US President Ronald Reagan (at the hotel in which he and some senior members of his delegation were staying) in order to exchange views on the important items on the agenda of the Cancun summit. L.K. Jha, G. Parthasarathi and I had accompanied her for this meeting. Reagan was assisted by Secretary of State Alexander Haig, Secretary of the Treasury Donald Reagan and Security Adviser Richard Allen. The meeting turned out to be a great disappointment for Indira Gandhi as Reagan appeared disinterested in, and was not well informed on, the major issues of concern to the developing countries including India. Indira Gandhi herself desisted from dwelling too much on these issues as she found, within a few minutes of the start of the talks, that Reagan was not focused on these matters. She, therefore, had let us (Jha, Parthasarathi and myself) do most of the talking and came in only on a few occasions, essentially to prod Reagan to express his views, but she elicited very little response from him. After this meeting, on the basis of Reagan's attitude, she reached the conclusion that nothing useful would emerge from the Cancun summit and that's what exactly happened despite all the hype and hoopla.

Indira Gandhi was back in Delhi on 28 October and there were no more foreign visits during the rest of 1981.

✧

Towards the last quarter of 1981, Indira Gandhi asked me to undertake a very delicate political mission to Kerala, my home state. She had brought to my notice, on several occasions earlier, that it was the disunity among the Congressmen in Kerala that had prevented them from forming a government. Also, she was keen on getting back into the Congress fold A.K. Antony and his group of Congressmen who had left the party after the Emergency. Kerala, at that time, was ruled by the Communist Party of India (Marxist) [CPI(M)]-led coalition government with E.K. Nayanar as the chief minister. This coalition had the support of both the factions of the Kerala Congress, a party that had been formed by some influential ex-Congressmen with strong pro-farmer inclinations.

An important partner in the coalition was the Congress (U) led by Antony. Antony had adopted an aggressively anti-Indira stand not only regarding the Emergency but also regarding several other issues. He had once boycotted a reception at the Calicut airport for Indira Gandhis in order to register his protest against her meeting with the Kerala bishops. He had also opposed the candidature of Indira Gandhi in the by-election to Parliament from the Chickmaglur constituency in December 1978. In fact, he had become more strident in his criticism of her than even some of the CPI(M) leaders in Kerala. He had always tried to project an image of himself as one who adhered to high principles without any compromise. However, after the disintegration of the dissident Congress factions, he probably began realizing that the political future for his group and similar outfits was bleak. He was convinced that the proper place for him and his followers was in the parent organization. His main worry was whether he and his colleagues would be treated honourably if they rejoined the Congress Party.

Fortunately for Antony and his supporters, Indira Gandhi herself was convinced that the Congress in Kerala could be strengthened only by reinducting the breakaway sections into the party. Her main obstacle in launching a unity drive loomed large in the form of K. Karunakaran, the leader of the Congress 'loyalists' in Kerala. He and his group fiercely opposed the rehabilitation of Antony and some of his colleagues in the Congress.

One day, after expressing her deep concern about the growing divisions within the Congress Party to me, she emphasized that she was very keen to get an objective assessment of the possibility of reuniting all Kerala Congressmen who had left the party at different stages in the past. She pointed out that she could not possibly entrust this task to senior colleagues of her own party as most of them were supporters of either Karunakaran or one of the many factions. According to her assessment, if credible assurances could be given by me to Antony and his group that they would be treated honourably if they returned to the Congress fold, she was confident that they would be quite willing to come back. She knew very well that the treatment that had been meted out by her to some important Congress leaders who had left the party and later rejoined it had not inspired much confidence among the former Congressmen. She was also sure that I would not be influenced in any way by Karunakaran's views on taking back the former Congressmen. She said that she would take further action on the return of the Antony group to the Congress only after I had presented my assessment of the situation in Kerala. Finally, she underlined the fact that I should undertake this mission discreetly, without too many people knowing about it as she was worried about the possibility of strong opposition being organized by the 'loyalist' group to the return of the Antony faction.

On 21 August 1981, I had an occasion to visit the Vikram Sarabhai Space Centre at Thiruvananthapuram on official work. I extended my stay in the state to meet Nayanar (the chief minister), Antony and several important leaders of the Congress (U), led by Antony. I also met several prominent non-party persons whom I knew personally and in whose political judgement I had a lot of confidence.

After holding extensive talks in Kerala, I was convinced that Antony and his colleagues were quite keen to re-enter the Congress.

They did not stipulate any preconditions, but only expressed the hope that they would be treated well. They were quite apprehensive about the treatment that Karunakaran would mete out to them. I also got the impression that about half a dozen legislators of the Antony group might not agree to return to the Congress and may prefer to carry on as a separate unit in the legislature. It also became quite clear to me that if the Antony group withdrew support to Nayanar, the Kerala Congress, under the leadership of K.M. Mani, would also walk out of the government, which would then lose its majority. On my return to Delhi, I apprised Indira Gandhi of my assessment. She asked me to continue to remain in close touch with the developments in Kerala.

On 19 November 1981, Karunakaran and Baby John (president of the Revolutionary Socialist Party and a highly respected and influential leader of Kerala) were guests for dinner at my residence in New Delhi. In response to a question from Karunakaran whether or not the RSP would support the Congress in case the Nayanar ministry fell, Baby John categorically stated on this occasion that his party would keep out of any new government.

I remained in close contact with various political leaders in Kerala during my trips to the state and I had kept Indira Gandhi fully informed about my assessment of the emerging situation there. Towards the end of 1981, events started moving very fast and the Antony group and the Kerala Congress (Mani) party withdrew their support to the Nayanar ministry, which eventually fell. On 24 December 1981 a new Congress-led coalition was sworn in with Karunakaran as chief minister.

Antony kept himself out of the ministry, as was his practice those days, but a senior leader of his party, Oommen Chandy, joined the Karunakaran Government as home minister. The Antony group continued to maintain its independent status as a partner in the coalition government.

✧

The year 1982 witnessed a sharp escalation of problems in sensitive areas such as Punjab, Jammu and Kashmir and Kerala, which I shall come to later. In early January 1982, Indira Gandhi had entrusted me with the important task of revamping the 20-point programme and preparing a draft for a new programme, which she was keen to announce on the second anniversary of her assumption of power.

To carry out this assignment, I consulted Dr M.S. Swaminathan, a renowned scientist, who was, at that time, the member in charge of agriculture in the Planning Commission. Dr Swaminathan's inputs proved very valuable. In fact, of all the inputs that went into the reshaping of the 20-point programme, his were the most significant. During the course of the 'revamping exercise', many eminent authorities offered their suggestions and guidelines, which I discussed with the prime minister. I also consulted, as suggested by Indira Gandhi, P.V. Narasimha Rao and R. Venkataraman (senior members in her cabinet) regularly to ascertain their views. The prime minister too passed on to me the suggestions she received from various chief ministers and senior members of her party. Finally, I produced a draft that met with her approval and later that of the cabinet as well. On the night of 14 January 1982, she announced the launching of the new 20-point programme in a broadcast over All India Radio.

In the same month, Indira Gandhi announced some major changes in her cabinet. The prerogative of carrying out cabinet reshuffles rested with the prime minister. This exercise involved dropping of some ministers, change of portfolios for some others, apart from the induction of new ministers. Such reshuffles occurred periodically, as and when she felt them to be necessary. The procedure Indira Gandhi followed for reshuffling was probably very different from that of other prime ministers before or after her. Most prime ministers usually consulted three or four senior cabinet colleagues before going in for a reshuffle. But Indira Gandhi had taken me into confidence at the very outset. After I joined the PMO in 1981, I was the first person she would take into confidence about her decision to make changes in the Council of Ministers. My first step was to prepare a chart that indicated the lacunae in representation from important states, castes and communities in the existing Council of Ministers. These lacunae needed to be plugged to make the Council of Ministers more representative. I also had to undertake an exercise to highlight how to group subjects or how to split certain ministries. Once the charts were ready, the prime minister specified to me the names of the ministers who were to be shifted or dropped. She also sent me a list of names to be considered for inclusion in the Council of Ministers. I was accorded full freedom to make suggestions for all the above categories and also to express my views with regard to each of the prospective candidates. Sometimes, my suggestions would be accepted straightaway and sometimes they would be held over for further consideration. Simultaneously, in the context of reshuffling she would invite suggestions from a few senior leaders of her party such as Uma Shankar Dikshit and Kamlapathi Tripathi. However, whomsoever she consulted was not given any information about other changes she had in view.

The problem that worried her the most was the paucity of talent in the Congress Parliamentary Party, which limited her choice of ministers considerably. Indira Gandhi herself had been holding the crucial portfolio of defence in addition to other portfolios such as atomic energy, space, science and technology, and ocean development. She was very keen to shed the defence portfolio, which was taking up a large amount of her time. She felt that R. Venkataraman (who was then the finance minister) would be ideal for this post. She had always treated some of her senior colleagues such as Venkataraman and Narasimha Rao with a good deal of deference and regard and whenever any changes had to be made in their portfolios she would be concerned as to how they would react. However, it was never her practice to take any of her colleagues into confidence about the changes she proposed to make. In fact, most of her ministers, either those who were dropped or those who were to be inducted, would come to know about the changes only on the day of the swearing in or, at best, a day earlier. She was very particular about maintaining the confidentiality of the cabinet changes. Consequently, the media also did not get to know about the changes till the day of the swearing in ceremony. In the case of Venkataraman her anxiety stemmed from the uncertainty whether he would consider the shift from finance to defence as a demotion. However, much to her surprise, she found Venkataraman very happy at the prospect of being entrusted with the defence portfolio, although she mentioned the proposed change just twenty-four hours before the swearing in took place.

The list of persons to be sworn in (in January 1982) was ready to be sent to the president only two hours before the time fixed for the actual swearing in ceremony (at 11:30 a.m.) because of a few last-minute changes made in the list earlier cleared by her. Indira Gandhi had considered G. Parthasarathi, known as GP to all his friends, for the post of commerce minister (holding the rank of minister of state with independent charge). GP was called into her room on the morning of the day fixed for the administering of the oath of office to inform him that she was planning to induct him into the Council of Ministers. I was waiting in the adjacent room to ensure that the final list was sent to the president without any further delay, when I saw GP coming out of the PM's room within two minutes of entering it. I was immediately called in by the prime minister, who told me that GP had declined the offer. Indira Gandhi, at that time thought that GP had refused because the rank offered by her was only that of a minister of state. However, people like me, who had known GP intimately, knew that the real reason was his aversion to hold any ministerial position. He was always content to remain in the background in the role of a trusted adviser to Indira Gandhi. I immediately suggested that she could probably consider Shivraj Patil, who was then minister of state for defence. She readily agreed with the suggestion, but this last-minute switch of portfolio meant a further delay. By the time the final list was ready for being sent to the president, it was already 9.45 a.m. and the PM decided to take the list personally to him. The president administered the oath to the new ministers at 11.30 a.m. on the dot, which was the time fixed for this ceremony.

Most unexpectedly, 1982 started with wild rumours circulating in Delhi that President Sanjiva Reddy was on a collision course with Indira Gandhi. The speculation was that he had made up his mind to dismiss her and induct a new Council of Ministers, made up of a broad-based coalition of three or four parties. Some of us in the PMO were aware of the growing trend of mistrust between the president and the prime minister. The events of 1969–70 – when Indira Gandhi supported V.V. Giri as the candidate for presidentship against Sanjiva Reddy (the official candidate of the Congress Party) and ensured the latter's defeat in the elections – had not been forgotten by the people at large and, therefore, the canard about an impending confrontation between the president and the prime minister could gain currency very quickly. The 'news' that was making the rounds in Delhi then was that more than one hundred Members of Parliament belonging to the Congress would desert Indira Gandhi and support a new coalition government. (The constitutional position is that the president cannot act except on the advice of the Council of Ministers, but it was vigorously argued by the initiators of the rumours that in a matter involving the prime minister, the president could not be expected to act on the advice of her cabinet.)

Indira Gandhi was aware that such rumours were being circulated. She did refer to them, though she personally did not attach much credence to them in the early stages. There were some busybodies in her own party who found that such rumours presented them a good opportunity to meet her regularly; they added their own mix of gossip and innuendo to make the rumours appear realistic. Meanwhile, the core group consisting of R.N. Kao, Krishnaswami Rao Saheb, T.N. Chaturvedi (home secretary) and myself met regularly to assess the validity of these rumours. Our assessment showed that there was very little basis for them. It should be remembered that Sanjiva Reddy had been in the habit of expressing his displeasure on certain decisions taken by the government to some of his friends who used to call on him. They, in turn, had been taking special delight in spreading the news about the president's growing unhappiness about the functioning of the government.

It was against this unusual background that the issue of Sanjiva Reddy's broadcast to the nation on the eve of the 1982 Republic Day (26 January) became the subject of a serious controversy between the president and the prime minister.

Over the years, the practice has been that the President's Secretariat prepares the draft of the president's Republic Day address and sends it to the PMO a few days earlier for clearance by the prime minister. The cabinet secretary and I had received reports that the draft speech prepared by the Rashtrapati Bhavan Secretariat, under instructions from the president, contained several critical comments on the working of the government. I had reported this matter to the prime minister. A crucial question discussed among some of us was whether the president could criticize his own government for its alleged failures or lapses in a parliamentary system of democracy. Such an event was unprecedented, and Indira Gandhi was determined to ensure that the well-established norms and procedures were followed by the president this time too.

At about 7 p.m. on 23 January 1982 I received the draft of the president's speech from his secretary, V.K. Rao, a former ICS officer of the Andhra Pradesh cadre whom Sanjiva Reddy had personally selected for this post. I found the contents to be highly critical of the government's performance and, in a few places, even downright condemnatory. I went through the speech carefully and marked those portions that I considered unacceptable. I immediately sought a meeting with the prime minister who was still in her office in South Block. As soon as I told her that I was unhappy with the draft she replied that she had already guessed it from the expression on my face. I requested her to go through the speech herself and particularly take note of the portions marked by me. However, after turning a few pages quickly, she handed the draft back to me and said in a very determined tone: 'I do not have to read it. I knew from your face what it contained as soon as you entered the room. This speech is not going to be broadcast in this form.' I was no doubt quite upset, thinking about a possible clash between the president and the prime minister and its consequences. I again requested her to read the speech carefully but she replied: 'What is there for me to read? You have read the whole thing and you have told me what it contains. What is important is to consider quickly the next step to take.' I realized that she was not going to make any compromises on this issue. When I suggested that the Cabinet Committee on Political Affairs (CCPA) should be convened immediately to consider the draft, she asked me to show it first to Narasimha Rao and Venkataraman and then meet her later in the night at her house.

Both Rao and Venkataraman agreed that there were many offensive sentences in the draft speech which had to be removed and that the president could not use his Republic Day message to castigate the government as he himself was part of it. When I went to the prime minister's house later in the night, Pranab Mukherjee was already there. He too went through the draft and agreed with my view that the portions marked by me should be either deleted or considerably toned down. The PM suggested that the speech should be redrafted and the objectionable sentences should be dropped. She also wanted a meeting of the CCPA to be held early next morning to consider the revised draft.

In this context, Sharda Prasad, information adviser to the prime minister, and I discussed the lines on which the draft could be revised. Sharda Prasad, a remarkable wordsmith, produced a revised draft by the morning of 24 January, well before the CCPA was to meet. The CCPA approved the revised draft and decided that the president should be advised formally by the prime minister that he should use only the new version for his address to the nation. The prime minister immediately sought an appointment with the president and was scheduled to meet him at 1 p.m. on 24 January. I accompanied her to Rashtrapati Bhavan. While the PM went to see the president in his office, I waited in the adjacent room. I was highly anxious as to what would be the consequences if they did not reach a consensus. After about forty minutes I saw Indira Gandhi and Sanjiva Reddy emerging from president's office and I could guess from the broad smile on the PM's face that the president had accepted the new draft. After reaching the prime minister's house, Indira Gandhi provided the synopsis of her meeting with the president. She told me that Reddy at first did not agree that there was anything objectionable in the first draft, but she insisted on his accepting the new draft and eventually he did so. Thus, a serious crisis, which otherwise would have led to grave consequences, was defused to the satisfaction of everyone.

✧

Time rolled on. Indira Gandhi visited London from 21 to 27 March 1982 and I had accompanied her on this visit. The main purpose of the visit was to inaugurate the Festival of India that had been organized by a team of experts under the guidance of Pupul Jayakar. During our stay in London, reports from Delhi informed us that Maneka Gandhi had decided to address a Youth Congress (I) Convention at Lucknow (scheduled for 28 March), which was being organized by Akbar Ahmad a friend of her late husband Sanjay Gandhi and later of Maneka. The relations between Indira Gandhi and Maneka had rapidly deteriorated over the past few months.

Maneka had become highly ambitious in that she wanted to play an active role in politics after the death of Sanjay and considered herself to be the political heir of Indira Gandhi. However, Indira Gandhi had no intention of obliging her, and the induction of Rajiv Gandhi as the All-India Congress Committee (AICC) secretary clearly drove home the point that it was Rajiv and not anyone else who would be Indira Gandhi's heir in Indian politics. Maneka was quite disappointed at what she thought was a move to sideline her. She soon started spreading stories about the alleged ill-treatment meted out to her in Indira Gandhi's household. Maneka's decision to sell the magazine *Surya* (of which she was the owner and editor) to a group of Rashtriya Swayamsevak Sangh (RSS) activists, without even informing Indira Gandhi, had caused a great deal of unhappiness to her and she had taken this act as an open defiance of her authority. The reported decision of Maneka to address the Youth Congress (I) Convention had greatly annoyed Indira Gandhi. She sent messages from London to her daughter-in-law to desist from any such move. For his stand, Akbar Ahmad was suspended from the Congress but this move did not deter him or Maneka from going ahead with the Lucknow convention. Media reports were speculating about the possibility of Maneka defying Indira Gandhi's instructions not to attend the convention and also about the likely repercussions of such an action. However, Indira Gandhi herself believed that Maneka would not take the final plunge and that she would eventually fall in line with her wishes. But Indira Gandhi was mistaken on this count.

While we were still in London, Maneka Gandhi had packed most of her possessions in steel trunks and had moved them from the prime minister's residence to her mother's house. On the prime minister's return to Delhi on 27 March she was asked at her press conference at the airport about her reaction to the reports that Maneka was planning to attend the Lucknow convention. Indira Gandhi replied in a very firm tone that such a convention would be considered an anti-party activity. However, Maneka attended the convention and addressed the participants for fifteen minutes. She then sent a letter to 'Dear Mummy' explaining her stand and promptly released it to the media. Indira Gandhi was quite angry over the contents of the letter becoming public. Maneka returned to her mother-in-law's residence from Lucknow on 28 March itself but did not meet her till the next day.

At about 8.30 p.m. on 29 March, I got a call from the PM's house summoning me there immediately. As I entered, R.K. Dhawan showed me the copy of a letter that Indira Gandhi had sent to Maneka, who was still staying with her. My immediate reaction was that she should not have sent such a letter, but Indira Gandhi obviously thought she had to set the facts right by putting everything in black and white. I found her quite distressed and upset over the entire episode. Maneka had met her earlier in the day and unpleasant exchanges had apparently taken place. Maneka had packed all her remaining stuff and was getting ready to leave. I tried my best to assuage Indira Gandhi's feelings by reminding her that she had faced much worse situations in her life with great courage and grit and that she should be able to confront the present crisis also with the same strength of mind. However, the personal aspects of the present crisis, especially the likelihood of a break in emotional bonding, were a bit too much for her. I could see that she was particularly upset by the fact that her grandson Varun would be taken away by Maneka. As a grandmother she had been doting over the child, who used to sleep in her bed every night. The thought of Varun being kept away from her caused her greater anguish than anything else. While I was closeted with Indira Gandhi, Rajiv suddenly stepped in to say that Maneka was planning to hold a press conference in front of the prime minister's house that night before leaving for her mother's house. However, we already had prior information about her plans to hold such a conference. Consequently, adequate arrangements had been made with the help of the police to ensure that no mediapersons came anywhere near the prime minister's house. In view of such a precaution, Maneka had to cancel her proposed conference. She gathered all her belongings and left the house with her child later in the night for her mother's residence.

It took only a couple of days for Indira Gandhi to come to terms with the departure of Maneka Gandhi. The prime minister was soon back in office, attending to her normal schedule of work as if nothing very material had happened in her life. In less than a week, the hullabaloo created in the media about Maneka's departure also subsided.

✧

In the first few months of 1982, Indira Gandhi was increasingly caught up in her campaign for the forthcoming elections to the state assemblies in Haryana, Himachal Pradesh, Kerala and West Bengal. In spite of her hectic efforts to win over the voters, the Congress could achieve success only in Kerala. This serious setback proved to be a source of considerable worry and disappointment to her. An unusually large flock of independents had been elected to the Haryana State Assembly and the different aspirants for power were indulging in unabashed horse-trading in an attempt to cobble a majority. The main rivalry was between the veterans Devi Lal (known as *Tau* or father's elder brother) and Bhajan Lal, each claiming to have the requisite numbers to take over the reins of power. Eventually, Bhajan Lal (a Congressman) was able to outwit his opponent and was invited by the governor to form the government. President Sanjiva Reddy (who was definitely not inclined towards the Congress) was very unhappy with the developments in Haryana and he even advised the prime minister to consider the option of imposing president's rule in the state. However, Bhajan Lal was able to prove his majority on the floor of the house and a Congress-led government came to power in Haryana.

The reverses suffered by the Congress in the state Assembly elections and the none-too-edifying developments in Haryana had greatly upset Indira Gandhi; I noticed that she had suddenly become very moody and depressed. The defeat of the Congress candidate by a big margin in the by-election to the Lok Sabha from the Garhwal constituency (then in Uttar Pradesh; now in the newly formed state of Uttaranchal) by H.N. Bahuguna (a former Congressman) was another unexpected setback for her party. In one of her conversations during the last week of May1982, she told me in all seriousness that she would like to resign from the post of prime minister and offer herself as a candidate for election as president after Sanjiva Reddy's term, which was due to end within a few weeks. She told me with a feeling of intense frustration that she had never been so unhappy in her position as prime minister as she was then. She sincerely felt, at that time, that it would be good for her and the country if a new prime minister were to take over from her and if she retired from active politics and made a bid for the Rashtrapati Bhavan. However, she had no idea then as to who would succeed her.

I was deeply shocked to see her in such a bleak and gloomy mood. I could discern that she was not making one of those usual attempts on her part to sound me out for my reactions to a hypothetical proposition. She was indeed very serious about quitting as both president of her party and prime minister of the country and strongly felt that such a step would mete out shock treatment to her party, thereby giving it a new stimulus. She was getting disgusted at the growing trend of thinking among her partymen that winning the election for the party was her sole responsibility and that they did not have to do anything more useful than making arrangements for her election campaigns in their constituencies. While I could sympathize with her in her mood of bitter disappointment, I knew that her party was in no position to throw up a leader in her place as prime minister. Moreover, as *president* of the Indian Republic, she would be absolutely helpless in our system of democracy to do anything to save the party. I could also see that, with the opposition parties in utter disarray, the chances of the country having a stable government were virtually nonexistent. I conveyed these views candidly to her. Fortunately, I noticed that she was slowly but surely shedding her mood of frustration. She realized that the remedy she had in mind was more dangerous than the disease! She never expressed any thoughts of quitting after May 1982, at least to me.

The year 1982 was to witness a crucial presidential election. Even though decisions on the choice of a suitable candidate were generally believed to be taken after extensive consultations with senior members of the government and the party, Indira Gandhi always held her cards close to her chest. As was the practice with her, she sounded me out on three or four occasions to ascertain my views on the subject. On all these occasions, I had suggested P.V. Narasimha Rao or R. Venkataraman, reinforcing my views with appropriate reasons. I pointed out that they were both very senior members of both the party and the government at that time. Both had gained considerable experience at the Central and state levels. I also thought that since the prime minister belonged to the north, it would have been appropriate to have a president from the south if a suitable person was available on the basis of merit. In my opinion on all these grounds, either of them should have been acceptable to her. From her reactions to my suggestions, I gained the clear impression that she had narrowed down her choice to Narasimha Rao as a suitable candidate for the post of president. I do not think that she ever gave him a hint or mentioned it even casually. I also kept my impression strictly confidential though I met Narasimha Rao regularly during the course of official work. When some of my friends in the media enquired about the names under consideration by Indira Gandhi, I simply said that she was still to make up her mind, though I personally believed at that time that she had decided in favour of Narasimha Rao.

However, by the middle of June 1982, certain new developments relating to the choice of the Congress Party's presidential candidate were taking place and I could sense that the name of Giani Zail Singh, the Union home minister, was engaging her attention. On 18 June, while discussing another subject with me, i.e., the names of certain persons – S.M. Burney and R.K. Trivedi – for the post of the chief election commissioner, Indira Gandhi very casually brought in the subject of the presidential election and made a very significant comment that Zail Singh possessed great 'political sagacity and shrewdness'. I quickly guessed that she had made this unusual observation only because she was now seriously considering him as the Congress Party's candidate. Given the political situation prevalent in the country at that time, I could see that she believed that the selection of a candidate from the Sikh community would be a sensible political move. Further, after the somewhat unpleasant relations she had with Sanjiva Reddy, she appeared to be keen to ensure that the next occupant of Rashtrapati Bhavan should be someone she could firmly rely on. This factor seemed to have considerably influenced her thinking. However, at this stage, I thought that I should express my views to her frankly. I told her on two or three occasions when the subject came up again that selection of a person like Zail Singh would not go down well with any section of public opinion in India including the Sikhs. I added that if it was her intention to select a person from the Sikh community for the presidential post, an ideal choice would be Swaran Singh, who had established a distinguished record as a very successful foreign minister and a highly efficient political administrator. When I found this name was not making any impact on her, I suggested another candidate, Darbara Singh, whose long political experience had made him a highly respected leader in Punjab. From her somewhat lukewarm response I could guess that the two names I had put forward were not acceptable to her. I then suggested that she could extend the area of choice to the non-political field and any eminent jurist from the Sikh community could be considered, but she did not appear to be happy with this suggestion either. I could then infer that she had made up her mind in favour of Zail Singh. One observation clearly revealed her thinking to me, when she declared abruptly that Zail Singh was very popular as the home minister all over the country and was particularly appreciated by the leaders of all political parties in the southern states.

A few days later I came to know what exactly had happened to tilt the scales in favour of Zail Singh. Even though, as a matter of practice, Indira Gandhi did not consult state political leaders with regard to a possible presidential candiate, the chief ministers of three southern states – Gundu Rao of Karnataka, M.G. Ramachandran of Tamil Nadu and K. Karunakaran of Kerala – had told Indira Gandhi separately (not giving the impression of making a concerted move) that they would prefer Zail Singh, a person from a backward community, to Narasimha Rao, a person belonging to an advanced community, though Rao was from Andhra Pradesh in South India. I also came to know that M. Karunanidhi, the leader of the DMK (Dravida Munnetra Kazhagam, the chief opposition party in Tamil Nadu), had also expressed similar views to the prime minister. Indira Gandhi did develop some doubts whether the people of the south would feel aggrieved if Narasimha Rao or Venkataraman were overlooked in favour of Zail Singh. But the fact that senior political leaders of the south had supported Zail Singh's candidature in preference to either Narasimha Rao or Venkataraman appeared to have reassured her that she was making a universally acceptable decision if she chose Zail Singh. It appears some MPs and MLAs (Members of Legislative Assemblies) from the southern states had also separately informed Indira Gandhi during this period that Zail

Singh's nomination would be well received in the south. It is not my intention to claim that these leaders from the south were persuaded by Zail Singh, or those close to him, to make such a recommendation as I had no direct links with any of them at that time. At the same time, I couldn't believe that these leaders were *voluntarily* offering their views to the prime minister on a subject on which she had not sought their opinions. Whatever the reality, I was convinced that their messages to the prime minister served as a basis for her taking a final decision to choose Zail Singh as the presidential candidate. Once I came to know of her final decision, I knew that there was little I could do to change her mind on this issue. I merely waited for the formalities to be completed.

Indira Gandhi held a meeting with Zail Singh in her South Block office a few days after she took the final decision to nominate him and she formally conveyed this decision to him. Zail Singh, of course, was delighted at the prospect of becoming the first citizen of the country. I should add here that before leaving South Block after his meeting, he walked up to my room at the end of the corridor and told me that he had just received the good news from the prime minister and that he would be asking his Secretariat, when elected, to work in full cooperation with the PMO as he had done during his tenure as home minister. He also thanked me personally for my cooperation in the past. I first congratulated him and then escorted him to his waiting car. It was indeed a very noble gesture on his part to have walked up to my office to greet me after receiving the 'glad tidings' from the prime minister.

A meeting of the Congress Parliamentary Party (CPP) was held on 21 June 1982 to approve of Zail Singh as the party's candidate for the office of president. For their part, the opposition parties had fielded Justice H.R. Khanna as their candidate, but when the results were announced, it was found that Zail Singh's tally of votes was much higher than what was expected by the Congress. The formal swearing in ceremony for the new president took place on 25 July 1982 and the outgoing president Sanjiva Reddy was given a formal sendoff at the Palam airport the same evening.

A few discordant notes were struck during the last days of Sanjiva Reddy's term in office.

Let me cite two instances. In the first instance, Sanjiva Reddy and his supporters had expected that the highest honour in the country, Bharat Ratna, would be conferred on him before he laid down office. In this context, his principal secretary, V.K. Rao, had sent out feelers to me and to the cabinet secretary, Krishnaswami Rao Saheb, during the first week of July. However, I knew that Indira Gandhi would never favour such a proposal due to the highly strained personal relations between Sanjiva Reddy and her. Nevertheless, it was my duty to ascertain her wishes in the matter. When I broached this subject, her response was clearly negative. She requested me to inform V.K. Rao that such a proposal could be considered only after the president had ended his term. This was a clear signal to me that she did not favour the proposal. However, I very politely informed V.K. Rao that the PM thought that it would be appropriate to consider such a proposal only after the president had relinquished office. The president got the message. The proposal was never brought up again at any point of time after he left Delhi.

In the next instance, Sanjiva Reddy wanted to host a dinner for the members of the diplomatic community on 15 July. He naturally expected that the prime minister would attend. However, she had already fixed up other important engagements for that day and was not in a mood to change her programme to attend the dinner. I failed to persuade her to cancel the other engagements, in spite of my earnest efforts. When Sanjiva Reddy came to know that the PM might not be present at the proposed party, he dropped the idea.

❖

President Zail Singh had been in office for hardly a month when, unfortunately, he suffered a serious setback to his health. On 20 August 1982, A.C. Bandopadhyay, the president's secretary, met me at my office at 7 p.m. and told me that Gianiji's old heart ailment had recurred a week earlier and his doctors had advised him to go to the United States of America for treatment. Zail Singh was feeling embarrassed at the fact of his having to go abroad for medical treatment so soon after he had assumed office. He was probably expecting that Indira Gandhi herself would suggest to him that he should seek expert medical help from the USA as suggested by his doctors. Heart surgery was not common in Indian hospitals in those days and there would have been nothing improper if the president had to go abroad for such an operation. I conveyed this message from the president to the prime minister. When she met Zail Singh two days later, she herself affirmed that necessary arrangements would be made for his treatment in the United States.

As time sped by, many significant events occurred. The passing away of Sheikh Abdullah (popularly known as Sher-e-Kashmir or lion of Kashmir) on 8 September 1982 was a major turning point in the history of that state. I had had the privilege of meeting him on a few occasions and I had been deeply touched by his generous hospitality and his care and concern to ensure my comfortable stay in the state. I met him last when I visited the state from 2 to 6 July 1982. When I called on him at his residence on the morning of 3 July, he was bedridden and appeared quite ill. He did not talk about any political issues; in fact, he was too ill to participate in any serious discussion. However, he summoned his personal assistant and gave him detailed instructions about the arrangements to be made for my comfortable stay in the different places in the state that I was scheduled to visit including the instructions that trout prepared in Kashmiri style should be served to me at these places. He was indeed a gracious and generous host besides being one of the most charismatic leaders of India. Sheikh Abdullah was succeeded by his son, Dr Farooq Abdullah, to whom we shall come back later.

During 1982 I again accompanied the prime minister on some of her foreign trips. Her itinerary included meetings with Prime Minister Margaret Thatcher of the UK in London (21–27 March); King Khalid of Saudi Arabia (17–20 April); President Ronald Reagan in the USA (27 July–5 August); and President Leonid Brezhnev in the Soviet Union (20–26 October).

Among the most important events in the country during 1982, I should particularly highlight the successful conduct of the Asian Games during November–December. India had very little experience in organizing such games. New facilities including stadia, swimming pools, hostels for athletes, new roads and flyovers had to be constructed. Although the process was underway, the projects had fallen far behind schedule. The preliminary work on these projects should have started at least three years before the event, but they were actually set in motion only by the middle of 1980 because the period 1977–79 witnessed a lot of political uncertainty, with two governments falling. Against such a background, the prime minister had placed Rajiv in overall charge of all projects and she also asked me to assist him wherever necessary. Rajiv himself was a novice when it came to dealing with government departments and their functioning, but he put in long hours of hard work every day in order to ensure that all projects were completed on time. He proved that he could succeed in providing the necessary motivation, drive and leadership for completing such a colossal task.

I had only one occasion to differ from Rajiv's opinions in matters connected with the Asian Games. After the conclusion of the games, his close aides had drawn up a very long list of persons involved in the conduct of the games for award of Padma honours. Rajiv had recommended to the prime minister that all the persons on the list be honoured. She handed over the list to me and asked for my recommendations. I found that the list contained far too many names. I told the prime minister that while it was true that they all deserved recognition and appreciation for their dedicated services, Padma honours should be given only to a very small number taking into account a variety of factors, especially the totality of their record and the importance of their services in ensuring the success of the event. I suggested that it would be adequate and appropriate if suitable entries were made in their character rolls. Eventually, we pared down the names to those who *really* deserved the Padma awards. I was happy to find that Rajiv came around to concur with my view when the reasons were explained to him. The list was finally cleared by the appropriate committee dealing with Padma awards and formally approved by the prime minister.

Immediately after the successful conclusion of the Asiad, many people had suggested to the prime minister that Rajiv should be entrusted with the responsibility of an important portfolio in her Council of Ministers, but she emphatically vetoed such suggestions.

The year 1982 closed with a highly unexpected and unpleasant development in Kerala. The state witnessed the outbreak of Hindu–Muslim riots in the Chaala Bazaar in Thiruvananthapuram. Kerala was well known for its unblemished record of communal harmony and when news of the riots reached Indira Gandhi in Bangalore (where she was camping during the election campaign), she sent me a message that I should immediately go over to the riot-affected areas and make a quick assessment as to what should be done by the Central Government in order to restore normalcy in the city as quickly as possible. I knew that the chief minister, Karunakaran, would not welcome my visit to the city. In fact, when I told him that I had been asked by the prime minister herself to make a first-hand assessment of the situation in the city, his response, as expected, was that I should postpone my trip. When the prime minister was informed of the chief minister's response she asked me to ignore it and proceed by the earliest flight to Thiruvananthapuram. I reached the city on 31 December and met a host of ministers as well as Karunakaran and Vayalar Ravi (the state home minister) apart from several senior government officials. I visited the Chaala Bazaar area and found the people in a state of great fear and tension. I also noticed that some undisguised attempts were made by some of Ravi's rivals to blame him for alleged lack of firmness in dealing with the riots, though I found that the home minister and the police officials had handled the problem as best as they could. In order not to allow the situation to deteriorate any further, I telephoned the cabinet secretary on the night of 31 December and requested him to arrange for 600 more personnel from the Central police forces to be sent to Thiruvananthapuram on an urgent basis. The cabinet secretary took immediate action on this front. Very soon the situation was brought under complete control due to the combined efforts of the state government and the Central police personnel.

✧

The year 1983 opened on a rather sombre note. Very serious political reverses were in store for Indira Gandhi. She had been actively engaged in hectic campaigning in Andhra Pradesh and Karnataka for Congress candidates contesting the elections to the state assemblies. Reports from intelligence sources and from her partymen indicated that Congress would face no difficulty in retaining power in both the states. However, when the results started pouring in on 6 and 7 January, Indira Gandhi realized how strong the anti-Congress wave had been in both the states. In Andhra Pradesh, the Congress suffered a stunning defeat at the hands of N.T. Rama Rao,* who had only very recently founded his new political party, the Telugu Desam. In Karnataka the ignominy was complete. Not only was the Congress swept out of power but also the chief minister, Gundu Rao, and many of his cabinet colleagues lost their seats. The results dealt a shattering blow to Indira Gandhi's personal prestige because the south had remained a strong Congress bastion despite the Emergency. After the Congress suffered defeat in Karnataka and Andhra Pradesh and with an AIADMK (All-India Anna Dravida Munnetra Kazhagam) government headed by M.G. Ramachandran already in power in Tamil Nadu, the party had lost its hold over virtually the entire south. Its position in Kerala, the only state in which it was in power, was already unsteady as the party was plagued with internal feuds and faction fights. Indira Gandhi was quite worried about the possible repercussions of these reverses on other states of the country. Maharashtra was ruled by a very weak Congress Government and in Bihar there was an imminent possibility of the government falling at any time.

On 8 January 1983 Indira Gandhi reviewed the situation in the aforementioned states at great length and shared her opinions with me. At the end of the review, when she asked for my suggestions on the further course of action, I emphasized that shock treatment alone could have a visible impact. I observed that, in my opinion, all the ministers at the Centre should be asked to submit their resignations and the Council of Ministers should be reconstituted

---

* N.T. Rama Rao was a former film star of the Telugu screen. He was renowned for his depiction of religious and mythological characters, especially Lord Krishna.

after dropping the non-performers and allotting full-time party work to the few senior and efficient ministers. I pointed out that if only the inefficient ministers were to be dropped, the move would create little impact. The entire exercise had to be seen by the people at large as an extensive shake-up and that new blood was being infused into the cabinet. I held the view that some senior posts in the party, above the level of All-Indian Congress Committee (AICC) secretaries, should be created for individuals of the calibre of Narasimha Rao and Pranab Mukherjee and the revamping of the party set-up should go side by side with that of the Central cabinet. I also suggested an immediate replacement of the chief minister of Maharashtra, where the government had already proved to be very ineffective. I felt that the the introduction of a short spell of president's rule in Bihar was imperative. In fact, I had been insisting on these changes even before the elections in Karnataka and Andhra Pradesh could be held.

Indira Gandhi's immediate reaction to my proposals was quite favourable. She appeared to be worried only about finding proper replacements for the senior ministers who were to be shifted for carrying out party work. She asked me to prepare draft proposals for a complete overhaul of the Council of Ministers. In this context, she mentioned the names of a few Central ministers who could be dropped without being given any other assignment either in the party or in the government. I submitted my proposals in the form of a note with an accompanying chart. However, after going through the documents she again said that it would be very difficult to find substitutes from the Congress echelons for senior ministers like P.V. Narasimha Rao and Pranab Mukherjee if they were to be reassigned to party work. I maintained my stand that if a few junior or inefficient ministers alone were dropped, such a step would have very little psychological impact on the people and what the present situation needed was a total shake-up.

Meanwhile, I was amazed to find how quickly some of Indira Gandhi's ministers could turn into carping critics when they saw that her position was becoming weaker. They started a whispering campaign to the effect that the party failed to win the confidence of the ordinary voters not because of non-performance of the ministers, but mainly because of Indira Gandhi's highly centralized style of running the government. I could see that some of the ministers who were quick to blame her for the electoral reverses had been the loudest in singing her praises in the past when she was leading the party from one victory to another.

I found that within a few days Indira Gandhi's initial enthusiasm for a total revamping exercise both in the party and the government had started waning. After some more rounds of discussions on the revamping exercise, in which Rajiv was also involved, a few changes were made in the party and the government. But these changes were merely cosmetic and could create little impact on the people. I felt that the prime minister had missed a good opportunity to inject a new dynamism into her administration, but I also realized that she alone could be the judge of what should be done and when and therefore did not press my views any further.

✧

Meanwhile, Assam had become a major cause of anxiety for the prime minister and all others in the government. The state was under president's rule and the Government of India had appointed R.V. Subramaniam, an experienced civil servant, as one of the advisers to the governor. (During president's rule, it is the state governor who runs the administration with the help of a group of advisers.) The main duty assigned to him was to ensure the peaceful and orderly conduct of elections to the Legislative Assembly. However, the All-Assam Students' Union (AASU) and its allies had given a call for total boycott of the elections and the mood of the people at large favoured it. Subramaniam was keeping me and the cabinet secretary regularly informed about the fact that he could not rely fully on the cooperation of the civil servants in Assam in the conduct of the elections. The main reason, he pointed out, was that many of them, particularly those at the middle and lower levels who were entrusted with the responsibility for holding elections, were strong sympathizers of the opposition parties. We, at New Delhi, sincerely felt that the state government needed the assistance of experienced officers from other states for the smooth conduct of the elections. After taking the prime minister's approval, we organized the temporary transfer of a large flock of IAS officers from the neighbouring states to Assam. We also made arrangements to send all the IAS probationers, who were still under training, to Assam to take on the various responsibilities involved in conducting elections. The cabinet secretary and the Union home secretary also made very quick arrangements for the despatch of adequate units of police forces to ensure that the elections were conducted without any hitch.

The security arrangements were no doubt satisfactory and the state went through the process of elections in February 1983. However, the regrettable aspect of the process was that the boycott of the elections by a majority of the people was equally successful. In many polling stations, the turnout was less than 10 per cent because even those individuals who wished to cast their vote were afraid to do so because of the fear of violence. There were a few polling stations where less than fifteen voters turned up. Nevertheless, the process of polling was duly completed and, naturally, those who were declared winners were mostly Congressmen who had bagged only a small fraction of the votes in their respective constituencies.

Unfortunately, the post-election violence assumed much larger proportions than that witnessed before and during elections. Nawgong district (in central Assam) was the worst hit by bloodshed, and the main targets were the refugees from Bangladesh who had settled down there in recent years. The original tribals of the Nawgong district had been dispossessed of their agricultural lands and they were waiting for an opportunity to take revenge on the refugees who had been assigned these lands. Tribals in large numbers descended from the hills and started attacking the helpless refugees living in the plains. The ghastly massacre that took place at Nellie was probably one of the cruellest the country had ever witnessed and the estimates varied from 500 to 1000. The media reports about this massacre shocked people all over India and there was a palpable fear that such incidents might take place in other parts of the state as well. Indira Gandhi rushed to Nellie and a few other affected areas and ordered immediate relief and rehabilitation measures for the affected people. The prompt action taken by the government to deal with the perpetrators of violence and to provide relief to the affected people helped only marginally in reducing the tension and turbulence in the state.

The Congress could form governments in Assam (and also in neighbouring Meghalaya) where it had emerged as the single largest party. However, the credibility of these elections was seriously questioned all over India, providing little comfort to the Congress in spite of its ability to take over the reins of power. The opposition parties soon launched a campaign for declaring the entire elections as null and void and for ordering fresh polls.

To add to the woes of the prime minister, her party lost all the four Lok Sabha by-elections held in February 1983 in Andhra Pradesh. On the whole, the impression that gained currency all over the country was that the Congress was rapidly losing its hold in most parts of India.

In the midst of all these anxieties and worries, we had to get into gear to make arrangements for holding the Summit Conference of the Non-aligned Movement (NAM) in Delhi (scheduled for March 1983). This exercise posed several unexpected and even dicey problems, which had to be quickly sorted out without causing diplomatic tensions. For instance, we received information that the Iraqis were flying in a few hundred armed guards to take care of the security of their president, Saddam Hussein, who was to attend the conference. We were suddenly informed that two Iraqis planes would be landing in Delhi in a short time with 190 fully armed security guards. There were also reports that the Cubans and the Iranians were bringing their own security guards to protect their heads of government. The Crisis Management Group (of which I was a member) met on 1 March 1983 to deal with the issue of foreign security guards. After a good deal of discussion, we decided that the Iraqis, who were reported to be already on their way, should be allowed to land with their security forces, but that no other delegation should be permitted to bring along armed guards.

When this decision was conveyed to the embassies of the participating countries, some governments kept insisting on their right to bring their own security personnel. They explained to us that they did not doubt the efficiency of the security arrangements by the host government, but they were only concerned about the danger posed by other delegations, which could contain elements inimical to their own countries. Eventually, we stood our ground firmly and insisted that these foreign delegations keep their guards within their own embassies as no foreign security personnel would be allowed to escort their VVIPs to the conference venue or any other place. We informed the various governments that we would take full responsibility for the security of the delegations. Eventually, all the governments concurred with our stand.

As the conference got underway, many pressing problems cropped up almost every day. Indira Gandhi, as the chairperson of the conference, spent practically the entire day and a good part of the night at Vigyan Bhawan, the venue of the conference. As I had also shifted my office to Vigyan Bhawan, I could hardly sleep for three or four hours. When the NAM conference ended on 12 March, everyone congratulated India for the excellent arrangements made and the prime minister for the efficient and graceful manner in which she had conducted the proceedings.

The summer of 1983 saw a rapid deterioration in the relations between Indira Gandhi and Dr Farooq Abdullah, the new chief minister of Jammu and Kashmir, who had come to power after the death of his father, Sheikh Abdullah. The elections to the J&K Assembly were due to take place in the first week of June 1983 and Farooq had made a public announcement to the effect that his party, the National Conference (NC), would fight the Congress in all the seventy-eight seats. Indira Gandhi was hoping that there would be an understanding between the Congress and the NC on the sharing of the seats, but Farooq's statement came as a big surprise to her. The state governor, B.K. Nehru, had informed me that despite the public proclamation, Farooq was really willing to reach an understanding with the Congress on the sharing of seats. In Delhi our main apprehension at that time was that if the Congress and the NC were to be pitted against each other, the anti-national forces, which were becoming very active in the state, would stand to gain the maximum.

Indira Gandhi felt happy upon receiving the message from the governor. She nominated Rajiv Gandhi and another seasoned Congress leader, K.C. Pant, to hold discussions with Farooq on the modalities of seat sharing. Farooq arrived in Delhi on 23 April 1983 and was expected to meet Rajiv and Pant over dinner for talks. I was called to the PM's house to participate in a strategy session to be attended by Indira Gandhi, Rajiv and Pant before they met Farooq. When asked for my views on the strategy for an alliance, I observed that if the Congress failed to get at least a few seats in the Kashmir Valley, which had a Muslim-majority population, such a situation would lead to a communal divide in the state. If the Congress were to emerge as the main winner in Jammu (a Hindu-majority region) and the NC as the sole winner in the Valley, J&K would present the picture of a state sharply divided on communal lines and such a scenario would be viewed as a great victory by the anti-national elements in the state. Keeping in mind these factors, I asserted that the strategy should be to help the NC to get some seats in Jammu and to ensure that the NC supported the Congress in bagging some seats in the Valley. Everyone affirmed that the top priorities should be to avoid a communal divide and to ensure the victory of the nationalist forces. I contended that if some seats had to be sacrificed for achieving this objective, neither side should back out. Rajiv and Pant held talks with Farooq on the basis of this strategy on the night of 23 April. On 24 April morning I was again called to the PM's house to attend a meeting. The objective was to assess the results of the talks with Farooq. Apart from the PM, Rajiv, Pant and myself, Narasimha Rao was also present at this meeting. Rajiv and Pant reported that the response from Farooq was positive and the chances of reaching an understanding for the sharing of the seats in both the regions were bright.

However, much to our dismay, the whole situation changed dramatically when Farooq returned to Srinagar. On home turf, he not only went back on his earlier commitment for an alliance with the Congress, but also was unwilling to come to Delhi for holding discussions on his new stand. However, he was eventually persuaded to reach the capital and a special plane was sent to fetch him on 25 April itself. This time around, he told Rajiv and Pant categorically that the NC would *not* enter into any alliance or understanding with the Congress as his mother was totally opposed to such a move. He further stated that he would be isolated in his party if he went against the wishes of his mother. The reasons given by him were probably genuine but what they revealed was that he was not a free agent who could take major policy decisions on behalf of the NC, whatever his personal inclinations may have been. The Congress was now left with no other alternative but to contest the forthcoming elections with the NC as its chief rival.

The election campaign that followed was a nasty and bitter one. Indira Gandhi mounted a vigorous offensive on behalf of her party throughout J&K, undaunted by violent incidents in a few places. On 19 May 1983, the Congress office in Srinagar was burnt down by the activists of the NC. Moreover, there were reports of attacks by the NC cadres on Congress offices and office bearers in different parts of the state. The Congressmen too were reported to have resorted to violence, though they claimed that they were merely acting in self-defence.

After the elections, the counting of votes (on 6 June) showed that the Congress had fared well in the Jammu region, while there was a strong wave in favour of the NC in the Valley. Persistent reports from the Congress workers as well as from intelligence agencies claimed that there had been large-scale rigging by the NC activists. A serious charge was levelled by the Congressmen against even the seniormost officials of the state that they had openly connived with the NC workers to fix the polls in several constituencies of the Valley. The J&K Congressmen alleged that their complaints about booth capturing and stuffing of ballot boxes with bogus votes had been ignored by the government officials and that the entire election process in the Valley had been a farce. Indira Gandhi was rather outraged by these reports but she was particularly furious at what she believed was the role of the officials of the state government in rigging of the polls. She was also very unhappy at what she described as the 'inaction on the part of the Governor B.K. Nehru'. I tried to explain to her that there was very little that the governor could have done to prevent rigging, but she was not prepared to accept my explanation on this subject. I realized that the entire matter had affected her very seriously and the alienation between her and Farooq had now become almost complete.

For his part, Farooq was very keen to mend fences with Indira Gandhi. When he called on me at my South Block office at 6.30 p.m. on 29 June, he expressed his disappointment at the manner in which Indira Gandhi had responded to the results of the elections. He told me that when elections were over and after the results had been declared, all the controversies should also be set aside. He felt that all feelings of bitterness should be discarded. 'Why is the PM annoyed with me?' he asked me, and added, 'I have not said a single sentence throughout the election campaign which can be described as a personal attack on her.' Farooq sought an appointment with Indira Gandhi but she did not oblige him. I told him that she was annoyed because of the dubious role played by the state government officials in the election. I also told him that she had received reports about the personal attacks made on her by some opposition leaders, including Farooq, at the gathering of the chief ministers of the opposition parties in Srinagar. In response to my statements he said in an emotion-charged voice: 'Farooq has not attacked and will not attack Indira Gandhi or her family in any gathering.'

I reported the details of Farooq's *tête-à-tête* with me to the prime minister, but she was not impressed, as she sincerely believed that the NC Government in J&K had rigged the election and Farooq himself had been indulging in a campaign of personal vilification against her. She was in no mood to forget or forgive and when I suggested that a prime minister should not refuse to meet a chief minister when the latter sought a meeting, she simply said that this was not the time to do so. I realized that the rift between the two had widened beyond any possibility of being bridged.

On 14 July at about 11.30 p.m. I was woken up by a call from PM's house. The caller told me that the prime minister wanted to see me urgently. I went to her house and found that Rajiv, Arun Nehru (a relative of Indira Gandhi who assisted her mainly with party matters) and the law minister, P. Shivshankar, had already assembled there. The topic of discussion related to the anti-national utterances of some of the leaders of J&K, particularly Mirwaiz Maulavi Farokh. We also focused on how the law and order authorities in the state had remained indifferent in dealing with such provocative speeches. The general consensus at the meeting was that if prompt action was not taken, J&K might slip into a state of anarchy and lawlessness and, consequently, the militant and the communal forces could gain the upper hand. Nobody wanted any reconciliation with Farooq; on the other hand, the overriding view was that he himself was responsible for creating such a situation. After the meeting ended at 2 a.m. (on 15 July), the PM asked me to prepare a note by the next evening on the steps to be taken to proceed legally against those elements indulging in anti-national activities.

On the southern front, the political turmoil in Kerala had been getting worse day by day. The Karunakaran Government was riven by sharp differences and was in great danger of not being able to survive for very long. As directed by the prime minister, I visited Kerala from 13 to 17 May 1983 to assess the situation there. G.K. Moopanar, AICC secretary, was also asked by the Congress high command to visit the state at the same time. I knew that it would be virtually impossible for me to make an assessment of the situation in a confidential manner when I was in the company of a prominent leader of the Congress Party. However, Indira Gandhi insisted that I should make my own independent assessment. Accordingly, I proceeded to Kerala.

The immediate cause of the crisis was the attitude of P.J. Joseph, the leader of one of the factions of the Kerala Congress Party (a new party formed due to a split in the parent Congress Party) and a minister in the Karunakaran cabinet. He had made some highly critical speeches against the Central Government, which was very odd for a minister in a Congress-led coalition government. I met Joseph (whom I knew well) at the guesthouse where I was staying in Thiruvananthapuram. I asked him why he was making such vitriolic statements, forgetting his position as a senior minister. He offered a long-winded explanation, the main thrust of which was that such statements were intended only to counter the moves made against him by his rival K.M. Mani, the leader of another faction of the Kerala Congress. I held discussions with senior Congress leders such as A.K. Antony, Vayalar Ravi and Oommen Chandy. I also met K.M. Mani of the Kerala Congress and Mohammed Koya of the

Indian Union Muslim League, both of whom were members of the coalition government. One persistent complaint made by almost everyone I met pertained to Karunakaran's style of working. Many believed that Karunakaran was trying to split some of the opposition parties through clever manoeuvring. While Karunakaran's critics wanted the important post of president of the Kerala Pradesh Congress Committee (KPCC) to be held by someone other than his own nominee, there was little agreement as to who should occupy this post. Antony was willing to take up the presidentship but he expressed strong doubts whether Karunakaran would cooperate with him. Karunakaran himself did not want Antony, Oommen Chandy or anyone associated with their group to be the KPCC president. He was unhappy with my very presence in Kerala because, according to him, it had created the impression that the PM doubted his abilities to handle the situation in the state. During my forty-five-minute session with Karunakaran, I tried to explain to him that Indira Gandhi was only trying to ease the situation for him and that the question of lack of trust in him just did not arise. Karunakaran, however, insisted that the change in the KPCC presidentship should be postponed for the moment. I left the state with the distinct impression that the coalition government was a house divided within itself: it was obvious that several factions within the Congress ranks were at odds with each other apart from sharp divisions existing between the Congress and its coalition partners. Upon my return to Delhi, I gave Indira Gandhi my candid assessment of the situation in Kerala (see also Chapter 9).

Indira Gandhi was scheduled to visit the United States during the last week of July 1983 but several irritants had crept into India's relations with that country, which raised some doubts whether an atmosphere of cordiality and trust would permeate her meeting with President Ronald Reagan. The US ambassador, Harry Barnes, had been maintaining very close contact with me. In fact, he used to call on me frequently to discuss bilateral issues. Nevertheless, I must point out that he had committed a gross indiscretion while bringing in the analogy of Puerto Rico in one of his references to the demand for 'Khalistan'. (Some sections of the Sikhs wanted a separate nation, 'Khalistan', to be carved out in North India.) The media had castigated him for this remark. When he called on me on 23 June, I told him very bluntly that it had been quite improper on his part to have made such a statement. He realized that he had committed a mistake, but great harm had been done by this statement to Indo-US relations. The US Secretary of State George Schultz was due to arrive at Delhi within a few days for holding a series of meetings with the prime minister and the Indian foreign minister. Consequently, Barnes's statement just a few days before Schultz's visit appeared particularly offensive. Nevertheless, on 30 June, Schultz held a very cordial and pleasant meeting with the prime minister that lasted for over ninety minutes. (This interaction helped a good deal in preparing the ground for her talks with President Reagan later.) Schultz and Indira Gandhi had a one-to-one meeting and I joined only in the last fifteen minutes. She gave me the gist of her talks with Schultz and asked me to also hold a one-to-one meeting with Schultz so that I could explain to him in greater detail the obstacles in our relations with the US. She also wanted me to highlight our expectations from the US for developing a more mature relationship between the two countries.

I met Schultz at the US ambassador's residence. After dinner, we moved over to the study. I explained to him how the US had misunderstood our country's stand on various issues in international fora and emphasized that it would be wrong to interpret India's stance as anti-US. I brought to his attention how certain anti-Indian groups, particularly the so-called 'Khalistanis', found support and sympathy in the US. I also mentioned the lack of understanding of Indian sensitivities on the part of Ambassador Barnes when he drew an analogy between Puerto Rico and 'Khalistan'. Finally, I drove home the point that the foregoing pinpricks were leading to hurdles in developing friendly and sustainable relationships between the two democracies. For his part, Schultz told me how impressed he was with Indira Gandhi and how very warm and sincere she was in improving the bonds of friendship between the two countries. He said he had the highest respect for her stand on the issues on which the two countries may have different perceptions. He told me that he had made a careful note of all my statements and attached great importance to them. After my meeting with Schultz I felt confident that the prime minister's visit to the United States (scheduled for later in the month) would go off very well. When I reported to the prime minister the details of my talk with Schultz, she expressed happiness at the fact that a little plain speaking had helped remove many of the misunderstandings that had recently crept into India's relations with the US.

The year 1983 saw the strengthening of the relations between M.G. Ramachandran, the chief minister of Tamil Nadu (popularly known as 'MGR'), and Indira Gandhi. The story of the ups and downs in their personal relations is an interesting one. MGR was particularly keen that the Congress should not enter into any electoral alliance or understanding with M. Karunanidhi, his main rival in the state. At the same time, he did not want to give Indira Gandhi the impression that he was himself very keen to have an electoral alliance with the Congress. He was no doubt interested in an alliance, but he wanted it to be on his terms, namely, that his party (the AIADMK) should contest the overwhelming majority of seats to the State Assembly, while the Congress could contest the majority of seats for the Lok Sabha. Indira Gandhi herself was in favour of an alliance on this basis, but details such as the number of seats to be contested and the constituencies to be allotted to each party were to be worked out at a later stage.

The relations between Indira Gandhi and MGR were fairly satisfactory (despite the occasional hiccup) during the Janata regime (1977–79) and she had even thought of contesting the by-election to the Lok Sabha from the Tanjavur constituency in Tamil Nadu. MGR himself had welcomed this idea, but later reportedly under pressure from Prime Minister Morarji Desai had withdrawn the offer of support. Such a reversal of stand had caused a good deal of unhappiness to Indira Gandhi. She eventually decided not to contest the election from Tamil Nadu but had not forgotten MGR's sudden volte-face.

In Tamil Nadu, some AIADMK activists had been making speeches severely critical of Indira Gandhi after her return to power in 1980. The party's publications propagated these speeches far and wide.

English translations of these speeches were regularly sent to the PM by her party members from Tamil Nadu. Their contents led to further estrangement between her and MGR. One day in September 1981, when she was flying to Madras from Delhi, a senior Congress leader from Tamil Nadu, R. Anparasu (who was travelling with her in the plane), gave her the English translations, with the Tamil originals, of a few such reports. I was also on the same plane and she called me to her cabin and showed me these newspaper cuttings. She was visibly annoyed at the personal attacks on her and she believed that such reports could not have been published without the knowledge of the chief minister himself. MGR was at the Madras airport to receive the prime minister and I could see that their brief meeting at the airport was hardly cordial. Before the cavalcade could leave the airport gates, she suddenly wanted her car to be stopped. After that, she asked me to request the chief minister to travel with her in her car. MGR was somewhat surprised at this sudden request, but he readily joined her. After reaching their destination, the Raj Bhavan, MGR told me that the conversation between the two had been very unpleasant. Indira Gandhi had kept asking him why he was encouraging such personal attacks on her by his party colleagues. He told me that he had pointed out to her that he did not want to enter into an argument with her in the car and that too in the presence of the driver and her personal security officer. His contention was that some Congress leaders were deliberately trying to cause a rift between him and the prime minister. He wanted me to caution Indira Gandhi about such insidious machinations. He further told me that he wished to maintain cordial relations with Indira Gandhi if she reciprocated. He wanted to talk to her directly without relying on Congress intermediaries. When I conveyed to Indira Gandhi the substance of my conversation with MGR, I noticed that her anger, was short-lived and that having let off steam, she did not nurse any ill-will against the chief minister. On the other hand, she disclosed that she had high personal regard for MGR and asked me to convey her sentiments to him. She specifically asked me to try to bring him round to a level of close understanding with her. When I conveyed Indira Gandhi's viewpoint to MGR, he was happy and affirmed that he fully reciprocated her sentiments.

Subsequently, several cordial meetings took place between MGR and Indira Gandhi; I was the only other person present in most of them. My main role was to interpret MGR's statements in Tamil into English and the prime minister's statements in English into Tamil. In a couple of earlier meetings, MGR had brought along with him M. Ramachandran, the state minister for electricity, but later on he dispensed with the minister and came alone. He relied on my presence at the meetings to keep things going smoothly. Neither of them referred to electoral alliances; probably both of them held the view that this subject should be brought up only at a much later stage. Be that as it may, the friendship between the PM and the chief minister had developed to such a stage that she used to consult him regularly on vital issues such as the Tamil agitation in neighbouring Sri Lanka for a separate state (*eelam*). She always looked upon MGR as a strong champion of national unity and he, in turn, showed great respect and regard for her, particularly for the manner in which she had defended the rights of the non-Hindi language groups against the overzealous attitude of certain pro-Hindi enthusiasts.

By around the middle of 1983, relations between Sri Lanka and India had come under tremendous strain. Reports of cruel repression of Tamils by the Sri Lankan troops had created great anxiety among the people of Tamil Nadu. In this context, many leaders felt that the Indian foreign minister, Narasimha Rao, should be deputed to visit Colombo in order to hold discussions with the Sri Lankan President Junius Jayawardene. When Indira Gandhi sought Jayawardene's reaction, the latter was quick to welcome a visit by Rao. Meanwhile, we had received reports that the Sri Lankan Government was approaching foreign governments like those of Pakistan, Bangladesh, the UK and the USA to seek military assistance to deal with the Tamil agitation. Our enquiries showed that these governments had no intention of offering such assistance to Sri Lanka for settling its domestic problem. To make matters difficult for the Central Government, the main opposition party in Tamil Nadu, the DMK, had announced a 'rail *roko*' (stop trains) agitation throughout Tamil Nadu on 4 August. MGR countered this agitation by announcing the cancellation of all trains in Tamil Nadu on that day. His view was that serious clashes could occur between the police and the demonstrators, resulting in large-scale violence and even deaths. He felt it would be prudent to avoid such a situation from arising in the state.

President Jayawardene talked to Indira Gandhi over the telephone on 5 August; he suggested that he would send his brother H.W. Janawardene as his personal envoy. His mission would be to discuss, with the representatives of the Government of India, the problem resulting from the Tamil agitation in his country. The PM accepted the offer readily and made a statement to this effect in Parliament. She nominated me to represent the Government of India for talks with Janawardene at the official level.

Janawardene arrived in Delhi on 9 August and was received at the airport by me and K.S. Bajpai, secretary in the Ministry of External Affairs. After the first round of discussions with me, he met Indira Gandhi on 10 August at her office in Parliament House; Bajpai and I were also present on this occasion. The PM expressed her concern at the severity of the repressive measures taken by the Government of Sri Lanka against the Tamils there. She also stressed the fact that India viewed with concern any role for foreign military forces to deal with Sri Lanka's domestic problems. She assured him that India was not in favour of seeking any solution that would affect the integrity of Sri Lanka as a sovereign nation, but also observed that India's stand always had been to support the demand of the Tamil people for an autonomous status within a federal set-up. Janawardene held a series of discussions with us at the official level and with some ministers of the Government of India. On the whole, his visit proved to be helpful in removing misunderstandings between the two governments on several crucial issues.

As the months went by, chief ministers belonging to the opposition parties made an attempt to come together, informally, on a common platform, in order to augment their bargaining power with the Centre. Their main objectives were to claim a larger share of Central funds and to seek a greater degree of autonomy for their states. Indira Gandhi believed that there was no need for any such collective action on the part of the chief ministers as they had always had the freedom to press their demands and claims with the Centre. She felt that their move was more a political ploy intended to embarrass the Centre than to promote the interests of the states. N.T. Rama Rao, the chief minister of Andhra Pradesh, was being projected as the unofficial leader of the group of opposition chief ministers. Indira Gandhi had been receiving reports about the likelihood of this move developing into a confrontation with the Central Government. She was very keen to talk to NTR to dispel his apprehensions, if any, on Centre–state relations. It was against such a background that NTR sought an early meeting with Indira Gandhi and she readily agreed. The meeting took place on 13 October 1983 in the prime minister's office. The PM was hoping that N.T. Rama Rao would stay at least for an hour or so and discuss with her all those matters that were of special concern to the opposition chief ministers, but the entire meeting lasted for hardly fifteen minutes. NTR spoke about the severity of the floods in his state and the need for funds for relief and rehabilitation. He also wanted increased Central assistance for some of the development projects in Andhra Pradesh. The PM was very prompt in offering help on these counts. After that, it appeared as if the chief minister had little else to say. Nevertheless, he very firmly asserted that he was mainly interested in the development of his own state and was looking forward to receiving due support from the Central Government. He affirmed that he stood for full cooperation between his state and the Centre and was definitely against any confrontational approach. The topic of the opposition chief ministers coming together for collective action, to press for their demands, was not mentioned at all.

After NTR left the PM's room, I asked Indira Gandhi why she did not utilize the opening provided by him by his comments on non-confrontation with the Centre. She replied that she did not expect the meeting to end so soon and, at any rate, she did not want to enter into a controversy with him on this issue. However, she suggested that I should ascertain from him whether he would like to meet her again to continue the talks and whether he wanted to discuss any other matter. If so, she told me to inform him that she would be glad to depute me to meet him. When this message was conveyed to NTR, I was informed that he would be happy to meet me.

When I informed Indira Gandhi about my proposed meeting with NTR, she asked me to use this opportunity to assure him specifically that all reports about attempts to topple his government were unfounded. She wanted him to know that the charge that she was responsible for the dismissal of the communist government led by E.M.S. Namboodripad in Kerala way back in 1957 was baseless. This decision, she declared, was taken by the Union home minister, Govind Ballabh Pant, and not by her as she was was then the president of the Congress Party. Rumours about toppling his government may have made the rounds, but people could not possibly be stopped from spreading them, particularly when some of them were not happy with NTR's utterances against the Centre. The PM quickly passed me a handwritten note, conveying her views on toppling state governments and it is reproduced here:

Assure him that we have never, and do not wish to, topple him or any other opposition government. Even in Kerala (EMS time), the responsibility was not mine but G.B. Pant's who was strongly against communism. We have asked our people to behave with dignity.

I called on NTR at 7 p.m. on 14 October 1983 at the Andhra Bhavan in New Delhi and conveyed to him the message specifically given by Indira Gandhi about the baseless rumours regarding toppling of his government. He repeated more or less what he had told Indira Gandhi at his earlier meeting with her: 'I am interested only in my state and its development. I have no ambitions to enter national politics. I came to power promising a better life for my people. Till now I had several problems – NGO [non-gazetted officers] strike, communal riots and cyclones. I now want to do something which will bring benefits to the people.' In fact, he was quite critical of the attitude of some of the opposition leaders, who, he felt, were only interested in a constant confrontation with the Centre, while his own interest was to only help the people of his state with the the Centre's assistance. Indira Gandhi was very happy to hear from me a full report of my talk with NTR.

❖

Meanwhile, the situation in Jammu and Kashmir had been steadily deteriorating. By around the end of 1983, a group of Congressmen in J&K, with the active support of Arun Nehru and Makhan Lal Fotedar (both of whom were very close to Indira Gandhi), appeared to have made up their mind to cause a split in the NC as the first step towards toppling Farooq's Government. Farooq's estranged brother-in-law (sister's husband), G.M. Shah, seemed to have entered into an understanding with this group according to which Shah, along with fourteen other MLAs, would quit the NC and form a government with the support of the twenty-six Congress MLAs. The arithmetic was just right as the magic figure of *forty* would be adequate to form a new government in the state, but there were some doubts whether Shah would actually be able to muster the support of fourteen NC MLAs when the final count was to be made. The strategy therefore they chalked out was to request the governor to dismiss Farooq as chief minister on their submitting a letter confirming the resignation of fourteen NC MLAs.

Personally, I strongly felt that the Congress Party would be taking a very wrong and dangerous step in ensuring the exit of Farooq from power by engineering defections through promise of ministership.

The proper course for the Congress would have been to wait till the NC split on its own, for which there were enough straws in the wind. Reliable reports indicated that Farooq was facing a rebellion in his party because of disenchantment on the part of some MLAs regarding his style of functioning. However, the group bent on ousting Farooq was not willing to wait that long; its members appeared to have made it their mission to topple the Farooq Government immediately without bothering about the means they were thinking of employing. They knew that I had been advising Indira Gandhi against getting rid of Farooq through contrived defection. Naturally, they were not happy about my stand on this matter. One day, at about 8 p.m., a phone call from the PMH informed me that a group of senior Congress leaders, which included Shafi Qureshi and Ghulam Nabi Azad, wanted to see me urgently to discuss the situation in J&K and that the PM would like me to meet this group as soon as possible. I readily agreed to meet them. This group met me in my office and vigorously put forth the argument that the Farooq Government should be dismissed in the best interests of the development of the state and the security of the nation and that a viable alternative could be formed. When I pointed that the right course would be to move a no-confidence motion against Farooq to test his majority, they appeared to be very unhappy at my suggestion. They forcefully contended that the move suggested by them was the only viable one and that I did not properly understand the political situation in the state. I told them that I was only expressing my personal view and the ultimate decision on the action to be taken would be that of the leaders competent to do so. They then left my office after expressing their disappointment at what they thought was my 'unhelpful attitude'.

Governor B.K. Nehru's stand was that he would not dismiss Farooq's Government unless it was defeated on the floor of the Legislative Assembly and if Farooq refused to resign even after suffering a defeat. The governor quickly became the target of sharp criticism by the Congress leaders of the state and their supporters in Delhi. I realized that whatever might be the correctness of the stand of the governor and my own personal views on this issue, the days of Farooq's Government were numbered and it was just a matter of time before he went.

NINE

1984

*T*HE PLAN TO TOPPLE THE FAROOQ ABDULLAH GOVERNMENT SUDDENLY came up against a major roadblock. When G.M. Shah became convinced that the Congress leaders were willing to pay any price to oust Farooq, he took the stand that he would form a government with the help of the fourteen defectors from the NC and that the Congress should support it from outside without joining; in other words, there would be no Congress ministers. Having gone so far, the Congress had no other alternative but to accept Shah's humiliating condition. By now, it had become very clear to me that the plan of the group in the PMH as well as the Congressmen in J&K to remove Farooq had Indira Gandhi's approval. After the meeting of the J&K Congress leaders with me, they had brought to her notice my 'unhelpful' attitude and expressed their unhappiness on my stand. She perhaps thought it necessary to make her position as unambiguous as possible to me as to what exactly she wanted in J&K. She made it clear to me that she agreed with the stand taken by her partymen and that of her cabinet members that Farooq had to be replaced. She made this view known to G. Parthasarathi also, who had expressed views similar to mine. I had no doubt in my mind that hers was an incorrect and even an unwise decision politically, but she had taken it after several months of deliberation and there was nothing more I could do to make her change her mind. Once the PM had made known to me her final decision, in unequivocal terms, I only had to facilitate its smooth implementation.

I informed B.K. Nehru of the PM's decision when he met me in New Delhi on 4 January 1984. His response was that the only honourable course for him to follow was to offer his resignation. As required by protocol, he wrote a letter, addressed to the president, resigning his office and requested me to hand it over to the prime minister, which I did. However, she did not take any action immediately; nor was the subject of resignation broached by either side when B.K. Nehru called on the prime minister on 5 January. However, the relations between them were noticeably strained and it became obvious to people like me that B.K. Nehru could not possibly continue as the Governor of J&K if the plan for removing Farooq was to be implemented.

The transfer of B.K. Nehru took place as expected. His new posting was as governor of Gujarat, an assignment that he heartily disliked. But he accepted the transfer without much protest and the line was now clear for 'Operation Remove Farooq'. Jagmohan (a person closely known to Indira Gandhi) was appointed as the new governor of J&K. However, a few more months had to pass before Farooq could be ousted. On 2 July 1984, twelve NC MLAs and one independent defected to G.M. Shah's side and they were paraded before Jagmohan, with the request that Farooq be dismissed immediately as chief minister. Jagmohan's initial reaction was that the state should be placed under president's rule. However, the Union cabinet met quickly and decided that the governor should explore the possibility of an alternative government being formed. By the evening of 2 July I received the news that G.M. Shah had been sworn in as the new chief minister; all the defectors were made ministers. The media was highly critical of the developments in the J&K state, particularly with reference to the manner in which a government made up of defectors had been allowed to be formed. Strangely, the reaction in the state itself was not as adverse as expected.

The removal of Farooq Abdullah continued to be severely criticized by the opposition parties in the country. The National Development Council (NDC) was scheduled to meet on 12 July at the Vigyan Bhavan (New Delhi) to consider the 'approach paper' on the Seventh Five-Year Plan. When the name of the chief minister of Andhra Pradesh was announced by the prime minister (to speak on the 'approach paper'), NTR started reading out a statement on behalf of the chief ministers of West Bengal (Jyoti Basu), Karnataka (Ramakrishna Hedge), Andhra Pradesh and Tripura (Nripen Chakraborty) registering strong protest at the removal of the Farooq Abdullah Government. The prime minister interrupted NTR to point out that the NDC was not a forum for political speeches, but he continued to read the statement amidst vehement protests from the Congress chief ministers and other ministers present in the auditorium. When calm was restored, the prime minister announced that NTR's statement would not be included in the record of the NDC proceedings. At this stage, the four opposition chief ministers staged a walkout. This was the first time in the history of the NDC that such an event had been witnessed. Immediately, a resolution was adopted by the NDC condemning the conduct of those chief ministers who had walked out of the meeting. At that time, MGR was staying at the Tamil Nadu guesthouse, but his electricity minister, M. Ramachandran, was present at the NDC meeting. He telephoned MGR to seek his permission to join the rest of the chief ministers in condemning the walkout. MGR readily agreed to his minister's request and he himself attended the afternoon session of the NDC as a gesture of support to the prime minister.

In early 1984 (on 4 February to be exact), developments in J&K had a ripple effect in other parts of the world. One of the most tragic incidents that shocked every Indian was the kidnapping of Ravindra Mathre, an attaché in the deputy high commissioner's office, in Birmingham (UK) by militants belonging to the Kashmiri Liberation Front (KLF). The militants demanded the release of Maqbool Bhatt, the leader of the KLF, who was facing a death sentence on murder charges. This was the precondition for sparing Mathre's life.

Indira Gandhi was very firm in her stand that Bhatt would not be released under any circumstances, which was conveyed to the militant group in the UK. The militants carried out the threat that they had held out and Mathre was brutally murdered. The militants also threatened further retaliatory measures against the government. Such threats only led to the stiffening of the government attitude, and the execution of Bhatt was immediately carried out (as per the judicial verdict). While people at large felt intense anguish at the killing of an innocent person like Mathre, they were, nevertheless, fully supportive of the government's stand not to yield to the militants' pressure tactics.

Apart from the tense situation in J&K, conditions in Punjab were causing alarm due to the Akali agitation and the demand by some Sikh fringe groups for a separate nation to be named 'Khalistan'. Terrorists were active not only in Punjab but also in the neighbouring areas including Delhi. Regular bomb blasts and killings became the order of the day. The police were forced to resort to certain special measures to deal with the situation. It was against such a backdrop that an unpleasant situation suddenly arose, in February–March 1984, when President Zail Singh himself a Sikh, alleged that his telephone was being tapped. This allegation turned out to be absolutely baseless upon thorough investigation, but the outburst did create an embarrassing situation for all concerned for a few days. Relations between Zail Singh and Indira Gandhi had started becoming discordant because of certain misunderstandings on the part of the president about the manner in which the Akali agitation was being handled by the government. Zail Singh wished to be consulted by the prime minister on all major steps to be taken by her in dealing with it. His view was that since he possessed an extensive knowledge of the politics of the state, he had a useful role to play in solving the problems there. Consequently, he expected the prime minister to consult him before taking any important decision regarding the ongoing Akali agitation. Indira Gandhi did not consider it necessary or even advisable to do so. On 28 February, the president, on the basis of some reports that were carried to him by people with an axe to grind, informed the minister for communications that his phone was being tapped and expressed his great annoyance at such an invasion of his privacy. The minister rushed to the prime minister requesting that a denial be immediately issued that there was no truth whatsoever in this allegation. The PM asked me to forthwith ascertain, from all possible sources, the veracity of the president's charge. After extensive investigation by all authorities concerned, the conclusion was that the president's phone was not tapped. The investigations revealed that telephones of a few Akali leaders in Amritsar were being tapped by the police and when the president spoke to them, the contents of his conversation with them naturally became known to the police. This state of affairs was wrongly interpreted as the tapping of the president's telephone at Rashtrapati Bhavan. I explained the entire situation to the prime minister. Later, the president himself came to know the truth of the matter and the issue soon died down without any further discordant notes being struck.

✧

On 19 July I accompanied the prime minister and her entourage on visits to Andhra Pradesh and Kerala. After landing at the Hyderabad airport the prime minister went to nearby Medak, where she laid the foundation stone for a new tank factory. After that, I, along with the defence minister, R. Venkataraman, visited the Defence Research Development Organization (DRDO) upon our return to Hyderabad. The scientists here were engaged in research related to missiles and electronic warfare under the guidance of eminent authorities such as Dr V. S. Arunachalam (director, DRDO) and Dr Abdul Kalam (who became president of India in July 2002). Indira Gandhi arrived there in the evening and spent about an hour in the laboratory, where Dr Arunachalam and Dr Kalam explained to her the details of the work being done there.

At that point of time, I was aware of the fact that the prime minister had decided to nominate Venkataraman for the post of vice-president of India, for which elections were scheduled to take place within a few weeks. She had not taken any of her colleagues in her cabinet or her party into confidence on this issue yet, though she had informed me of her decision a few days earlier. I was also aware of the fact that she had not informed Venkataraman himself about her decision as she had not yet found a suitable opportunity for doing so. While we were having tea under the *shamiana* (a huge tent),

I reminded her that there were hardly a few days left for filing the nomination for the post of vice-president and that she could use the opportunity of Venkataraman's presence there to convey her decision to him. She then moved over to the place where Venkataraman was standing along with some of the senior officers of the DRDO and took him aside. She then informed him about her decision and returned very quickly to the place where I was standing. She told me that she had conveyed the news to Venkataraman but that he did not appear to be very excited about it. She said that Venkataraman seemed to be so happy in the Defence Ministry that he did not feel overjoyed at the prospect of his elevation to the post of vice-president. However, according to Indira Gandhi, he had told her that he would gladly accept whatever position she offered him.

The PM reached Thiruvananthapuram from Hyderabad at about 8.30 p.m. on 19 July itself. A.K. Antony met her at the Raj Bhavan the same night. Later, Antony called on me in my room in the Raj Bhavan and said that he was very unhappy at the unfriendly attitude of K. Karunakaran towards him. Antony's chief grievance was that Karunakaran was using every opportunity to 'slight' him, as he described it.

Karunakaran was scheduled to meet Indira Gandhi on 20 July morning at the Raj Bhavan. Before that meeting, Indira Gandhi had asked me to inform him of her decision to nominate Antony as a general secretary of the AICC. She thought that conveying this decision to Karunakaran before he met her would be useful. She wanted me to meet her again before Karunakaran himself was called in by her. Those who are not familiar with Indira Gandhi's style of working may wonder why she chose to send out feelers and messages in advance to the concerned persons, but this was how she worked in certain situations and, by then, I was quite used to her methods. When I mentioned the fact to Karunakaran he, without any hesitation, expressed great satisfaction. I had no reason to doubt the genuineness of his happiness at that time.

After my conversation with Karunakaran in the portico (in front of the main suite where Indira Gandhi was staying), I entered her room to convey Karunakaran's reaction. She was quite happy to hear that Karunakaran (and his supporters) would warmly welcome the idea. However, what transpired between Indira Gandhi and Karunakaran at the meeting in her suite was totally in contrast to what I had expected. Indira Gandhi, after a brief session with Karunakaran, straightaway went to attend a function at the Belhaven Palace (at Thiruvananthapuram) in connection with the inauguration of the new Southern Command of the Indian Air Force. Immediately after the function, she rushed to the airport to fly back to Delhi. (I was planning to stay back in Kerala for a couple of days more.) Before boarding the plane, she took me aside and briefly told me that Karunakaran had expressed great unhappiness at her decision to appoint Antony. I felt extremely unhappy with Karunakaran's contradictory statements. I wondered why he had adopted 'a dual policy' particularly when he knew very well that I was playing the role of an emissary of Indira Gandhi. He probably underestimated Indira Gandhi's trust in me and thought that she would keep his statements to herself. Another probability was that Karunakaran honestly believed that Antony should not be trusted with such a vital responsibility in the party, taking into account the fact that he had chosen to go against Indira Gandhi when she was facing a serious crisis. But all this did not explain the exuberant manner in which he welcomed the news when I first conveyed it to him.

Anyhow, I was determined to find out from Karunakaran at the earliest opportunity as to why he had made different statements to me and Indira Gandhi. I got the opportunity within a few days, when Karunakaran was called to Delhi by Indira Gandhi. I met him at the Kerala House on 10 August and confronted him point-blank. Karunakaran was taken aback by the frankness with which I expressed my unhappiness as he had probably not expected Indira Gandhi to tell me what exactly she had heard from him. He began to hedge and then stated that there was some misunderstanding on the part of Indira Gandhi about what he had told her and that he would clear up the matter during their meeting.

Karunakaran met the PM at 12.15 p.m. on 10 August. She bluntly informed him that she was going ahead with her decision on Antony. After her meeting with Karunakaran, Indira Gandhi asked me to

202 |I THROUGH THE CORRIDORS OF POWER

inform Antony that she wanted to meet him the next day itself. Antony made a dash to Delhi and first met Indira Gandhi and later Rajiv Gandhi on 11 August. They informed him of the decision to appoint him as a general secretary of the AICC. He, naturally, felt happy on hearing this news.

I had not given Antony even the slightest hint about his prospective appointment till he heard the news directly from Indira Gandhi. In those days Antony had considered me as his ardent well-wisher; he looked upon me as one who had played a very fair and just role in ensuring his honourable rehabilitation in the Congress Party. He had himself told me that my honest assessment of the situation in Kerala had been an important factor in her making up her mind about the respectable return of himself and his colleagues in spite of very strong opposition from Karunakaran.

Meanwhile, the prospects arose of my being scheduled for a top post in the UN. Around August 1984 I had received information from S.K. Singh, India's ambassador in Vienna, that my name was being seriously considered in influential quarters in the UN for the post of director-general of the UNIDO and that my candidature could receive good support if the Government of India decided to sponsor me officially. V.P. Singh, India's commerce minister, had visited Vienna to attend a meeting of the UNIDO and, during his stay there, he had also come to know that my chances were bright if the Government of India was willing to nominate me. As stated earlier, I had worked in the UN for over ten years in various positions. On his return to Delhi V.P. Singh informed the prime minister (through a letter dated 17 August 1984) about the same. I was expecting that the prime minister herself would bring up this subject. However, she remained silent on this topic for some days, though S.K. Singh had been calling me to enquire about the stand of the government. After about a week or so, in one of my morning meetings with her, she suddenly brought up the subject of developing countries losing the services of experienced officers to the UN while these countries needed their services much more than the international organization did. At that point of time, M.S. Swaminathan was being considered for a senior position in the FAO and I thought she was making this observation in that context. She then suddenly handed over V.P. Singh's letter to me and remarked in a lighter vein: 'I hope you are not going to be one of those whom the UN wants to take away' and kept on laughing as if the whole issue deserved no serious thought. The relevant extracts from V.P. Singh's letter (of 17 August 1984) are given here:

> Next year the UNIDO is likely to be converted into a specialized agency. Election fever for the Director-General was on, as the present Director-General is due to retire.
>
> There was mention that India could also make a bid if a suitable candidate was fielded, and in this connection the name of the Dr P.C. Alexander found circulation who is well-known and highly respected in the international fields. I think we should consider this possibility as it will be of particular interest to us. However, we will have to butt in early in the game before countries get firmly committed to the going candidates. The strategy will also have to be planned well in advance...

I deciphered from her reaction that she was against my quitting my present job to take up a UN post and she was only waiting for me to confirm that I was not inclined to switch over. I quickly replied that I would not have quit my UN job in 1981 had I wanted to make a career there. She was happy with my reaction and promptly changed the subject.

August 1984 witnessed some dramatic developments in Andhra Pradesh. Around noon on 16 August, the director of the Intelligence Bureau (IB) gave me the somewhat startling news that Governor Ram Lal had issued orders dismissing NTR as chief minister and appointing Bhaskar Rao in his place. NTR had just returned from the US after undergoing heart surgery and, without holding any consultations with him, the governor appeared to have come to the astonishing conclusion that he had lost his majority. The governor also felt that Bhaskar Rao, who had defected from NTR's party, was in a position to form a government with the support of the Congress. NTR was naturally taken aback by this unexpected development and requested the governor to convene the State Assembly immediately so that he could prove that he still enjoyed the support of the majority of the legislators. The governor refused to oblige; instead, he invited Bhaskar Rao to form a new government. Bhaskar Rao had paraded ninety-one persons before the governor, claiming that they were MLAs who supported him. The governor, however, had not verified whether all those presented before him were really MLAs or whether some outsiders too had helped in swelling the ranks. Ram Lal refused to accept NTR's request to allow his supporters to be presented before him (the governor) to prove that NTR still enjoyed the majority. To me these reports seemed incredibly strange and I wanted to verify, before meeting Indira Gandhi, whether anyone in Delhi had any prior knowledge about these astounding events. The director (IB) confirmed that his organization did not have any prior information about these developments; they came to his knowledge only after they had actually taken place. I called up Makhan Lal Fotedar (a close aide of the prime minister) to find out whether he had any prior knowledge about these goings-on, but his response was that this was a bolt from the blue. R.K. Dhawan (another confidant of Indira Gandhi and her family) told me that he had talked to the governor on the phone after hearing the news and that the latter had confirmed that Bhaskar Rao was being sworn in by him as chief minister.

The majority of the people in Andhra Pradesh reacted to NTR's dismissal with great revulsion and anger. They came out on the streets in hordes in several towns in the state to protest against the high-handed action of the governor.

I called on the prime minister at her house immediately after ascertaining the facts from all available sources. She too did not have any prior information about this matter and appeared to have been completely taken by surprise. By then information had reached us that a few opposition leaders, namely, Atal Behari Vajpayee, H.N. Bahuguna and Farooq Abdullah, were rushing to Hyderabad to meet NTR. The reports from Andhra Pradesh revealed that the demonstrations by the crowds were turning violent and the police had to open fire in several places. We also received information that NTR was planning to bring the MLAs supporting him to Delhi in order to parade them before the president. Parliament was then in session, but could not transact any business because of noisy protests by the opposition MPs. I met the prime minister on the afternoon of 18 August and suggested that she should make a statement in Parliament emphatically denying any involvement on her part or on the part of anyone in the Central Government in the entire affair. She was quite receptive to my suggestion and said that she would do so at the appropriate time.

The allegation that the PM or some members of her inner circle had been involved in the 'Andhra drama' was gaining currency very fast. The public at large appeared to believe that Governor Ram Lal could not have acted on his own. The opposition leaders raised the cry of 'democracy in danger' and announced that they were launching a countrywide 'save democracy' agitation. Some newspapers even published reports that Ram Lal would not have taken such a step without support from the Centre. When I informed some of my close journalist friends that Indira Gandhi had no prior knowledge of these developments, their response was that it would be very difficult to convince the common man.

On 21 August, at about 8.30 a.m., MGR called me from Madras. He insisted, vehemently at that, that the PM should not delay the announcement in Parliament disowning any knowledge about the governor's action. When I informed him that she herself was considering such a step, he warned that any further delay would cause irreparable damage to her name. I met the PM at 10 a.m. in Parliament House and gave her MGR's message. I, too, forcefully suggested that she should make the announcement in Parliament that day itself. Meanwhile, the opposition tabled a vote of no-confidence against the government. In the face of this development, some of Indira Gandhi's senior cabinet colleagues were of the view that instead of the prime minister making a *suo moto* statement disowning any responsibility for the governor's action as proposed by me, the government should ask for a debate on the no-confidence motion first. Their stand was that since a no-confidence motion had already been tabled, a discussion on that motion should receive priority over any other issue. Once again I expressed my strong conviction to the prime minister that if her statement was delayed merely because of procedural wrangles, the public would draw the conclusion that the

Centre was attempting to hide something and that was why she should herself seek an opportunity for making a statement. At this stage, she called in a few more of her senior colleagues for a discussion on the strategy to be followed in Parliament. By about 10.45 a.m., it became clear that she and her senior colleagues were in favour of accepting my suggestion about the PM making a statement that day itself. She asked me to draft a statement as quickly as possible, which I did sitting in front of her and handed over the draft to her. She made a few changes and rushed to the Lok Sabha immediately after the 'question hour' ended at noon. I watched the proceedings from the official gallery.

Madhu Dandavate, a highly respected leader, who had held ministerial positions during Morarji Desai's tenure as PM, speaking on behalf of the opposition parties, launched a blistering attack on Governor Ram Lal and chief minister Bhaskar Rao. He spoke for about forty-five minutes, before taking a pause. The PM then developed a doubt whether a *suo moto* statement by her would be proper since Dandavate himself had not, so far, made any allegations against her. She sent me a note from her seat, which was a normal practice with her. I replied on that note itself that her statement was not only for the MPs but also for the entire nation wanting to know the truth. In my reply, I also added that Dandavate himself would soon make the charge against her as his speech so far clearly indicated that he was preparing for such an attack. Sure enough, in a few minutes, Dandavate trained his guns directly on Indira Gandhi, alleging that without the prior approval of the Central Government the state governor *could not* have taken such a step. The PM immediately availed of this opportunity and made a statement to the effect that she had no part to play in, or knowledge of, the Andhra episode. She was heckled in the Lok Sabha by the irate opposition members, who became obstreperous while she was making her statement. However, she did not yield any ground and completed it. She then went straight to the Rajya Sabha and made the same statement there too.

Indira Gandhi's categorical statement about her non-involvement in Ram Lal's action made big headlines in all the newspapers on 22 August. However, NTR still stole the show as he arrived in Delhi on the same day with all the MLAs supporting him and paraded them before the president. Charges and countercharges about impersonation and the use of false identity cards flew thick and fast, but, on the whole, the prime minister's statement in Parliament had blunted the edge of the opposition's allegation of her involvement in this murky episode.

To continue the story of the Bhaskar Rao Government, the Legislative Assembly met in Hyderabad on 11 and 12 September 1984, but could not transact any business because of disorderly and chaotic scenes in the house. The opposition parties levelled the charge that Bhaskar Rao, with the support of the Congress, was trying to prevent any voting on the confidence motion by going in for stalling tactics in the Assembly. However, a clear signal was sent to the governor that the period of one month earlier fixed by him, within which the confidence vote had to be held, should not be extended under any circumstances. Bhaskar Rao knew that the game was over for him and submitted his resignation, which was announced on 16 September. On the same day, NTR was sworn in as chief minister again.

NTR called on the prime minister on 5 October 1984 at her office in New Delhi. His mood had changed for the better and the unpleasant experiences of the previous month did not appear to have caused any ill-will or estrangement in him. Indira Gandhi herself was extraordinarily courteous and friendly to him. NTR repeatedly thanked her for her message of condolences on the demise of his wife, addressing her very warmly as 'our beloved prime minister'. He highlighted the severe drought conditions in some of the districts of Andhra Pradesh and, in response, the PM assured him that she would, at the earliest opportunity, visit those districts. It was indeed a cordial meeting; it turned out to be the last between them.

On 13 October 1984, the prime minister received the news that MGR was suffering from serious kidney ailments and that he may have to go to the US for treatment or else specialists from there may have to be flown in to Madras. On 16 October the PM decided to go over to Madras to see MGR. G. Parthasarathi and I accompanied her on this visit. I had telephoned the state governor in advance to

inform him to ensure that ministers and others coming to the airport to receive the prime minister should not bring flowers or garlands. We went straight to the Apollo Hospital where MGR had been admitted. MGR could hardly speak, but he was able to recognize the prime minister, GP and me. He motioned to the doctors to raise him up, but the PM asked him to remain lying and not to exert himself. She tried to pep him up: 'Chief minister, please look after yourself and get well quickly. You have fought many battles and shown great courage in your life. You will show the same courage in this crisis too.' MGR became emotional and tried to say something, but words were not forthcoming. GP and I then went very close to the bed and MGR smiled at us. After that, Indira Gandhi talked to MGR's wife, Janaki Ramachandran, who was in the room for a few minutes. She then met the team of doctors, one of whom informed her that the Indian doctors were quite competent to look after MGR and national prestige may be hurt if doctors from outside were brought in. Indira Gandhi's response was that national prestige was not at stake here but MGR's life was valuable to the whole nation. The PM next met the ministers in MGR's cabinet for about half an hour at the Raj Bhavan, after which she immediately flew back to Delhi.

Three days later, four doctors from the US arrived in Delhi and were flown to Madras by a special flight arranged by the Central Government. The prime minister had instructed that an Air India aircraft be kept ready to transport MGR to the US if found necessary. However, the US doctors were of the view that his condition at that point of time was not stable enough to stand the strain of a journey. MGR survived this critical phase and lived on for a few more years.

While the Andhra Pradesh contretemps and MGR's health continued to engage our attention, we had to deal with another crisis of a totally different nature: the hijacking of an Indian Airlines Corporation (IAC) plane from Chandigarh by a group of Sikh militants. The plane was allowed to land first at Lahore by the Pakistan authorities and later at Karachi. Krishnaswami Rao Saheb, the cabinet secretary, and I, after holding discussions with M.K. Rasgotra, foreign secretary, and other members of the Crisis Management Group thought that we should request the prime minister to speak to President Zia-ul Haq of Pakistan, seeking his help to deal with the hijackers. I met the prime minister at her house around 8.40 p.m. on 24 August and requested her to speak to President Zia on the hotline, which she readily agreed to do. I was present in her room when this conversation took place. Zia started off by complaining that India had never appreciated Pakistan's help whenever it had intervened in hijacking cases at the request of the Indian Government. Indira Gandhi pointed out to him that his impression was not correct; at any rate, she continued, she wanted him to resolve the present crisis promptly without raking up any controversies about past incidents. Zia then promised that he would do everything in his power to save the lives of the passengers and the crew. We waited till 1 a.m. the next morning to find out what exactly the authorities in Pakistan would do, but were quite disappointed to hear that they had done virtually nothing in response to the PM's request. Rao Saheb and I then hurried over to Narasimha Rao's house to chalk out a further course of action. After that we decided to obtain the PM's permission to inform Pakistan that we would have no objection to allowing the hijackers to go to the US if they would leave the plane and the passengers behind safely. We went to PM's house at 1.30 a.m. and woke her up to tell her about this proposal. She readily agreed with it. Narasimha Rao then spoke to General K.M. Arif, chief of staff to President Zia, and conveyed the message to him. However, within an hour or so, much to our disappointment, we came to know that the Pakistanis had allowed the hijackers to take the plane along with the passengers to Dubai.

We then made attempts to persuade the authorities in Dubai to return the plane, the passengers and the hijackers to India. Various options and suggestions were put forword to them. The authorities in the USA, which was the preferred destination of the hijackers, were also consulted simultaneously. After prolonged exchanges with authorities in both countries, in which Rasgotra and Romesh Bhandari of the Ministry of External Affairs actively participated, lasting over a week, a satisfactory formula was evolved by which the hijackers could be brought back to India from Dubai. This nerve-racking experience convinced us that Pakistan would do little to help us during crisis situations. On the other hand, we were happy to discover that we could depend on the cooperation of the UAE and US Governments when faced with an emergency of this nature.

Two important visitors called on me in the last week of October 1984. The first was Richard Murphy, the US assistant secretary of state, who visited Delhi to clear the misunderstandings created by a statement made by the US ambassador in Islamabad that his country would assist Pakistan in case of an attack by India. The obvious implication of this statement was that India was a potential aggressor. Murphy's meeting with me lasted for an hour and a half. I explained to him how both in 1965 and 1971 India had been the victim of aggression by Pakistan and how Pakistan's military leaders, unfamiliar with the norms of democratic functioning, made grave mistakes in assessing the political situation in India. I also brought to his notice the fact that Pakistan had used the arms supplied by the US against India in the 1965 and 1971 wars, though Washington had always maintained that such weapons were intended only for Pakistan's defence against possible attack from Afghanistan or the Soviet Union. For his part, Murphy clarified that the US had no intention of supporting Pakistan in any war against India and that the US had never considered India as an initiator of conflict.

My second visitor was Humayun Khan, Pakistan's ambassador to India. He spent about an hour with me and, after underlining the fact that his government was quite unhappy seeing the recent deterioration of relations between the two countries, stated that President Zia had asked him to ascertain whether or not Indira Gandhi would agree to resumption of talks between the two countries. My response was that unless some tangible evidence of a change in Pakistan's attitude towards India could be provided, these was no point in resuming the talks and I also highlighted the damage caused to Indo–Pak relations as a result of Pakistan's active support to militant groups indulging in terrorist activities against India. I told him that we had garnered reliable information about the source from which the hijackers of the IAC plane had procured the pistols at the Karachi airport. I pointed out that at least the act of handing over the terrorists wanted by India, who were then in Pakistan, would have been an encouraging gesture to build up a cordial and amicable atmosphere for talks. He declared that preconditions like these for talks would not be acceptable to Pakistan and the return of terrorists should be the outcome of the talks and not before them. I left him in no doubt about our strong reservations about the usefulness of talks, as I knew very clearly the prime minister's own thinking on this issue. When I reported the details of this meeting to the PM, she fully agreed with the stand I had taken.

✧

On 26 October 1984 V.R. Nedunchezhian, finance minister of Tamil Nadu and the seniormost member in MGR's cabinet, came to meet the prime minister in connection with seat-sharing arrangements as the AIADMK was keen to finalize an electoral alliance with the Congress. The formula he offered contained a clear-cut demarcation: the Congress should contest one-third of the Assembly seats and two-third of the Parliament seats, while the AIADMK would contest the remaining seats. He also stated that the AIADMK was in favour of conducting simultaneous elections for both the Assembly and the Parliament. Indira Gandhi straightaway agreed to the formula, but stressed that for the present this arrangement should be kept confidential.

On 27 October, Indira Gandhi suddenly decided to make a dash to Srinagar. The next day when I asked her the reason for her impulsive visit, she replied that she wanted to see the Chinar trees shedding their leaves, a sight that she had always found fascinating. (The magnificent Chinar tree is symbolic of Kashmir.)

I noticed that she was looking somewhat worried when I met her on 28 October as she said that she had received reports from reliable sources in Srinagar that disclosed large-scale Pakistani infiltration into the Kashmir Valley. She also discussed the latest situation in the Punjab with me. Suddenly, she telephoned General A.S. Vaidya, chief of the Army Staff, to come over to her office. General Vaidya turned up within ten minutes and briefed her about the security situation in Punjab and J&K. He assured the PM that there was no danger of any large-scale Pakistani infiltration taking place either in Punjab or in Kashmir and the reports, which the PM would have received, did not quite reflect the reality on the ground.

After General Vaidya left, she turned to the subject of President Zail Singh's somewhat cold attitude towards her, a subject that she had discussed with me on several occasions before. She underscored the fact that she was trying to fulful his wishes on most issues to the maximum extent possible, but she could not understand what was making him behave so strangely of late. She asked me whether I had noticed her talking to him at the airport (on 22 October) when he was on the verge of leaving on a visit to Mauritius. I replied in the affirmative and told her that, in my view, the conversation did not seem to be a very pleasant one but, I did not think it proper to ask why.

She narrated to me what exactly had transpired. According to her, she told him that she was very unhappy at his changed attitude towards her, to which his reply was that he too had reasons to be unhappy, but would specify them at a later date and added: 'If I come back alive after this visit, I would have a lot to talk to you.' Indira Gandhi was rather amazed at these words but did add that he was in perfect health and should not be talking in such terms, especially when he was proceeding on a foreign visit. After seeing off the president the PM boarded an Indian Air Force (IAF) plane on a tour of Uttar Pradesh.

When she narrated this incident to me, I told her that she should not have chosen such an occasion for expressing her unhappiness. Her response was: 'I felt I had to talk to him plainly and therefore I did so. I had to do it and I did it.'

On 29 October, the prime minister undertook a whirlwind tour of Orissa. She touched many places in the state and addressed a slew of meetings, each of which was attended by large crowds. She returned to Delhi at 8.45 p.m. and I met her at 9.10 p.m. at her house. She appeared quite tired and also somewhat irritable. The reason was not hard to figure out. She was rather peeved that the itinerary in Orissa for her meetings had not been very intelligently fixed. She had to criss-cross the state many times, leading to unnecessary stress and fatigue. Earlier in the day, the car escorting Priyanka and Rahul, her grandchildren, had been involved in a minor collision with another car, but, fortunately the children were not injured. However, the news of the accident appeared to have upset her. She had always been intensely worried about the security of the members of her family, particularly about that of her grandchildren. She probably suspected some foul play in this collision. When I met her, she had not even changed the sari (orange in colour) that she was wearing while travelling in Orissa earlier in the day. She was wearing the same sari when she made that prophetic 'Every drop of my blood...' speech earlier in the evening at a public meeting in Orissa. The words of this now-immortal speech had got imprinted in the minds of millions of viewers when this scene was repeatedly shown on television screen after the tragedy of 31 October. The sari looked uncharacteristically crumpled on a person who was always very meticulous about ensuring that her apparel was spotless and spick-and-span. Since I found her unusually tired, I wanted to be brief during our meeting in which I needed to discuss some important matters with her besides, of course, giving her a quick report on the latest developments in Punjab. Towards the end of the meeting, I told her that I was leaving for Bombay early the next morning along with the cabinet secretary, to attend meeting of the Atomic Energy Commission (AEC), of which I was a member. She then called R.K. Dhawan to her room and informed him that she would not be going to her office at South Block the next day and asked him to cancel all the engagements fixed for her there on 31 October.

There has been some speculation in the media as to what exactly was the urgent matter that I discussed with her on 30 October night. In fact, the leader of the BJP, Atal Behari Vajpayee, had made a public demand that I should make known to the people the subject of my talk with her. Extracts from Vajpayee's statement in the *Indian Express* (30 November 1984) are reproduced here:

COUNTRY MUST KNOW WHAT SHE TOLD ALEXANDER

BJP president A.B. Vajpayee said here yesterday that the country has a right to know the important matters which Mrs Indira Gandhi discussed with her Principal Private Secretary, Mr P.C. Alexander, on the night of October 30 as stated by the latter in a Press interview.

In a statement, Mr Vajpayee said according to the Press interview, Mr Alexander had said that his "last meeting with her was on the night of October 30 at 9.15 p.m. I will not say anything about the subjects I discussed with her. All that I can say is that we discussed some very important and urgent matters and she gave me instructions about the further action to be taken on them".

Mr Vajpayee said the "country has a right to know what were these very important matters which Mrs Gandhi needed to decide so urgently at night immediately on her return from a hectic tour of Orissa..."

I did discuss some important issues with the prime minister and because of the sensitive nature of the subject, I did not, at that time, reveal to anyone what I had discussed; nor do I think I should now.

✧

Krishnaswami Rao Saheb (the cabinet secretary) and I left for Bombay at 6.45 a.m. on 31 October 1984. We went by helicopter from the airport to the Bhabha Atomic Research Centre (BARC) complex. We spent a few minutes talking to Raja Ramanna, chairman of the AEC, in his office. Ever since the Punjab situation had started becoming very serious, the cabinet secretary and I had worked out an arrangement that both of us would not be absent from Delhi at the same time so that one of us was always available in the capital to assist the prime minister in dealing with any unforeseen serious developments. This was the first occasion in 1984 that both of us were being absent from Delhi together and, unfortunately, this happened to be the day when a monumental tragedy in recent decades in the history of India took place.

We moved on to the committee room at 10 a.m. Ramanna, in his welcome remarks, mentioned how happy he was to see both the cabinet secretary and me attending a meeting together away from Delhi which, in his view, showed how much the law and order situation had improved in the country. Ramanna had hardly spoken two or three more sentences, when someone rushed in to inform me that there was an urgent call from Delhi. The call was from my office, but the message was shocking beyond words. My personal assistant told me in a trembling voice: 'I have very bad news Sir, the prime minister has been shot this morning and taken to the Medical Institute [The All-India Institute of Medical Sciences (AIIMS), New Delhi]. Her condition is critical.' I was stunned and asked him to repeat what he had just told me to make sure that I had heard him correctly. He repeated his words and I told him to inform everyone concerned that cabinet secretary and I were rushing back to Delhi. Within minutes the AEC arranged a helicopter to transport us to the airport. On that particular day many important persons were out of Delhi: the president was in Mauritius, Home Minister Narasimha Rao in Andhra Pradesh; and Rajiv Gandhi and Pranab Mukherjee in Calcutta. We got into the special plane at 11.30 a.m., all the time cursing ourselves for being away from Delhi when our presence was most needed there.

Around 12.30 p.m. the pilot told me that he had just received a message from the IAC office in Delhi that 'work was in progress'. He said that this message meant that surgery was still going on. However, after a few more minutes he approached me again with the new message that 'the worst fears are confirmed' and added, 'this means she is dead'. The pilot also informed me that the prime minister had been shot by her own security guards at her house. Rao Saheb and I were deeply worried as to what would be the situation in Delhi at that stage and who would be managing the crisis there.

We reached Delhi at 1.15 p.m. and were immediately driven to AIIMS, where her body was lying. As we neared our destination, we found thousands of people gathered all around the hospital and along all roads leading to it. The news of her death had not yet been announced and the crowds were desperately waiting to know the truth. The mood was sombre and marked by grief and anxiety. We were quickly taken to the eighth floor, where the postmortem examination was going on. A few ministers and some close friends of Indira Gandhi, such as G. Parthasarathi and Pupul Jayakar, were standing in the verandah. I asked for Dr K.P. Mathur, personal physician to the prime minister, who was inside the operation theatre. He came out and told me, with tears rolling down his face, 'all is over, the body is being stitched up'. Rao Saheb and I held a hasty consultation session with each other. We decided that Rao Saheb would go over to his office immediately and convene a meeting of the Crisis Management Group, which would take the necessary action as per the emerging situation. I was to remain at AIIMS to deal with the situation arising there. My first act was to clear the verandah in front of the operation theatre on the eighth floor, allowing only the senior ministers and a few close friends of Indira Gandhi to remain. A room on this floor was quickly readied and a visitor's book was placed there so that those who came up there could record their condolences in the book if they so wished. I placed V.S. Tripathi, joint secretary in the PMO, in charge of regulating the entry of people to the verandah.

The vice-president, R. Venkataraman, arrived at 2.45 p.m. to pay his condolences. A message had been flashed to us by then that Narasimha Rao's plane (from Hyderabad) would be landing in Delhi shortly and he would be coming straight to the institute.

It was my firm conviction as soon as I received the news of the tragedy that the most feasible arrangement would be to have Rajiv sworn in *immediately* as prime minister without going in for an interim prime minister. I held hurried consultations with Shivshankar and B. Shankaranand, senior ministers in Indira Gandhi's cabinet, who had rushed to AIIMS. They both expressed their strongly held view that Pranab Mukherjee should not be sworn in as interim prime minister, although he was high up in the hierarchy. Indira Gandhi had not formally nominated anyone as second in command in her cabinet though, informally, Mukherjee occupied such a position. By then chief ministers from the Congress-ruled states had arrived at the institute and were standing together on the eighth floor in one section of the verandah. I knew that a final decision on the succession issue could be taken only by Rajiv who was already on his way to Delhi from Calcutta. However, I thought it would be prudent to quickly ascertain the views of the chief ministers, the ministers and other senior members of the party present there on the question of succession. I sought the opinions of N.D. Tewari (chief minister of Uttar Pradesh), Janaki Ballabh Patnaik (chief minister of Orissa), Bhajan Lal (chief minister of Haryana) and Shiv Charan Mathur (chief minister of Rajasthan) and discussed with them the idea of having Rajiv sworn in as prime minister, thereby discarding the option of having an interim prime minister. All of them enthusiastically agreed with this idea. I then went to another section of the verandah and highlighted the salient points, to those present there, of my brief talk with the chief ministers. I found that everyone was in agreement with the suggestion that Rajiv should be administered the oath forthwith. (I was convinced that an interim arrangement with Pranab Mukherjee as prime minister, even for a very brief period, would not be acceptable to any senior Congress leader present at the institute.) Within a few minutes, Narasimha Rao reached the eighth floor. We embraced each other, without being able to control our tears. I told him quickly that there was unanimity among all the chief ministers and the ministers present at the institute that Rajiv should be sworn in directly as PM and he fully endorsed the proposal.

A few minutes earlier Maneka Gandhi had turned up on the eighth floor along with her son Varun. She was about to enter the room adjacent to the operation theatre when Mohammed Yunus, a very close friend of the Indira Gandhi family, whispered to me that Maneka should not be allowed inside the room. But I quietly pacified him through appropriate gestures. Maneka went inside the room without even noticing Yunus's exchange with me.

Rajiv arrived at 3.15 p.m. along with Pranab Mukherjee and Arun Nehru (one of Rajiv's cousins). After greeting us with folded hands, Rajiv quickly went inside the room adjacent to the operation theatre, where his wife Sonia Gandhi had been standing near the wall and sobbing. His face was filled with anguish, but he was trying to be calm and composed without being overly emotional.

I quickly told Pranab Mukherjee that everyone had agreed that Rajiv should be administered the oath of office as PM without going in for an interim arrangement. Without any hesitation, Pranab Mukherjee gave his assent to this suggestion. A group of individuals, with malicious intent, later spread a canard that Pranab Mukherjee had staked his claim to be sworn in as interim PM and had to be persuaded with great difficulty to withdraw his claim. The obvious objective was to create discord between Rajiv Gandhi and Pranab Mukherjee. But I should record here the true fact that Pranab Mukherjee had readily endorsed the suggestion I made to him.

While Rajiv was inside the room with Sonia, a serious controversy was brewing among the persons standing on the verandah of the eighth floor. Arun Nehru took me aside and told me in a very serious tone that Rajiv should be sworn in immediately by the vice-president without waiting for the president's arrival, scheduled for 5 p.m. Arun Nehru confirmed that he had obtained the approval of all the ministers present there as also that of the Lok Sabha speaker, Balram Jakhar. Parthasarathi and many others also strongly supported the proposal.

I was quite surprised to find that Arun Nehru and almost all the dignitaries present on the eighth floor believed that a swearing in by the vice-president was necessary to ensure Rajiv's assumption of office without any complication. They were of the view that President Zail Singh could not be trusted to accept Rajiv's nomination without a formal election by the Congress Parliamentary Party. They were genuinely apprehensive that because of the recent deterioration in the relations between Zail Singh and Indira Gandhi, he might use his position to prevent Rajiv from becoming prime minister and may administer the oath to Pranab Mukherjee as interim prime minister. Such a development could lead to serious difficulties as far as Rajiv's election later was concerned. I was more aware than anyone else present on the eighth floor of AIIMS at that time about the gravity of the strained relations between Indira Gandhi and Zail Singh. However, I was quite convinced that it would be ethically very wrong and politically very unwise if the president were made to feel that he had been deliberately denied the exercise of his most important responsibility, namely, choosing the prime minister and administering the oath of office to him. I was seriously worried that if Rajiv were administered the oath by the vice-president, Zail Singh would view this step as a challenge to his authority and may even take the extreme step of not recognizing the oath administered by the vice-president. Anyway, the president was on his way back to Delhi as quickly as possible. Zail Singh had not authorized the vice-president to exercise his functions in his absence.

While such thoughts were whirling around in my mind, I was also quite conscious of the fact that I had no official standing or authority to enforce my own views on the late prime minister's senior colleagues in her party. Whenever I had done so in the past, I did so with the confidence that I had the backing of the prime minister, but, theoretically, I had ceased to be principal secretary the minute Indira Gandhi was no more. I decided to take a determined stand on the issue of administration of the oath of office, as I wanted to ensure that the correct procedures were followed in such a crucial matter. No one at that time questioned my authority to press on with this line of action because the individuals present there always had great regard for me and trusted my sincerity. I turned to Shivshankar, the Union law minister, and asked whether or not he agreed with my views. He replied that he agreed that my stand was legally valid, but he was not prepared, at that point of time, to support it. Everyone knew very well that there was no time for holding a meeting of the Congress Parliamentary Party to formally elect Rajiv as leader. Recognizing this practical difficulty, I suggested that the Congress Party's Parliamentary Board could formally recommend Rajiv's name to the president, which could be ratified by the CPP later. However, Arun Nehru, supported by a few like-minded individuals, was quite firm in his stand that no risk could be taken in this matter. He asked me, in a very defiant tone, as to who would accept the responsibility for the consequences if Zail Singh refused to administer the oath to Rajiv. My immediate response was that the person who was the most concerned about, and who would be most affected by, this decision was Rajiv and, first of all, his own wishes in the matter ought to be ascertained. Arun Nehru declared that he would go into the room where Rajiv was standing with Sonia and talk to him, but I pre-empted him and I quickly went inside the room.

What I saw on entering the room was Rajiv clasping Sonia with both hands and earnestly conveying to her the message that he considered it his duty to take on the responsibility as prime minister. Sonia was holding him tightly and tears were rolling down her cheeks. She was pleading with him not to yield to the forceful request of his party colleagues to accept the top post. Rajiv was kissing her forehead repeatedly and trying to convince her that his duty was to abide by the decision of his party. Time was ticking away and I was very keen to talk to him. I went near the couple and gently touched Rajiv on the back of his shoulder to indicate that I had some very urgent work with him. He released himself from Sonia's arms and turned around to talk to me. Knowing that I would not have disturbed him unless the matter was very urgent and confidential, he quickly led me to the bathroom attached to the room so that we could talk without being noticed by anyone else who may enter the room.

I briefly informed him that the proposal of Arun Nehru and most of his senior partymen present there was to have him sworn in as prime minister by the vice-president without waiting for the arrival of the president, as they were concerned that Zail Singh might not agree to administer the oath to him without being first elected as leader by the CPP. Moreover, he may insist on appointing Pranab Mukherjee as interim prime minister, which could cause complications later. I then explained all the reasons why I personally felt that the correct and even prudent course would be to wait till the president arrived and asked him (Rajiv) for his own wishes on this matter. Rajiv listened to me patiently and, much to my relief, told me that he fully agreed with my views and that the risk, if any, was worth taking. He said he would talk to Arun Nehru later, but that I, for my part, should go ahead with making the necessary arrangements for the swearing in by the president, presuming that he would agree with the proposal. I came out of the bathroom and conveyed Rajiv's decision to everyone present on the eighth floor. Nobody raised any objection after that.

Time was racing by. At 4.10 p.m. Pranab Mukherjee and Narasimha Rao went to 1, Akbar Road to arrange for the meeting of the Congress Party's Parliamentary Board, which was to recommend to the president the nomination of Rajiv by the party for the post of prime minister. By this time, Krishnaswami Rao Saheb came to the eighth floor and we both met Rajiv again in the bathroom, to ascertain his views as to who all should be sworn in as ministers. Rajiv's immediate reaction was that the entire team of Indira Gandhi should be administered the oath. The cabinet secretary took his leave and made a dash for his office to make arrangements for the oath-taking ceremony and I made a beeline for 1, Akbar Road to meet Narasimha Rao and Pranab Mukherjee. All the ministers in Indira Gandhi's cabinet were present at 1, Akbar Road and I informed them about Rajiv's decision that he wanted all of them reinducted and requested them to be present at Rashtrapati Bhavan at 6 p.m. for the oath-taking ceremony. As swiftly as possible, the Congress Parliamentary Board passed a resolution nominating Rajiv Gandhi as the party's candidate for the post of prime minister and recommending his appointment for the consideration of the president. Rajiv had decided to wait at AIIMS for the arrival of the president as the news had been flashed that Zail Singh would be reaching the institute directly from the airport. I went along with Narasimha Rao and Pranab Mukherjee in the same car to Rashtrapati Bhavan and Buta Singh (another minister) followed us in another car. The plan was that Narasimha Rao and Pranab Mukherjee would meet the president as soon as he reached there from AIIMS and present to him the letter officially approved by the Congress Parliamentary Board.

Suddenly, a totally unexpected development took place. At the inner entrance to the Rashtrapati Bhavan, our car was stopped by a junior functionary. Although he recognized me (sitting in the front seat) and also the home minister and the finance minister (sitting in the back seat), he made it a point to glance through the document that contained the official list of visitors who were scheduled to meet the president that evening. Since our names were not on the list, he refused to let our car in. I stepped out of the car to reveal my identity and brought to his notice that two senior ministers were also present in the car. He replied that he knew our identities but he had no authority to let us in. My nerves were already on edge as a result of the severe mental strain imposed by the last few hours and I shouted at the top of my voice asking him to open the doors instantly to let our car in. He was, of course, merely doing his duty, but he did not appear to realize that that was not the occasion to satisfy the formalities for taking an appointment with the president, particularly when he knew who the three of us were. The man who had blocked our car then immediately signalled the sentry to open the gate and we went inside. The cabinet secretary later told me that he could hear my voice even from his office; probably my rage had got the better of me.

My top priority was to draft a condolence resolution to be moved at the first meeting of the Council of Ministers. While I was preoccupied with it, Rao Saheb darted in to tell me that he had just received a call from Rajiv to the effect that only Narasimha Rao, Pranab Mukherjee and Shivshankar were to be sworn in as ministers on that day; further expansion would be made after a day or two. This sudden change on Rajiv's part led to a somewhat embarrassing situation because all the ministers had already arrived at the Rashtrapati Bhavan and were waiting to be sworn in at 6 p.m.

Zail Singh reached Rashtrapati Bhavan along with Rajiv within a few minutes of these fast paced events; Arun Nehru and R.K. Dhawan also arrived there close on their heels. I met the president in his office immediately on his arrival and informed him that Narasimha Rao and Pranab Mukherjee were waiting to meet him. They were immediately called in and they gave the letter to the president. I came to know later that the president, as soon as he had arrived at AIIMS, had informed Rajiv that he wanted him to be sworn in as prime minister without going in for an interim arrangement. Thus, all apprehensions and misgivings on the part of the Congress leaders had proved unwarranted.

We all assembled at the magnificent Ashoka Hall at 6 p.m., the time fixed by the president for the ceremony. There was a delay of about forty minutes in the arrival of some of the dignitaries such as the president, the vice-president and Rajiv Gandhi at the venue as they were discussing some crucial matters among themselves in the president's office. Just five minutes before the start of the ceremony for oath taking, Arun Nehru informed me that Rajiv had decided to include Buta Singh also in the list of ministers to be inducted in the cabinet on that day.

The entire ceremony of administering the oath to Rajiv and his four cabinet colleagues was completed in twenty minutes and the first meeting of the new cabinet was held in the Rashtrapati Bhavan itself immediately thereafter. As soon as the cabinet met, the prime minister asked me to read out the resolution of condolence from the paper on which I had written it out rather hastily. I did so with my voice trembling; I also faced great difficulty in controlling my emotions. Everyone present was in a rather sombre and grim mood and we stood up silently, offering a prayer, for two minutes. The cabinet then took a series of decisions. The cremation was fixed for 3 p.m. on 3 November at Shanti Van (near Raj Ghat). The body was to be brought to 1, Safdarjang Road, Indira Gandhi's residence, immediately from AIIMS and from there it was to be taken to Teen Murti House (the official residence of Prime Minister Jawaharlal Nehru, where Indira Gandhi had lived for seventeen years) at 7.30 a.m. on 1 November. It was to lie there in state till the morning of 3 November. The news of her death had not yet been officially announced. It was decided that the announcement should be made immediately after the cabinet meeting.

From Rashtrapati Bhavan, Rajiv left for AIIMS to take his mother's body to 1, Safdarjang Road. I stayed back to brief Sharda Prasad, the PM's information adviser, about the cabinet decisions, which he was due to announce to the media immediately. The cabinet secretary and I held a hurried discussion about various arrangements to be made for the following three days and we left for our respective homes very late on that fateful night. I was quite aware of the need for informing Rajiv, as soon as possible, that I had ceased to be principal secretary to the prime minister and decided to do so the next day.

I went to 1, Safdarjang Road early in the morning (at 6.30 a.m) on 1 November along with my wife Ackama. Indira Gandhi's body was kept in the dining room and a few ladies who were close to her were sitting around and singing bhajans; Ackama joined them. Indira Gandhi's face appeared calm and serene in spite of the fact that her body had been riddled with nearly twenty bullets the previous day.

On 1 November 1984, the departure of the cortège from 1, Safdarjang Road was delayed a little as the face appeared to show some signs of swelling and family members wanted to be sure that the embalming had been done satisfactorily. The doctors, after careful examination, certified that there was no defect at all in the embalming. The body was lifted by Rajiv and some of us close to Indira Gandhi on to the gun carriage, which had been drawn up to the porch of the building from which Indira Gandhi used to depart in her car for her various assignments. Narasimha Rao, Pranab Mukherjee and I followed the gun carriage in my car. The journey from 1, Safdarjang Road to Teen Murti Marg took half an hour. Upon reaching our destination we lifted the body and took it to the room facing the porch of the Teen Murti House. We carefully laid the body on the specially erected platform with the upper part of the body slightly elevated so that the mourners passing through the porch could see her face properly.

Huge crowds had by now entered the premises of the Teen Murti House and were impatient to have a 'darshan' of Indira Gandhi. Rajiv and members of his family performed their *pranams* (salutations) first. I laid a wreath on behalf of the Prime Minister's Office and then a few more close friends followed suit.

The crowds by now had started moving towards the porch to get a glimpse of her face. Within a short time, we found that the hordes were becoming hysterical. Some people started shouting '*khoon ka badla khoon*' (blood for blood) in great anger. I was standing by Rajiv's side inside the room receiving some VIPs who had come to pay their last homage. Rajiv came on to the porch several times to pacify the crowds and asked them not to shout such slogans. However, fresh waves of people, overcome by uncontrollable emotions, surged forward demanding vengeance and the police had a very difficult time in controlling them.

At about 1.30 p.m. the multitude inside the premises of Teen Murti House became quite unmanageable in spite of all the efforts made by the police. Some individuals appeared to have worked themselves into such a state of intense frenzy that we were genuinely apprehensive that they might break open the doors and windows of the Teen Murti House in order to get inside. The cabinet secretary and I rushed immediately to the PM's House to apprise Rajiv of our apprehension that the police might not be able to control the situation at Teen Murti House. He decided that the Army should be called in immediately and given charge of the security arrangements there.

By this time information was pouring in that some places in the city had witnessed large-scale riots marked by murder, arson and pillaging and the police had not been successful in handling the situation. Rajiv agreed with us that here too the Army should take over the responsibility for maintaining law and order in the entire city. When Rao Saheb and I went back to Teen Murti House, we faced tremendous difficulty in negotiating our way to the place where the body was lying in state in spite of the police officers trying to clear the way. We noticed that frenzied mobs were banging on the window panes and doors of Teen Murti House in a desperate effort to get in. We telephoned the chief of Army Staff forthwith to inform him of the urgent need to send troops to the Teen Murti House to restore order there. By about 3 p.m. the Army contingent arrived and took charge to control the situation, after which the crowds became somewhat orderly and well behaved.

At 4.30 p.m. the ambassadors of various foreign countries resident in Delhi started arriving to pay their last respects. I stood by the side of Rajiv when he met them and acknowledged their condolences till about 6 p.m.

✧

By the evening of 1 November the riots had spread to many parts of the city and reports of the massacre of innocent Sikhs and destruction of their properties began coming in. A Control Room was quickly set up in the Cabinet Secretariat where the cabinet secretary, the home secretary and I spent most of our time in dealing with the problems as and when they arose. We were deeply worried about the likelihood of the situation in the city getting out of hand at a time when we had to receive large contingents of important foreign dignitaries who were coming to Delhi from all parts of the world to pay their homage to the departed leader.

✧

On 2 November a large number of prominent leaders from abroad came to the PM's Akbar Road office to offer their condolences, including Margaret Thatcher and Yashuhiro Nakasone, the prime ministers of the UK and Japan, respectively. The US delegation led by George Schultz (secretary of state) consisted of former ambassadors to India such as J.K. Galbraith, Robert Goheen, Daniel Patrick Moynihan and some senators who were close friends of Indira Gandhi. I was with the new prime minister when the VIPs started calling on him at 11.30 a.m. Some of them spoke very touchingly about Indira Gandhi; in fact, Senator J.S. Cooper broke down when he recalled his close friendship with her. Margaret Thatcher, dressed in solemn black, spoke with intense emotion about her warm friendship with Indira Gandhi and said how anguished she had felt when she came to know about the assassination.

After the VIPs left, Rajiv told me that he wanted me to continue as his principal secretary. He briefly discussed with me the functions handled by the senior officers in the PMO and stated that he would consider going in for a few changes in the PMO Secretariat and the PM's House after he had settled down.

✧

From 1, Akbar Road, I went to the Control Room in the Cabinet Secretariat. Here, more reports of killings and maiming of Sikhs and looting of their properties were flowing in from virtually all parts of the city. Very early on the morning of 2 November, Mother Teresa (whom we knew quite well) telephoned my wife to inform her that she had found most of the camps for the Sikhs (riot victims) to be in a miserable condition. When Mother Teresa said that she was setting out to visit other camps immediately, Ackama told her that she would accompany her. Pranab Mukherjee's wife too joined them and the trio went around the most affected areas in the forenoon of 2 November. They were perceptibly shaken by the horrible state of affairs they saw in these places. A few groups of kindhearted citizens had come forward at great risk to their life with food and drinking water for riot victims in some camps, but in the majority of the camps, even the basic necessities were not available. When the helpless people recognized Mother Teresa they started weeping. They beseeched her to provide them with water and blankets, as winter had set in. Obviously, the arrangements made by the Delhi Administration were totally inadequate to deal with magnitude of the problem in most camps. When my wife informed me about the abysmal conditions in these camps at about 2 p.m., I became convinced that only by entrusting the Central Government officers with the responsibility for providing relief could something be done for the affected people. I met the prime minister at 3 p.m. and recounted in detail the conditions in the camps as was described to me by my wife. He was shocked to hear my report. When he asked me as to what course of action needed to be taken, I replied that he should issue orders making the Central Government officials directly responsible for carrying out the relief work. I pointed out that the Delhi Administration was just not capable of handling such a massive exercise. I assured him that if he issued such an order, a committee of secretaries could be constituted as a 'Special Action Group' under the direction of the cabinet secretary. Such an arrangement, I emphasized, would help a great deal in bringing immediate relief to the beleaguered victims. He promptly agreed with my suggestion and added that he would like the cabinet secretary and me to report to him on the steps taken by 9 p.m. that day.

Rao Saheb immediately constituted a Special Action Group of the secretaries of the Ministries of Defence, Home, Transport, Health, Food, Commerce and Civil Supplies. He convened the first meeting of the group within a few minutes. A programme of action was chalked out and responsibilities of each member were clearly spelt out. Secretaries were instructed to ensure that relief reached *all* the camps in the city by 8 p.m. that day and that we should be kept informed regularly of the progress. Within an hour, relief in the form of tents, medicines, blankets, food and water started flowing into the camps. Temporary telephones were installed in all the camps to facilitate quick communication and the secretaries themselves started visiting the camps to guide the officers and other personnel deputed for duty there.

The lieutenant-governor of Delhi, P.G. Gavai, and some senior officers of the Delhi Administration were not very happy that the Central Government ministries and agencies had been handed over direct responsibilities for a task which was legitimately under their jurisdiction. Their views were, however, ignored; they were unambiguously told that they should take instructions from then on directly from the Special Action Group. By 8.30 p.m., the cabinet secretary and I received reports from the secretaries of every ministry/ department concerned that relief materials and facilities, including telephones and sanitary arrangements, had been put in place for all the camps. More importantly, proper security arrangements were made in every camp and, in sensitive locations outside each camp, senior officers were placed in charge of armed patrols to deal with emergency situations. Instructions were given to all ministries and departments of the Government of India that topmost priority should be accorded to the relief work and action should be taken without waiting for prior approval by the Finance Ministry or other authorities. In other words, red tapism should not obstruct humanitarian exigencies. I should state in this connection that Krishnaswami Rao Saheb handled the entire situation very capably and adroitly, displaying extraordinary qualities of leadership in crisis management. At about 9 p.m. Rao Saheb and I reported to the prime minister the encouraging results of the emergency operations undertaken by the Special Action Group.

In spite of all the arrangements made and all the precautions taken by the Central authorities for ensuring the security of the Sikhs affected by the riots, reports of violence against them continued to pour in from several parts of the capital. When the prime minister came to know about these reports, he decided that 'shoot-at-sight' orders should be enforced wherever rioters were seen indulging in violence or arson. These orders were given wide publicity in the media and through public announcements and they had a salutary impact in controlling the incidents of killing and looting.

Throughout the day and the night of 2 November, huge crowds continued to stream through Teen Murti House. The queues appeared unending. Nevertheless, it was decided that the public 'darshan' should be stopped at 6 a.m. on 3 November in order to prepare the body for the cremation and for making arrangements for the large group of VIPs to join the funeral procession.

A suitable site at Shanti Van had been selected for the cremation early on 3 November and work had started there for erecting the cremation platform. Also, meticulous arrangements for ensuring security for the large number of people, including several VIPs from foreign countries who were expected to attend the cremation, were being carried out. A stream of dignitaries such as chief ministers, governors and other special invitees (who were to join the funeral procession) started arriving at Teen Murti House from 10 a.m. onwards on 3 November. While the body was being prepared for the cremation, the governors and the chief ministers waited in the adjacent hall in Teen Murti House. I announced to them the arrangements made for the funeral procession and when and where they had to get into their cars to join the procession and other such details. Rajiv and members of the family arrived at 11 a.m. and went into the room where the body was kept. The president and the vice-president arrived by 11.30 a.m. to pay their last respects. I also offered my last *pranams* and waited for my turn to join the journey. The gun carriage was pulled by a team of soldiers, airmen and sailors and immediately behind the carriage Field Marshal Sam Manekshaw and the three chiefs of the armed forces took their positions. They were followed by Rajiv and the members of his family, the president, the vice-president, the chief justice of India, speaker, cabinet ministers and others, according to the sequence specified by protocol. The president, the vice-president and the governors took off from the Safdarjang Road premises and proceeded direct to Shanti Van. The cabinet secretary, the home secretary and I were travelling in the same car. We took another route and reached the cremation grounds well ahead of the cortège.

At the cremation site, I found that the seating arrangements made for the VIPs, particularly for the visitors from foreign countries, were not adequate, i.e., all of them could not be possibly accommodated. Consequently, I requested all the governors, who had already occupied the sofas reserved for them, to sit on the durries placed in front, so that their seats could be given to the guests from abroad, who would find it very awkward and uncomfortable to sit on the ground. Everyone cooperated, although some of them were subjected to inconvenience. I took along Mother Teresa, who was sitting in the VIP enclosure, to the place where the priests were singing bhajans (devotional songs), and she said a few words of prayer. President Zail Singh, who had arrived at the cremation site a little earlier, noted that no provision had been made for kirtans (religious recitation) by Sikhs. He immediately rectified this lapse. By this time the cortège had arrived at the entrance to the cremation site. At 3.15 p.m. the body was lifted out of the gun carriage and carried on the shoulders of Rajiv and other members of the family to the funeral pyre. All of them then went on to the cremation platform. The formal military and religious ceremonies connected with the cremation took about forty minutes. Rajiv lit the funeral pyre and he, along with other close relatives, went round the pyre putting sandal sticks into the fire. This moment in history shall remain imprinted in my memory forever. The president left at 4.45 p.m. followed by the foreign VIPs. The prime minister and members of his family departed at 5.30 p.m. and immediately after that so did we (the cabinet secretary and I).

By the time I reached home, after attending to other urgent work, it was well past midnight. Just then I received a telephone call – from the prime minister on an important matter and in answer to a query from him I replied 'Yes Sir'. All these years I had addressed him only as Rajiv and this was the first time that I was calling him 'Sir'. There was an embarrassing pause for a few seconds on the other side and then the prime minister asked me very softly: 'Dr Alexander why did you "Sir" me. You should not be doing that.' I then replied: 'From 31 October evening you are the prime minister of India and I am your secretary. I should address you either as "Mister prime minister" or "Sir". "Mister prime minister" sounds too formal for me. I would therefore prefer to address you as "Sir".' There was long pause at the other end of the telephone and obviously realizing that I had to observe a new protocol in my dealings with him, he resumed his conversation with me.

TEN

The Akali Agitation

A VARIETY OF ARTICLES AND BOOKS HAVE BEEN WRITTEN AND WILL continue to be written on Indira Gandhi's handling of the Akali agitation in Punjab, culminating in the military operation in June 1984. This operation, code-named 'Operation Blue Star', entailed an attack on the Golden Temple, Amritsar, Punjab. (The Sikhs regard this temple as their holiest shrine.) Most of these publications are highly critical of the manner in which she dealt with this agitation. Some writers have accused her of acting in haste by calling in the Army; they contend that she should have continued with the efforts for finding a *negotiated solution* to the problem. A few others have lambasted her for not taking action much earlier than June 1984, when, in their view, the police force could have proved adequate to evict the militants entrenched in the Golden Temple premises. Yet another criticism is that even while entrusting the operation to the Army the strategy should have been to flush out the militants by laying siege to the temple, by cutting of communication and transport facilities as well as the supply of food and water, instead of opting for a frontal assault.

As one closely associated with all behind-the-scenes discussions, decision-making processes and strategies concerning the Akali agitation during the period 1981–84, I am perhaps more in the know of the facts on this subject than most others who have written about it. I have always been conscious of my responsibility as a witness to history to present the facts correctly to the people at large. However, since I continued to occupy some important public offices after my tenure as principal secretary to the prime minister, I did not have the freedom to write about this subject till now.

After quitting as governor of Tamil Nadu in 1990, I had started publishing a series of articles describing my years with Indira Gandhi (which were later collated and published as a book in 1991). I wanted to include in it all the facts I knew about the Akali agitation in Punjab and how Indira Gandhi dealt with it. When I informally consulted Rajiv Gandhi for his opinion, he expressed his anxiety that the publication of certain facts might lead to unnecessary controversies. His advice was to postpone publication for some more time. But 'this some more time' turned out to be more than a decade as I was governor of Maharashtra till July 2002. Now that I am free from the trammels of office, I can place the full facts about the Akali agitation, as I knew them.

✧

Before proceeding to deal with the agitation launched by the Akalis in 1981, it would be necessary to give a brief historical background.

The Sikh community had always been in the forefront of the nationalist movement in spite of the fact that a large number of them had been serving in the Indian Army during the British rule. Many Sikh youths took to Army service as an honoured profession, while others had readily responded to the call of the national leaders and actively participated in various agitations against the foreign rule. One section of the Sikhs, however, was engaged in a different type of agitation from the early 1920s, i.e., for the protection of not only the interests of the Sikhs but also their separate identity as a community.

Even though the Sikhs were originally converts from the Hindu community, and many of their festivals, customs and rituals are common, they have always remained a separate community distinct from the Hindus. There exists some ambiguity as to what this 'separateness' really involved when the Sikhs resorted to words such as 'panth', 'qaum' and 'nation' to describe their community. Until the demand for 'Khalistan' (a separate sovereign state to be carved out of India) was raised by some militant groups within the community, their insistence on a separate identity meant a separate community. The demand for 'Khalistan' itself was confined to some groups of Sikhs living in foreign countries and had little support from the Sikh community in India. However, there has always been an undercurrent of fear among some sections of the Sikh community that they might lose their identity and get slowly absorbed into the Hindu fold unless they took special care to protect and preserve their distinctiveness.

The formation of assemblies of Sikhs, called Singh Sabhas, to ward off the growing influence of the Arya Samaj in the closing decades of the nineteenth century may be considered as the first organized effort by the Sikhs to protect their identity. From the early 1920s, they have been engaged in one agitation or the other in order to safeguard their religious interests. The agitation during 1920–25 to liberate their gurdwaras from the control of the *mahants*, who were accused of 'Hinduizing' the worship there, was the first major movement launched by the Sikhs. They gained a historic victory in 1925 when, after five years of agitation, the British conceded to the Shiromani Gurdwara Prabandhak Committee (SGPC) the right to manage their gurdwaras in Punjab. The Akali Dal (or Akali Party), which was formed during the mid-1920s, became the main forum for these groups to ventilate their grievances and has continued ever since as a party for championing both religious and political causes.

The urge for a separate identity in the post-independence (post-August 1947) years took the form of a demand for the Punjabi Suba or a separate state of Punjab within the Indian Union. The establishment of the States Reorganization Committee by the Centre in 1953 to consider the question of redrawing the boundaries of states on the basis of language provided an excellent opportunity to the Akalis to intensify their agitation. What they wanted was not merely a Punjabi-speaking state, but a state where the Sikhs would form the majority. This was a demand *based on religion* and not on linguistic identity, which therefore was not accepted by the Central Government.

The denial of a separate state for the Punjabi-speaking people, while the claims of most other linguistic groups were agreed to by the government, provided the Akalis with one motivating force badly needed to start a mass agitation, namely, grievance based on discrimination, on the basis of which they tried to win the support of the Sikh community. However, this move failed to get the backing of the majority of the community in the elections that followed.

The Akalis continued to maintain the posture of being the sole champions of Sikh rights and interests and tried to build up their political base by claiming to be crusaders against discrimination by the government. The Sikhs had undergone great hardship and intense persecution during the reign of some fanatic Mughal rulers. However, such trials and tribulations had failed to break their morale; they had always emerged stronger and more determined in the defence of their rights. Sufferings and sacrifices, therefore, always had a strong appeal to the Sikh psyche. The Akalis alleged that their religion was again in danger and tried to imbue their agitation with the characteristics of a religious crusade.

❖

The demand for a separate Punjabi Suba had been rejected by Jawaharlal Nehru as communal in nature, but, in 1966 Indira Gandhi conceded their request, though in a modified form, in an effort to win the goodwill of the Sikh community. Two new states, namely, the Hindi-speaking states of Haryana and Himachal Pradesh, were carved out of Punjab. The Sikhs had only a marginal majority in the remaining portion of the erstwhile state of Punjab, but they were happy that at last they had acquired a state where their community would be in a majority. However, the formation of two new states carried within it the seeds of further discontent.

The most important cause of dissatisfaction for the Akalis was that Chandigarh, the prestigious capital of the undivided state, had not been allotted to Punjab alone. A commission appointed by the Central Government headed by Justice J.C. Shah had recommended that Chandigarh – the city beautiful – should be the capital of the new state of Haryana only. However, this recommendation was not implemented and the city continues to be the joint capital for both the states, but administered by the Central Government as a Union Territory. The people of Punjab, both Hindus and Sikhs, considered it as the natural choice for the state capital and had expected that Haryana would be asked to build a new capital of its own. Justice Shah's recommendation allotting Chandigarh to Haryana triggered off protests and agitations in Punjab. Eventually, Chandigarh became the central issue of all the agitations launched by the Akalis who projected this as a deliberate act of injustice against the Sikhs.

In October 1969, the death (by fasting) of a highly respected leader of Punjab, Darshan Singh Pheruman, on the issue of allotting Chandigarh to Punjab, created an explosive situation. As a consequence, the Akalis were able to whip up a lot of support. Sant Fateh Singh, a charismatic leader, announced his intention to court death by immolating himself within the precincts of the Akal Takht (Amritsar) if the demand for the transfer of Chandigarh to Punjab was not conceded by the Central Government.

At this stage, Indira Gandhi intervened again and announced that Chandigarh would go to Punjab in toto, and, as a concession to the sentiments of the people of Haryana, a part of Fazilka *tehsil*, including Abohar in Ferozepur district of Punjab, would be transferred to Haryana. She also announced that a commission would be appointed to settle other claims and counterclaims for the readjustment of boundaries between the two states. These decisions were never implemented as the Akalis were unwilling to agree to the transfer of Abohar-Fazilka to Haryana, and Chandigarh continued to be the most intractable issue in all the agitations launched by the Akalis. Indira Gandhi's announcement on Chandigarh enabled Sant Fateh Singh to desist from his attempt at self-immolation but the Akali agitation against the government continued unabated.

With the passage of time, the list of grievances of the Akalis become longer. A turning point in their agitation was reached when a comprehensive charter of demands was formally approved by the party at its meeting at Anandpur Sahib on 16–17 October 1973. There have been different versions of the Anandpur Sahib resolutions, but the one published by the party described as the 'basic postulates of the Shiromani Akali Dal' has been acknowledged as the authentic version.

The Anandpur Sahib resolutions were a collection of vague and loosely worded suggestions and ideas that were partly an articulation of certain goals and objectives and partly a strident criticism of the Congress Party and the Central Government. The Akali's main concern about the preservation of the separate identity of the Sikhs comes out clearly in these resolutions. The Akali Dal is described as 'the very embodiment of the hopes and aspirations of the Sikh Nation'. With respect to the political goal of the Akali Dal, the resolutions point out that it 'is determined to strive by all possible means to have all those Punjabi-speaking areas deliberately kept out of Punjab such as Dalhousie in Gurdaspur district, Chandigarh, Pinjore, Kalka and Ambala Saddar (in Ambala district), the entire Una *tehsil* of Hoshiarpur district, the "Desh" area of Nalagarh, Shahabad and Gulha blocks of Karnal district, Tohana sub*tehsil*, Rati block and Sirsa *tehsil* of Hissar district and six *tehsils* of Ganganagar district in Rajasthan, merged with Punjab to constitute a single administrative unit where the interests of the Sikhs and Sikhism are specifically protected.'

The foregoing extravagant territorial claims were never insisted upon at any of the talks that the Akali Dal held with the Central Government's representatives during 1981–84. The only one put forward was that referring to Chandigarh. Probably, the Akalis realized only too well that if all the territories claimed in the Anandpur Sahib resolutions were added to Punjab, Punjab's identity as a Sikh-majority state might get compromised.

The most important part of the Anandapur Sahib resolutions was the one which referred to Centre–state relations: 'In this new Punjab and in other states, the Centre's interference would be restricted to Defence, Foreign Relations, Currency and General communication; all other important departments would be in the jurisdiction of Punjab (and other states) which would be fully entitled to frame their own laws on these subjects for administration. For the above departments of the Centre, Punjab and other states [would] contribute in proportion to [their] representation in the Parliament.'

The aggressive anti-Congress attitude of the Akalis was reflected in the resolution on foreign policy: 'The Shiromani Akali Dal strongly condemns the foreign policy of India framed by the Congress party. It is worthless, hopeless and highly detrimental to the interests of the country, the nation and the [*sic*] mankind at large.'

It may be pointed out here that even though Centre–state relations often figured in the talks between the Akalis and the government representatives, the former had never defined what exactly the federal set-up of their choice should be. The foreign policy which they condemned as 'worthless and hopeless' was never even casually mentioned in any of these talks. The Anandpur Sahib resolutions did not contain any of the religious demands of the Akalis that were to find top priority in the list of demands in the early 1980s.

The Anandpur Sahib resolutions, on the whole, did not create any serious impact on the community and they remained dormant for a long time. During 1977–80, the Akalis were running the government in Punjab in coalition with the Jana Sangh and were partners in the Janata Party Government at the Centre. During this period, it is important to note that the Akalis never raised the cry of Sikhism in danger; nor did they mount any pressure on the Central Government for the transfer of Chandigarh to Punjab. They launched the agitation only after they lost the elections in Punjab (1980) and ceased to have a share in the power equation at the Centre. This move led to the criticism against the Akalis that their agitation was really armed at gaining power, which they had failed to get through the democratic process of election.

When the agitation was launched, the Akali Dal was led by a triumvirate consisting of Harcharan Singh Longowal, Prakash Singh Badal and Gurcharan Singh Tohra, each having a distinct field of activity, but each in a way complemented the other. The head of the triumvirate was Longowal, the president of the Akali Dal. He was a religious figure respected by the community as a sant and had no political ambitions of his own. He could not converse in English and even his knowledge of Hindi was limited. He generally kept a low profile, but all calls for *morchas* (movements) and *bandhs* (total closure) on behalf of the Akali Dal were issued in his name, as were all party statements. Badal, who was the chief minister of Punjab during the Janata period, was the most articulate and was the acknowledged candidate for chief ministership if the Akalis were to regain power. Tohra, who had been president of the SGPC for several years, exercised tight personal control over the management of the gurdwaras. Like Longowal he too had very little knowledge of English and was not considered to be an aspirant for chief ministership. But he had acquired the reputation for being adept at manipulations and manoeuverings and was always a power to be reckoned with in Akali politics. The supremacy of the triumvirate was unquestioned in the party and for, all practical purposes, the triumvirate was the Akali Dal, till a new and much younger leader appeared on the scene with a new political philosophy and strategy of action in the form of Jarnail Singh Bhindranwale.

✧

In 1977, at the relatively young age of thirty, Bhindranwale rose to become the head of the Damdami Taksal, a fanatic religious group, which commanded tremendous respect in the Sikh community.

The Damdami Taksal, with its headquarters at Chowk Mehta (about 60 km from Amritsar), had been founded by one of the legendary heroes of the Sikh community, Baba Deep Singh, with the avowed object of producing intrepid warriors to protect the sanctity of the Golden Temple at Amritsar from the attacks of Ahmed Shah Abdali, the eighteenth-century Afghan conqueror.

True to the traditions of the Damdami Taksal, the new head took upon himself the responsibility of ensuring that the orthodox practices and original tenets of the Sikh religion did not get eroded or diluted by Hinduism or by certain new sects that had started attracting followers from the Sikh community. He also launched a crusade against the growing laxity on the part of the youth in observing the strict discipline and the immutable code of conduct of the Sikh faith.

One of the religious sects, which the orthodox Sikhs considered heretic, was the Nirankaris, who became the focused target of Bhindranwale's wrath. He started making highly provocative speeches from the precincts of the Golden Temple, instigating violence against them. The first major act of violence, which was to trigger off a series of such violent attacks in Punjab, took place in April 1978 when the Akalis were in power in Punjab and were partners in the Central Government. A group of Sikh militants, inflamed by a highly volatile anti-Nirankari diatribe of Bhindranwale, marched from the Golden

Temple to the venue where the Nirankaris were holding their convention and tried to assassinate the head of the Nirankari sect, Baba Gurbachan Singh. The Nirankaris, who were better prepared and better armed, fell upon the assailants and killed twelve of them. In the clash, three Nirankaris also lost their lives. The killing of the twelve Sikhs immediately set in motion a series of vehement protests by the Akalis and, in the bargain, Bhindranwale emerged as the main leader of the anti-Nirankari crusade. Meanwhile, a new party, called the Dal Khalsa, had been formed, which soon attracted the militant sections of the community. This party also became the main platform for Bhindranwale's activities.

Bhindranwale's public posture was that he was not interested in political activities and that his sole concern was the protection of the purity of the Sikh faith. But in Akali politics, there was no dividing line between religion and politics and for Bhindranwale also such a distinction had little relevance. Subsequent events showed how Bhindranwale's religious zeal got mixed up with Akali politics, leading to disastrous consequences for the Sikh community in particular and the country as a whole.

Bhindranwale's anti-Nirankari campaign continued unabated and reached a turning point with the cold-blooded murder of Baba Gurbachan Singh in April 1980 at his residence in New Delhi. By this time, Indira Gandhi had returned as the prime minister, and a respected Congress leader, Darbara Singh, had become the chief minister of Punjab. The murder of the Nirankari Baba sent shock waves through the country. What was more shocking was the reported statement of Bhindranwale that the assassins of the Nirankari Baba deserved to be weighed in gold and honoured at the Akal Takht. People were soon to get used to this type of blatant glorification of violence by Bhindranwale in the name of religion.

Akali politics itself took a new turn on 9 September 1981 when Lala Jagat Narayan, a respected editor of a newspaper and an elderly leader of the Hindu community of Punjab, who had strongly condemned the anti-Nirankari utterances and activities of Bhindranwale, was shot dead while travelling from Patiala to Jullundur. The police suspected Bhindranwale to be behind this murder and the Punjab Government issued a warrant for his arrest.

What followed later that month was a sordid episode of clumsiness, betrayal and bungling, which was to lead to sharp escalation of violence and confrontation between the Akalis and the government. When the arrest warrant was issued, Bhindranwale had gone to Chandokalan in Haryana. The government could have quietly carried out the arrest without publicizing its intention to do so and thus inviting a spate of avoidable violence. Bhindranwale escaped from Chandokalan and took refuge at the gurdwara at Chowk Mehta in his home territory. The Punjab police pursued him and surrounded the gurdwara where a large number of his followers had collected to forcibly prevent the arrest. The authorities vacillated and started negotiating with Bhindranwale to obtain his agreement for arrest. After five days of negotiation, Bhindranwale offered himself for arrest, but only after he had made a highly provocative speech. The arrest sparked off large-scale violence, resulting in the death of eleven supporters of Bhindranwale and injuries to many others.

The news of Bhindranwale's arrest and the ensuing death of many of his followers in police firing led to the outbreak of fresh violence in many parts of Punjab. Consequently, the authorities found themselves in open confrontation with the militant sections of the Sikh community all over the state. A cascade of violence soon seemed to engulf Punjab. Three Sikhs on motorcycles fired at Hindus in a market place at Jullundur in the violence following Bhindranwale's arrest; four persons were killed and twelve injured. On 21 September 1981, six Sikh militants opened indiscriminate fire at a bazar at Taran Taran, killing three persons and injuring thirteen others. On 26 September, a bomb exploded at the Central Telegraph Office at Patiala. On the same day, a goods train was derailed between Rayya and Butari railway stations in Amritsar district as a result of sabotage. Railway tracks were found tampered with in many other places and several incidents of bomb explosions were reported. On 29 September, an Indian Airlines plane was hijacked by Sikh militants to Lahore in Pakistan.

While violence and terrorist activities were spreading like wildfire across the state, the personal enmity between Darbara Singh, the chief minister of Punjab and Giani Zail Singh, the Union home minister, continued unabated, thereby seriously impairing the effective handling of the situation. Darbara Singh levelled a serious charge, confidentially, to the prime minister against Zail Singh that he had helped Bhindranwale to escape from Chandokalan. For his part Zail Singh accused Darbara Singh of ineptitude in handling the whole affair.

Events took a totally different turn when Zail Singh announced in Parliament that there was no evidence to connect Bhindranwale with the Jagat Narayan murder. Consequently, Bhindranwale was released on 15 October 1981. All that Bhindranwale needed was the halo of being the innocent victim of malicious persecution by the government and the government handed it to him on a platter. Bhindranwale's unconditional release considerably enhanced his prestige in the community and he emerged centre-stage as a great hero. He had been vociferously protesting that he had been needlessly implicated in the murder case. Moreover, the government's announcement of his innocence after a period of unnecessary detention showed up the powers that be in very poor light and exposed them to vitriolic castigation by the Akalis and the Sikh militants. It was against this background that Prime Minister Indira Gandhi decided to hold direct talks with the Akali leaders on the demands they had been persistently making.

✧

The first in the long series of talks initiated by the government in an attempt to find a peaceful solution to the Punjab imbroglio was held at the prime minister's office at Parliament House, New Delhi, on 16 October 1981.

The Akali delegation for the talks consisted of Longowal, Badal, Tohra, S.S. Barnala and Balwant Singh. The prime minister was assisted by Cabinet Secretary Krishnaswami Rao Saheb, Home Secretary T.N. Chaturvedi and me. For the first round of talks, Indira Gandhi did not want to involve the home minister, Zail Singh; consequently, no other minister was invited.

A pertinent question has often been asked as to why Indira Gandhi did not bring in Zail Singh the first time around, or on all subsequent occasions, except one, even though some other senior cabinet ministers were actively involved. One of the reasons could be that she harboured serious apprehensions that the presence of Zail Singh may lead to a stiffening of the attitude of the Akali leaders participating in the talks. The seniormost among them heartily disliked Zail Singh; this dislike had been aggravated during his tenure as the chief minister of Punjab. The Akalis seemed to believe that Zail Singh would be more interested in breaking the unity among the Akalis than in finding a solution to the problems. In fact, they believed, rightly or wrongly, that Zail Singh had been secretly grooming Bhindranwale to become a rival power centre in Punjab in order to weaken the Akalis' hold over the Sikh community.

Moreover, Indira Gandhi's conviction was that both Zail Singh and Darbara Singh should be kept out of the parleys, as she was apprehensive that their participation may provide another opportunity to both of them to try and undermine each other. She was particularly insistent that the internal politics of the Congress Party in Punjab should not be allowed to affect the outcome of the talks in any manner.

Another relevant question raised is: why did a strong leader like Indira Gandhi allow both Zail Singh and Darbara Singh to continue in their respective positions despite the fact that she knew that their mutual hostility was harming not only her party but also the interests of Punjab? The widely held view was that Zail Singh's appointment as home minister (in early 1980 when Indira Gandhi returned to power) could be largely attributed to the support he had received from Sanjay Gandhi, who, at that time, was playing a very important role in the politics of the country. Since I was not working with Indira Gandhi during that period, I cannot claim to have personal knowledge on this subject. All that I can say is that she was becoming increasingly unhappy with the continuing feud between Zail Singh and Darbara Singh. The latter had, on some occasions, complained to her about the home minister's attempts to run the Congress Party in Punjab by 'remote control' from Delhi. Indira Gandhi had hoped that upon becoming the Union home minister, Zail Singh would cease to behave as if he was still the leader of a Congress faction in Punjab. For his part, Zail Singh had always held the view that Darbara Singh's handling of the law and order situation was inept and had severely aggravated the problems in the state. He had not kept this opinion a secret; he expressed it in his talks with senior officials such as the cabinet secretary and me. However, Indira Gandhi was not contemplating any change in the positions of Darbara Singh and Zail

Singh. The underlying reasons were that both were dedicated party men and both were very loyal to her personally. Nevertheless, as mentioned in Chapter 7, Indira Gandhi's relations with Zail Singh became strained during the latter part of his tenure as president. Darbara Singh had perforce to be replaced when the law and order situation in Punjab suddenly worsened as a result of a sharp escalation in terrorist activities.

Yet another dimension could be that Indira Gandhi was aware of the fact that in 1981 the Congress in Punjab did not have many leaders of the stature of Zail Singh and Darbara Singh. In other words, no one there could replace them and, therefore, she was not inclined to do so at that point of time. With the alienation of Swaran Singh (a veteran Congress leader and a former Union minister), Zail Singh and Darbara Singh had emerged as two of the top leaders of the Congress in Punjab and the removal of either of them or both from their positions was seen by her as unnecessary or untimely.

❖

The Government of India had received from the Akali leaders in September 1981 a list of forty-five demands grouped under various subheads: religious, political, economic and social. One of the main grievances mentioned in this list was 'denial of internal autonomy to the state'. Another referred to 'rejecting the Anandpur Sahib resolutions and following a policy of divide and rule by inciting communal tensions'. Under the subhead 'economic demands', a series of shortcomings of a general nature had been mentioned. These included: (1) the failure to establish a dry port at Amritsar; (2) overall increase in prices; (3) a paucity of heavy industries in Punjab; (4) the failure to introduce a group insurance scheme in Punjab; (5) payment of non-remunerative prices for agricultural produce; and (6) non-payment of unemployment allowance.

In October 1981 the forty-five demands were whittled down to fifteen. The unconditional release of Bhindranwale was at the top. The revised list, consisted of certain 'religious' demands as well as 'political and economic' ones.

The religious demands included the following: (1) permission for Sikhs to carry *kirpans* (short, curved swords) in domestic and international flights; (2) passing of an All-India Sikh Gurdwara Act; (3) grant of holy city status to Amritsar; (4) installation of 'Harmandir Radio' at the Golden Temple to relay *kirtans;* and (5) renaming of the Flying Mail as 'Harmandir Express'.

The political and economic demands included the following: (1) the restriction of the powers of the Central Government on the lines recommended by the Anandpur Sahib resolutions; (2) merger of all Punjabi-speaking areas with Punjab; (3) granting a licence for a new bank in the place of the Punjab and Sind Bank 'which should be under Sikh control'; and (4) remunerative prices for agricultural products by linking them to the price index of industrial products.

The discussions at the meeting on 16 October 1981 focused mainly on the religious demands and on the transfer of Chandigarh to Punjab. As Bhindranwale had been released one day prior to the meeting, the demand for his release became a non-issue. The political and economic demands were never raised at the talks and, in fact, faded out of the agenda during subsequent discussions as well. The talks were held in a cordial atmosphere and the Akali leaders were assured by Indira Gandhi that their demands, particularly the religious ones, would be given urgent consideration.

Soon, it became clear that the Akali triumvirate (Longowal, Badal and Tohra) and the other two moderate leaders (Barnala and Balwant Singh), while disassociating themselves from the terrorist activities unleashed by Bhindranwale and his group, were trying, at the same time, to use terrorism as an instrument to pressurize the government to fulfil their demands. They pointed out that the Sikhs would eventually choose the path of terrorism if the government did not accept the demands of the moderates now. Their tactics involved forcing the government to appreciate their stand that they themselves could not settle for anything less even if they wished, because of the growing support for the militants within the Sikh community. The top-level Akali leaders did not do anything to discourage terrorism. In fact, they did not even openly condemn terrorism, while they still had the power and influence over the community because they thought that the parallel violence unleashed by the militants could strengthen their bargaining position with the government. But as subsequent developments showed, they lost control over the course of events, and the monster of terrorism, once allowed to thrive, could not be tamed or controlled by them.

On the day Indira Gandhi was holding talks with the Akali leaders (16 October 1981), the militants struck at a vital target: the Punjab Government Secretariat itself. Niranjan Singh, an IAS officer belonging to the Nirankari sect, was attacked and seriously wounded and his brother killed. More acts of violence and terror soon followed. On 23 October, Mohinder Pal, a Hindu *sarpanch* (headman) of Panchta village in Kapurthala district was slain. The terrorists exploded a bomb on 14 November right in the office of the deputy inspector general of police, Patiala, proving that they could strike even at heavily guarded places. On 19 November, a police party was fired upon at village Daheru in Ludhiana district; an inspector of police and a constable lost their lives. Needless to say, these attacks led to considerable demoralization among the police forces.

Against the background of rapidly spiralling violence, Indira Gandhi held a second round of talks with the Akali leaders on 26 November 1981 at the Parliament House, New Delhi. The Akali delegation consisted of the same five leaders who had come for the first round. This time around the prime minister was assisted by Narasimha Rao, the minister for external affairs, Krishnaswami Rao Saheb, the cabinet secretary, T.N. Chaturvedi, the home secretary, and me. Once again, Home Minister Zail Singh was left out.

The religious and territorial demands again dominated the discussions. Indira Gandhi explained to the Akali leaders that there had never been any formal recognition of Banaras as a holy city, as claimed by them, as a precedent in support of their demand for such a recognition for Amritsar. As regards banning of the sale of liquor and tobacco in Amritsar, she explained that the local authorities in Hardwar (then in Uttar Pradesh) and Kurukshetra (Haryana), two other important pilgrim centres, had imposed restrictions on the sale of meat and liquor in certain demarcated areas and similar restrictions including those on sale of tobacco could be imposed within the precincts of the Golden Temple at Amritsar too. On the question of installing a radio station within the Golden Temple, it was explained that no private group was allowed radio broadcasting facilities anywhere in the country and no exception could be made in this case. However, the prime minister affirmed that the government would arrange for the relay of *kirtans* from the Golden Temple through the Jullundur station of All India Radio. The Akalis were asked to provide the necessary facilities for arranging such relays.

Regarding the demand for carrying *kirpans* on international flights, the delegation was informed that Air India (India's international airline) was bound by worldwide rules and regulations and could not make any exception in favour of one group of passengers. As regards flights on domestic airlines, the government was prepared to allow the Sikhs to carry *kirpans* but of smaller sizes.

Whereas the government's willingness to grant the foregoing concessions was adequate to assuage the genuine concerns of the community, it was disinclined to accept the demand for an All India Gurdwaras Act covering all historical gurdwaras straightaway. The government forcefully maintained that such an enactment would affect the rights of the gurdwaras in states outside Punjab. Therefore, consultations with the authorities of all such gurdwaras were necessary. The Akalis themselves were not clear as to what they meant by 'historical' gurdwaras; nor did they have an agreed list of such gurdwaras. The discussions on this issue remained inconclusive at this meeting, but Indira Gandhi thought that there would be general satisfaction among the Sikhs as a result of the readiness with which the government came forward to fulfil their demands wherever possible.

As mentioned earlier, one of the demands of the Akalis had been that an express train should be named after the Golden Temple or Harmandir. In the original list of forty-five demands, the Akalis had charged the government with deliberate discrimination in not naming 'any train as Golden Temple Express while 15 trains have been named after other religious places'. In the revised list of fifteen demands there was a specific suggestion that the Flying Mail be renamed as 'Harmandir Express'. The government representatives pointed out that they had no objection to naming a train after the Golden Temple, but they would not agree to the ban of tobacco on the train or entertain any request to maintain any religious association with the train. Some media reports revealed the Flying Mail's notoriety for always running late and the inappropriateness of associating the name of such a train with a holy place! The Akalis themselves realized later that if this demand was accepted by the government, it may turn out to be an embarrassing achievement for them and, therefore, did not press for it.

Another subject that cropped up during these talks was the dispute regarding the sharing of the surplus waters of the rivers Ravi and Beas between Punjab and Haryana. In this context, the Punjab agriculturists had always maintained that the formula announced in May 1976 by the Government of India had been unfair to Punjab and required a review. The main support for the Akali Dal came from the agricultural classes and, therefore, the Akalis had assumed the role of a champion in safeguarding the interests of the Punjab farmers. In the revised list of fifteen demands, they had asked for the 'handing over of dams and headworks in the state to Punjab and redistribution of river waters as per national and international rules'. What, in effect, they were demanding was the scrapping of the 1976 notification and a much larger share of river waters for Punjab. Indira Gandhi was, from the beginning, sympathetic and had asked us to examine the possibility of accommodating the Akalis' demand on this issue without, at the same time, damaging the interests of the neighbouring states such as Haryana and Rajasthan. She assured the Akalis that she herself was looking into the entire problem of equitable sharing of waters and she was hopeful of providing Punjab an increased flow and that discussions were going on between the officials of the Central Government and those of the Governments of Punjab and Haryana. We were all optimistic about finding a satisfactory solution to this problem.

We got the distinct impression that the Akalis were fairly satisfied with the assurances given by the prime minister and we sincerely thought that the Akali leadership would not opt for a confrontation with the government. But it soon became clear that the moderate leadership of the Akali party was fast losing its grip over the agitation and the militant sections in the community were no longer under the control of the Akali triumvirate.

The militants stepped up their terrorist activities immediately after the talks, thereby frustrating any chance of reaching a peaceful settlement with the government. On 29 November 1981, a massive explosion took place within the gurdwara at Chowk Mehta, in which three inmates were killed. It conclusively proved that this gurdwara was being used for the preparation and storage of explosives. The government had been regularly receiving reports on the procurement and hoarding of arms and explosives by the followers of Bhindranwale. The reports also indicated that many gurdwaras were being used for the training of terrorists and storing arms. Intelligence reports clearly pointed to the possibility of large-scale escalation of violence by the Sikh militants, who had declared publicly that they were against *any compromise on their demands*.

Meanwhile, Indira Gandhi decided to announce a fresh deal on the sharing of surplus waters between Punjab and Haryana in the hope that it would satisfy the Punjab farmers and help defuse the tension that had been built up on this issue. She herself held several discussions with the officials dealing with this subject and also with the chief ministers of Punjab, Haryana and Rajasthan. Finding a formula to satisfy both Darbara Singh and Bhajan Lal, the chief minister of Haryana, was not easy, but she used the full potential of her prestige and authority as much as her persuasive skills to make the chief ministers agree to a new formula, which she thought was fair to all parties concerned. The estimated availability of surplus waters on the basis of which the earlier allocation formula had been arrived at was 15.85 million acre feet (MAF). Subsequent studies by the Central Irrigation Department, which were not seriously disputed by any party, showed that a total of 17.17 MAF was now available for allocation. According to the new formula arrived at after Indira Gandhi's discussions with the chief ministers in December 1981, the entire additional water available for allocation was to be given to Punjab alone. Thus, Punjab's share was raised to 4.22 MAF, whereas Haryana's share remained at 3.50 MAF. An agreement was also reached that until such time as Rajasthan was in a position to utilize its full share, by completing the canal infrastructure required for this purpose, Punjab would be allowed to use that surplus water.

All those who had participated in the protracted discussions leading to this agreement were convinced that Punjab had been given a fair deal. They also felt that for Haryana, the possibility of the early completion of the Sutlej–Yamuna link canal was adequate compensation for not getting any increase in its share. But our optimism was soon proved to be misplaced, as the Akalis condemned the December 1981 agreement as a betrayal of Punjab's interests and announced their decision to intensify the agitation on this issue. Further, as will be explained later, the Akalis started extending their claims on all surplus waters, thereby frustrating all attempts to reach a settlement among the states concerned.

Sensing the possibility of further escalation in the intensity of the agitation, Indira Gandhi made one more attempt to find an agreed solution to the demands of the Akalis by inviting their leaders for a third round of talks. These talks were held on 5 April 1982 and lasted well over two and a half hours. For the first time, Zail Singh, the Union home minister, was invited to participate in the talks, though he remained silent throughout. The Union finance minister, Pranab Mukherjee, also attended this meeting. Krishnaswami Rao Saheb, T.N. Chaturvedi and I were the government officials present. The Akali delegation consisted of, besides the triumvirate (Longowal, Badal and Tohra), Balwant Singh, Bhan Singh, P.S. Oberoi and Ravi Inder Singh.

Right from the commencement of the meeting it was clear to us that the Akali leaders had come prepared to force a breakdown of the talks. They vehemently criticized the December 1981 agreement on the sharing of waters and questioned the bona fides of the government in withdrawing the case on this issue, which had been filed by the previous Akali Government in the Supreme Court. Indira Gandhi's repeated assurance that she would find other ways of compensating Punjab, if the Akalis still felt aggrieved by the December 1981 agreement, made no impact.

The Akalis brought up various other issues in support of their view that the government was discriminating against the Sikhs. Their grievances included: (1) alleged reduction in the recruitment of Sikhs to the Indian Army; (2) persistent harassment of Sikh farmers in the Terai region of Uttar Pradesh; and (3) the denial of second-language status to Punjabi in Haryana, Rajasthan and Himachal Pradesh. We, the officials present at the meeting, furnished relevant facts and figures to prove that there had been no discrimination against the Sikhs on any of the points raised by them, but they were unwilling to accept our data and explanations.

Indira Gandhi was scheduled to make an official trip to Punjab on 8 April to inaugurate the Sutlej–Yamuna link canal. The Akalis found in this visit too good an opportunity to miss: they planned to stage a demonstration that would attract attention all over India. The irony of the entire situation was that the construction of the Sutlej–Yamuna canal had been agreed to by the Akalis themselves when they were in power in Punjab (1977–80). They had already succeeded in whipping up intense passions among the Sikh farmers about the alleged betrayal of their interests by the ruling Darbara Singh Government. They had unleashed the propaganda that Indira Gandhi was sacrificing the interests of the Punjabi Sikhs in order to win the support of the Hindus of Haryana and Rajasthan. Consequently, the Akalis asserted that they were compelled to call for a protest meeting to launch the mass agitation that they had been trying to organize in support of their various demands.

Despite such provocations, Indira Gandhi tackled the situation with immense patience and great tact. In fact, she was quite accommodative in her responses, contrary to the accounts put out by the Akalis and to some versions that have since appeared in different publications. Immediately after leaving the meeting venue, the Akalis unilaterally announced that the talks had failed. They appeared to be determined not to lose the political mileage gained by holding a mass protest demonstration at the same place and date as announced for the prime minister's meeting. Moreover, they wanted to create the impression that the protest was being organized by them since the talks had failed in spite of all earnest efforts for a peaceful settlement on their part.

✧

For their part, the chief ministers of Punjab and Haryana strongly felt that the protest demonstration to be organized by the Akalis on 8 April 1982 should be banned and that force should be used, if necessary, to prevent them from going ahead with their programme.

Indira Gandhi was away on a visit to Jammu on 6 April. I met her at the airport immediately on her return on the same evening and reported to her the views of the two chief ministers. She did not agree to their proposal to ban the demonstration. Instead, she decided to advance the inaugural function to 11 a.m. on 8 April from the previously scheduled time of 3 p.m. so that there would be no possibility of a clash between the two groups of people attending the two meetings. Eventually, nearly two lakh people flocked to attend the inaugural meeting addressed by Indira Gandhi and the Akali protest later in the day attracted relatively very little attention.

The Akalis, however, did not give up their idea of a *morcha* (movement) on this issue. On 24 April, they launched a *nahar roko*, or 'block the canal', agitation. In spite of repeated attempts to gain mass approval on this issue, the agitation petered out without getting any appreciable support from the Sikh farmers.

The Punjab agitation by now was being conducted at two levels: at one level by the Akalis through protest meetings, *nahar roko* and other such demonstrations, and, at the other, by the militants through provocative acts of deliberate violence.

According to the 1981 census, the Sikhs accounted for 60.75 per cent of Punjab's population and the others for 39.25 per cent. Bhindranwale adopted tactics that would provoke communal incidents and frighten the Hindu minority in Punjab and force as many of them as possible to leave the state. The militants simultaneously wanted to bring into Punjab those Sikhs who had settled down in large numbers in other states such as Haryana, Rajasthan, UP and Bihar. For decades, the Sikhs and Hindus had been living in perfect harmony and friendship in these places; the former had no desire whatsoever to migrate to Punjab. But according to the calculations of the militants a large-scale influx of Sikhs into Punjab would make it a decisive Sikh-majority state and would eventually lead to the realization of their goal, i.e., acquiring a separate sovereign state called 'Khalistan'. They were not particularly bothered about the huge human cost involved in uprooting millions of people and about the killing of innocent Sikhs and Hindus who did not harbour any hatred for each other. They were convinced that killing of innocent people was justifiable if such killings helped their cause. Consequently, they deliberately resorted to blatant acts of sacrilege to provoke Hindu–Sikh clashes.

On 26 April 1982, two severed heads of cows were found hanging in two Hindu temples at Amritsar and as news of this outrageous act spread, it inflamed Hindu feelings. For the Hindus this heinous deed was the ultimate affront to their religious sentiments. The audacity of this sacrilege made many Hindus take to the streets in different parts of the state. What was more provocative was the statement issued by an organization known as the Dal Khalsa claiming responsibility for this act.

Indira Gandhi was deeply shocked by these events and was rather worried about the possible repercussions on other states. She asked us to immediately alert the law and order authorities in all North Indian states to remain vigilant to prevent a possible backlash from the Hindu community. She instructed that they should take the strictest possible measures to put down communal violence if it flared up. She was constantly relaying us instructions over the telephone till very late on the night of 26 April about the steps to be taken in regions with large Sikh populations such as Delhi, Haryana and some parts of UP to prevent any retaliatory action by the Hindus. She mentioned to me several times how the communal carnage of the partition days spiralled out of control because of the failure of the authorities to anticipate backlashes. She emphasized that this incident should not be allowed to reach to such a situation. By early morning of 27 April reports came to us from all potential trouble spots that there had been no major backlash on the part of Hindus. These reports indicated that even though the police had to resort to *lathi*-charges and use of tear gas in some places, the situation on the whole in Punjab and the neighbouring states had remained peaceful. The expectation of the militants that they could provoke a major communal holocaust had been frustrated mainly by the good sense prevailing among the common people. On 1 May 1982, the government declared two organizations, namely, the Dal Khalsa and the National Council of Khalistan, as unlawful.

When the militants found that their attempts to provoke large-scale Hindu–Sikh clashes had failed, they unleashed a series of indiscriminate killings without bothering as to who the victims were.

Their main objective was to create conditions of panic and anarchy. On 22 May, four Sikh militants opened fire in the main bazar at Patti in Amritsar district, killing four persons and injuring several others. On 27 June, three Sikhs on a motorcycle fired at three Hindus in Amritsar town. On the same day, Joginder Singh Sant, the propaganda secretary of the Nirankari Mandal, was shot at and injured at Dhabuji in Amritsar district. In connection with this incident, the police arrested Bhai Amrik Singh, president of the All-India Sikh Student Federation (AISSF) and a close associate of Bhindranwale. On 19 July, Bhindranwale launched a *morcha* to protest against Amrik Singh's arrest and exhorted Sikh youths to court arrest in front of the deputy commissioner's residence. On 21 July, Sikh militants hurled a bomb into the main bazar of Moga in Faridkot district. A rickshaw puller died and five others were wounded.

The opportunity provided by the call for a *morcha* by Bhindranwale was instantly seized upon by the Akali leaders to launch a *dharam yudh* (religious war) against the government. Thus, two simultaneous movements against the government were on: one launched by Bhindranwale to secure the release of Bhai Amrik Singh and the other by the Akali leaders in support of their various demands. Bhindranwale decided to merge his *morcha* with the *dharam yudh*. By acquiescing in this 'merger', the Akali leaders tacitly condoned the terrorist activities of militants. For the first time, the fig leaf, attempting to cover the fact that the Akali leadership was against the Bhindranwale-type of terrorism, was removed and now both the moderates and the militants joined hands in a no-holds-barred war against the government.

On 4 August 1982, the day the *dharam yudh* was proclaimed, an Indian Airlines plane on a flight from Delhi to Srinagar via Amritsar was hijacked with 126 passengers on board, by a Sikh militant, and was forced towards Lahore. The plane was refused permission by the Pakistani authorities to land there and was brought back to Amritsar, where the hijacker was arrested.

On 20 August, another Indian Airlines plane, on a flight from Jodhpur in Rajasthan to Delhi was hijacked and again taken to Lahore. Again, the Pakistani authorities refused permission and it was then diverted towards Amritsar. The hijacker was killed at Amritsar airport in a shoot-out. On the same day, Darbara Singh, the chief minister of Punjab who was on a visit to Rahon in Jullundur district, was attacked with hand grenades by some Sikh militants. Darbara Singh escaped unhurt, but eighteen persons, including the education minister of Punjab, sustained injuries.

An unfortunate accident occurred on 11 September 1982 resulting in the death of more than thirty Akali agitators when the vehicle carrying them rammed into a moving train at an unmanned railway crossing at Taran Taran. This was clearly an accident, but it was given a sinister twist by Bhindranwale who stridently declared it as a deliberate killing of Sikh agitators by the government. Such a statement from Bhindranwale could have been expected, but what was astounding was that even Longowal concurred with Bhindranwale. Whether or not the Akali leaders really believed in the version put out by them, the very fact that such a statement could be issued by them was indicative of the depth to which their relations with the government had sunk after the launching of the *dharam yudh*. The agitators who died in this accident became instant martyrs. Violent demonstrations were held in several places to protest against the so-called 'deliberate killings'. One such massive demonstration was held on 11 October 1982 in front of Parliament House, New Delhi. This demonstration marked the conclusion of a mourning procession that had started from Anandpur Sahib carrying the ashes of the victims of the accident. By organizing this demonstration in New Delhi, the agitators were trying to drive home the point that they could take their *dharam yudh* right up to the capital.

As the *dharam yudh* spread rapidly and grew in intensity, the fact that the militants had acquired considerable expertise in using bombs and explosives became evident. On 26 October 1982 two hand grenades were thrown at a Dussehra procession near the Golden Temple, killing a Hindu youth and a constable and injuring many others. Explosions occurred on 12 and 13 November at various places in Jullundur, Faridkot and Gurdaspur districts, affirming the fact that the militants could strike simultaneously in several places at will.

In a bid to intensify their efforts, the Akalis announced that they would carry the agitation right up to the venue of the Asian Games in Delhi, due to commence on 19 November 1982. Elaborate

preparations had been going on for many months for the first-ever
mega event to be hosted by India and teams from almost all Asian
countries and observers from all over the world started arriving in
Delhi. In spite of receiving intelligence reports on the Akalis' plans
to obstruct the Asiad, none of us in the government really thought
that they would ever go to such an extent. The Sikhs were ardent sports
lovers and many of them were representing India in the Asian Games.
Above all, the Sikhs were second to none in their zeal for defending
the honour of the country and no one could believe that the Akalis
would do anything to damage the country's fair name by disrupting
an international sports event. As the date for the commencement of
the Asiad approached, the militants began stepping up the scale of
violence. They resorted to new techniques of terror by going in for
sophisticated explosive devices. The leadership of the Akali Dal appeared
to have accepted terrorism as a component of the *dharam yudh*.

A large section of nationalist-minded Sikhs were by now getting
seriously concerned at the growing rift between the government and
members of their community. They were particularly anxious to
discover the increasing support that the militants were receiving from
the younger generation. One such nationalist Sikh was Amarinder
Singh, a descendant of the Patiala royal family. He was a Congress
MP but had established very close contacts with most of the top Akali
leaders and enjoyed their trust. He was particularly close to Ravi
Inder Singh, former speaker of the Punjab Assembly and an active
Akali loyalist. These two young men and a few like-minded individuals
were also concerned at the alienation developing between the Sikhs
and the Hindus and were particularly worried at the prospects of
the Akali agitation slipping into the hands of the militants. They were
keen to do whatever they could to prevent this eventuality. Amarinder
Singh was a confidant of Indira Gandhi and he knew Rajiv well. He
had met me at my residence on several occasions to express his
anguish at the rapidly worsening situation in Punjab and offered his
services to bring the senior Akali leaders back to the negotiating table
if the government would welcome such a move. He pointed out that
the talks at the prime minister's level had not led to a solution,

though the Akalis had succeeded in securing satisfactory assurances from her on most of their religious demands. Therefore, Amarinder Singh suggested that the government could consider holding informal talks with the Akali leaders at levels lower than the prime minister's to begin with. He felt that such talks had to be held secretly without any publicity. If the secret talks proved satisfactory, the Akali leaders could go in for further talks with the prime minister. Amarinder Singh's expectation was that the Akali leaders would be more flexible in their stand during the secret talks.

The prime minister readily agreed to the suggestion of government representatives holding informal secret talks with the Akali leaders. She asked me to go ahead with making arrangements and I conveyed the PM's message to Amarinder Singh, who promptly confirmed that the Akali leaders would arrive in Delhi for talks on 16 November. In order to maintain the secrecy and informality of the talks, we all agreed that the venue should be my residence located at 27, Safdarjung Road, New Delhi.

On 15 November evening, Amarinder Singh came to my residence along with Balwant Singh and Ravi Inder Singh for an informal exchange of views. I told them that the prime minister's instructions were to explore all avenues for an early settlement, but at the same time, the agitators should not get the impression that the government would make concessions under the threat of violence at the forthcoming Asian Games. They assured me that the Akali leaders were coming for the talks in a spirit of cooperation and goodwill and expressed optimism about the prospects of reaching a settlement.

As scheduled, the talks started on 16 November at my residence in an atmosphere of amity and cordiality. The Akali delegation consisted of Prakash Singh Badal, Balwant Singh, Ravi Inder Singh and R.S. Bhatia. The government was represented by Defence Minister R. Venkataraman, Home Minister P.C. Sethi, Law Minister Shivshankar, Home Secretary T.N. Chaturvedi and myself. Amarinder Singh was present throughout the talks as an observer. He intervened only to iron out differences or make a helpful suggestion.

We did not face any serious difficulty in arriving at an understanding on the various religious demands as the prime minister herself had already indicated the government's positive response during her earlier meetings with the Akali leaders. We agreed to put this understanding in writing as part of the minutes of the discussions.

On the sharing of river waters, the government representatives agreed with the Akali demand that the entire issue should be referred to a tribunal to be appointed by the Supreme Court. The Akalis were opposed to the agreement of December 1981, which they described as a betrayal of the interests of the Punjab farmers. By agreeing to refer the dispute to a tribunal now, the government was, in fact, making a major concession to the Akalis.

On the question of Centre–state relations, the Akalis did not have a clear stand. All that they seemed to be interested in was in getting a commitment from the government that a committee of experts would be appointed to go into all aspects of the matter.

Chandigarh proved to be the most vexatious issue at these talks. The government side pointed out that Chandigarh could be transferred to Punjab without any delay, but there should be a simultaneous transfer of the Abohar-Fazilka region to Haryana. But the Akalis insisted on the immediate transfer of Chandigarh without any quid pro quo. We explained that if the Central Government agreed to the transfer of Chandigarh to Punjab without any territorial concessions to Haryana, this step may mark the end of one agitation in Punjab, but it may also mean the start of a new one in Haryana. In spite of prolonged discussions on various alternative suggestions regarding the territorial issue, we could not reach any agreement on Chandigarh. Hence, we decided that the talks should be resumed on 17 November.

When we met again at my residence on 17 November, the discussions centred mainly on the question of the transfer of Abohar-Fazilka to Haryana. The Akalis suggested that the agreement reached on other issues could be announced including that on the transfer of Chandigarh to Punjab, but they persisted that the claims of Haryana on Abohar-Fazilka ought to be referred to a committee. The government side could not agree to this demand, as it would be unfair to Haryana. The meeting concluded without arriving at any agreement on the territorial issue. Eventually, it became clear that if no satisfactory agreement on the Chandigarh issue could be reached, the agreements on other issues would *not* lead to the withdrawal of the agitation by the Akalis.

In a bid to salvage something, the Akali side informally put forward a suggestion to me on 18 November that the government could announce an agreement on all issues including the transfer of Chandigarh to Punjab, but state that the discussions on the future of Abohar-Fazilka would be resumed after the Asiad. Potentially dicey factors such as the threat of demonstrations at the venue of the Asiad and that of the disruption of the games were looming large. Consequently, considerable public interest was focused on the results of the talks. Home Secretary Chaturvedi and I consulted the three cabinet ministers (who had participated in the talks) on the new suggestion received from the Akali side. All three agreed that an announcement on the lines proposed could be made. They felt that there was never any doubt about the claim of Punjab over Chandigarh; the only controversial issue was the transfer of territory, as compensation, from Punjab to Haryana. By announcing the postponement of the discussions on this issue to a date after the Asiad, we were not in any way prejudicing the interests of Haryana. At any rate, the formal transfer of Chandigarh to Punjab would not have taken place *without* a satisfactory settlement of Haryana's claim on Abohar-Fazilka. All of us who participated in the talks (on behalf of the government) agreed that we should recommend the acceptance of the new Akali suggestion to the prime minister. We also agreed that, after getting the final clearance from Indira Gandhi, the home secretary should fly to Amritsar on 18 November itself to obtain the concurrence of Longowal and his colleagues in the Akali Dal high command to this suggestion and then announce the decision over television and radio on the same day (i.e., 18 November) itself.

At this stage, some unforeseen developments took place, which prevented the formal conclusion of the proposed agreement between the government and the Akalis. Just an hour or so before the home secretary was to board the special plane for Amritsar, carrying with him the draft of the minutes of the talks, we had to suddenly face very strong opposition to the whole proposal from an unexpected source.

Bhajan Lal, the chief minister of Haryana who had been informed of the proposal, adopted a determined stand against any deferment of the decision on Abohar-Fazilka. He also strongly opposed the reference of the river waters issue to the Supreme Court as he believed that this was merely a ruse to prevent the construction of the Sutlej–Yamuna link canal. His stand was that if the decision on Abohar-Fazilka was to be deferred, that on Chandigarh should also be. He claimed to have secured the support of a few senior Union ministers during interactions with them.

The main reason put forward, by the cabinet ministers against the announcement, was that the people in general would view it as a surrender to the Akali threat of disrupting the Asiad and it would only result in further strengthening the position of the militants. Some ministers underscored the point that the transfer of Chandigarh to Punjab without simultaneous transfer of territory from Punjab to Haryana would be considered by the people of Haryana as sacrificing their interests in order to placate the Akalis. The prime minister quite unexpectedly agreed with these views; consequently, it was decided that no announcement need be made on the lines of the draft minutes of the talks which had been prepared. The home secretary's proposed trip to Amritsar was cancelled. Thus, despite hectic negotiations lasting three days, the situation was back to square one.

The Akalis as well as some political commentators have since described this decision as a turning point in the recent history of Punjab. They have expressed the view that if the Central Government had agreed to announce the agreement reached with the Akalis, the Punjab agitation would have come to an end and peace could have been established in the state.

As against this view, those individuals who have defended the decision not to make any announcement have maintained that such a claim amounted to an oversimplification of the issues involved. In their opinion, the most controversial issue of the transfer of territory was yet to be resolved and the announcement would have only meant postponement of the resolution of the problem. They have insisted that the Akalis would *never* have agreed to the transfer of Abohar-Fazilka to Haryana (as several subsequent rounds of discussion on the subject revealed) and without a settlement accepted by both states, no lasting peace in Punjab and Haryana could have been established. Further, they have pointed out that the Akalis had been constantly shifting their position and escalating their demands.

Consequently, even after getting the concessions announced by the government, they would have continued their agitation by coming up with some new demand.

Whatever the justification for the apprehensions expressed by those who defended the government's decision, I am one of those who hold the view that the powers that be really missed a good chance for establishing peace. It is true that the Akalis themselves were not one homogeneous group (differences existed among the diverse factions); as a result, any settlement agreed to by one section may have been later disowned by another. At that stage, Bhindranwale and his followers (i.e., militants) were steadily gaining the upper hand in the agitation; they may have continued the agitation, ignoring the settlement reached with the Akali leaders. In spite of all these potential risks, my conviction is that it would have been safer to go ahead with the announcement of the points of agreement already reached. Such an announcement would have helped a great deal in defusing the tensions that were steadily mounting. If the Akalis later went back on their commitment, they would have stood exposed in the eyes of the public. Consequently, the government's stand would have received greater moral support from the people. A settlement of the type that had been reached in our talks could not have been viewed by the general public as a surrender to the militants as had been made out by Bhajan Lal and his supporters. There was absolutely nothing in the agreement that could be interpreted as a surrender to the militants. On the issue of transfer of territories to Haryana, there was little danger of any serious dissatisfaction resulting among the people of that state if the leaders had agreed to explain the full facts to them. But they chose to oppose the decision on the plea that the people of Haryana would not accept them.

The failure to make the announcement on 18 November contributed a great deal to the increase in tension and made the government vulnerable to the charge of succumbing to pressure exerted by the Haryana lobby. The announcement of the decision may not have brought lasting peace to Punjab, but there was at least a slim chance of a settlement and it was certainly worth a try.

✧

A most unexpected fallout of this decision, which developed into a major sore point during subsequent negotiations and dealings with the Akalis, was the unimaginative manner in which the Haryana police handled a sensitive assignment. They had been entrusted with the task of preventing the entry of potential troublemakers from Punjab to Delhi via Haryana for holding demonstrations at the Asiad venue on 19 November. Perhaps, the decision of 18 November proved to be crucial on this score, but this was a totally unanticipated and definitely avoidable development.

In the absence of any agreement between the Akalis and the government, the decision of the former to stage demonstrations at the venue of the Asiad and to disrupt the games stood. Hence, the government's efforts now turned to the tightening of the measures to avert such demonstrations. The opening of the Asiad by President Zail Singh was scheduled to take place at 3 p.m. on 19 November and the governments of the states neighbouring Delhi as well as the Delhi Administration swung into action to prevent Akali demonstrators from reaching Delhi by all means. The Haryana policemen took upon themselves the responsibility to search practically every Sikh who was travelling through the state to Delhi from the early hours of 19 November. Intelligence reports indicated that the demonstrators would travel by different routes in twos and threes and regroup themselves in Delhi for disrupting the opening ceremony. The Haryana police, therefore, stopped almost every vehicle that carried a Sikh passenger in it. They searched the vehicle and the passengers to make sure that no arms were hidden and no suspected terrorists would reach Delhi. Many Sikhs were prevented from proceeding to Delhi and most of them happened to be bona fide travellers who were not even remotely involved in the Akali plans for holding demonstrations. What was most galling was that even some highly respected and well-known retired Sikh generals and judges were not spared by the overzealous Haryana police and were subjected to the humiliating experience of being physically frisked. The explanation that the Haryana police gave later was that they could not recognize who the traveller was or what his background was without questioning him or her and that, in this context, they did not want to take any risk whatsoever.

The grand opening function of the Asiad took place without any demonstrations anywhere near the venue of the games and those in charge of the security arrangements in Delhi and Haryana were very pleased that they had effectively prevented all attempts at mischief by the Akalis and the militants. But little did they realize that their excessive zeal in detecting potential troublemakers had resulted in inflicting a deep scar on the self-respect and pride of a large number of peace-loving and patriotic Sikhs who earlier never had any sympathy for violence or terrorism. These people were profoundly hurt by the fact that they had been subjected to the indignity of a physical search merely because they were Sikhs when all non-Sikhs, including those travelling along with them in their vehicles, were allowed to proceed without any impediment. They had been treated as suspects, with criminal intentions to disrupt the Asiad, merely on the basis of their being Sikhs. Such suspicion wounded their pride and sense of patriotism.

When statements appeared in the media over the next few days from some eminent Sikhs about the ignominious experience they had to undergo at the hands of the Haryana police on the roads, the Akalis promptly described such treatment as a deliberate act on the part of the Central Government and the Haryana state government to humiliate the Sikh community. This one incident won for the Akalis immense support from those sections of the Sikhs, which, till then, were quite unsympathetic to their *morchas* and *dharam yudh*. No amount of explanation that the police personnel had overreacted and that there had been no instructions from higher political levels to search every Sikh traveller passing through Haryana could help to assuage the wounded feelings of the Sikhs. This unfortunate incident has continued to rankle in the minds of Sikhs ever since.

To Bhindranwale, this event was a godsend. He exploited to the maximum the value of this incident in his sermons to foment anti-Centre and anti-Hindu feelings among the Sikhs. Even the senior leaders of the Akali Dal used this incident to rouse the feelings of the Sikhs against the Central Government and the atmosphere, which was already surcharged with bitterness, was getting increasingly tense. The militants started stepping up their terrorist activities and incidents of bomb attacks on the residences of some Congress members were reported. Murderous attacks took place on some Nirankaris on 24 December 1982 and 10 January 1983. Indira Gandhi deputed the three cabinet ministers who had participated in the earlier talks with the Akalis (Venkataraman, Sethi and Shivshankar) to go over to Chandigarh on 11 January 1983 in an attempt to defuse the tension through talks with the Akalis. But their mission did not produce any worthwhile results.

✧

Amarinder Singh again took the initiative for the resumption of talks with the Akalis and sought the good offices of Rajiv Gandhi for this purpose. He informed me that the Akali leaders were willing to hold talks with Rajiv on all issues *ab initio* and requested me to ascertain the prime minister's reaction to the proposal. Indira Gandhi was keen to get the negotiations restarted and readily agreed to the suggestion.

The talks between Rajiv and the Akali leaders were held at my residence (27, Safdarjung Road) on 17 January 1983. For the first time, G.S. Tohra, the influential chairman of the Shiromani Gurdwara Prabandhak Committee (SGPC), was brought in by the Akalis. Apart from Tohra, the Akali delegation consisted of Badal and Ravi Inder Singh. Besides Rajiv Gandhi, our team was made up of the cabinet secretary, Krishnaswami Rao Saheb, and myself. Amarinder Singh was present as an observer as usual.

The talks started at 3 p.m. and went on for five and a half hours. We noticed that the Akalis were in a rather defiant mood this time and had adopted a more rigid stand on various issues. In fact, they raised many more new demands; they now appeared to be unwilling to accept the formulations on some of the issues agreed to by them during the talks in November 1982. The reverses suffered by the Congress Party in the Assembly elections in Andhra Pradesh and Karnataka held a week earlier had weakened the prestige of the government and seemed to have encouraged the Akalis to take a tougher stand. They probably felt that the government was in a weaker position now compared with what it was in November 1982 (when the talks were last held) and probably wanted to exploit this situation to their advantage.

Rajiv went through the various demands of the Akalis, item by item, and tried to obtain their concurrence in the form of a written document, which could then be submitted to the prime minister for her final approval. But, as already mentioned, the Akalis upped the ante, and came up with many more demands.

The government's stand on the question of the All-India Gurdwara Act had been that they would initiate consultations immediately with the authorities in charge of those gurdwaras in various states (besides Punjab) and come up with proposals that could be finalized in further discussions with the SGPC. But Tohra and Badal insisted that the government introduce the Bill in the forthcoming budget session of Parliament. When we pointed out to them that it would be difficult to complete consultations with all parties concerned in such a short time, they asserted that they could not wait longer than the budget session for this purpose. On the question of transfer of Chandigarh, the Akalis insisted that it should be done *without* handing over Abohar-Fazilka or any other territory from Punjab to Haryana.

Tohra spoke most of the time in Urduized Punjabi, which needed translation often. He was courteous and polite in expressing his views but the stand he took on the Gurdwara Act was quite uncompromising. Badal, soft-spoken and sophisticated, probably did not want to be seen as less ardent than Tohra in support of these demands and was tougher than before on both the Gurdwara Act and the Chandigarh issue. On the question of river waters, they both underscored the point that the Akalis would not settle for anything less than a reference to the Supreme Court, irrespective of the views of Haryana on this matter.

Rajiv tried his best to budge the Akali leaders from their extremely rigid positions on these issues by suggesting various alternative formulae, but the latter were not in a mood to make any concessions. I left the meeting for about half an hour (at 7 p.m.) to report to the prime minister in her South Block office on the disappointing trend of the talks. She stressed that the endeavour for reaching a satisfactory settlement should continue in spite of the rigid stance adopted by the Akalis now. Although we made all possible efforts, no agreement could be reached on any issue when the talks concluded.

Indira Gandhi did not want to accept the breakdown of the talks as final. She always believed that a solution could be reached through negotiations if both sides kept the dialogue going. The next day, 18 January, she sent Venkataraman, Sethi and Shivshankar again to Chandigarh to pick up the threads where they had been left off on 11 January. But the new round of talks again yielded no results.

✧

On 21 January 1983, Indira Gandhi held a meeting with the leaders of the opposition parties in order to enlist their support for, and involvement in, her efforts to find a peaceful solution to the Punjab problem. She explained to them in detail the government's stand on the various demands made by the Akalis. Some of the opposition leaders, particularly Charan Singh (a former prime minister) emphasized that the government should not grant any concession to the Akalis that would prove harmful to the interests of Haryana; instead he declared that the authorities concerned should be very firm in dealing with such demands. Others, such as Inderjit Gupta and Piloo Mody, were in favour of a more conciliatory approach in the larger interests of establishing peace in Punjab. One suggestion that emerged from this interaction and which the prime minister readily accepted was that tripartite talks, involving government representatives, leaders of the opposition parties and the Akalis, ought to be held to explore the possibilities for a peaceful settlement.

A tripartite meeting was accordingly held on 24 January 1983 at the Parliament Annexe in New Delhi. Six members of the Union cabinet – Venkataraman, Sethi, Narasimha Rao, C.M. Stephen, Shivshankar and Bhishma Narain Singh – and Cabinet Secretary Krishnaswami Rao Saheb, Home Secretary T.N. Chaturvedi, Special Secretary (Home) P.P. Nayyar and I, represented the government. Much to our surprise, the Akali triumvirate chose not to attend the meeting themselves, but instead fielded a second-level team consisting of S.S. Barnala, Balwant Singh and Ravi Inder Singh. Some of the opposition leaders disparagingly described the Akali delegation as a 'B Team'. Charan Singh and Atal Behari Vajpayee sent only their deputies to attend the meeting.

The tripartite talks were taking place under the shadow of a threat by the Akalis that they would intensify the agitation; they proposed to ask *all* Akali MPs and MLAs to resign. The opposition leaders repeatedly appealed to the Akalis not to precipitate a crisis by resigning from the legislative bodies. The tripartite discussions continued for two days, 24 and 25 January 1983, but there was no meeting ground on any issue whatsoever. The topic of river waters took up a considerable part of the time. At one stage, the Akali representatives appeared to be satisfied with the government's offer to refer the matter to the Supreme Court. But after further discussions among themselves and with their senior leaders, they changed tracks and adopted a rigidly uncompromising position on this issue too. Amarinder Singh arranged a meeting for them with Rajiv Gandhi on 25 January night in the hope that Rajiv might succeed in persuading them to be more accommodative. This meeting too was unproductive.

On 26 January evening, Amarinder Singh met Indira Gandhi and Rajiv at the prime minister's residence to report on the reactions of the Akalis after they had met Rajiv the previous night. I was present at this meeting. The message he conveyed was that the Akalis were not in favour of any compromise on any of the issues and had decided to go ahead with their plan to resign from all legislative bodies and to further intensify the agitation.

The prime minister urgently called a meeting of her senior cabinet colleagues later in the night and apprised them of the Akali decision. The outcome of the meeting was that the home minister would issue an appeal to Longowal asking him and his colleagues to desist from taking any precipitate action. Amarinder Singh took along a copy of the appeal that night itself to Longowal who was in Amritsar, but it made no impact on the Akali leaders. On 27 January, the Akalis submitted letters, thereby formally resigning from Parliament and the legislative assemblies, though the resignations were to come into effect from a later date.

Despite a series of setbacks, Indira Gandhi did not give up her efforts for peaceful negotiations and decided to reactivate the tripartite discussions, which were eventually held at the Parliament Annexe on the afternoon of 8 February 1983. This time around the government team consisted of five Union ministers – Venkataraman, Sethi, Narasimha Rao, Shivshankar and Bhishma Narain Singh – and Cabinet

Secretary Krishnaswami Rao Saheb, Home Secretary T.N. Chaturvedi and myself. The Akalis were represented by the same 'B Team'. Most opposition parties were represented by their leaders and in a few cases by their deputies. Among the prominent opposition leaders were L.K. Advani, Madhu Dandavate and H.K.S. Surjeet.

Earlier in the day, the government team had held a meeting at the same venue with the chief ministers of Punjab, Haryana and Rajasthan and the leaders of the opposition parties. The objective was to explore the possibility of arriving at a consensus on the dispute relating to territories and river waters before meeting the Akali representatives. Various alternative suggestions were discussed at the tripartite meeting, but a consensus proved elusive.

✧

Since the tripartite discussions on 8 February 1983 remained inconclusive, it was agreed to hold another meeting two days later. However, a big shock was in store for us when the river waters issue was taken up for discussion on 10 February. The Akalis, for the first time, moved the goalposts and took the stand that the proposed reference to the Supreme Court should cover not only the agreements of 1976 and 1981 but also the settlement of 1955. They demanded that the allocation of waters between pre-partition Punjab and Rajasthan should be reopened, as, according to them, Rajasthan had been allotted more than its legitimate share under this settlement.

This new stand came as a huge disappointment to people like me who had participated in all the negotiations with the Akalis before and had believed that they had accepted the government's offer to refer the issue to the Supreme Court without any preconditions. We pointed out to the Akalis that the 1955 agreement was not open to renegotiation at that stage. After the partition of India, there was a continuing dispute between India and Pakistan on the sharing of the waters of the Punjab rivers. Pakistan had maintained that India would not be able to fully utilize the waters it had claimed. In response, New Delhi had contended that India needed these waters to irrigate the arid Indus basin in Rajasthan. The Indo–Pakistan agreement on sharing of the Indus waters had been arrived at by accepting India's claim regarding the waters for use by Rajasthan as legitimate and valid. Rajasthan had, after the agreement of 1955, built up a vast irrigation infrastructure at tremendous expense to utilize these waters. The Akalis now not only wanted the settlement on Rajasthan's share to be reopened but also insisted that the sharing of the waters of the Yamuna be taken into account in determining the quotas for Punjab and Haryana.

The opposition leaders who attended the tripartite meeting expressed their resentment in strong terms at this opening of a new 'can of worms' on the part of the Akalis. They felt that this move was unacceptable. The tripartite meeting ended on a note of disappointment.

In spite of the inflexible attitude of the Akalis, efforts for reaching an agreement through tripartite discussions were not abandoned. More such discussions were held at the Parliament Annexe on 15, 18, 19 and 20 February 1983. In all these meetings, the Akalis were represented by the same 'B Team'. The government team remained the same except that Buta Singh replaced Bhishma Narain Singh at the meetings on 19 and 20 February because, by then, the latter had quit the Union cabinet. L.K. Advani, H.K.S. Surjeet and Madhu Dandavate were among the senior opposition leaders who attended all the four meetings. During the negotiations, the Akalis appeared to have softened their attitude towards Rajasthan's quota of river waters, but they refused to commit themselves to a definite position on this issue; the uncertainty about their stand on river waters persisted. On the territorial dispute, their firm stand was that Chandigarh should be transferred to Punjab and Abohar-Fazilka should also remain in the same state.

While talks with the Akalis were in progress at various levels, there had been no let-up in the spate of violence in Punjab and in other places in North India. On 31 January 1983, Mohinder Pal, the elder brother of Jogindernath (a member of the Punjab Legislative Assembly), was shot dead at Amritsar. On 16 February an inspector of police was shot dead in village Kirijah in Amritsar district. On 8 March, bomb blasts occurred in the underground Palika Bazar (New Delhi) and the Inter State Bus Terminal (Delhi). The Akali leaders had by now given up even the pretence that their agitation was being conducted in a non-violent manner. They gave a call for recruitment of *'shaheedi'* (martyr) volunteers in order to constitute a suicide squad. On 4 April 1983 they announced the launch of a *rasta roko* (block the road) agitation in Punjab. The Akali stance now became one of open confrontation with the government with an obvious potential for instigating large-scale violence.

The *rasta roko* agitation led to large-scale disruption of normal life across Punjab. The blockades seriously affected the movement of goods and commodities and, by extension, trade in most towns besides causing tremendous hardship to travellers. The agitators frequently resorted to violence, forcing the police to open fire in several places. Two executive magistrates and 175 police personnel sustained injuries while the death toll was 21.

Violence and concomitant terror continued to escalate. A series of incidents of pillaging and robbery marked April 1983. On 6 April, a large quantity of rifles and ammunition were stolen from the Home Guard armoury at Ferozepur. On 20 April, Rs 3 lakh was looted from a branch of the Punjab and Sind Bank in Jullundur district.

The most daring and dastardly of all the crimes committed during this period was the murder of A.S. Atwal, the deputy inspector general of police, Jullundur, outside the main entrance of the Darbar Sahib in Amritsar on 25 April 1983. Atwal, a competent and highly respected Sikh police officer, had just come out of the Golden Temple after walking round the *Parikrama* and after prostrating himself before the Granth Sahib as every devout worshipper does when he or she visits the temple. He was walking towards the main gate with the *prasad* – holy offering – he had received from the temple in his hands when he was shot dead by a bunch of militants. Bhindranwale had marked Atwal out for retribution as he had dealt with terrorists very sternly, as any conscientious police officer would have done. The most disturbing part of this tragic episode was that none of Atwal's bodyguards or the policemen who were on duty near the temple made any attempt to nab the assailants, who escaped without any difficulty.

The murder of Atwal sent shock waves all over the country. There was a public clamour that the police should enter the Golden Temple and arrest Bhindranwale and his collaborators for this crime. At this point of time Bhindranwale was staying in Guru Nanak Niwas, one of the outhouses of the Golden Temple. The Akalis had always maintained that the outhouses formed part of the temple, and, therefore, enjoyed the same sanctity as the temple itself. There was nothing in the history or religious traditions to support this claim, but generally the outhouses and rest houses attached to the Golden Temple had been treated as 'out of bounds' for the police. Reports trickled in that these places were being used as torture chambers, where the opponents of Bhindranwale were treated brutally. These places were apparently used to hide guns, explosives and other armaments. For this reason alone, the people at large felt that they did not deserve to be treated as sacred. Even if they were to be treated as part of the Golden Temple, the activities for which they were utilized should not have conferred on them any immunity from police action, especially in a case involving murder.

A good deal of discussion took place between the authorities in charge of law and order in the Punjab administration and their counterparts in the Central Government about sending the police into Guru Nanak Niwas to arrest Bhindranwale. Longowal, instead of condemning this heinous crime, sent out a clarion call to his followers to the effect that it was their duty to prevent the entry of the police into the temple. (The rest houses and outhouses were of course included in his definition of the temple.) The issue was now projected by the Akalis as one of protecting the purity of the Golden Temple and any suggestion about police entering its precincts, to arrest those accused of murder, was denounced as violating its sanctity. The entire situation became a highly sensitive one and, eventually, it was decided at a fairly high political level that the police need not enter Guru Nanak Niwas to make the arrests.

In retrospect, I must state that the decision not to send the police to arrest Bhindranwale and to search for the killers of Atwal within Guru Nanak Niwas and other neighbouring buildings was a grave error. If, at that point of time, the police had nabbed Bhindranwale and conducted a search of these premises for concealed weapons and criminals, as was their legitimate duty and right, the militants would have learnt a lesson and viewed the police action as a warning against further escalation of violence. In fact, had the police attempted the aforementioned tasks, the majority of Sikhs would have accepted their action as the proper response expected of any law-enforcing agency and would not have treated it as violation of the sanctity of a place of worship. Probably, the pattern of violence and terror in Punjab would have received a hard knock, if not a smashing blow, by such a quick response. Thus, such a decision only encouraged the terrorists to become more daring in their crimes and reassured them about the immunity of their sanctuaries.

More audacious crimes followed. On 29 April 1983, a sum of Rs 22,000 was looted by militants from a branch of the Punjab National Bank in Amritsar district. (They also walked off with a gun in the process.) There was a macabre aspect as well. Corpses of torture victims appeared in the temple premises on 4 May, 23 May and 11 June, testifying to the fact that the militants were stepping up their violence against those not cooperating with them. Bank robberies were reported from various places in Punjab such as Kapurthala, Gurdaspur and Jullundur. Murderous attacks on Nirankaris at Hoshiarpur and Amritsar were also reported.

Meanwhile, the government began to receive information about the growing rift between Longowal and Bhindranwale. Bhindranwale had by then turned openly hostile against the ostensibly moderate 'style' of the Akali leaders. He branded them as 'agents of the government' in his diatribes. What he wanted was an all-out war against the government as well as major communal clashes, which could lead to a massive exodus of the Hindus from Punjab. Longowal was basically against instigating communal conflicts; he wanted the agitation to be directed only against the Central Government and the state governments. At the same time, he was becoming increasingly anxious about the propaganda unleashed against him by Bhindranwale. Consequently, he felt obliged to intensify the agitation in order not to be overshadowed.

Longowal not only did not condemn Bhindranwale's extremely provocative tirades but also did not denounce the heinous crimes perpetrated in the name of religion. He and his senior Akali colleagues seemed to think that the best way of retaining their leadership over the agitation was to step up its scale and intensity. As a result, they gave a call for a *rail roko* (block trains) agitation on 17 June 1983. The large-scale violence and killings, which occurred during the *rasta roko* agitation, did not deter them in any way from going in for this more dangerous form of agitation. However, the government decided to act with caution as it did not want to endanger the safety of thousands of railway passengers. It ordered the suspension not only of all rail traffic but also the operation of state transport buses in Punjab. Nevertheless, the agitators indulged in unlawful activities such as cutting signals and telegraph wires. They also 'ensured' extensive destruction of railway property. In fact, the agitators interpreted the government's cautious action as a sign of weakness on its part.

The tide of violence engulfed Punjab and neighbouring regions. Assassinations, looting of banks and bomb attacks on police stations continued unabated during the latter part of 1983. Bhindranwale's speeches became more and more inflammatory and provocative. He called upon Sikhs to arm themselves with guns and grenades. Killing of innocent people by terrorists riding on motorcycles had become a common occurrence. Bhindranwale openly exhorted each village to raise a team of three youngsters with one revolver each and a motorcycle. He also wanted every Sikh boy to keep 200 grenades with him. These irresponsible diatribes shocked people all over the country but the senior Akali leaders did not seem to disapprove.

Towards the close of 1983, Bhindranwale unleashed a string of terrorist attacks specifically targeting the Hindus. On 28 September, five Hindus enjoying a morning walk at Jagraon in Ludhiana district were fired at indiscriminately; all of them suffered serious injuries. Two days later, a Hindu medical practitioner was shot dead in his clinic at Patti in Amritsar district. On 4 October, Madan Mohan Dhawan, a Hindu merchant, was pumped with bullets in his shop at Jandiala; he succumbed to his injuries later. Reports of more attacks on Hindus at Jullundur, Taran Taran and Hoshiarpur poured in.

❖

A most shocking incident took place on 5 October 1983 when a private bus plying between Amritsar and Delhi was hijacked at a place called Dhilwar and forced towards another place called Nurpur Labana. The hijackers segregated the six Hindu passengers from the Sikhs and shot them dead. News of this outrage stirred the entire nation and president's rule was imposed in Punjab on 6 October in an effort to tackle the worsening situation more effectively.

The promulgation of president's rule was followed the next day by the declaration of Punjab as a disturbed area under the Punjab Disturbed Areas Ordinance. The Armed Forces Special Powers Ordinance was promulgated on 15 October, giving the Punjab administration special powers to deal with the growing violence in the state.

There was widespread expectation that the Punjab administration under president's rule would be able to end terrorism or at least control it to some extent. But terrorism continued unabated. In fact, the situation deteriorated further. Hardly a day passed without violent incidents and murderous attacks on Hindus. Looting of shops, passenger buses, banks and petrol stations became daily occurrences. On 21 October 1983, the Sealdah–Jammu Tawi Express derailed near the Gobindgarh railway station as a result of sabotage, killing 19 persons and injuring 129.

On 19 November, there was a repetition of the dastardly bus hijacking incident. A Punjab Roadways bus on its way to Moga was diverted to Rasoolpur village and four Hindu passengers were shot dead. On 21 November, two bombs were thrown at the Hanuman Temple at Yamuna Nagar. On 3 December, the idols of Krishna and Subhadra at the Ramtirath Holi complex were broken and the clothes on the idols were burnt.

These attacks on Hindus, their temples and properties were planned deliberately in order to create widespread Hindu–Sikh animosity, but fortunately, the traditional bonds of harmony and friendship between the two communities survived these grave acts of provocation. Bhindranwale's rabid communal attitude could best be discerned in his unrestrained outburst about a relatively minor incident which took place in Rajasthan on 26 November. An attempt was made by some Hindu fanatics to set fire to a gurdwara at Churu.

Only the gate was broken; nothing else was damaged. Bhindranwale responded with a highly provocative statement condemning this incident and held out the threat that if Sikhs were attacked in other states, every Hindu in Punjab would be killed. Parliament was then in session and many members demanded the immediate arrest of Bhindranwale.

✧

Bhindranwale, who had established himself in Guru Nanak Niwas, began developing apprehensions that the police may actually arrest him there. He and his armed followers, therefore, moved to the Akal Takht, which was considered next only to the Harmandir Sahib as far as sacred status was concerned. The Akal Takht was considered specially holy because it was in this shrine that the Granth Sahib, which was read in the Golden Temple every day, was brought for safekeeping. Anyone setting up living quarters within the Akal Takht would have been castigated for committing a great act of sacrilege. But Bhindranwale with his group of followers, armed with sten guns, grenades and other varieties of weapons and ammunitions, defied the authority of the priests who were responsible for the management of the temple. The most regrettable part of the entire episode was that the senior Akali leaders did not think it proper to protest against this highly objectionable act. There were reports of a conflict, almost taking the form of a physical confrontation, between the followers of Longowal and those of Bhindranwale at Guru Nanak Niwas just before Bhindranwale actually moved into the Akal Takht. However, after that, the Akali triumvirate did not choose to make his occupation of the Akal Takht an issue and tacitly acquiesced with the *fait accompli*.

From then on, Bhindranwale began directing his 'crusade' involving killing, arson and looting from within the sacred precincts of the Akal Takht, free from fear of arrest by the police or retaliation by aggrieved groups or individuals. The year 1983, which had witnessed killings and destruction of property in the name of religion on a very high magnitude, thus closed with a highly sacrilegious act committed by one who claimed to be the staunch defender of Sikh traditions and religious practices. No Akali leader denounced this step. They were either unwilling to speak up or were mortally afraid to do so. In the process, they were really surrendering the leadership of the movement they had launched and this fell into the hands of Bhindranwale with disastrous consequences, as the events of 1984 were soon to prove.

✧

From early 1981 onwards, reports reached the Government of India that the terrorists were the beneficiaries of large sums of money from certain Sikh organizations based in foreign countries. Other reports revealed that arms and ammunitions were being smuggled into Punjab through Pakistan for use by the terrorists; these reports also showed that Sikh militants were being trained in Pakistan on how to use firearms.

Here, a brief historical account would be in order. In the post-Second World War years, there had been large-scale migration of Sikhs to the United Kingdom, the USA and West Germany in search of employment. These countries had, in the past, welcomed labour forces from developing countries because of the acute shortage of manpower. A fairly sizeable number of Sikhs had settled down in Canada long before Second World War. By and large, the Sikhs had made worthwhile use of the opportunities available in these affluent countries. Many had achieved tremendous success in fields such as real estate, hotels, transport and retail trade. The older generation of Sikhs in these countries continued to maintain close contacts with their friends and relatives in India through visits and business transactions. However, a new generation had grown up in these countries, which had little first-hand knowledge of the homeland of their ancestors, but who were keenly interested in the politics and fortunes of their fellow-religionists in India.

One characteristic feature of the Sikhs settled in the Western countries was their cultural isolation from the host communities. The gurdwaras they had built in these countries served not merely as places of worship but also as centres for sustaining their emotional links with India in general and Punjab in particular. A conspicuous feature of the Sikh community, as with most other Indian communities settled abroad, was that they were divided on group, party and caste lines as in India. Thus, there were ardent supporters of the Congress

Party among the Sikhs living abroad and also equally strong supporters of the Akalis and of the militant groups within the Akali fold. As in India, the supporters of the militants were more vociferous and demonstrative than the others and, therefore, were more conspicuous in the community. Some younger people in the community were supporters of 'Khalistan'. Most of them had been carried away by the rhetorical utterances of extremists such as Bhindranwale and had convinced themselves that the ultimate goal of the Sikh community in India was the establishment of a separate sovereign state. For some Sikhs settled abroad, the championing of the cause of their fellow-religionists in India provided them with an excellent opportunity to play the role of leaders of the community.

One of the most active proponents of the 'Khalistan' movement abroad was Dr Jagjit Singh Chouhan, who founded a National Council of 'Khalistan' in London in 1980. He proclaimed the establishment of the so-called state of 'Khalistan', based in London, with himself as the president. He took upon himself the role of the philosopher and prophet of 'Khalistan' and started putting out statements and pamphlets justifying the demand for a separate state for the Sikhs. Ganga Singh Dhillon, president of the Nankana Sahib Foundation of Washington, was another prominent Sikh leader canvassing support for 'Khalistan'. While these two leaders were relatively more restrained in their support for violence, there were other Sikh organizations openly advocating violence and terrorism to achieve the goal of 'Khalistan'. One of them was the Dal Khalsa operating from the UK and another the Babbar Khalsa operating from Canada. They also actively sought the support of Pakistan in the fight against what they called their common enemy: the state of India.

The secessionist organizations of Sikhs based abroad were regularly supplying arms and funds to the militants through various channels, including their agents in Pakistan. The militants also derived a good deal of emotional support from the fact that some of their fellow-religionists living abroad were behind them in their secessionist activities.

✧

After Bhindranwale lodged himself in the Akal Takht, he felt sufficiently emboldened to intensify his campaign of violence. Throughout January

1984, a series of incidents of bomb throwing, looting of buses and killing of innocent people totally unconnected with government or politics rocked Punjab and neighbouring regions.

Militants specially targeted Central Government offices and establishments. On 28 January alone, three railway stations were set on fire in Sangrur district. On the same day, telegraph wires were cut at the Gurney railway station in the same district.

While the spate of arson and terror unleashed by the militants continued unabated, efforts for a settlement through negotiations with the Akali leaders were still being made. The Akali leaders were sounded out on their willingness to resume secret talks; they promptly conveyed their positive response through Amarinder Singh and eventually resumed the dialogue, with Rajiv Gandhi, on 24 January 1984, at a guesthouse in New Delhi.

The Akalis were represented by Tohra, Badal and Ravi Inder Singh. Rajiv was assisted by the cabinet secretary and me. Amarinder Singh was also present in his role as an observer. The talks lasted from 9.30 p.m. till midnight and the possibility of reaching an agreement on some of the contentious issues appeared bright. We quickly readied the draft framework of an agreement, which could be sent to the prime minister for her approval. The Akali leaders, however, did not commit themselves to the document but stated that they would let us know their reaction in a few days, i.e., after consulting their colleagues. But the message that the Akalis sent across was that they would *not* agree to any compromise on the territorial and river waters disputes; instead, they insisted on the government accepting their old rigid stand on them.

In spite of the reverses and setbacks, India Gandhi did not give up hope. On 7 February 1984, she called for a meeting of the opposition leaders and apprised them of the Akalis' stand on various issues. These leaders suggested that the tripartite talks, which were last held in February 1983, should be resumed and another effort made to seek a settlement through such discussions.

Consequently, a tripartite meeting was held at the Parliament Annexe on 14 February 1984. This time the Akalis came in with a formidable array of leaders: Badal, Tohra, Barnala, Balwant Singh and R.S. Cheema (a legal luminary). The opposition parties were also represented by a distinguished spectrum: Jagjivan Ram, Atal Behari Vajpayee, L.K. Advani, Chandrashekhar, Biju Patnaik, Madhu Dandavate and H.K.S. Surjeet. The government was represented by P.C. Sethi, Pranab Mukherjee, Shivshankar, Buta Singh, Cabinet Secretary Krishnaswami Rao Saheb, Home Secretary Chaturvedi, special secretaries in the Home Ministry, P.P. Nayyar and Prem Kumar, and myself.

At this meeting, which began in the morning, the Akalis had to listen to a good deal of plain speaking from the opposition leaders, particularly from Chandrashekhar and Patnaik about the rigidity of their stand on the territorial and river water disputes. However, the Akalis refused to budge from their stand. The meeting adjourned at 4.30 p.m. for the day.

The tripartite meeting resumed the next day. Narasimha Rao reinforced the government side. Again, the discussions did not lead to any solution on any issue.

Even as the talks were going on the next day, news came in that violence had broken out in several places across Haryana. This time, it was the Hindus who had attacked the Sikhs. The immediate provocation was that Hindus in Punjab had been fired at by police forces on 14 February as they had called for a hartal on that day. The death toll was eleven.

The government's apprehensions had come true. These alarming reports agitated the Akali leaders who wanted to return to Punjab immediately. The meeting, once again, remained inconclusive. After the discussions on 14 and 15 February, the Akalis were just not interested in attending any more meetings as they found that practically all the opposition leaders had been highly critical of their extremely rigid stand.

The violence sparked off in Haryana provided a good excuse to the militants, if they needed any, to escalate their terrorist activities in Punjab. Armed bands of Sikh militants struck indiscriminately at several places, resulting in a huge loss of innocent lives. On 21 February, three Hindu temples were damaged in Bhatinda. In a shooting incident on the same day at the main bazar of Kahnuwan in Gurdaspur district, six Hindus were killed and eight injured. On 22 February, four persons were killed and two injured at Lopoke

Bazar and three killed and four injured at Valtoha, both in Amritsar district. Shooting incidents became rampant across the state. The death toll between 15 February and 1 March in various incidents crossed the forty-five mark.

On 16 February, the militants opened fire from inside the Golden Temple complex at personnel of the Central Reserve Police Force (CRPF) who were on duty there; they returned the fire. On 18 February, the Akali leaders announced that they would not participate in tripartite meetings convened by the government any more. This announcement was expected, but what was ironical was that the Akalis' statement blamed the government for the violence that broke out in Punjab and Haryana on 14, 15 and 16 February.

✧

While the government continued with its efforts to reach a satisfactory solution to the various disputes, the Akalis sprang a surprise by raising a totally new demand. They wanted Article 25, Clause (2) Subclause (b) of the Constitution to be amended, deleting the provision which states that reference to Hindus in this article shall be construed to include Sikhs, Jains and Buddhists. It needs to be pointed out that Article 25 has always been considered an important provision to protect the interests of the Sikhs as it recognizes their special religious rights.

Hitherto, neither the Akalis nor any other section of the Sikhs, including the militants, had considered the provisions in Article 25 as in any way weakening the separate identity of the Sikhs. Even the Anandpur Sahib resolutions, very comprehensive in their coverage of the community's demands, had not brought up this matter. But the Akalis suddenly hit upon some portions of Article 25 as something harmful to their identity as a separate community. They gave a call for a demonstration scheduled for 27 February 1984 in support of the demand for amending Article 25. One phase of the demonstration entailed burning pages of the Constitution containing Article 25.

The call for the public burning of the Constitution hurt the sentiments of all patriotic Indians. Moreover, it came at a time when passions had been roused to fever pitch by the large-scale killings and other acts of terrorism rocking Punjab. The Bharatiya Janata

Party (BJP) called for a 'bandh' in Delhi to register its protest. President Zail Singh was very unhappy that the Akali demonstration was adopting such a defiant mode. Some reports indicated that he tried to talk to Longowal over the telephone in order to dissuade him from going ahead with his plans but was rebuffed. To those of us who were in the know (about the developments unfolding in Punjab), this act provided more evidence of the scant respect the Akali leaders had for Zail Singh. The president issued a statement expressing his strong disapproval of this type of demonstration, which he felt was an affront to the Constitution.

The Akalis were not at all deterred by the nationwide protest against the proposed demonstration involving burning some pages of the Constitution. The senior Akali leaders themselves decided to participate in these 'burning' acts. Badal quietly slipped into Delhi, disguised as a truck driver, thus eluding the police. He reached Gurdwara Bangla Sahib in the heart of Delhi on 26 February night. On 27 February he and four others emerged in front of the gurdwara and publicly burnt a copy of Article 25 much to the discomfiture of the Delhi Police, who then arrested them. Barnala, Tohra and some others performed the 'burning' act in Chandigarh and were also arrested. Thus, all the senior Akali leaders were behind bars, whereas Bhindranwale continued to enjoy immunity ensconsed in his Akal Takht residence.

On 28 February, the Union home minister made a statement in Parliament, providing the background to the talks the government had been conducting with the Akali leaders. He also highlighted the extent to which the authorities had gone to accommodate the Akali demands on various issues. He drew attention to the fact that in spite of repeated requests from the government for assurances from the Akali Dal that places of worship would not be used for storing of arms or for harbouring criminals, this party was unwilling to offer any. He reiterated the government's keenness to find solutions through negotiations but, at the same time, warned that it would 'take every possible step to stamp out violence ruthlessly, whatever may be the cost'.

The home minister's statement in Parliament helped in keeping the nation informed about the reality regarding the Akali demands and the government's response to them. Public opinion was quite supportive of the government stand, but there was also a strong undercurrent to the effect that the authorities should act more firmly to curb terrorism and punish those guilty of crimes. The alleged soft approach of the government in dealing with terrorists and its hesitation to send the police inside the gurdwaras to seize weapons and arrest the wanted culprits came in for increasing criticism. Most of this criticism was targeted against Indira Gandhi personally. People started asking why she, who exhibited great courage and firmness in dealing with the Pakistanis during the 1971 Bangladesh war, was now showing weakness in dealing with terrorists who were trying to destroy the integrity and unity of the nation. Indira Gandhi was quite aware of the barbs being hurled against her handling of the Punjab agitation, but she still firmly believed that solutions should be found through negotiations and that eventually good sense would prevail on the agitators. She instructed us to explore possibilities for the resumption of talks with the Akalis in spite of the bitterness caused by the 'burning' incidents.

A former ambassador, Gurbachan Singh, who had visited the jailed Akali leaders in Chandigarh, informed me on 16 March 1984 that they were not willing to hold talks unless released unconditionally. He added that they were not prepared to suspend their agitation, even for a short period, so as to facilitate negotiations. They probably relized that any call by them for suspension would have little impact on the militants. In fact, the militants were no longer following the instructions of the Akali leaders; they were indulging in a spree of carnage, arson and looting, irrespective of the stand taken by the senior Akali Dal leaders.

The militants soon began targeting prominent political leaders. On 9 March 1984, the vehicle carrying Ved Pal, the deputy speaker of the Haryana Assembly, was attacked near Karnal (Haryana) by terrorists (riding on a motorcycle) with sten guns. The driver of the car was killed but Ved Pal escaped unhurt. On 13 March, an attempt was made on the life of Darbara Singh, former chief minister of Punjab at a gurdwara at Nangal, where he had gone to attend a cremation ceremony. Darbara Singh escaped unhurt, but six others were injured in the melee. On 27 March three well-known dignitaries,

Ved Prakash, Dr Joginder Singh and Roop Lal, were assaulted while returning home in a jeep after attending a Nirankari conference at Dhanauala in Sangrur district. Ved Prakash was killed and the other two were seriously injured. On 28 March, Harbans Singh Manchanda, a prominent Sikh leader and president of the Delhi Gurdwara Prabandhak Committee, was assassinated in New Delhi.

✧

While lethal attacks on prominent leaders continued and other grave crimes such as looting of banks and sabotaging railway lines were being committed, we were, as instructed by the prime minister, continuing our endeavours to bring the Akali leaders back to the negotiating table. We received reliable information that they would be prepared to come for talks, without insisting on being released first, provided all of them could be brought together at a single venue.

In this context, we contacted Longowal, who, in turn, ascertained the views of the other Akali leaders. We were finally informed that they were ready to resume talks. The prime minister nominated Narasimha Rao to conduct the negotiations. Our main problem was to locate a suitable secret venue in Chandigarh where the jailed Akali leaders could be brought to, undetected. An unoccupied private house in Chandigarh was arranged as the venue for the talks on the night of 27 March.

As government representatives, Narasimha Rao, cabinet secretary (Krishnaswami Rao Saheb), the new home secretary (M.M.K. Wali) and I flew to Chandigarh by a Border Security Force (BSF) plane. We reached there at 9.30 p.m. and went straight to the venue without being noticed by anyone. Tohra, Barnala, Balwant Singh Ramuwalia and R.S. Cheema, who had been brought earlier to the house from the jail, were waiting for us there. The discussions, which lasted till 2 a.m., focused mainly on Chandigarh and Article 25 of the Constitution.

The issue relating to the amendment to Article 25 did not prove difficult to resolve. Narasimha Rao pre-empted all discussions on this topic by telling the Akalis that the government had no objection to the amendment provided they themselves were quite clear about the exact terms in which the article should be amended.

The future of Chandigarh, as expected, proved to be a tough proposition. A suggestion emerged that the city could be partitioned between Haryana and Punjab along the Madhya Marg line. Such a partition would result in the loss of several government buildings for Punjab. However, Narasimha Rao assured the Akalis that their state could be adequately compensated. Punjab could opt for the construction of newer and better buildings in its section of Chandigarh. The Akalis appeared to favour the idea of partitioning Chandigarh, though not along the line of partition proposed. Various permutations and combinations were examined with the help of the maps of Chandigarh spread on the table. However, there could be no finality about the talks as the Akalis wanted us to consult Badal, who was then lodged in Tihar Jail, New Delhi. After that, the Akali leaders were taken back to the jail and we returned to Delhi by 3 a.m.

Our next task was to ascertain the views of Badal. Narasimha Rao, the cabinet secretary, the home secretary and I met Badal at a guesthouse in Vasant Vihar, New Delhi, where he had been brought from jail on 28 March evening. Badal vehemently opposed the suggestion of partitioning Chandigarh. Incidentally, we also discovered that his own house would have gone to the Haryana part of Chandigarh if the city was to be partitioned on the lines we had discussed earlier at the meeting in Chandigarh. He, however, was agreeable to the continuation of talks on all issues. The talks concluded by 7.30 p.m. and Badal was taken back to jail.

For the next round of negotiations, we decided that instead of talking to Badal separately in Delhi and to the other leaders in Chandigarh, the proper course would be to hold talks with all of them together at Chandigarh. Therefore, on the night of 29 March, we took along Badal in a BSF aircraft to Chandigarh, where the other Akali leaders had assembled. The venue was the same private house where we had met two days earlier. The government team, besides the four of us, had a new entrant: the special secretary in the Home Ministry, Prem Kumar.

The talks, which lasted from 9.30 p.m. till 2.30 a.m., centred on the issue of Chandigarh. Towards the end, the Akali leaders appeared to be agreeable to the partitioning of Chandigarh provided Punjab got thirty-eight of the forty-seven sectors. Even on these terms, the Akali leaders were not ready to give any definite assurance. All they said was that we should contact Longowal, to whom they would convey their views, and he would inform us directly of the final decision of the party. We returned to Delhi at 3.30 a.m. bringing Badal with us; he was sent back to Tihar Jail.

We reported the outcome of our talks to the prime minister on 30 March. A few days earlier, she had received a long letter from Longowal listing the various demands of the Akalis. The letter was mainly intended to counter the charge that the Akalis were shifting their stand frequently and were coming up with new demands to keep their agitation alive. A reply indicating the government's position on the various points raised in the letter was in the process of being drafted, and the prime minister was only waiting for the outcome of the secret parleys (in which some of us had been continuously engaged from 27 March onwards) before she could finalize the reply.

The Akalis had already given a call for a mass protest demonstration for 2 April 1984. On this occasion, more than 50,000 persons were expected to court arrest after burning copies of the Constitution. They were really turning on the heat by intensifying their *dharam yudh* at a time when Bhindranwale and his cohorts were perpetrating indiscriminate violence and terror all over the state. They were well aware of the fact that a demonstration of this nature would lead to extensive violence and that the extremists would seize this opportunity to create conditions of anarchy all over the state. They knew very well that they could not exercise any restraint on the extremists who were conducting their own agitation independently. Still, they went ahead with this call for a massive protest demonstration. We requested the Akalis to call off the agitation proposed for 2 April, but they refused to do so unless a substantial concession was granted by the government vis-à-vis their demands.

Bhajan Lal (the chief minister of Haryana) arrived in Delhi on 30 March. He immediately raised serious objections to the idea of partitioning Chandigarh on the lines suggested by the Akalis. As usual, he had drummed up support for his stand from some senior ministers and stood his ground firmly against the formula suggested. We had also not recommended the partition of Chandigarh on the lines proposed by the Akalis as we were convinced that would have been unfair to Haryana. In the reply to Longowal, therefore, no indication was given about the government's stand on partitioning Chandigarh. Instead, all the options open for a solution to the territorial dispute were outlined. The government's stand on various other demands also was spelt out clearly. On the question of amendment to Article 25, the government expressed its willingness to accept the Akali demand unreservedly. Our hope was that since the Akalis' demand on the issue of Article 25 had been accepted, they would call off the demonstration proposed for 2 April. The letter to Longowal was sent by 9 p.m. on 30 March and he was requested to send a definite reply by 31 March about the demonstrations scheduled for 2 April.

Longowal's reply reached us by the afternoon of 31 March. Much to everyone's relief, he agreed to call off the demonstrations in response to the government's acceptance of the Akalis' demand on Article 25. He sent a draft statement, which he proposed to issue, subject to the government making a statement conceding the Akalis' demand on this issue. The Akali draft was more in the nature of a victory statement, but the government did not object to that since it had agreed to accept the Akali demand without any reservation. The government's statement was issued at 6 p.m. on 31 March and, within an hour, Longowal issued his statement shelving the demonstrations scheduled for 2 April. At last, a solution was found for the 'burning' problem and we thought that this step would mark the beginning of peace in Punjab.

But our hopes were soon belied. Bhindranwale, according to the reports that reached the government, was very angry at the compromise agreed to by Longowal, especially the cancellation of the demonstrations. He fervently urged his followers to step up the violence and terrorist activities in order to sabotage all prospects for peace. More ghastly crimes soon followed.

On 1 April, R.N. Sharma, the principal of a college in Ferozepur, was riddled with bullets. The next day, Harbans Lal Khanna, an ex-MLA and district president of the BJP in Amritsar, was shot dead along with his gunman. In the violent incidents that occurred during the funeral procession of Khanna on 3 April, eight persons were killed and nine injured. Another shocking incident was the firing on

V.N. Tiwari, MP, at his residence on that day. Tiwari succumbed to his injuries later.

The graph depicting murder, looting and destruction of government properties attained its peak during April 1984. Various incidents of robbery in running trains took place. Reports of growing tension between the followers of Longowal and those of Bhindranwale filtered in. On 13 April, the day of the Baisaakhi festival (an important occasion for the Sikhs), the two rival groups published pamphlets, accusing each other of betrayal of the Sikh cause. The rival groups were engaged in killing each other's members. The murder of Surinder Singh Sodhi, a close associate of Bhindranwale, on 14 April, magnified the schism between the Longowal and the Bhindranwale camps. The murderer was immediately killed and, three days later, Baljit Singh Kaur, who was suspected to have been involved in the murder of Sodhi, was killed and her mangled body was found lying near Walla village in Amritsar district inside a gunny sack.

✧

The government made yet another effort to defuse the situation by resuming talks with the Akali leaders. As already mentioned, Badal was lodged in Tihar Jail (New Delhi) and other senior leaders in a Chandigarh jail. A message was sent to Longowal that the government was willing to release the Akali leaders to enable them to take part in talks, but much to government's surprise, the leaders did not want to be released. They probably wanted to avoid a confrontation with Bhindranwale who, by now, was calling all the shots. Or else, they wished to retain the halo of being 'martyrs' for a cause. Nevertheless, Longowal sent a message to the government that the Akali leaders would be willing to participate in talks while remaining prisoners. He suggested that the talks be held in Chandigarh. This suggestion meant transporting Badal from Tihar Jail to a suitable venue in Chandigarh, where the other Akali leaders also could be brought.

On 21 April 1984 around 8 p.m., Narasimha Rao, Pranab Mukherjee, Krishnaswami Rao Saheb, M.M.K. Wali, Prem Kumar and myself boarded a special plane for Chandigarh. We took Badal with us. The weather throughout the flight was quite rough because of a severe dust storm and, at one stage, we were doubtful whether we would be able to make it to Chandigarh at all. Eventually, we did. We held talks with the Akali leaders at the airport lounge itself, which had been carefully segregated from visitors and airport employees. Badal, Tohra, Barnala, Balwant Singh Ramuwalia and R.S. Cheema represented the Akalis at these talks.

We found the Akali leaders in a very uncompromising frame of mind. They appeared to be apprehensive to even stick to their earlier commitments because of the growing support gained by Bhindranwale from fervent youngsters of the Sikh community. Probably, they did not want to be branded as 'betrayers of the Sikh interests' by Bhindranwale and, therefore, they took very extreme positions on all issues. Bhindranwale, though not physically present at the meeting, was the real deciding factor at the talks. On Chandigarh, the Akali leaders ruled out partition on any lines. They insisted on Punjab getting the whole of Chandigarh and also on retaining Abohar-Fazilka. On other issues, such as river water sharing, their stand was equally rigid. The talks were a complete failure and we returned to Delhi at about 2.30 a.m. the next day, bringing Badal with us.

❖

Soon a very disturbing situation developed at Moga, one of the smaller towns of Punjab. Reliable information pointed to the fact that a large band of extremists had occupied the gurdwara there (along with a stockpile of arms and ammunition) and that, in their midst, were present many suspects wanted by the police in connection with specific crimes such as murder and robbery.

On 1 May, a BSF contingent surrounded the gurdwara and asked the extremists to surrender along with their weapons. The BSF laid siege to the gurdwara preventing anyone from going in or escaping. The extremists retaliated by opening fire at the BSF and demanded that the siege be lifted. On 2 May, the police received instructions to flush out the extremists and to use force if they tried to break out with their weapons. Tension mounted across Punjab over the Moga situation. Reports came in about large congregations of Sikhs from outside converging on Moga to assist the besieged 'victims'. On 3 May, however, the extremists agreed to hand over to the police all the suspects. More than 350 persons came out of the gurdwara and the police arrested sixteen of them and seized their weapons. There was no occasion to resort to force as the extremists had realized the wisdom of surrendering. However, this incident created a lot of commotion all over the state and the predictable hue and cry about the police violating the sanctity of the gurdwaras rang loud and clear.

Meanwhile, the government was privy to reliable reports that the gulf between Longowal and Bhindranwale could no longer be bridged. Longowal and his senior colleagues had by now become almost irrelevant in deciding the future course of the agitation. Moreover, they had lost all authority and control over the *morcha* they had started. Longowal called a meeting of his senior followers inside the Golden Temple complex on 27 April in a attempt to reassert his authority. However, much to his discomfiture, a sizeable section of the invitees walked out of the venue and went over to the Akal Takht, where Bhindranwale had set up his headquarters and pledged their allegiance to him. Longowal then made a feeble attempt to persuade the priests in charge of the Golden Temple to oust Bhindranwale from the Akal Takht. The priests were duly alarmed at the manner in which the temple was being converted into a headquarters for terrorist operations. Their timid protests made little impact on the extremists. All that they could do now was to issue a statement to the effect that killings or shootings should not take place from within the temple complex. Bhindranwale's reply to this statement was a contemptuous warning to the priests that they would be turned out of the temple if they tried to dictate terms to him. The priests meekly accepted the reality of the situation that they were no longer in control of the temple and stopped protesting.

The militants had by now almost succeeded in creating conditions of anarchy in many parts of Punjab. One of their most dastardly acts was the killing (on 10 May) of the eighty-five-year old Giani Pratap Singh, former *jathedar* of the Akal Takht, at his residence in Tahli Chowk in Amritsar. The government released the Akali leaders on 10 May, hoping that they, who had the legal responsibility for the management of the temple, would make a serious attempt to throw out the militants. This expectation proved to be misplaced as they had neither the will nor the power to achieve their objective. Having allowed 'the Bhindranwale phenomenon' to grow unchecked and having used it to their advantage in their manoeuvrings against the government, they now found that they had themselves become its victims, though they were unwilling to accept this fact openly.

The government had received information that the extremists had already piled up huge stocks of arms and ammunitions inside the Golden Temple and that they had been regularly using the *karseva* (a form of service performed by devotees) vehicles for bringing in more weapons. These vehicles had not been, in the past, subjected to any check by the police as they were supposed to be used for carrying the material required for performing religious rites and services. The police now started examining these vehicles and this move led to protests by, and often resistance from, the extremists. On 12 May, the Central Reserve Police Force (CRPF) tried to stop a *karseva* truck for inspection. The militants present in the fleeing truck fired at the police before the vehicle was stopped. A large quantity of arms and ammunition was recovered from it, but the militants managed to sneak into the temple.

On 12 May yet another shocking incident took place. Romesh Chander, the editor of the *Hind Samachar*, Jullundur, and the son of Lala Jagat Narayan (who had himself been killed by the terrorists in September 1981), was gunned down by extremists. This killing led to protests all over North India, underlining the government's inability to protect the lives of innocent citizens in Punjab.

A series of attacks on the police forces followed. On 13 May, a CRPF party was fired at near Pakhowal in Ludhiana district, killing one constable. The next day, hand grenades were thrown at a CRPF camp at Ghuman in Gurdaspur district, resulting in injury to six policemen. On 16 May, a head constable, Raj Singh, who was driving a scooter towards Ajnala in Amritsar district was shot at and injured; his scooter and wrist watch were taken away. Five days later, Hardayal Singh, an assistant subinspector of police, was shot dead near Raipur Araya in Jullundur district. On 22 May, a grenade was flung at a CRPF truck in Amritsar, injuring two persons. These attacks on the police personnel and camps and the manner in which the assailants evaded arrest in most cases created a feeling of despair and fear among the people. They saw the police forces being reduced to helplessness and put on the defensive by the militants.

A serious development took place in Amritsar, which further exposed the weakness of the Punjab police. This was the occupation of as many as seventeen houses surrounding the Golden Temple by the extremists. The militants started fortifying these houses under the very nose of the police. They were armed with light machineguns and automatic weapons and constituted the first line of attack in their war strategy against the government. The armed militants inside the temple had organized themselves into an effective fighting force under the command of retired Major General Shabeg Singh.

Immediately after the release of the senior Akali leaders, the government sent a message to Longowal asking him to depute a team for the resumption of talks. Frankly, the government was, at that time, not fully aware of the extent to which the Akali leaders had become ineffective in controlling the situation. The government knew of the rift between Longowal and Bhindranwale and also the fact that the extremists were acting independent of Longowal's instructions. Still, he was officially the president of the Akali Dal and the 'dictator' of the *morcha*. The Golden Temple and the other gurdwaras in Punjab were legally under the control of the SGPC, of which Tohra was the president. The government, therefore, continued to entertain the hope that if a settlement could be reached with Longowal and his colleagues, it could still help in restoring peace in Punjab.

Longowal and his senior colleagues themselves were fully aware of the magnitude of the danger that had been posed by Bhindranwale to their authority. But they kept up the pretence that they were still in charge of the agitation and that it was they who decided its course. If they had shown the courage to come out openly, even at this stage, to condemn the violence and terror that had been dragging Punjab into anarchy and called off the *dharam yudh* and extended their cooperation to the government for reaching a peaceful settlement, events would not have taken the tragic turn they did over the next month. These leaders were genuinely appalled at the violent course that the *dharam yudh* launched by them had taken and were bitter over the fact that their movement had been hijacked by Bhindranwale and his group of militants. They were particularly unhappy that the sacred places of worship had been converted into arenas for staging murderous attacks on innocent people. They were equally bitter over the reality that the authority of the priests appointed by the SGPC had been emasculated and that their writ no longer ran in the management of the holy places and even in the most important of all temples, the Golden Temple. It would have required great courage on their part to declare openly that they would not condone murder and mayhem in the name of religion and the gross misuse of the places of worship for terrorist activities, whatever their quarrels with the government might be. But instead of showing such courage, they tried to maintain the façade that they were still directing the agitation. They chose to swim with the current and, in an attempt to reassert their control, they gave a call on 23 May for intensifying the agitation from 3 June through a very explosive programme of non-cooperation. Longowal issued a statement that, from 3 June onwards, no one should pay land revenues, charges for canal waters and electricity dues. The most provocative demand was that he wanted all movement of foodgrains out of Punjab to be stopped from that date. He and his senior colleagues in the Akali Dal probably thought that by giving such a call for this highly disruptive form of agitation, they would go one step ahead of Bhindranwale himself in their confrontation with the government. They did not realize that by calling for this new agitation at that stage, they were setting fire to the powder keg on which they themselves were sitting.

It was at this stage that Indira Gandhi came to the conclusion that any further attempt at peaceful negotiations with the Akali leaders would be an exercise in futility. However, she did not want to miss even the faintest chance of a settlement through negotiations and, therefore, she asked us to get in touch with Longowal once again and ascertain his willingness to depute a team of senior leaders for talks.

On 25 May, the government received a message from Longowal that he would send Badal, Tohra and Barnala to Delhi for talks which, he insisted, should be kept secret as on previous occasions. Narasimha Rao, Pranab Mukherjee and Shivshankar met the three Akali leaders at a guesthouse in Vasant Vihar, New Delhi, on 26 May. The cabinet secretary, the home secretary and myself were also present, but this time the negotiations on behalf of the government were conducted exclusively by the ministers. The talks lasted from 9 a.m. till 3.30 p.m., and after a brief interval, continued again from 8 p.m. till 9 p.m. The Akalis did not grant any concession on *any* issue. In a last bid for reaching a compromise on the territorial dispute, they were asked whether some villages either from Abohar or from any other region of Punjab could be transferred to Haryana in compensation for that state surrendering its claims on Chandigarh, but they would not consider this option. In fact, they had lost the political backing required for any compromise and were persistently sticking to their original rigid positions. The discussions came to a close with a promise that they would let us know their final decision on various issues after consulting Longowal. The government never heard from them and this proved to be the last of the meetings with the Akali leaders before the Army action.

I have recounted here the full details of the series of meetings the government held with the Akali leaders covering the period October 1981 to May 1984 to clearly bring how keen Indira Gandhi had been to seek a solution *through peaceful negotiations*. The importance she attached to these negotiations can be gauged from the fact that she herself attended the first three meetings. It was only when the Akali leaders themselves suggested that secret talks might be more helpful to iron out the differences that she withdrew from direct talks and deputed her political colleagues and other senior officials to conduct the negotiations. When the Akalis expressed their wish to go in for informal secret meetings with Rajiv Gandhi, she had readily agreed. When the opposition leaders put forth a suggestion that it might be helpful to hold tripartite meetings, she again concurred. On the whole, *twenty-six* meetings at very high levels of the government, each one lasting several hours, were held with the Akalis during the two and a half years preceding the military action in June 1984.

Before moving on, a brief analysis would be in order. The basic flaw in the Akali agitation was that the triumvirate who started it completely lost control over its tempo and found themselves sidelined by the militants. In the early stages, the Akali leaders thought that they could use the militants in order to pressurize the government, but this stage lasted only for a year or so. The militants contemptuously ignored the Akali leaders as 'toothless tigers' irrelevant to their scheme of things. The fundamental error committed by the Akali leaders was that even *after* they realized that they had been displaced, they insisted on maintaining the charade of being in charge of the *dharam yudh*. The Akali leaders themselves had started pulling in different directions. There were reports that Tohra was, at one stage, trying to make his peace with Bhindranwale by ignoring the authority of Longowal. Badal wanted to keep all the options open and finally lost all. Longowal put up the semblance of a fight to assert his authority, but by the time he did so, it was too late. The other Akali leaders did not count for much. Eventually, the Akali leaders became too weak and too insecure in their position to accept a settlement even when they were convinced about its overall merits.

As one who knew Indira Gandhi's thought processes well and as one who participated in all the talks, I can assert, on the basis of direct knowledge, that she sincerely believed till the very last minute that a solution could be found through talks and, therefore, wanted to avoid the use of force. There have been some highly mischievous reports that Indira Gandhi had initiated these talks and kept up their momentum only to create the impression of seeking a settlement through negotiations but that she had always planned to crack down on the Akalis. Nothing could be farther from the truth. She had always dismissed all suggestions about deploying the Army to deal with the Punjab agitation and believed that the Akali leaders would eventually come round to accepting a peaceful settlement. When the law and order situation started deteriorating in Punjab, she arranged for reinforcements from the CRPF to assist the Punjab police; at that stage, she rejected the suggestion to call in the Army. But the fast-paced events of April–May 1984 coupled with the complete collapse of the authority of the Akali leaders and the failure of the Punjab police to cope with the highly sophisticated weapons of the extremists finally forced on her the decision to send in the Army.

❖

It was a case of the proverbial 'last straw'. The Akalis declared on 23 May 1984 their intention of intensifying the agitation by calling for stoppage of movement of foodgrains out of Punjab as well as a refusal to pay taxes and other charges due to the government from 3 June. This call was a virtual invitation to anarchy, which the state police would have found almost impossible to handle in addition to having to cope with the daily (heavy) quota of killing, destruction of government properties, looting of banks and other crimes. It was immediately after this call by Longowal, on 25 May to be precise, that Indira Gandhi finally made up her mind to summon the Army. She sent for General A.S. Vaidya, the chief of Army Staff, and asked him to keep the Army on alert as the civilian authorities may require its help to deal with the situation in Punjab. General Vaidya told her that he had already ordered certain troop movements in anticipation of such a demand and that he would be able to move the forces in adequate numbers into the major trouble spots in Punjab at short notice. The prime minister specified to General Vaidya that the top priorities of the Army would be to effectively curb terrorism and violence, provide security to the people and restore normalcy in Punjab. These tasks involved flushing out the terrorists from their hideouts in certain gurdwaras, their arrest and the seizure of their weapons. Her expectation was that the very presence of the Army and the demonstration of its strength through flag marches would, by themselves, act as deterrents. Consequently, she felt that there would not be any need for use of excess force by the Army.

Nearly forty gurdwaras in different places in Punjab had been taken over by the extremists. These gurdwaras were reported to be having adequate stocks of arms and ammunition as well as food and water to enable the militants to offer long-drawn-out resistance if any attempt was made to flush them out. When General Vaidya met the prime minister on 25 May, he explained to her his strategy as to how the Army planned to accomplish the mission assigned to it. He pointed out that he would move a sufficient number of troops into Punjab to deal quickly with the situation in different places simultaneously. The gurdwaras that had been seized by the extremists would be surrounded by the troops who would prevent movement of water, food, weapons and men into these places and force them to surrender. He said that a similar siege operation would be mounted in the Golden Temple using a larger number of troops. According to his strategy, the troops would fan out to all the trouble spots in the state and thus would be able to prevent movement of troublemakers towards Amritsar, which would be the main scene of the flushing out operations. The prime minister was assured by Vaidya that there would be a maximum *show* of force, but minimum *use* of it. She repeatedly told the general that in any operation *no damage should be done to the temple buildings and particularly to the Harmandir Sahib*. She also told him about the meeting with the Akali leaders, which had been scheduled for 26 May. Although she was not very optimistic about the outcome, she, nevertheless, brought to his notice that if there was a favourable response from the Akalis at the talks, he would be immediately informed about it. Otherwise, she instructed him that he should proceed with all the necessary arrangements to restore order and peace on the lines discussed between them. As stated earlier, the talks with the Akalis ended in total failure.

On 27 May at 10.30 a.m. the cabinet secretary, senior security adviser, R.N. Kao, and I held a meeting with Vaidya at the Cabinet Secretariat to discuss the follow-up of the decisions conveyed to the general and the details of the Army operation. We informed Vaidya that the talks with the Akalis on 26 May had failed. For his part, Vaidya told us that the soldiers would be moving in, in sufficient numbers, and that they would establish themselves properly in all the trouble spots over the next four or five days in order to be able to start the operations on 2 June.

We decided, in consultation with Punjab Governor B.D. Pande, the further measures that needed to be taken by his administration.

I would like to state here categorically that the military operations, which the prime minister authorized on 25 May 1984 and which Vaidya discussed with us on 27 May, were confined to the *siege and flushing out operations* in the identified gurdwaras in different places and in the Golden Temple at Amritsar. Till that point of time, there was no reference to any plan except for an effective siege of the buildings involving cutting off telephones, electricity, water, food and inflow of men and weapons. However, there were major and sudden changes in the plan that had been approved by the prime minister on 25 May and discussed with us in considerable detail by Vaidya on

27 May. Vaidya, after a quick visit to Punjab and after consultations with his senior colleagues in the Army, sought an urgent meeting with the prime minister on 29 May to inform her of some important changes in the plan. He met Indira Gandhi at her South Block office on 29 May and explained to her the revised plan and the reasons for the change. R.N. Kao and I were present at this meeting. K.P. Singh Deo, minister of state for defence, joined the meeting a little later but had to soon leave (as soon as Vaidya had explained his new plan) to attend to some other urgent work relating to the Punjab situation.

Vaidya told the PM that he had discussed the plan of the siege with Lieutenant General K. Sundarji and other senior officers directly in charge of the operations and it was now their considered view that while the plan of siege could be followed in respect of all smaller gurdwaras then under the control of the extremists, it would not be practical to follow this plan in the case of the Golden Temple. Instead, he said, there would be a quick seizure of the hideouts of the terrorists inside the temple using minimum force. This seizure, he said, would entail a commando operation *inside* the Golden Temple, which would be conducted with such swiftness and surprise that it would *not result in any damage* to the temple buildings.

Needless to say, the prime minister was taken aback by this sudden change of plan. She was quite perturbed at the suggestion of the use of force *inside* the temple and asked Vaidya several questions seeking clarification. She enquired as to what would happen if the terrorists put up stiff resistance? She also wanted to know how long it would take to subdue such resistance and particularly as to what would happen if the terrorists took refuge in the inner sanctum where the Guru Granth Sahib was placed. She asked him why the previous strategy of siege and flushing out was being discarded so soon (after all, Vaidya had outlined it only on 25 May). She also sought details about the comparative analyses in terms of loss of life and damage to the temple with respect to the two plans. Another question she raised was whether such an action inside the temple would have any adverse effects on the loyalty and discipline of the Sikh jawans in the Indian Army.

Vaidya explained that what he was now proposing was the result of very detailed discussions he had had with Sundarji, who was the person in direct command of the operations and had his full endorsement. He pointed out that a siege could lead to a mass upsurge among the Sikhs in the countryside and mobs might start moving towards Amritsar, galvanized by religious frenzy. In such an eventuality, the Army may have to open fire in several places in the state to prevent such mobs from reaching the vicinity of the Golden Temple. Even if the mobs from outside Amritsar could be stopped, he felt serious problems would be faced in preventing the frenzied mobs within Amritsar from entering the temple or attacking the Army from behind. He also thought that Bhindranwale may force the priests in the temple to issue a *hukumnama* (diktat) asking the people to assemble in the Golden Temple in large numbers. If that happened, he observed that it would be difficult to distinguish between the troublemakers and ordinary people and the siege may become ineffective. Vaidya affirmed that, after weighing the pros and cons of the two options, he, without any hesitation, would agree with his senior colleagues that no time should be lost by going in for a siege; instead the Army ought to make a quick entry into the temple and take the terrorists by surprise.

On the question of adverse reaction among the Sikh jawans, Vaidya was quite reassuring. He declared that there need not be any apprehension on this score as the Sikh jawans constituted a highly disciplined and loyal force and they would always accept the orders of their senior officers. He also clarified that the extremists holed up inside the Golden Temple would be given adequate time to consider the option of surrender without resistance and there was every possibility of their accepting that option when they realized the odds against them.

Vaidya spoke with such confidence and calmness that the new plan he was proposing appeared to be virtually the only option open to the Army. He said that the other option was fraught with dangerous consequences and hundreds of innocent people may fall victim to firing along the roads leading to Amritsar and in the vicinity of the Golden Temple. He noted that Army casualties could also be heavy as the siege may last several days in view of the reaction to be expected from the frenzied mobs. On the other hand, he emphasized that the new plan would be executed so quickly that everything would be over by the time the people came to realize what was happening. On the question of damage to the temple, Vaidya asserted that *strict instructions* would be given to the Army to ensure that no damage was caused to the temple buildings under any circumstances.

The convincing manner in which Vaidya explained the pros and cons of the two plans left the prime minister with no other option but to ask him to go ahead with the plan proposed by him. On 29 May, when Vaidya was explaining to the prime minister so eloquently and with so much confidence about the soundness of his new plan of operation, he himself could never have anticipated that events would take the turn they eventually did.

After Vaidya left the room, the prime minister told Kao and me that she was accepting the general's advice since he was, after all, the person responsible for delivering the goods. She added that during the Bangladesh war in 1971, she never interfered with the decisions of those in command of the field operations. She used to discuss with the senior generals the broad objectives and apprise them of the important political considerations to be kept in view, but would leave the decision on the specifics of the operation entirely to them. In other words, she respected the professional judgement of the generals.

Events now started moving very swiftly. All paramilitary and armed police forces stationed in Punjab and the union territory of Chandigarh were placed under the command of the Army. Chandigarh itself was placed under the charge of the governor of Punjab.

On 1 June 1984, some extremists fired upon a BSF contingent from inside the Golden Temple; the contingent promptly returned the fire. The firing continued intermittently during the afternoon and resulted in seven persons inside the temple and three outside losing their lives and sixteen persons inside and nine outside being severely injured. This 'test firing' looked like a probing on the part of the extremists to ascertain the reaction of the armed forces stationed outside the temple.

✧

Indira Gandhi addressed the people over national television and radio on the night of 2 June, just a few hours before the new agitation called by the Akalis was to start. In her address, she recapitulated the various concessions offered by the government to accommodate the Akalis' demands. Even at that last minute, she offered to sit round a table to find a solution through discussions. Addressing her 'Sikh brothers and sisters', she reminded them how Sikhism was born as a faith to bring together people of different religions and how the great Gurus taught love and tolerance. 'Let not a minuscule minority among Sikhs', she declared, 'be allowed to trample underfoot civilized norms for which Sikhism is well known and to tarnish the image of a brave and patriotic community.' She concluded by making an impassioned appeal: 'Even at this late hour, I appeal to the Akali Dal leaders to call off their threatened agitation and accept the framework of the peaceful settlement we have offered. Let us join together to heal wounds. The best memorial to those who have lost their lives is to restore normalcy and harmony in the Punjab which they loved and served. To all sections of Punjabis I appeal: *'Don't shed blood, shed hatred.'*

As anticipated, there was no response either from the Akali leaders or the militants to this appeal. The government announced on the night of 2 June that the Army had been called in to support the civil authorities. Lieutenant General Ranjit Singh Dayal, a Sikh himself, was appointed as adviser (security) to the governor of Punjab and Major General Kuldeep Singh Brar, another Sikh officer, was placed in direct control of the operations inside the Golden Temple.

Some of the Akali supporters close to Dayal's family tried to persuade him to turn down the assignment. He was one of the senior-most among the Sikh officers in the Army hierarchy at that time and some of his friends thought that if he refused the assignment and resigned on religious grounds, this move would be viewed as a great victory for the Sikh cause and might encourage some other Sikh officers also to follow suit, thereby causing considerable embarrassment to the government not to mention the resulting problems. But Dayal was a good soldier and a patriot. He informed his friends that he would not be true to his profession, his country and his religion if he shirked his duty. As subsequent events showed, Dayal and scores of other brave and patriotic Sikh officers and jawans proved their commitment to their country and their profession by performing the duties assigned to them with exemplary courage and loyalty.

On 3 June, the Army moved swiftly into action in various places suspected to be the strongholds of the militants. They laid siege to thirty-five gurdwaras in different parts of Punjab. However, many extremists were able to escape from the gurdwaras through exits unknown to the Army personnel. The flushing out operation in the gurdwaras outside Amritsar was a relatively painless one, except in Patiala, where the militants offered stiff resistance. The operation there was conducted by a Sikh officer, Major General Gurdial Singh, who was able to clear the temple of all extremists as a result of very quick action. By 4 June night, practically all gurdwaras outside Amritsar were cleared of extremists and the Army had arrested most of them and confiscated their weapons.

✧

The main action at the Golden Temple commenced on 5 June 1984. Appeals were repeatedly made over the loudspeakers asking the militants to come out of their hideouts and surrender along with their weapons. The Army had pinned great hopes on these appeals and had expected that most of the militants would respond positively upon seeing for themselves the strength of the forces assembled against them. But only 129 persons came out of the temple in the first lot. Some managed to escape without even being noticed by the armed forces.

Finding that the militants were not in a mood to surrender, the Army proceeded to the next stage of the operations, namely, entering the temple through a commando operation. Most unexpectedly, the commandos came under heavy fire. It was *only then* that the Army commanders realized that they were up against an enemy well entrenched in secure positions within various unapproachable labyrinthine passages inside the building and very well equipped with machineguns and other heavy weapons.

It is not my intention here to recount the details of the operations inside the temple as they have been more than adequately described in various publications. Here, the important point to be stressed about the operation is that the Army found itself suddenly faced with a situation that it had not anticipated and for which, therefore, it had not been prepared. It was obvious that the information that the commanders had gathered about the weapons and men inside the temple was grossly inadequate and they had started the operations on the basis of insufficient data. At the start of the operations, the clear-cut instructions received by them specified that there should be no damage to the buildings. But very soon, the Army officers realized that the plan they had in mind would not work and the soldiers were becoming sitting ducks for the well-entrenched and well-armed militants.

The entire strategy and tactics had to be changed quickly. Eventually, armoured personnel carriers and tanks had to be brought in to tackle the new situation that confronted the Army. At that point, they realized that there was no possibility of ensuring the surrender of the militants without causing damage to the buildings. The only redeeming feature was that the Harmandir Sahib itself would not be damaged in this operation.

At one stage during the operation, there was a report to the effect that Bhindranwale and a group of armed men had sneaked inside the Harmandir Sahib and were firing at the soldiers from the sanctum sanctorum itself. On 6 June, at about 3.30 a.m., the Punjab governor, B.D. Pande, telephoned the cabinet secretary to inform him that firing was continuing from Harmandir Sahib and it was suspected that Bhindranwale was commanding the attacks from there. The governor was seeking the prime minister's instructions as to how should the Army respond in the light of the earlier instructions that no damage was to be caused to Harmandir Sahib. The cabinet secretary consulted me as to whether fresh instructions should be obtained from the prime minister on the governor's message. The governor himself did not have any definite information whether or not Bhindranwale was actually present inside the Harmandir Sahib. Moreover, prime minister's instructions about Harmandir Sahib to Vaidya were very clear, namely, that the structure should not be damaged under any circumstances. We both decided that it would not be necessary to disturb the prime minister at that time of the night to ask for instructions on a matter on which she had already given clear guidelines. The cabinet secretary contacted Vaidya and the latter assured him that there were suitable plans to deal with such situations and that the commanders were well aware of them.

The Army exhibited tremendous restraint while following the explicit instructions *not to cause any damage to Harmandir Sahib*. The soldiers faced a grave risk and suffered many casualties. But the situation regarding Akal Takht, from where the main attack was being mounted against the Army, was different. Here, the Army had to resort to heavy artillery against the militants who were using machineguns from within the Akal Takht. Eventually, the casualties as well as the damage to the Akal Takht proved to be heavy.

At about 4.30 a.m. on 7 June, Prem Kumar, special secretary (home), who was continuously monitoring the action through messages over the telephone and by wireless from Amritsar and, in turn, had been keeping me informed, telephoned to confirm the report received earlier that *Bhindranwale was dead* and his body, which was lying in the basement of the Akal Takht, had been identified. I conveyed this vital information on the phone immediately to the prime minister.

The operations in the Golden Temple were over by 7 June, but new cans of worms were being opened. These events, again, had not been anticipated by the senior officers of the Army. Again, they were taken by surprise. The most serious of these developments was the mutiny by Sikh jawans in a few Army units.

The news of the Army operations on 6 June, resulting not only in the killing of Bhindranwale but also in serious damage to the Akal Takht, was splashed in newspapers all over India. The immediate fallout was that a large number of Sikhs felt very unhappy and very upset. What enraged them was not the killing of Bhindranwale and some of his followers, but the damage caused to the Akal Takht. Unconfirmed rumours spread, like the proverbial wildfire, that the Akal Takht had been razed to the ground; that Harmandir Sahib itself had been badly damaged; and that even the Guru Granth Sahib (the holiest book of the Sikhs) had been riddled with bullets. Exaggerated versions about alleged atrocities by soldiers and alleged killings of Sikhs in large numbers in different places in Punjab were doing the rounds. These rumours reached some military cantonments with all sorts of embellishments, and some religious fanatics among the Sikh jawans made highly inflammatory speeches appealing to their co-religionists to rise in revolt and march to Amritsar to defend their temple and their religion.

On 7 June, about 500 soldiers belonging to the 9th Battalion of the Sikh Regiment stationed at Ganganagar in Rajasthan mutinied. Seizing Army vehicles, they drove through the streets of the town shouting slogans against the government. As Ganganagar borders Pakistan, some mutineers, not being clear about their objectives, fled across the porous border. K.P. Singh Deo, minister of state for defence, telephoned me very early on 8 June morning about the outbreak of the revolt but also told me that he had been assured by Vaidya that this was an isolated incident and there was nothing to worry about. But soon similar incidents, some on a larger scale, flared up in other places, which indeed caused some anxiety. The most serious incident was the mutiny at Ramgarh in Bihar at the Sikh Regimental Centre where large batches of fresh Sikh recruits under training broke open the armoury and carried away a big cache of weapons to the military vehicles they had seized. Brigadier S.C. Puri, the commander of the centre, was shot dead by the mutineers. They drove away in the seized vehicles and headed in the direction of Amritsar shouting slogans against the government. Soon reports poured in about revolts by Sikh jawans in Alwar (Rajasthan), Jammu, Thane and Pune (both in Maharashtra), though the number of soldiers involved in these cases was small.

Indira Gandhi was quite perturbed at the news of the mutiny. What shocked all of us was the fact that such incidents, however small the numbers involved were, could take place at all in the Indian Army. It was unthinkable for most Indians that soldiers of the Army, noted for the highest standards of loyalty and discipline, could revolt. Vaidya kept his cool despite all these alarming reports. He kept on assuring us that the problem would be tackled without any difficulty and solved in a day or two. He proved to be correct. The mutineers were quickly intercepted and brought to book and normalcy was restored expeditiously. When the full details about these revolts emerged later, everyone felt reassured by the unshakeable loyalty and discipline on the part of the Sikhs in the Indian Army, because it was found that a large number of soldiers who mutinied were indeed raw recruits. Not a single Sikh *officer* joined the revolt or lent even indirect support to the mutineers.

Looking back on the Army operations in Punjab, some questions have caused serious concern. First, should the top-level generals, Vaidya and Sundarji, have changed the plan of action with regard to the Golden Temple on the apprehension that the earlier plan of going in for a siege would have been frustrated by frenzied mobs? Second, when they opted for the Army entry into the temple, should not the officers in charge of the operations have collected the necessary intelligence about the deployment of the militants within the temple, the arms and ammunition under their control and other such relevant facts before sending in the commandos? And third, should not the senior officers in command of the various Army units consisting of large numbers of Sikh soldiers have explained to the jawans in advance factors such as the real reasons behind the Army operation, the demands of the agitating Sikhs and the various measures the government had been taking to fulfil them? Also, should they not have taken necessary precautions against possible misinformation and disaffection among the ranks?

Some of the aforementioned questions have been raised not only by laymen but also by experienced Army officers. For his part, Sundarji has explained to some of his friends the reasons that made him and his chief change the plan of operations so suddenly. The most important reason given was that Bhindranwale would have asked the religious-minded Sikhs to congregate in their thousands at the Golden Temple to prevent the Army operations there; such a development would have led to either massive use of force by the Army against the mobs or abandonment of the siege itself. In support of this argument, Sundarji has clarified that the Army had intercepted messages going out to the countryside from Bhindranwale and his people from inside the Golden Temple asking the Sikhs to rush to Amritsar in large numbers to defend the temple. Even if such messages had gone out, can one come to the conclusion that the ordinary people in the countryside would have obeyed such commands from Bhindranwale and flocked to Amritsar as Sundarji had feared?

Let me put forward my analysis. The Sikhs are, by and large, a religious-minded people and when a call is given that they should rise in defence of their religion, a positive response can be expected from a large number. But their response would also depend on who gives the call, for what purpose and in what circumstances. During the three years when Bhindranwale dominated the Punjab scene, he never had a mass following in the Sikh community. All the killings, lootings and attacks on government properties were carried out by individuals or groups consisting of a few extremists. The Sikh masses had never approved of such activities. On the other hand, there was growing resentment among large sections of the Sikhs at the manner in which the agitation was developing into a Hindu–Sikh confrontation. Bhindranwale himself did not rely on mass support for his activities; in fact, he had only contempt for the politics of Longowal and other Akali leaders who were always anxious to gain the support of the masses. Therefore, it is very doubtful whether the Sikh masses would have responded to Bhindranwale's call in such large numbers as to have caused a real threat to the powerful Indian Army. Even if some crowds tried to march to Amritsar the Indian Army, with its massive presence all over Punjab, with the support of the large police force placed under its command and with the cooperation of the large silent majority among the Punjabi population, could have controlled them and prevented them from interfering with the operations in Amritsar. The mobs, if any came forward, could have been handled through the effective imposition of curfew and other appropriate action.

The clear-cut instructions to the Army from the prime minister were to flush out terrorists from the temples without causing damage to the temple buildings. How an experienced general could assure the prime minister on 29 May that the Army would be able to flush out the extremists from the Golden Temple by direct commando action, without causing damage to the buildings, is something I have not understood. This aspect leads to the next question: had the Army commanders collected the required information about the strength and deployment of the extremists inside the temple? It becomes clear from the details relating to the operation that the commanders came to know about the nature of the weapons and the strength of the extremists *only after* they found that the commandos whom they sent in first could make little headway and were being picked off by the extremists from extremely well-fortified positions inside the temple. The officer in command, Major General Brar, is reported to have told the media later that he found his infantry 'in danger of being massacred' and it was at that stage that he was compelled to send in the tanks. The question that any layman would ask is: why did Army intelligence fail to assess the strength and deployment of the terrorists *before* deciding on the plan of entry by the commandos? The Golden Temple was easily accessible to intelligence teams for several weeks before the operations started and the collection of all the data necessary on the militants' strength and positions would not have been a difficult job. If correct information about their numbers and weapons was available to the Army commanders, it is doubtful whether they would have gone ahead with the changed plan of operations in the manner they did, which later necessitated the entry of tanks.

Sundarji's oft-quoted statement to the press that the Army units went inside the Golden Temple 'with humility in their hearts and prayers on their lips' shows their noble intentions. Another statement of his reveals the secular credentials of the armed forces: 'We in the Army hold all places of religion in equal reverence.' There was no pressure from any high political level that the operations should be completed before a particular date. It was entirely for the Army commanders to decide as to when they should start the operations and, therefore, there cannot be any complaint from any quarters that adequate time was not given to the Army for gathering intelligence.

The next question focuses on the failure to judge correctly the mood and the possible reaction of the ordinary jawans. As I have stated earlier, this was a problem anticipated by the prime minister herself and she had specifically asked General Vaidya whether there would be any adverse reaction, and if so, what he proposed to do. The senior Army officers apparently never thought that an operation like this could really infuse intense frenzy in some of their men and, therefore, did not take the precaution of explaining the reasons properly to their juniors in advance. The top brass should have put it in no uncertain terms that the objective of the Army action was not the capture of the Golden Temple or other places of worship, but to flush out the militants who had forcibly occupied these places and converted them into arsenals and centres for directing acts of terror and violence. They should have emphasized the fact that for several weeks, before the military operation, ordinary worshippers did not have free access to the Golden Temple because the entire area had been converted into a fortified place. The main tasks of the Army, they should have explained, were to hand over the temple to its rightful and legal managers and to restore normal religious services there for the benefit of the worshippers. If the issues involved had been put in proper perspective, probably even the few cases of revolt that occurred may not have. There had indeed been a failure somewhere at the top levels of the Army command to take these normal precautions.

Whatever may be the explanations and justifications for the sudden change of the plan of operation, I can definitely state on basis of the clear knowledge of Indira Gandhi's thinking at that time that she agreed to the revision of the earlier plan at the eleventh hour strictly on the assurance given to her that the whole operation would be completed swiftly and without any damage to the buildings within the Golden Temple complex. Obviously, the Army commanders sincerely believed that they would be able to fulfil this assurance. Their failure resulted from their going ahead with the operation without being fully aware of the real situation inside the temple. Brar has stated in his book *Operation Blue Star: The True Story* (UBSPD, New Delhi, 1993) that he was getting ready to leave on a month's holiday for Manila on 1 June 1984, but was suddenly asked to report to Sundarji on that date. When he did so, he was informed by the general that he was to be placed in charge of Operation Blue Star. He was not familiar at all with the situation inside the Golden Temple. All his knowledge about the problem and the means for tackling it came from the briefing he had received on 1 June. As a brave and disciplined soldier he accepted the assignment even though he had not been given the time to get adequately prepared.

None of the senior officers, including Sundarji who was mainly responsible for the sudden change in the plan, asked for more time to prepare for the operation. If they wanted more time, the prime minister would have readily agreed to their request. But they set the target date for the operation themselves presumably under the impression that a surprise attack would result in a quick victory and went ahead with the operation on 5 June. The lack of proper preparation before launching the operation undoubtedly led to the most unexpected reverses for their plans.

Indira Gandhi did not consider Operation Blue Star a mistake. The mistake was in the *manner of implementing* the decision and not in the decision itself. It was Indira Gandhi's consistent policy not to criticize the Army either in private or in public even if she was convinced about the lapses in the implementation of the decision.

The fallout of the Army operations in the Golden Temple brought in its wake more problems than possibly anticipated. The most important development was a new mood of defiance and militancy among the priests of the Golden Temple. They had been keeping a low profile when Bhindranwale had been operating initially from Guru Nanak Niwas and later from the Akal Takht. They were so cowed down then that they had not protested even when Bhindranwale threatened to throw them out. After the Army had cleared the temple of all the extremists, the priests developed the courage to assert their authority. They announced that no repairs to the Akal Takht would be approved by them till the Army withdrew completely from the temple and its attached buildings.

Immediately after the operations of 6 and 7 June, the Army personnel tried to clean up the place and to attend to some urgently needed repairs to the walls, floors and ceilings. President Zail Singh was scheduled to visit the Golden Temple on 8 June and a large phalanx of photographers and reporters would be accompanying him. The Army tried to spruce up the premises to the extent possible within the short time available, but the Akal Takht was in a shambles and needed a few weeks for restoration to its original state. The recitation of *kirtans* had been resumed, but regular visits by worshippers had not yet been permitted. The priests took the stand that they were responsible for the management of the temple and, therefore, for the repairs to the Akal Takht, but that they would start the repairs only after the Army was withdrawn from the temple. The prime minister was quite firm in her stand that the Army would not be withdrawn till the repairs were completed and the Akal Takht was restored to its original condition. She believed that if the Army was withdrawn, the priests and the Akali leaders would prevent all efforts to repair the Akal Takht and would keep the buildings in their ruined condition in order to whip up anger among religious-minded Sikhs against the government. Her fear, based on reliable intelligence reports, was that the Akalis and the groups of militants wanted to keep the damaged Akal Takht in that condition as a monument to the alleged repression of the Sikhs by the government and build a new Akal Takht near the site of the ruined building. She was, therefore, determined to keep the Army within the temple premises till the Akal Takht was rebuilt and deputed Buta Singh (a Sikh), the then Union minister for works and housing, to make quick arrangements for the work of repairs and reconstruction.

Buta Singh began visiting Amritsar by special plane or helicopter very frequently after the Army action. He carried out negotiations with the priests to arrive at a mutually agreeable arrangement for the rebuilding of the Akal Takht. On 19 June, Buta Singh was engaged in one such round of talks with the priests at Amritsar. At about 8.30 p.m., the prime minister saw a news item flashed by both the agencies UNI (United News of India) and PTI (Press Trust of India) attributing to Buta Singh a statement at Amritsar that the prime minister had accepted the demand of the priests to hand over the temple to them and that the Army would be withdrawn by 20 June. She was very upset and angry at this news and asked me to contradict it straightaway. We tried our best to establish contact with Buta Singh at Amritsar but could not. He was expected back in Delhi later in the night, but even without waiting for his return, the news was contradicted through a statement that we hastily drafted and the next day's newspapers carried the official announcement that 'there was no decision to hand over the temple to the priests till the repairs to the buildings were completed'.

It was quite unlike Buta Singh to exceed his brief, particularly when he had strict instructions from Indira Gandhi herself. Everyone, including Buta Singh, knew about the prime minister's firm stand that the Army would *not* be withdrawn from the temple premises before receiving credible assurances from the priests that they would not allow the militants to regain possession of the temple. Buta Singh flatly denied the next day (i.e., 20 June) that he had given any assurance to the priests about the Army's withdrawal. He vehemently asserted that he had been 'misquoted' by the media. Anyhow, the timely contradiction (on 19 June) made it amply clear to the priests that the government would not make any compromise on its stand on the withdrawal of the Army.

The prime minister wanted to hand over control of the temple to the priests and withdraw the Army after completion of repairs to the buildings but only upon securing credible assurances from them that they would ensure that the premises would not be allowed to be used by the extremists again. She also wanted a thorough revamping of the Punjab Administration. Unfortunately, B.D. Pande, the governor, had come in for a lot of undeserved flak from the president and also from some prominent Punjab politicians. The governor, on his own, could not have done anything to change the course of events in Punjab; nevertheless, he submitted his resignation. On 23 June, Indira Gandhi paid a brief visit to the Golden Temple. She was quite shocked by what she saw there and became more convinced than before that the Army's presence there was definitely needed for some more time. She told me on her return to Delhi that replacements should be immediately found for the governor, the chief of the police and the advisers. K.T. Satarawala, the lieutenant governor of Goa, was considered as Pande's successor, and I talked to him about the proposed move. He was not very happy at the prospect of going to Punjab but accepted the appointment, in deference to the prime minister's wishes.

The situation in Punjab remained as bewildering as before. The three senior Akali leaders, Longowal, Badal and Tohra, were still in jail. Many second-level leaders had also been arrested. The Army had launched combing operations all over the state and many persons suspected of involvement in terrorist activities had been rounded up and remanded to custody. There was a vacuum as far as the management of the temple was concerned because most SGPC members had been put behind bars. The priests were trying to project themselves as the custodians of the temple. Some of them had even assumed for themselves the role of being the authentic spokesmen for the Sikh community. It was against such a backdrop that the priests announced that they would themselves organize the *karseva* for the repairs if the Army was withdrawn. The prime minister was not prepared to accept the assurance of the priests on its face value and the stalemate on the reconstruction of the buildings continued. Buta Singh's efforts at reaching an understanding with the priests yielded no results.

✧

No appreciable abatement in violence occurred despite the large-scale combing operations by the Army and the arrest of many extremists and others suspected to be their supporters. The government was facing more or less the same tense situation in Punjab as it existed before the Army action. The tension was aggravated further by an incident that took place on 5 July 1984. At about 3.30 p.m. an Indian Airlines Airbus, which left Srinagar for Delhi and Bombay, was hijacked by Sikh extremists who wanted to take the plane to Lahore, Pakistan. The plane was running out of fuel and the pilot wanted to land at Amritsar, but the hijackers insisted on taking it to Lahore. After discussing the situation with the prime minister, we conveyed clearance at about 6.30 p.m. that the plane may be taken to Lahore. We requested the Pakistani authorities in Lahore and Islamabad not to permit refuelling and remained continuously in telephonic contact with them. At about 10 p.m. the hijackers announced their demands: all arrested members of the All-India Sikh Students' Federation (AISSF) should be released and that the hijackers should be paid $20 million in cash. The demands were rejected straightaway. The hijackers appeared to be about ten in number and the passenger count on board the aircraft was about 240. Nerve-racking negotiations with the hijackers went on throughout the night of 5 July and continued till about 1.30 in the afternoon the next day. The Pakistani officials conducted the negotiations; eventually, the hijackers surrendered unconditionally. The Government of India had sent a group of commandos to Amritsar to stand in readiness in case a swift operation was permitted by the Pakistani authorities. Finally, the hijackers were granted asylum in Pakistan and the passengers returned to India in a Pakistani plane.

While Indira Gandhi was greatly relieved at the fact that all passengers had returned to India safely, she was not particularly happy about the asylum given to the hijackers. From the time the plane landed at Lahore, all negotiations with the hijackers were handled exclusively by the Pakistani officials; in fact, they did not allow the Indian ambassador, who had rushed to Lahore, to take any part in them. The hijackers seemed to have agreed to surrender primarily because they had been promised asylum in Pakistan.

When the government's attempts at persuading the priests to organize *karseva* for repairs to the Akal Takht failed, Buta Singh came up with an alternative: enlisting the services of Baba Santa Singh, the head of a group of Nihangs,* not so widely accepted as a sant or high priest by the Sikh community in general, but otherwise having good credentials to perform tasks like *karseva*. Almost a month had gone by without any organized efforts for the restoration of the building and the prime minister was determined that the work should not be put off any longer. Santa Singh's services were, therefore, accepted and the Baba and his Nihangs promptly started *karseva* after performing the prescribed religious rites. Multitudes of pious Sikhs from all over Punjab and neighbouring states voluntarily took part in the process of repair and restoration. Visuals of hundreds of Sikh men and women clearing debris and carrying head-loads of bricks, cement and other construction materials appeared daily on the TV screens, much to the annoyance and discomfiture of not only the priests in the Golden Temple but also the extremists. The priests issued a notice to Santa Singh, threatening to excommunicate him for his alleged irreligious act in organizing *karseva*. Santa Singh also received several threats to his personal safety. By now he had moved into the temple complex along with his Nihangs and he quite contemptuously dismissed the priests' notice of excommunication and the threats from the extremists. The priests declared Santa Singh *Tankhaiya* (excommunicated), but this 'stigma' did not deter him, or the hundreds of voluntary workers who were performing *karseva* every day, from continuing with their work. The legions of voluntary

---

* Nihang Sikhs are warriors whose origin can be traced back to a tradition begun by the tenth Sikh Guru – Guru Gobind Singh (1666–1708).

workers kept on increasing even after the *hukumnama* (diktat) issued by the priests. The priests, as a consequence of their accommodative behaviour towards the extremists during the occupation of the temple by Bhindranwale, had lost much of their moral authority among the community and thus their *hukumnama* had got devalued.

The Akalis and the extremists were getting frustrated at the smooth progress of the reconstruction work. In spite of the initial doubts about Santa Singh's credentials and abilities, he proved to be an effective leader capable of engendering and sustaining religious fervour and enthusiasm among the voluntary workers, who toiled ceaselessly round the clock in batches. On 11 August, the nationalist groups among the Sikhs organized a 'Sarbat Khalsa'* attended by over one lakh of their brethren at Amritsar; it was this event that provided the moral sanction for the ongoing *karseva* for the restoration of the Akal Takht. The presence of the *jathedar* of Gurdwara Patna Saheb, one of the recognized high priests of the Sikhs, at the function lent weight and prestige to the Sarbat Khalsa. This development further infuriated the extremists.

✧

Another hijacking took place on 24 August 1984. It appeared as if the extremists could again strike at will as in the days before the Army action. We were informed at about 8.30 that morning that an Indian Airlines plane on its flight from Chandigarh had been hijacked by Sikh extremists and had been forced to fly to Lahore. On all such occasions the Crisis Management Group members in the Cabinet Secretariat would come together immediately and continue to operate from there till the imbroglio was resolved. The group met at 9 a.m. and, within a few minutes, the information was flashed that the hijackers were insisting on being given free passage and visas to the USA. The Pakistanis had allowed the plane to take off from Lahore without informing us. The plane later landed at Karachi.

I went to the prime minister's residence at about 8 p.m. to apprise her of the current situation on the hijack drama. I conveyed to her the suggestion of the Crisis Management Group that she may consider

---

* Literally 'the entire Sikh nation'.

talking to President Zia-ul Haq of Pakistan directly on the hotline. She agreed do so in order to seek his intervention in ensuring that the hijackers were sent back to India. I was with her when the call came through at 8.40 p.m. I could discern that Zia was not exactly warm in his response to the proposal. He started off by asserting that India had not been very appreciative of Pakistan's role in previous hijacking incidents and, therefore, his country's intervention would again be criticized in India, despite all his efforts. Indira Gandhi responded that there was no such criticism in India as stated by him and, at any rate, he should now try to cooperate without raking up previous controversies. Zia then switched tracks and asserted he would do everything possible to save the lives of the crew and the passengers. Indira Gandhi offered to send commandos from India, but Zia countered by saying that Pakistan had enough equipment and troops at Karachi to handle the situation. We got the impression that Zia would order a commando operation immediately, but we found even after four hours had gone by that nothing was happening. It now became obvious that Pakistan would not help us.

At about 1 a.m. (on 25 August) the cabinet secretary and I went to Narasimha Rao's house for consultations. From there the three of us rushed to the prime minister's house. She was asleep, but had to be woken up. We apprised her of our apprehensions. We obtained her permission to inform the Pakistanis that we had no objection if they wished to send the hijackers to the USA from Karachi provided they would allow the crew and passengers to return to India. Narasimha Rao spoke to General K.M. Arif in Pakistan, whom he knew personally and conveyed this message. General Arif repeated what President Zia had said earlier. We realized again that the Pakistanis were not going to do anything on the lines suggested by us. Within an hour or so, they allowed the plane (along with the crew and passengers) to take off from Karachi and fly towards the Gulf. Dubai permitted the plane to land on its soil, where from then on, the scene of negotiations shifted to.

We contacted Harry Barnes, the US ambassador to India, to seek the permission of the authorities in Washington to send the hijackers to that country as requested by them. Fortunately, the officials in both Dubai and the USA were quite cooperative and after a good deal of negotiations between Delhi and Dubai as well as Delhi and the USA, an agreement was finally reached that the hijackers would be allowed seven days asylum in UAE. After that, they would be given travel documents and tickets to proceed to the USA. M.K. Rasgotra, India's foreign secretary, was actively involved in these negotiations. At about 8.45 p.m., our ambassador in Dubai, Assiz Ishaque, who had played a very useful role in the negotiations with the Dubai authorities, informed me telephonically: 'Sir, the drama has ended happily and our people are all safe and back in the airport lounge.'

Even though the passengers returned home safely, we continued our efforts to get the hijackers back to India. Ambassador Barnes informed us that it would be very difficult to extradite the hijackers to India once they reached the US, because they could claim political asylum and, if granted, a prolonged legal battle may ensue. Consequently, we explored different alternatives for getting the hijackers back to India. We deputed Romesh Bhandari, secretary in the Ministry of External Affairs, for conducting negotiations with the Dubai authorities on this issue. Finally, after a week of continuous negotiations, for which Bhandari's services proved very helpful, it was agreed by all parties that the hijackers would be escorted in a US plane, from Dubai to India, by a team of trained commandos whom we had sent to Dubai for this purpose. All arrangements worked satisfactorily and the hijackers were brought to Delhi on 2 September 1984.

The persistent and successful efforts undertaken by the government to secure the return of the hijackers to India were appreciated virtually all over the country, but the Akalis and the extremists were not particularly pleased. They had already reverted to the war path on the issue of the Army withdrawal from the Golden Temple and the alleged atrocities of the soldiers who were engaged in combing operations against the terrorists. There were complaints from the priests about the alleged irreverential behaviour of our soldiers within the Golden Temple like smoking and drinking alcohol. The Army authorities, who had investigated these complaints, found them baseless; nevertheless, the complaints persisted and a lot of bitterness was created on this account.

✧

The Sikh priests announced that they would organize a 'World Conference' of Sikhs on 2 September 1984 to focus upon the situation resulting from the Army action in the Golden Temple. This conference was held in a gurdwara in Amritsar and was adroitly utilized by the priests to assert their authority as the authentic leaders of the Sikh community. Fiery speeches set the tone at the conference. The speakers castigated the government and the Army for their alleged repressive measures against the Sikhs. The conference fixed 30 September as the deadline for the Army's withdrawal and the handing over of the temple to the priests. The conference resolved to launch a statewide agitation commencing on 1 October and to march to the Golden Temple to seize it by force, if the government failed to accept their demands. The conference proclaimed President Zail Singh and Union Minister Buta Singh as *Tankhaiya* for their alleged 'anti-Sikh activities'.

Given the ultimatum issued by the priests and the various defiant resolutions passed by the 'World Conference', the situation was almost back to square one, except that the place of Bhindranwale was now occupied by the priests, although they were not publicly advocating violence and terrorism. The central issue this time was transfer of the temple to the control of the priests and withdrawal of the Army from its premises.

While the reconstruction of the Akal Takht was going ahead at top speed, Indira Gandhi asked us to make arrangements for a peaceful transfer of the temple to the priests upon completion of the work. But she insisted that the priests give an undertaking that the temple would not be allowed to be misused by the extremists in future. In negotiating the terms for transfer of the temple with the Akalis as well as with the priests, the government used the good offices of a well-intentioned intermediary (who enjoyed the trust and respect of the Sikhs), namely, Aswini Kumar, former, head of the Punjab Police. He met me many times in his informal capacity as intermediary and finally informed me that the acting president of the Akali Dal, Prakash Singh Majithia, had indicated his willingness to come for secret talks, if they had the approval of the prime minister. The prime minister agreed to the idea of holding such talks and authorized Narasimha

Rao and me to represent the government. We met Majithia at a government guest house in Vasant Vihar, New Delhi, on 15 September evening and found him to be quite reasonable in his attitude. He was keen to reach an arrangement satisfactory to both the government and the Akalis. We told him that since the work of reconstruction and repair of the building was almost complete, the prime minister was quite willing and even keen to withdraw the Army and hand over the management of the temple to the priests and the SGPC. We, however, insisted that the government, should receive a written undertaking from the SGPC and the priests that they would no longer allow the temple to be occupied by the extremists or to be used for storage of arms or for terrorists and secessionist activities by any group. We also suggested that as a gesture of goodwill, the priests should withdraw the *Tankhaiya* decree against Zail Singh, Buta Singh and Santa Singh. A few civil cases had been filed against Santa Singh, which we wanted to be withdrawn. We assured Majithia that all security forces, including the Army, would be withdrawn and the temple would be handed over to the SGPC and the priests immediately on receipt of such an undertaking. Majithia agreed that the terms were fair and reasonable. He said that he would return on 20 September for further talks on this matter after consulting the priests and his colleagues in the Akali Party.

The talks had been held in strict secrecy, but President Zail Singh received a full account of the discussion from one of his sources within the Akali Party. He was furious on this count. He expressed his annoyance to Narasimha Rao for holding talks with the Akalis on crucial matters without taking him into confidence and angrily asked him: 'How can an Alexander and a Narasimha Rao hold discussions on such matters without informing me?' Narasimha Rao explained that the talks were held according to specific instructions of the prime minister and that any agreement regarding withdrawal of the *hukumnama* against the president would definitely be cleared with him before finalization. Zail Singh expressed the same view to Indira Gandhi though in much softer terms when she called on him later.

Narasimha Rao and I held another meeting with Majithia on 20 September at the same venue. The talks lasted from 6.30 p.m.

to 8 p.m. Majithia informed us that the priests were totally opposed to dropping the *Tankhaiya* against Santa Singh; they had no such problems with Zail Singh or Buta Singh. On the question of giving a written undertaking as demanded by the government, Majithia told us that the priests had suggested that they would instead give a solemn assurance orally from within the Harmandir Sahib. Majithia wanted all points of agreement to be put in writing so that he could obtain firm confirmation from the priests and all others concerned on that basis.

Narasimha Rao and I discussed the matter with Indira Gandhi on the night of 20 September itself and, as directed by her, prepared a 'non-paper' containing the agreed terms to be passed on to Majithia informally. This document was handed over to Majithia the next morning and he left for Amritsar immediately for consultations with his colleagues and the priests.

Indira Gandhi and Narasimha Rao met Zail Singh on 22 September and apprised him of our talks with Majithia and the terms and conditions on which the temple was to be handed over to the priests. It was on this occasion that Zail Singh informed the prime minister for the first time that he was planning a visit to the Golden Temple. She tried to dissuade him from doing so as it would upset the process leading to the agreement that was being hammered out with the priests and the Akalis very cautiously and in the face of tremendous odds. But the president appeared determined to visit the temple. Under these circumstances the prime minister decided, on the night of 25 September, to announce the withdrawal of the security forces from the temple and hand over the premises to the priests, thereby avoiding a new controversy involving the president.

Once an announcement was made, the government lost the leverage to secure from the priests the assurances it had insisted upon. As stated earlier, the government had been assured that the priests would make a solemn statement containing the required undertaking sitting in front of the Guru Granth Sahib inside the Golden Temple. This act would have been a more binding assurance than any written undertaking. But now the government had to be content with just a public statement issued by the priests before handing over the temple to them. The priests felt very jubilant at the fact that they were getting control of the temple without giving the solemn assurances before the Guru Granth Sahib as earlier agreed to by them.

Having announced the decision to hand over the temple, the first task was to get Baba Santa Singh out of there. Santa Singh had developed a very foul temper by now. He was rather angry that Zail Singh, who visited the temple on 27 September and spent quite some time with the priests, had not met him. He expressed his annoyance to all those who visited him and persistently complained that the government was slighting him after having used his services during a time of crisis. The priests had set 6 a.m. on 29 September as the time to begin their *Ardhas* (a form of prayer) at the temple, but in spite of persistent persuasion and pressure Santa Singh refused to leave earlier. When he finally agreed to quit on 29 September, it was only after fixing 7 a.m. as the time for his *Ardhas*. Nerve-racking negotiations continued with Santa Singh on one side and with the priests on the other, and, finally, late in the night of 28 September, Santa Singh agreed to wind up his ceremony by 10 a.m. the next day and the priests agreed to commence theirs at 11 a.m. Santa Singh's comments about the manner in which he was being hustled were very bitter and, at one stage, he even threatened to court arrest. Finally, he agreed to leave in peace and marched out of the Golden Temple with his Nihangs at 10.10 a.m. on 29 November. Immediately thereafter, R.V. Subramaniam, adviser to the governor, handed over the keys of the *Tosha Khana* (treasury) to the priests and the government withdrew the troops guarding it.

Just at this time, a most unexpected development took place, which almost led to a breakdown of the entire handing over proceedings. I was following very closely the developments in the temple on 28 and 29 September through reports coming over the telephone and I constantly kept the prime minister informed. Suddenly a report was flashed that a bunch of extremists had raised pro-Khalistan slogans from inside the temple and that they were planning to reoccupy the temple immediately after the withdrawal of the troops. At about 10.50 a.m. on 29 September, Indira Gandhi called me over to her office and instructed me not to proceed with the handing over of the rest of the buildings until we received unequivocal assurances from the priests about their readiness to prevent misuse of the temple by secessionists and terrorists. I found her in an extremely agitated and angry mood. She repeatedly emphasized that under no circumstances should terrorists be allowed to use the temple again. She was insistent that the priests be made to accept this responsibility and, if they did not agree to do so, status quo should continue till they agreed.

Fortunately, for the government, Subramaniam was a very experienced administrator, who could handle dicey situations with firmness and tact. My problem was that I *had to* contact him before he handed over possession of the remaining buildings to the priests. He was inside the temple somewhere negotiating with the priests and in those days, when mobile phones were not available, communication was not all that simple. I dashed off messages to four different persons in Amritsar that Subramaniam should contact me immediately. I came to know later that Subramaniam was already in the process of completing the formalities for handing over the remaining buildings, but fortunately my message to the Intelligence Bureau officer in Amritsar reached him in the nick of time. Subramaniam immediately called me. I quickly conveyed the PM's instructions to him and asked him to come over forthwith to Delhi for urgent consultations. The handing over of the buildings was stopped just two minutes before the appointed time.

Subramaniam and Lieutenant General Gowri Shankar, who had succeeded Lieutenant General Dayal as security adviser to the governor, rushed to the capital. The three of us met the prime minister together at her office on 29 September afternoon. She told Subramaniam and Gowri Shankar in a very firm tone that the priests *must* accept the responsibility for keeping the extremists out of the temple and there could be no compromise whatsoever on this condition. She sternly added that if the priests declared that they had no control over the extremists, the security forces should continue to remain in the temple.

The prime minister's apprehensions about the inability of the priests to keep the extremists out of the temple were proved correct by some ugly incidents that took place in the temple on 1 October 1984. The day was being observed as the 'Bhog' day. While the religious ceremonies were going on, about 200 extremists forcibly snatched the microphone from the priests and started shouting anti-government slogans into it. Some of them waved Khalistan flags and made highly provocative speeches in its support. The priests could not control the situation and, at about 3.30 p.m., the police entered the temple and seized the flags and nabbed nearly 150 extremists. The Army stood in readiness to enter the temple and to assist the police, if found necessary. Fortunately, the police could carry out the arrests and restore peace on its own. This incident served to convince the extremists and also the priests that the government would not hesitate to send the armed forces into the temple if the occasion demanded.

An unfortunate sequel to this incident was that the priests came out on 2 October with a totally distorted account of the happenings inside the temple. Instead of condemning the extremists for again trying to misuse the place of worship in their very presence, the priests laid the blame squarely on the government and betrayed their inability or lack of will to face the realities of the situation. The home minister issued a strong statement warning the extremists that the government would deal very sternly with all anti-national activities.

The priests, meanwhile, had been persisting with their demand for the transfer of the remaining buildings in the temple complex to their control. Subramaniam had, in his several rounds of discussions with them, insisted that they should accept responsibility for preventing the entry of the extremists into the temple and all the buildings attached to it as a precondition for the aforementioned transfer. Finally, the priests agreed to accept that responsibility and to include this clause specifically in the minutes of his discussions with them. A copy of the agreed minutes was handed over to them and they acknowledged it in token of their acceptance of their responsibility. On 5 October the prime minister agreed that the control of the remaining buildings could be handed over to the priests.

The process of handing over the buildings started on 8 October and was completed the next day. The effort involved in removing the debris and broken and burnt furniture from these buildings was rather time consuming. One of the lockers in the buildings contained

Rs 15,000 in Pakistani currency apart from several cartridges. They were confiscated by the government.

In view of some positive developments, such as the handing over of all the buildings to the priests, the withdrawal of the security forces from the temple complex and the understanding reached with the priests about preventing future misuse of the temple and its premises by the extremists, we expected that all controversies would end and normal religious activities would be resumed in the temple. The priests organized a *karseva* on 11 and 12 October to clean up the temple tank. Thousands of people participated in this voluntary effort to remove the silt and dirt and restore the tank to its original condition marked by cleanliness and purity. Some opposition leaders also participated in the *karseva*. The temple soon reverted to its normal schedule of worship, and Sikhs and Hindus from all over started thronging the temple in their thousands.

On the surface, there was an appearance of normalcy as far as the temple was concerned, but it was obvious to everyone that the extremists were nursing their grievances and trying to resume their subversive activities though not so openly as before. Tension continued to simmer beneath the surface and the general feeling was that the problems had only been set aside for the present, but not solved.

Many people have asked me a crucial question: why did Indira Gandhi fail to inform President Zail Singh in advance about entrusting such sensitive operations to the Army? Some have queried whether it was because he was a Sikh. Nothing can be more absurd an assumption than this because all those who knew Indira Gandhi well also knew that she had absolutely no prejudice against, or dislike of, the Sikh community. On the other hand, she had the highest regard and respect for the community and the thought of any discriminatory action based on their religion would never have entered her mind. In fact some of the senior military officers such as General Dayal, Major General Brar and Major General Gurdial Singh, who were entrusted with the responsibility for the Army operations in Punjab, were themselves Sikhs. The only reason I can think of as to why she did not inform President Zail Singh about her decision on the final stages of Punjab operations was that her relations with him by then were strained to the extent of her losing full trust in him. (I have already dealt with this aspect in Chapter 9.) Another reason may be that the way the operation inside the Golden Temple turned out was quite unexpected and she could not have anticipated the seriousness of the damage caused.

These explanations may not be adequate for not informing the president about so important a decision as calling in the Army for operations inside the Golden Temple premises. In fact, it has even been argued by some that her failure to keep Zail Singh informed about seeking the aid of the Army was itself the chief reason for their strained relations. The matter of not informing the president about the Army operations never arose in any of her talks with me either before or after the operations and therefore I cannot say anything more about this topic based on personal knowledge.

ELEVEN

With Rajiv Gandhi

RAJIV GANDHI HAD DECIDED THAT HE WOULD ATTEND OFFICE ONLY after the mourning period of twelve days was over. However, I had been meeting him regularly at his residence to discuss official matters and had also been sending him the relevant files.

By 5 November 1984, Delhi had almost returned to normal though some of the displaced members of the Sikh community, particularly, women and children, were still living in the temporary camps.

The last remains of Indira Gandhi were collected from the funeral pyre on 5 November and kept in thirty-five urns under a tree at the same place in the Teen Murti compound where Jawaharlal Nehru's ashes had been kept some two decades earlier. Pupul Jayakar had informed Rajiv that Indira Gandhi had told her (Pupul) a few days before her death that her mortal remains should be scattered over the Himalayas, for which she had developed a great fascination right from her childhood. Rajiv decided to fulfil this wish. Hence, he requested the chief ministers and governors to take the urns containing the lasts remains to their respective capital cities for *darshan* by the people and return them to Delhi within five days. After that, the ashes were to be scattered over the Himalayas on 11 November.

The urns were transported to the Hindon airport at Ghaziabad (in Uttar Pradesh, neighbouring Delhi) from where they were to be taken by Rajiv in a plane. A solemn send-off ceremony was conducted at the Teen Murti compound. The three service chiefs saluted the urns and the bands played a farewell tune when they were being placed on a decorated truck. One urn was placed in a helicopter in which Rajiv, Sonia, two or three close family members and I travelled to the airport at Ghaziabad. He stepped down from the helicopter first and I then stepped down the ladder holding the urn in both hands and handed it over to him. (This was an honour that Rajiv accorded to me.) After brief prayers Rajiv took off in an IAF aircraft with all the urns containing the mortal remains to scatter them over the Himalayas. The rest of us returned to Delhi by the same helicopter immediately after the departure of the IAF aircraft.

On 9 November the prime minister held a fairly long discussion with me about holding general elections as early as possible. He asked me to ascertain the views of the chief election commissioner, R.K. Trivedi, about advancing the dates to the last week of December 1984, if possible. Trivedi agreed to fix 24 and 27 December as the dates for polling and 28 December as the date for counting of votes.

From then on elections dominated the attention of the media and political parties, some of which had been taken by surprise. The opposition parties were sharply divided and could not reach any agreement about setting up a joint front against the Congress. N.T. Rama Rao, the chief minister of Andhra Pradesh and head of the Telugu Desam Party, was interested in cementing an electoral understanding with the Congress so that certain number of seats could be contested by that party in his state. However, in spite of prolonged discussions, an agreement on the number of seats that the TDP would leave uncontested could not be reached. Eventually, the Congress fought the elections in Andhra Pradesh on its own.

Another decision taken by the prime minister was to request the vice-president, R. Venkataraman, to be the chairman of the committee for instituting a suitable memorial for Indira Gandhi. According to convention, the president of India should have been its chairman, but Rajiv personally thought differently.

Rajiv decided that he would begin attending his office at South Block from 12 November, by which date the mourning period would have ended. A slew of senior functionaries of the Ministry of External Affairs wanted to welcome the prime minister along with me at the entrance to the South Block (which housed a few ministries). I pointed out to them that this was Rajiv's visit to the PMO and not to the South Block; I firmly told them that only I would be present to receive him on his arrival. Rajiv arrived at 10.30 a.m. and I greeted him by offering him a single red rose. I then escorted him to his office where he spent about 20 minutes.

Within a few days of the announcement of the election dates, Rajiv started his whirlwind tour to different parts of the country. Almost every day he would come back from his election campaign well past midnight and would leave again before 5 a.m. Very often, I had to meet him at 1.30 a.m. or 2 a.m., when he reached home from the airport, to take oral orders on important matters and later record them on file.

On 30 November 1984, a train of events was set in motion that later proved to be crucial in my career as principal secretary. On this day I received a telephone call from the director of the Intelligence Bureau (DIB) that he wanted to meet me urgently on a very important matter. On meeting, he conveyed to me the startling news that my private secretary and some of the personal assistants working in my office were being suspected of passing on confidential information and copies of confidential documents to certain commercial establishments in the city. I was shocked beyond words that such activities could take place in the PMO and told the director to go ahead, with all the resources at his command, to identity those involved in such criminal activities. None of my staff, including my private secretary who supervised the day-to-day functioning of the stenographers and clerks, had been appointed by me. Having inherited them from the previous regimes, I had just carried on by utilizing the staff members already there on the obvious assumption that they had all been cleared by the concerned departments of the government from the security angle. I had also assumed that the intelligence agencies had carefully checked their antecedents and character before inducting them into this office and therefore I had considered them trustworthy and reliable.

The DIB brought to my notice that further confidential investigations would be necessary to verify the truth of the charges against them and that this process would involve shadowing them during their after-office hours to keep a continuous watch over their movements for some days. I told him that he should take whatever steps were found necessary to ascertain the truth and no mercy should be shown to anyone found indulging in such activities.

The room containing the workplaces of my private secretary and stenographers was just opposite my own office room. Whenever I had some very sensitive matters to handle, I would make them bring their typewriters inside my room for typing out letters or notes for which I would be giving dictation and personally ensure that the relevant pages in their notebook and the carbon papers were destroyed in the incinerator kept behind my chair. I knew that, in spite of such precautions, there was no foolproof method of preventing leakage of information or pilfering of documents by those bent upon committing such crimes. Anyhow, what I was immediately interested in was to ensure that the investigations proceeded without any hitch and all those involved in these activities were brought to book. I asked the DIB whether anyone of them should be placed under suspension straightaway but he replied that such a step would alert others who were involved in these activities. He said that some private secretaries and personal assistants working in certain other places such as defence, economic affairs, commerce and the Rashtrapati Bhavan were also suspected to be involved in these activities. He felt that all those under suspicion should continue to work without developing any doubts in their minds that they were under scrutiny. I fully agreed with him and assured him that the staff in my office would not get even an inkling that their activities were under investigation. I immediately informed the prime minister about the information I had received from the DIB and he agreed that every effort should be made to find out all those involved in such activities. Though I was deeply disturbed at the information I had received, I took special care to ensure that no one in my office got wind of the fact that the police were keeping a close watch over them.

One of the most tragic events of the 1980s was the leakage of highly toxic gas from the Union Carbide plant at Bhopal (on the night of 2–3 December 1984) resulting in the death of several hundreds of people and serious injuries of various types, particularly of the eyes, to several thousands. There was widespread panic in Bhopal that one more tank in the plant containing poisonous liquid may also start leaking, causing more deaths and injuries. Arjun Singh, the chief minister of Madhya Pradesh, met the prime minister at his house to provide the details about the large-scale loss of life and injuries and the measures taken to provide relief to the affected people. I was present at this meeting that took place very early in the morning a couple of days after the tragedy occurred. Some of Arjun Singh's political enemies had let loose a whispering campaign that the state government had failed to ensure that the industrial establishment of the Union Carbide in Bhopal strictly observed the required safety measures in the plant. Consequently, Arjun Singh appeared to be worried about Rajiv's possible reactions on this matter. He was at great pains to explain that the entire responsibility for the tragedy fell on the Union Carbide Company and its management should be punished for their gross negligence. Rajiv did not raise the question of the state government's responsibilities regarding safety measures and Arjun Singh was visibly relieved.

After obtaining prior permission, the president of Union Carbide, Warren Anderson, arrived at Bhopal on 7 December, but was promptly arrested by the local police. Immediately after his arrest, we received information that he was being sent to Delhi and had been permitted to return to the United States. The situation in Bhopal and the controversy as to who was actually responsible for the failure to detect the lapses in the safety arrangements in the plant were becoming highly embarrassing to the state government.

I received information that the prime minister would return to Delhi after his election tour at 2 a.m. on 9 December and that he wanted a meeting of the Cabinet Committee on Political Affairs to be held at 3.30 a.m. at his house to consider the situation in Bhopal. Dr S. Vardarajan, an eminent scientist, had been deputed to Bhopal along with a team made up of specialists and technical personnel for recommending the immediate measures to be taken to provide relief to the affected persons. He had also been requested to attend the meeting of the CCPA. A scheme for the transfer of the people living near the Union Carbide plant to safer places was approved by the CCPA. The meeting of the CCPA ended by 6 a.m. I stayed on for some more time with the prime minister to obtain his instructions on some urgent cases. It was at that stage that he told me to prepare a note for a major revamping of the Central cabinet and keep the proposals ready so that he could take up this exercise immediately after the election results were announced.

Meanwhile, the Justice (C.K.) Thakkar Commission, which had been appointed to enquire into the assassination of Indira Gandhi, had started functioning. On 13 December, I met Justice Thakkar at his residence (at his request) to brief him about the arrangement of work in the PMO and about the people working in the Prime Minister's House. I was somewhat surprised to note from some of his questions that he was harbouring a deep suspicion about the involvement of some persons in the PM's house in Indira Gandhi's assassination. He pointedly asked questions about R.K. Dhawan's role in continuing to retain some security guards belonging to the Sikh community even after receiving information from the intelligence agencies that the conduct of these guards had been suspect.

Investigations conducted by the group under the chairmanship of Anand Ram and the enquiry by the Justice Thakkar Commission appeared to be following one lead: 'the needle of suspicion' was pointing towards R.K. Dhawan in the conspiracy for the assassination of Indira Gandhi. I held another informal meeting with Justice Thakkar at his request and he asked me several questions about Indira Gandhi's relations with Dhawan during the last few months before her assassination. He wanted to gather more information, particularly about the strained relations between Indira Gandhi and Zail Singh. He also quizzed me about Indira Gandhi's alleged suspicion that Dhawan had been meeting Zail Singh very frequently and supporting the president who was opposed to the prime minister's policies in dealing with the Punjab agitation. I related to Justice Thakkar how the relations between Zail Singh and Indira Gandhi had soured during the last few months before her assassination. I told him that while I did not fully support the style of Dhawan's working in the PMH, I would never believe that he had any role at all in the conspiracy in her assassination. I very firmly asserted that Dhawan had remained fully loyal to her all through his service and it was unthinkable that he would ever be a party to the assassination of a person whom he served so sincerely. After listening to me he replied: 'Dr Alexander you are too good a gentleman to believe that some others can be wicked. Your difficulty is that you apply your standards to others.' In other words, he was telling me that he did not accept my assessment of Dhawan's role in the conspiracy to assassinate Indira Gandhi.

On 17 December 1984, the prime minister arrived at his house at 1.45 a.m. after a hectic campaign tour. I immediately met him and presented to him my proposals on the reorganization of the ministries and departments and the changes in the Council of Ministers. The PM discussed these proposals at some length with me and pointed out the major changes in the senior portfolios which he wanted to make immediately after the elections. He appeared to be quite confident that he would get the two-thirds majority in the Lok Sabha. In fact, the MARG opinion poll, organized by *India Today* magazine, had predicted that the Congress would bag 360 seats.

The Planning Commission also was to be reconstituted, as was the usual practice with the change of government at the Centre. In one of my discussions with the prime minister, I recommended that Dr Manmohan Singh (who was then the governor of the Reserve Bank of India) could be considered for the post of deputy chairman of the Planning Commission, R.N. Malhotra, secretary, Economic Affairs, could be appointed as governor in Dr Singh's place and Abid Hussain, who was due to retire as secretary in the Ministry of Commerce, be appointed as a member of the Planning Commission. On 20 December, the PM accepted the proposals made by me.

After obtaining the PM's informal approval I requested Dr Manmohan Singh to meet me in my office for holding consultations on the composition of the Planning Commission. He suggested the names of Hiten Bayya and Raja Chelliah. I prepared a note for the PM's formal approval for the reconstitution of the Planning Commission, which was submitted to him immediately after the elections were over and was cleared by him straightaway.

Just five days before the counting of votes, Prannoy Roy, today a well-known TV celebrity and psephologist, who had then just begun his career in India, met me in my office. He asserted with absolute certainty that, according to his estimates, Rajiv's party would bag more than 400 seats in the Lok Sabha. This number was probably the highest ever predicted for the Congress in any election. I immediately informed Rajiv, who was more circumspect in that he hoped to win around 380 seats. When the results started pouring in on 28 December 1984, the fact that the Congress would cross the 400-mark predicted by Roy became obvious. Ultimately, the Congress swept the polls everywhere except in Andhra Pradesh, where it managed to scrape through with just six or seven seats. In most states the Congress victory was almost total.

On 29 December, I spent nearly two hours discussing with the prime minister various significant matters such as the reconstitution of the ministries as well as the various departments of the Central Government, the induction of new ministers into, and the dropping of some others from, the cabinet. When I met the prime minister again at 9 a.m. on 31 December, he had finalized the list of the ministers after making a few last-minute changes. One change was the induction of K.R. Narayanan as the minister of state in place of Vakkom Purushothaman whose name he had earlier approved. (I am particularly mentioning this fact as this decision marked the beginning of a new political career for Narayanan, which later propelled him to the top position as the president of India.)

The Council of Ministers met briefly on the last day of 1984. Immediately after the meeting, the prime minister told me very firmly that he had decided that R.K. Dhawan be relieved of his duties in the PMH and asked to 'proceed on long leave'. Later, I came to know that the prime minister had received a letter from Justice Thakkar expressing strong reservations about the desirability of Dhawan continuing to work in the PMH.

I reached PMH at about 8 p.m. along with Gopi Arora (joint secretary in the PMO), and Dhawan as usual received me with great courtesy and warmth without having any idea as to what was to happen to him soon. In a few minutes Dhawan was called in by the prime minister to his room and told of his decision while Gopi Arora and I waited in Dhawan's room. This session took an unusually long time, almost forty-five minutes.

When Rajiv informed Dhawan that he had to 'proceed on long leave', the latter was understandably shocked as well as anguished by the abruptness of the entire episode. He was stunned by the fact that his *loyalty* to Indira Gandhi was being questioned and, that too, so soon after her death. He asserted his innocence and wanted to know the specific charges against him. To cut a long story short, I firmly told him that the PM's decision was final and that he should leave *all* materials behind and hand over all the keys to Gopi Arora. Dhawan, for his part, insisted that he would hand over the keys only to the PM, who took possession of them. By about 10.45 p.m. Dhawan left the PMH empty-handed. All the almirahs and tables were sealed and the room closed.

In the normal course, the prime minister could have told Dhawan about his decision directly as he was working in the PMH and not in the PMO, which was under my administrative supervision. However, he had decided that when he conveyed his decision to Dhawan I should be present at the PMH to ensure that it was promptly carried out. It was somewhat embarrassing for me to tell Dhawan that he had to go immediately but it was my duty to do so as the PM wanted me to handle this matter personally.

As requested by the PM, I began looking for a substitute for Dhawan as special assistant to the PM. A few friends suggested the name of P.A. Venkataraman, who had worked with the former prime minister, Lal Bahadur Shastri, in the same capacity. After verifying his credentials from the intelligence agencies, I recommended him to the PM, who duly appointed him.

✧

The early days of January 1985 proved to be very hectic for the PM and, by logical extension, for me too. He held a series of meetings with secretaries in groups, who briefed him about the work going on in their respective ministries. Both the cabinet secretary and I were present in all such meetings. Since Parliament was also in session, Rajiv had to be fully up to date for the various sessions every day. On the whole, I found that my workload had suddenly increased considerably and I had to put in much longer hours than before every day.

The day 18 January 1985 turned out to be a black day in my service as principal secretary. Early in the morning that day, the startling news was conveyed to me that my private secretary and three personal assistants working in my office had been arrested the previous night on charges of leaking information from my office to certain commercial concerns in Delhi. Apart from the aforementioned individuals, a few groups in the Rashtrapati Bhavan, in the Ministries of Defence, Commerce and in the Department of Economic Affairs had been supplying certain business establishments photocopies of confidential documents. As a reward, it appears that they were provided money as well as expensive liquor. The members of these groups were also nabbed. The news of their arrests, however, had not yet appeared in the newspapers as it missed the deadline for printing. I was deeply anguished that such a serious crime could take place in my office. My immediate reaction was that I should own the moral responsibility for the misdeeds of my staff and submit my resignation. I did not bother to find out what course the secretaries in the other ministries/departments concerned were planning, but I thought that I ought to put in my papers. Moreover, I was also greatly concerned about the prestige and reputation of the prime minister, who had just emerged victorious in the general elections with a massive majority of over 400 seats in the Lok Sabha.

I could meet the prime minister at his office in Parliament House only at about 3 p.m. to inform him about my decision. While I was closeted with the prime minister, his senior cabinet colleagues, Narasimha Rao, V.P. Singh and S.B. Chavan came in along with the cabinet secretary to discuss with him the crucial Anti-defection Bill. I thought I should finish my business with the prime minister as quickly as possible. Consequently, in their presence, I told him that I would like to talk to him alone. He signalled to them to leave and I hurriedly told him that in view of the recent developments I had decided to submit my resignation, owning moral responsibility for the lapses of those working in my office. He immediately asked: 'Why should you resign because of this? Rao Saheb (the cabinet secretary) is leaving in a few days and if you are also leaving it will cause serious problems for the administration.' My response was that even though I was not in any way connected with the misdeeds of the personal staff working with me, my resignation would serve as a good gesture for maintaining the reputation of the PMO. By this time, H.K.L. Bhagat, minister for parliamentary affairs, peeped in to remind the PM that his presence was urgently required in Parliament. The PM said: 'We shall discuss this later.' He quickly collected his papers and rushed out of the room along with Bhagat.

A meeting of the cabinet was scheduled for 6 p.m. at Parliament House. I participated in this meeting and, as usual, expressed my views on the various items that came up for discussion. At the end of the meeting I again met the PM in his office. The PM's response was as follows: 'It is very unfortunate that this has happened but I do not want to lose your services. Can you suggest how to make use of them? Why not you go as high commissioner to London?' At that point of time, I was not in a proper frame of mind to discuss my future posting. I merely told him that I was not particularly interested in a foreign assignment but that my future posting could be discussed at a later stage. The PM replied: 'Yes, we can discuss this later. I am sorry Dr Alexander that things have happened like this.' I then thanked him for all the kindness and courtesy he had extended to me. I shook hands with him and left his room at about 8.30 p.m. and went straight home.

I had not spoken a word about the developments of the day to my wife Ackama till then because I felt that I should spare her the inevitable mental anguish. She was used to my coming back from office late in the night almost every day and she probably thought that this was just another day. I then broke the news to her with the words: 'This has been my last day in office. I have resigned.' She remained quite cool and composed in spite of the seriousness and suddenness of the news. I narrated the events of the day. 'We shall face the situation together,' she responded: 'You badly need some rest and now you have the opportunity to look after your health,' she added. For the past four years or so, every day meant a gruelling eighteen-hour schedule for me, replete with tremendous tension and anxiety. I had often thought of going on at least a month's leave but could hardly manage a couple of days. Now that I had an opportunity to go on a vacation, I was not particularly happy in the manner in which it had materialized.

The news of the arrest of persons from various ministries/ departments dominated the headlines of all the newspapers on 19 January and subsequent days. On 22 January, the prime minister made a brief reference to what was branded as the 'spy scandal' while replying to the three-day debate on the motion of thanks to the president for his address. In the course of the speech in the Lok Sabha, he referred to my resignation and declared: 'There is nothing against him but it was in the best traditions of civil service that he has taken this decision.' The loud thumping of the desks which greeted this statement spoke volumes about how much the members appreciated my work. The editorial (on 20 January 1985) in the *Hindustan Times* made the following observations, which reflected the mood of the media and the public:

> The saddest part of the whole incident was that Prime Minister's Principal Secretary P.C. Alexander felt constrained to tender his resignation in the best traditions of the service. Alexander was of course not personally involved and he could have had no knowledge that his long time Assistant who had presumably been cleared by security officials was engaged in anti-national activities for personal gain. Alexander upheld the highest traditions and principles of the administrative ethos in offering his resignation; but we strongly feel that the offer to resign from a good, efficient and innocent man should not have been accepted. Alexander had done excellent work for the past four years; in fact he had not taken a single day off during that period, often to be in an 18 hours' stint [sic].
>
> In any case, it was known that the unremitting rigours of a high-pressure job and long hours were beginning to get to him and he would have normally wished to retire in another year. That would have been a graceful conclusion to a distinguished career. It is a terrible pity that it should have ended in the manner it did. The Prime Minister would doubtless find it difficult to obtain a suitable replacement.

In spite of the overwhelming support and sympathy extended by the media and the members of the public, a discordant note was struck by one or two journalists and one political party, namely, the CPI(M). E.M.S. Namboodripad, the leader of this party, came out with a statement that the prime minister should not have expressed such warm sentiments about me till the investigations into the entire episode were completed. His views were repeated by some of his colleagues, particularly by those belonging to Kerala, my home state. However, these occasional barbs did not make much of an impact.

A stream of visitors flocked to my residence. My friends in the civil service along with ministers and Members of Parliament, who had known me closely, called upon me. A good number of journalist friends also turned up. An important visitor on 23 January was A.K. Jain, proprietor of the *Times of India* group of publications. Within a few minutes of starting the conversation, he admitted that he had come specifically to offer me the post of chief editor of the *Economic Times*, one of the renowned newspapers published by the *TOI* family. He told me that I could specify later the terms of appointment acceptable to me and he would straightaway accept them. However, I told him, without any hesitation, that I was definitely not interested in taking up such an assignment. Earlier, an emissary on his behalf, Ram Taneja, had also sounded me out about the same job.

While I was on leave, I came to know that Rajiv had been weighing the options of posting me either as high commissioner to London or as governor of Maharashtra. Since I had expressed the view (on the 'black day' 18 January) that I was not keen on taking up a job outside India, probably he was considering me for the second post. In fact, he had just appointed Idris Latif, the governor of Maharashtra, as India's ambassador to France. The post of the high commissioner to London had also been lying vacant for some time. By this time, the media had begun speculating about my future posting. Also, some newspapers and magazines castigated intelligence agencies of the government as well as the Ministry for Home Affairs (MHA) for the manner in which the whole 'spy scandal' had been handled. *India Today* (in its issue of the second fortnight of February 1985) pilloried the MHA and the Intelligence Bureau for what it called the inept handling of the entire affair. In fact, the article had called for the resignation of the home minister for the manner in which the government had treated senior officials whose staff were found to be involved in spying activities. The writer also chastised the government for pressurizing senior secretaries like S.C. Sareen and J.S. Baijal to quit their jobs though they had not offered to do so on their own as they felt that they were not responsible for the crimes committed by their staff. The highly respected journalist, Nikhil Chakravartty, in his journal *Mainstream*, termed the government's handling of the spy episode as 'juvenile'. Another magazine, the *Onlooker*, in its cover story in the last week of February 1985, stated that I had been the victim of vindictive action by some top men in the intelligence agencies who were trying to settle some personal scores with me. However, I kept myself completely aloof from these controversies, and refused to meet any journalist or make any comment on the recent events.

Rather unexpectedly, a Bombay newspaper, *Daily* (belonging to the *Blitz* group) published a report under a banner headline: 'ALEXANDER – GOVERNOR'. My photograph had also been printed along with the report that I had been appointed governor of Maharashtra. After that, I was flooded with calls from journalists, mostly from Bombay and Delhi, asking me to confirm or deny this report. My only response to all such enquiries was that I would inform them if I received any definite information on any posting. In fact, I was then totally engrossed in making arrangements for the wedding of my daughter, Rajani, which was to be solemnized on 10 April at Delhi. Consequently, I had neither the time nor the inclination to meet the eager beavers of the media to comment upon the government's handling of the 'spy episode' or my future posting.

The uncertainty in this context was put to rest on 26 April when Rajiv deputed his cousin and a well-known politician, Arun Nehru, to convey a message to me that he would very much like to use my services as high commissioner to the UK rather than in any gubernatorial position. Arun Nehru emphasized that the prime minister believed that the situation in the UK, where the Sikh militants had become very active, required the presence of an experienced and competent individual with good knowledge of the country's political and economic problems. The PM thought that I fulfilled the requisite criteria.

✧

The formalities for my appointment as high commissioner were completed in record time. The news of my new posting became public when *The Hindu* published it on 2 May 1985. Other newspapers soon picked up this story. Long before I came to know about my London assignment, I had decided to visit my home state Kerala for a few days from 14 May onwards.

On my return on 3 June, I called on Rajiv. During our thirty-minute meeting, he made a significant observation: 'I kept the post vacant so long, as I was keen to have you there. It is going to be a tough one but I have full faith in you.' I explained to him the main policy change that Indira Gandhi had initiated to bolster India's relations with the UK towards the latter part of her prime ministership. I sought confirmation from him that he also wished to continue with the same policy, which he gave. Several instances of misunderstanding had cropped up in the past between India and the UK, but in the last two years preceding her death, Indira Gandhi had established a very close personal friendship with her British counterpart, Margaret Thatcher. In fact, both the prime ministers had been making determined efforts to strengthen the relations between the two countries. Indira Gandhi's new policy, as she had explained to me, was to use the UK's good offices for forging friendly relations with the US too. I brought to the attention of the prime minister that I was aware of the fact that certain middle-level officers in the Ministry of External Affairs were pursuing their own agenda of needless confrontation with the UK. Such belligerent posturing had caused some strains in our bilateral relations. Rajiv told me that he was in complete agreement with the policy initiated by Indira Gandhi. He affirmed that I had the full freedom to chalk up my own strategy for handling Indo–UK relations. He assured me that I did not have to bother about the views of some MEA officials regarding my strategy and that I would have his full support in doing what I considered to be in the best interests of our country. He added that if I encountered any obstructionist attitude on the part of the MEA officials, I should telephone him personally and he would deal with such situations promptly. I was quite heartened to receive such an assurance from the prime minister. In fact, such confidence enabled me to function in my new assignment without being unduly bothered by the irritants that were often created by some MEA mandarins.

TWELVE

In the UK

I ARRIVED AT THE HEATHROW AIRPORT, LONDON, ALONG WITH MY WIFE on 19 June 1985. Our reception committee consisted of an official of the British Foreign Office, the deputy high commissioner, Romesh Arora, and his wife and all the senior officials of the Indian Mission. My first official duty was to send a letter from the airport itself to the British secretary of state for foreign affairs informing him of my arrival. We had taken with us our Tibetan terrier Rudolf, a favourite of our family for ten years, but he had to be sent away to a kennel to be quarantined for six months as per UK laws. We then proceeded to our official residence at 9 Kensington Palace Gardens, where I had stayed earlier on several occasions during my official visits.

On 21 June I called on Sir John Richard, the chief marshal of the Diplomatic Corps. He informed me that I could officially present my credentials to Queen Elizabeth on 27 June and he explained in great detail the formalities of the ceremonies involved on this occasion. He actually rehearsed for me the entire proceedings, commencing with my entering into the room and ending up with a talk with the Queen, which he pointed would not exceed three minutes. I next went over to my office at India House and in the afternoon called on some of the senior officers in the British Foreign Ministry, starting with Sir William Hardinge, deputy undersecretary. He welcomed me warmly and exclaimed joyously: 'We threw our hats up in sheer joy when we first heard about your appointment!' I had come to know Prime Minister Margaret Thatcher and many of her senior ministers and officials fairly well in my previous official capacity in Delhi. Consequently, I was no stranger to them; nor were they to me.

Within four days of my arrival in London, a serious tragedy occurred. An Air India flight originating from Montreal crashed at Cork on the Irish coast, killing all the 350 passengers and 22 crew members. It was believed that Sikh militants had sabotaged this aircraft. Even though India had a separate ambassador in Dublin and he was handling the situation arising out of the tragedy very efficiently, I considered it my duty to give him full assistance. Hence, I remained in touch with him continuously. Ambassador Kiran Doshi had a small staff in his mission and I had asked my colleagues in the UK to chip in to help to the maximum extent possible. Many relatives of the crash victims wanted to visit the site of the accident and participate in the funeral rites. The logistics involved were efficiently handled by our mission.

On 29 June, I called on the British foreign secretary, Sir Geoffrey Howe, at 10.30 a.m. and Baroness Young, the minister of state at 3 p.m. I expressed India's grave concern about the terrorist activities carried on by the UK-based Sikh militants and emphasized the vital need for close surveillance by the British intelligence authorities on their activities. The foreign secretary readily agreed to take strict action to curb the undesirable activities of the Sikh militants. He told me that whenever I needed any help in this matter, I could meet him or telephone him. At 5 p.m. I called on Sir Anthony Auckland, the permanent secretary in the Ministry of Foreign Affairs.

The British prime minister, whom I had the privilege of knowing fairly closely during my years as principal secretary to the prime minister, was kind enough to agree to receive me on 25 June, which was within six days of my arrival in London. The senior officials in the Foreign Office had told me that normally a new ambassador or high commissioner would have to wait for almost ten weeks before they could meet the PM. They were truly amazed to find that she had acceded to my request for calling on her so quickly! (I had met her last when she had called on Rajiv Gandhi after the assassination of his mother.) When I met her at 10 Downing Street, she spoke to me with great warmth of her close friendship with Indira Gandhi and also how much she felt concerned about the personal security for India's young prime minister, Rajiv Gandhi. I did not want to miss this opportunity, though it was my first call on the prime minister, to convey to her our very serious concern about the freedom with which a certain group of Sikh militants based in the UK were carrying on virulent anti-India propaganda. I mentioned particularly the activities of Jagjit Singh Chouhan, the self-styled president of Khalistan and the leader of this group. I brought to her notice that just the previous day Chouhan had been given an opportunity to express his pro-Khalistani views on the Independent Television though people everywhere had been horrified by the huge loss of life resulting due to the sabotage of the Air India plane. She assured me that immediate action would be taken to curtail his anti-Indian activities. At the end of our talks, which were interspersed with frequent expressions of deep sorrow by Margaret Thatcher at the tragic assassination of Indira Gandhi, I told her that Rajiv had specially asked me to inform her of his warm personal friendship and regard for her and convey his assurance that he would like to carry forward the policy initiated by his mother to strengthen Indo–UK relations. Mrs Thatcher reciprocated the sentiments very warmly and paid me a great compliment by saying that Rajiv had selected the most suitable person as high commissioner to further this objective. I thanked her for agreeing to meet me so soon after my arrival. She then extended to me the honour of escorting me all the way from her office to the portico of 10 Downing Street. This is an honour, which under protocol, is reserved only for some selected heads of government.

The ceremony for the presentation of credentials (on 27 June) was quite an impressive one. The traditional pomp and splendour associated with this ceremony were very much in evidence. At the Buckingham Palace I presented the credential papers to the Queen and declared: 'I have the honour to present letters withdrawing the credentials of my predecessor and presenting my commission of appointment.' She took the papers and promptly passed them on to Sir Anthony. I had been told earlier that the Queen would talk to me for about three minutes. However, much to the surprise of the senior officers present in the room and to my own surprise, the conversation lasted nine minutes! She asked me about my tenure with Mrs Indira Gandhi. She briefly expressed her sorrow at the Air India tragedy and added how sad it was that the world was plagued by so much violence and terrorism. She then asked me how long I had served as principal secretary to Rajiv Gandhi. Obviously, she had been briefed well about the circumstances in which I had resigned from that post. She led me on to that subject by asking me why I decided to put in my papers. I then told her about the spy incident and how I felt I should submit my resignation as a moral gesture. She then volunteered a comment that I had acted very honourably in offering to quit. When this conversation was over, the doors were opened for eight of my senior officers to come in one by one. I introduced each one of them to the Queen in the order of seniority. These officers then left the room. The chief marshal then announced 'Shrimati Ackama Alexander' and my wife stepped into the room. The Queen briefly spoke to her. After two more minutes of exchange of pleasantries, we bowed and took leave of the Queen and returned to Kensington Palace Gardens.

A small party was held at Kensington Palace Gardens when champagne bottles were opened for our senior officers and the British guests from the Foreign Office. The assistant secretary of the Foreign Office then highlighted the fact that I had established a record among all ambassadors and high commissioners for having been able to call on the foreign minister, the prime minister and the Queen within a week of my arrival. They were obviously conveying the message that the UK government attached high importance to my appointment as India's high commissioner.

When I started regular work in the mission, I found that the methods of functioning needed a good deal of streamlining and reorganization. The distribution of the job functions among the various wings of the mission was not quite balanced. As a result, large areas existed in the form of 'no man's land' and no one seemed to be directly responsible for items that fell into this category. Moreover, considerable overlapping of functions was prevalent. It took me about a month to bring about a rational restructuring. I instituted the practice of calling a meeting of all heads every Monday at 10 a.m. sharp. These weekly meetings provided me an excellent opportunity to evaluate the progress of work in the various wings and to sort out problems through discussions and coordinated action. We also used these meetings to discuss important political developments of the week, which were of interest to India. This interaction enabled the senior officers to know the stand they should take in their dealings with their counterparts in the UK Government. These meetings also proved to be good brainstorming sessions. Some of my colleagues in the mission at that time were well informed about political issues and competent in the analysis and resolution of a variety of problems. I found the contributions of deputy high commissioner, Salman Haider (later secretary in the MEA), the military attaché, Brigadier Satish Nambiar (later lieutenant general), K. Padmanabiah (later home secretary) and the air attaché, Air Commodore S.K. Sareen (later air chief marshal) particularly useful.

The most important change introduced was in the systems and practices followed for the issue of passports and visas. I had noticed long serpentine queues every day around the India House building waiting for these precious documents. Standing for long hours in the bitterly cold winter months, particularly during days of heavy snowfall, was a harrowing experience. In most cases, on submitting their applications, after a long excruciating wait, they were told to return another day specified to them by the officials to collect their passports or visas. They had to undergo the ordeal all over again. I held several rounds of discussions with my senior colleagues so as to ascertain how the entire process could be speeded up.

The most useful suggestion was to *computerize* the entire procedure. Colonel A.K. Aggarwal (later lieutenant general) undertook this formidable task. The logistics involved in this process were complex. For instance, additional space on the ground floor had to be found (to be used as a waiting hall); half a dozen more counters had to be constructed; additional computers and the related paraphernalia had to be purchased; and extra staff had to be deployed. Moreover, all the proposals and the expenses to be incurred had to be formally cleared by the Government of India. When I mentioned the costs involved to the prime minister, he did not demur. I immediately sent the proposals to the GOI for formal sanction, pointing out the fact that the PM had approved the scheme in principle. Within a month, the new procedures were introduced and proved highly successful. A prospective candidate could get his or her passport or visa on the same day itself. Those seemingly interminable queues became a thing of the past.

Another setback, which struck me within a few days after my joining, stemmed from the fact that some middle-level officers in the MEA had been trying to run the day-to-day administration of the mission by remote control from New Delhi. The post of high commissioner had often remained vacant for long periods in the past and deputy high commissioners had been holding charge during such periods. This state of affairs had provided the opportunity to the aforementioned officers to carry out their scheme. I noticed that this practice was continuing even after the regular high commissioner had taken charge. I also found that some junior Foreign Service officials in the mission had fallen into the habit of seeking guidance from New Delhi without heeding the instructions of the high commissioner. Often, they sought such guidance on the pretext that policy matters were involved. I made it amply clear to my officers in the mission that this practice should stop forthwith and that whatever instructions they needed should always be obtained from me and, if instructions or guidance from New Delhi were needed, I would take the appropriate steps myself.

In spite of my specific directions, I noticed that one or two officers were still referring cases in a routine manner for instructions to New Delhi. Consequently, I had to issue written orders to these officers strictly prohibiting such a practice. It took sometime for me to establish a proper system of discipline and control, but such an improvement eventually helped in the expeditious disposal of pending cases.

In a few cases, I had to speak to the foreign secretary and to the minister for external affairs in New Delhi about unnecessary interference of some middle-level MEA officials in the functioning of the mission. To their credit, they promptly took action to stop such practices. An illustrative example deserves mention here to reveal how tightly some officials in the MEA wished to control the mission. The British had announced their intention to withdraw from the UNESCO as a mark of protest against what they, the US and some developed countries had considered the anti-Western attitude of the UN body. Many developing countries and practically all the Commonwealth countries felt concerned at this proposed move, as they believed that it would weaken the organization and reduce its power to help the developing countries. The high commissioners of the Commonwealth countries met at the Jamaican Mission in London to discuss the repercussions. After that, it was decided that a formal note should be presented to the British Foreign Office expressing the concern of the Commonwealth countries on the proposed action by Britain.

A small group of high commissioners, including those of Canada, Australia and India, was authorized to call on the foreign minister in order to convey the views (through a letter) of the Commonwealth countries. Accordingly, I went along with this group and presented the letter. It became very clear to us after meeting the minister that the UK was firm in its decision to withdraw from the UNESCO. However, we derived the satisfaction that we had brought to London's notice the concern of the Commonwealth countries. The message we conveyed was consistent with the known stand of the Government of India on this issue. However, much to my surprise, a telex message was received from New Delhi by the counsellor of the mission dealing with political matters to the effect that the MEA wished that I had obtained its formal clearance before joining the group. I was initially quite surprised and later distinctly annoyed when the message was brought to my notice. I immediately called up Romesh Bhandari, the foreign secretary, and told him in no uncertain terms that such a message should not have been sent by his ministry. I also asserted that I had no intention of seeking prior clearance whenever I took any action that was *consistent* with the declared policy of the

Government of India. Bhandari was somewhat embarrassed at my outburst. He clarified that the message had not been authorized by him. Obviously, the systems of control and discipline within the MEA were not ideal ones.

Almost immediately after my arrival in London, I found that a good deal of my time and attention would have to be devoted to resolving the problems arising due to anti-Indian activities of certain groups of Sikh militants based in London. The Indian community in Britain in general was at that time badly divided; more so was the smaller Sikh community within the Indians staying there. The division between the Sikhs loyal to the Akali Dal and those loyal to the Indian National Congress was pronounced. A new line of division cutting across party affiliations was that between the small sections of militants, which were very virulent in their anti-Indian tirade, and the large but silent members of the majority who were loyal and devoted to their country of origin. With the recurrence of extremist violence in Punjab following Operation Blue Star, the militants had stepped up their anti-Indian activities in Britain. They mainly targeted the nationalist Sikhs, most of whom were law-abiding and peace-loving citizens. Several such Sikhs remained under a continuous threat of attack from the extremists. Jagjit Singh Chouhan, a long-time resident of the UK, had been carrying on a vigorous and vicious anti-Indian propaganda among the Sikhs through provocative writings in his newspaper and his speeches in some of the gurdwaras that had come under the control of the militants. With the spurt in terrorist activities by the extremists in the Punjab, Chouhan had become more militant in his writings and speeches. By describing himself as the 'president of Khalistan' in exile, he was behaving as if he was the acknowledged leader of the entire Sikh community in the UK. Ever since my arrival in London, I had been receiving representations from many prominent nationalist Sikh leaders that the UK Government had not been taking sufficiently strong action to curb the violent activities of the militants. I had to keep in constant touch with the senior officials and ministers of the British Government all through my tenure as high commissioner. My prime objectives were to convey to them the deep concern of the Government of India about the activities of the extremists and to underline the need for providing ample protection to the lives and properties of the nationalist sections of the Indian community.

On 12 July 1985, Sir Geoffrey Howe, the British foreign secretary, invited me for lunch at his residence. This was a one-to-one meeting so that we could speak to each other freely and frankly. Howe told me that the British Government was keen to evolve a new relationship with India; he assured me that he would do everything within his power to achieve this objective. I used this opportunity to emphasize how anxious the Indian community, and particularly the nationalist Sikhs, felt about the activities of Chouhan and his colleagues in the 'Khalistan' movement. He replied that his government was quite aware of these developments and promised that effective action was being planned to deal with all unlawful activities.

Another instance when I had to intervene was when a report reached me that certain militant Sikhs in a place called Smithwitch were planning to conduct a football tournament named after Satwant Singh and Beant Singh, the assassins of Indira Gandhi. I called on Leon Briton, the secretary of state for home, and pointed out to him that such a tournament would greatly hurt the feelings of the Indian community. He promised me that such a tournament would not be allowed to take place; and he fulfilled his promise promptly.

Chouhan did not remain idle. He created another discomfiting situation in an attempt to embarrass the Indian community in the UK by inviting a team of three persons from Ecuador, the leader of which was a former president of that country. This team was taken to various gurdwaras, where they gave out assurances that Ecuador would be glad to recognize the government of 'Khalistan' in exile. The ex-president and his team-mates obviously enjoyed the lavish hospitality extended to them by Chouhan and his associates and did not mind giving such astounding assurances, though they had neither the authority nor the intention to fulfil them. I met the ambassador of Ecuador in the UK and sought a clarification from him about the status of these visitors and the views of his government on their utterances. He affirmed that they were here in their private capacities and their views did not represent those of the government or of any important party in his country. He promised that on behalf of his government he would issue a statement to this effect, which he did immediately.

On 16 January 1986, I was informed that Santa Singh Sandhu, a prominent follower of the Akali Dal leader Sant Longowal, had been shot at by extremists. I visited him in the hospital. He had sustained grievous injuries but luckily he survived. This attack created a sense of fear among the Indian community in the UK and representations poured in from various groups of nationalist Sikhs requesting my intervention with the British Government for making immediate arrangements for their protection.

The most serious violence unleashed by the extremists took the form of an attack on Tarseem Singh Toor, a prominent and respected nationalist Sikh leader of London. He was gunned down in his shop at about 10 p.m. on 23 January 1986. Later in the night, I came to know that he had succumbed to his injuries. Even before I took over as high commissioner in London, I had known Toor as an outspoken critic of the extremists. His assassination, coming so soon after the attempt on Sandhu's life, created tremendous panic among the entire group of moderate Sikhs. I called on the new home secretary, Douglas Hurd, and explained to him how the community felt insecure and demoralized at the assassination of a respected leader such as Toor. Hurd's stand was that his government had taken these events seriously and no effort would be spared to arrest the culprits. In the succeeding days, Scotland Yard on its own started tightening the security arrangements for me as well as for the Indian Mission. There was a report in the *Mail* that the extremists might try to kill an Indian diplomat, which prompted Scotland Yard to be more vigilant. Chouhan stepped up his anti-Indian activities. He issued a statement, immediately before the date fixed for the cremation of Toor, disclaiming any responsibility for the spurt in terrorism in recent days, but making a vicious personal attack on me by stressing the fact that I had been close to Indira Gandhi, who had been the main target of his campaign for several years.

The Government of India had deputed A.P. Sharma, former governor of Punjab, and G.S. Dhillon, a prominent Congress leader, to participate in Toor's funeral, scheduled for 5 February. I visited the crematorium along with the visitors from India at 3.15 p.m. on the cremation day. There was a large solemn gathering of the Indian community at this place. David Waddington, minister of state (home), was present to represent the British Government. A brief religious ceremony was held at the crematorium and then we all went to the neighbouring temple for the memorial service and condolence meeting. Over a thousand people attended the service and the meeting. Sharma, Dhillon and I along with a few other members of the Indian community in London made brief speeches on the occasion. Rumours abounded that the militants might disturb the meeting and create law and order problems there, but the British authorities had made very tight security arrangements and the proceedings passed off without any incident. However, the nationalist Sikhs in the UK continued to feel very unsafe.

Rajiv Gandhi's first official visit to the UK as prime minister was scheduled for October 1985, i.e., within four months of my assumption of duties as high commissioner. I personally began supervising all the arrangements necessary to make his visit a grand success. The British authorities had made it clear to me that they attached special importance to Rajiv's visit and wanted to take this opportunity to further strengthen relations between the two countries. In fact, during a casual conversation at the Queen's garden party on 17 July, Prince Charles told me that he would like to meet Rajiv when he visited London.

Rajiv Gandhi and his entourage arrived at Heathrow airport at 10.45 a.m. on 14 October 1985. Margaret Thatcher received him at the airport though protocol norms did not demand her presence there. Rajiv and Sonia stayed at our residence. On 15 October morning Rajiv met a large group of senior British ministers and also the leaders of the opposition parties such as Niel Kinnock and David Owen. This meeting was followed by a formal meeting between the two delegations headed by their respective prime ministers. Mrs Thatcher explained how economic sanctions imposed on South Africa would affect the jobs of over a million British nationals in that country. She also pointed out that the British economy itself would be badly affected by the sanctions, which, in turn, would compel her government to cut aid to developing countries. Rajiv spoke very forcefully about the moral dimension involved in the sanctions against the apartheid policies of the South African Government. In spite of the warmth during the talks and the mutual respect shown by the two prime ministers, there was no meeting ground on the issue of sanctions against South Africa. This meeting was followed by a glittering function at Mansion House hosted by the Lord Mayor of London. From there we went to Hatfield to see the British Air Spaces Industry. On our return, Rajiv interacted with Indian journalists for about forty minutes and then attended a press conference. In the evening, I hosted a reception at 9, Kensington Palace, attended by 200 people. At about 9 p.m. Mrs Thatcher arrived at our residence to take formal leave of her Indian counterpart. The meeting between the two prime ministers lasted for about half an hour. Later in the night, Rajiv and his delegation left for the airport for their return journey.

I have stated earlier in this chapter about the sharp divisions between the extremists and the nationalists in the Sikh community and how I, as the high commissioner, had to seek the intervention of the British Government very frequently in dealing with the problem of militancy. Disputes and dissent existed in other communities as well, though in a different form. Very often, such schisms were caused by personal rivalries and the unbridled ambitions of some leaders to gain influence over the community. One unfortunate feature of such squabbles and conflicts was that sometimes the Indian Mission and the high commissioner personally had, in the past, been sucked into them. Such a situation had resulted in the prestige of the mission being tarnished. One may well claim that in a million-strong Indian community, as in the UK, dissent was unavoidable. However, what was avoidable was the attempt of some individuals to drag the high commissioner into their quarrels. During my previous term of office in New Delhi, I was aware about these conflicts and the principal characters involved in them. I was determined to steer clear of all such controversies. However, some of these 'bigwigs' successfully enlisted the support of a few top Congress leaders in Delhi and some high-level officials. Such a state of affairs sometimes led to needless embarrassment for the mission. In spite of my earnest efforts to avoid getting dragged into such politics, I was not entirely successful. Let me mention a case in point.

The Gujarati community in Britain had decided to instal a plaque in the house where India's 'iron man', Sardar Vallabhbhai Patel, had stayed while he was a student in London in the pre-independence era. The Greater London Council (GLC) had agreed to the proposal. But very soon a controversy arose as to who should play the 'leadership role' in organizing this function. C.B. Patel, the editor of *New Life*, (a newspaper popular among the Gujaratis) attempted to get the plaque installed, but his efforts were frustrated by a rival faction led by Praful Patel, a powerful businessman. Praful Patel, on the basis of his influence with some officials in the MEA, had managed to take over the function on 31 March 1986. The event seemed to have obtained the 'stamp of approval' from New Delhi. He had succeeded in securing the presence of a few prominent Congress leaders from New Delhi, such as R.L. Bhatia, at this function. The chairman of the GLC, Ken Livingston, had agreed to do the honours, thus according the function a formal British approval as well. As this function was meant to honour the memory of one of the greatest personalities of modern Indian history and as it had obtained the approval of the GLC, I decided to attend it. On arrival at the function venue, I saw a distressing scene. One faction that backed Praful Patel was standing on the side of the road close to the house, raising slogans in praise of Sardar Patel. A much larger bunch, led by C.B. Patel, was standing on the opposite side of the road carrying placards. The latter were shouting loudly, denouncing everyone who had come there to participate in the function, including the high commissioner. I felt very upset and embarrassed that these rival factions had thought it fit to use this solemn occasion to settle scores with each other. Anyway, the guests from Delhi and I made brief speeches and the plaque was installed in the midst of shouts and demonstrations.

The aforementioned incident led to an unedifying sequel. C.B. Patel had planned a trip to India in the last week of November 1986, but unknown to the Indian Mission or to Patel himself, some of his opponents in London had managed to get his name blacklisted with the help of some obliging officials in the MEA. I came to know of this development only on 27 November, the date on which Patel was to fly to India, when he came to see me and complained about the delay in issuing a visa to him. I spoke to the foreign secretary, who readily agreed that the visa could be granted. However, when Patel reached Bombay with the visa issued by the mission, the police detained him, as instructions on removal of his name from the blacklist had not yet been communicated to them. I had to intervene again to sort out the imbroglio. However, C.B. Patel had to suffer the agony of being detained at the airport for over eight hours. Here was another sordid instance of officials in Delhi backing one group or another in the internecine rivalry, that too in Britain.

I should, however, point out here that during gala occasions such as cultural events, sports and games, the members of the Indian community in the UK always came together, demonstrating their unity and loyalty to the country of their origin. They wholeheartedly participated and were deeply involved in all the activities. Such enthusiasm was particularly evident whenever cricket matches between the Indian team and the English team or between the Indian and Pakistani teams in Britain were scheduled to take place.

I retain fond memories of the cricket match at Lords (on 10 June 1986) when India emerged victorious against England. Huge Indian crowds were present at the stadium. They wanted to join the victory celebrations at the end of the match. I was watching the match from my enclosure, but once it ended, I rushed to the balcony of the dressing room to join Kapil Dev (the Indian captain) and his men who were overwhelmed by the cheering of the vast Indian community present on the grounds. I noticed the famous batsman Sunil Gavaskar reacting to this historic win with tears of joy in the privacy of the dressing room.

I should also mention here my experiences during the famous Ascot races (held on 17 June 1986), which were regarded as a major national event. The gentlemen in the main enclosures were attired in formal dark dress complete with tail coats and top hats because the Queen and the members of the royal family were also attending the races. My wife Ackama and I were seated in the diplomat's enclosure next to the royal enclosure. At about 2.30 p.m. Queen Elizabeth and Prince Philip arrived in their coach followed by the other members of the royal family in a ceremonial procession. Within an hour or so, I was informed by the marshal of the Diplomatic Corps that the Queen would like me and my wife to join her for tea in the royal enclosure; we were soon escorted to that area. I was seated to the right of the Queen and Ackama to the right of Prince Philip. The topic of conversation was horses, about which my wife and I were totally ignorant. I did not want to display either my ignorance or lack of interest, and therefore maintained the diplomatic posture of an eager listener as long as horses dominated the discussion at the table. After some time, the Queen turned to me; she evidently wanted to focus on more serious subjects. She referred to the forthcoming visit of prime minister Rajiv Gandhi to London, and here I was on quite familiar territory! That was the time when the Commonwealth prime ministers were rather agitated about the rigid stand of South Africa on apartheid and about Britain's stout opposition to imposing sanctions against that country. The Queen enquired about the Indian prime minister's proposed visit to Mexico to attend the meeting of the six-nation summit. I briefly explained the main issues that would be discussed there. She expressed sympathy at the sufferings of the blacks in South Africa and hoped that the meeting of the Commonwealth prime ministers in August would help in finding a satisfactory solution to the problem.

Rajiv Gandhi's second trip to London was scheduled for two days: 3 and 4 August 1986, but spilled over to 5 August. This time he was accommodated in a hotel where the other visiting heads of Commonwealth countries were staying.

Whenever Rajiv found an opportunity to talk to me alone, he would express his views candidly on all matters that worried him the most. He also dwelt on the behaviour of some of his close aides and colleagues who were also known to me. I was travelling with him in his car from the airport to the hotel when he whispered to me that he had been noticing a major change in the attitude of Arun Nehru towards him and that he was feeling very unhappy at some of Arun's doings. At that time, no one in Delhi was even remotely aware of the level to which the estrangement between them had reached and I myself had little idea that their relations had become so severely strained. Arun Nehru had, in his dealings with me and during telephonic conversations, been behaving as if nothing serious had happened between him and Rajiv. On the other hand, the impression I gained was that he was still as close to him as he was when I left the post of principal secretary to Rajiv a year earlier. I realized the significance of the information Rajiv conveyed to me, but kept it strictly to myself even when I met Arun Nehru later on several occasions.

Here, a very amusing incident connected with Rajiv's visit comes to my mind. I was hosting a dinner at my residence on 3 August for the ministers and some senior officials who were accompanying the prime minister. Rajiv Gandhi was then attending a banquet at the palace. While the dinner in my house was almost reaching its end and my guests were about to tuck into the dessert, I received information from the Scotland Yard men assigned to me that Rajiv was arriving at my residence in a couple of minutes! I rushed to the door to receive him after requesting my guests to remain at the table and continue with the dessert. Rajiv arrived at about 10.30 p.m. escorted by an unusually large security force. The men in charge of Rajiv's security had received information about a threat to his life at his hotel and had decided to divert his car to my residence instead. The PM whispered to me the reason for the diversion and we quickly made arrangements for him to spend the night at our house. What amazed me the most, as I was taking Rajiv to the dining table, was the incredible sight in front of me. Some of my distinguished guests had hurriedly placed their unfinished wine and champagne glasses in front of my seat at the table so that they could retain their image as teetotallers in the PM's eyes. In the process, more than a dozen goblets wound up in front of my seat! I wonder what Rajiv thought! The PM, however, did not have to stay in my house that night as the security personnel got the 'all-safe' clearance signal within forty-five minutes and he was escorted to his hotel suite.

The vetting of the draft communiqué to be issued by the Commonwealth prime ministers took up a considerable amount of the prime minister's time. In fact, on 4 August Rajiv had been with us continuously from 3.30 p.m. to 11.00 p.m., trying to produce a draft acceptable to all Commonwealth delegations. Mrs Thatcher, however, refused to endorse the call for sanctions against South Africa, whereas the other heads of government firmly stood their ground on this issue.

Rajiv Gandhi held a press conference on 5 August in which he put forth India's view. He left for the Heathrow airport immediately after that.

Indo–British relations again took a downturn on certain matters, which should never have been allowed to deteriorate. Let me cite one illustrative example. A major issue on which the Government of India took an unnecessarily unhelpful stand was the signing of an extradition treaty between India and the UK. On 4 December 1986, Foreign Secretary Geoffrey Howe invited me for a breakfast meeting at his residence. His basic objective was to focus on what he called 'lack of proper response from India' on the question of the extradition treaty. Negotiations on the treaty had been going on for quite some time between the two governments. In fact, the Government of India had been very keen in the past to get the treaty ratified as it would have helped in getting back at least some of the militants who were indulging in various crimes against India by using the UK as a safe haven. However, most inexplicably, at some point of time, the GOI started giving the impression that it was not as serious about the treaty as it was before. I explained to Howe that certain provisions in the treaty needed modification and that we expected greater accommodation from the British Government on these provisions. He observed that they could be cleared through discussions but his main grouse was the slow pace at which negotiations were proceeding. He suggested that the discussions on the treaty be raised to higher levels between the two countries. I conveyed these views to the Government of India, but for several months after that, hardly any progress took place.

N.D. Tewari, the new minister for external affairs, who was passing through London in March 1987, suggested that Salman Haider (the deputy high commissioner) visit Delhi in order to discuss the matter with the concerned officials in the Home Ministry and the MEA. After such a discussion, he could come up with a clear draft acceptable to the Government of India. Salman undertook the visit, but reported to me on his return that he found little enthusiasm on the part of the MEA officials to reach a speedy agreement on the treaty. Tewari next suggested that I make one more attempt to negotiate with the high-level politicians in the UK to ascertain whether any further concessions on the part of the British Government were possible. Accordingly, I again met Howe on 7 April and Timothy Renton, minister of state (home), on 14 April, and put forward a few specific suggestions for improving some of the provisions in the treaty but the British interlocutors appeared to be reluctant to accept some of my suggestions. More urgent interaction was necessary at the official level to arrive at an agreed draft, but nobody in New Delhi appeared to be keen to deal with the matter with the priority it deserved. I was greatly disappointed at such a lackadaisical attitude and came to the conclusion that nothing more could be done by the high commission. I left the matter to be handled in New Delhi according to its own scheme of priorities.

One particular directive from the MEA again highlighted its lack of vision and arbitrariness in dealing with heads of missions. Towards the end of November 1986, A.P. Venkateswaran, the foreign secretary of India, sent out a circular to all heads of missions with instructions that copies of reports from such heads to the MEA on various matters should *not* in future be marked to the PMO as had been the practice till then. This circular was totally unacceptable to me as I felt that it was my duty to keep the prime minister informed of some of the crucial developments. The prime minister himself had been seeing copies of my reports marked to him and, in some cases, he had asked for more information on the topics covered in the reports. In a few cases, he had personally written to me on some vital points I had raised in the reports. I spoke to Venkateswaran on the phone, forcefully putting across the message to him that the MEA could not arbitrarily deny to the heads of the missions their right to keep the PM informed directly about crucial matters. I also told him that the MEA could not also impose restrictions on the right of the prime minister to hear directly from his ambassadors or high commissioners. I informed him that as far as I was concerned, only I had the right to decide what reports should go to the PM and what reports should be sent only to the MEA. I pointed out that while the MEA had its own right to offer its comments and advice to the prime minister on the reports sent by the heads of mission, it had no right to deny them the freedom to inform the PM directly on matters they considered specially important. I also clarified that as high commissioner in London, I was not an MEA official and restrictions of the type stated in the circular would not be binding on me. Venkateswaran accepted the validity of my arguments and promptly agreed that I could ignore the circular. I followed up this conversation with an official letter detailing my views and his response. I was happy that the officials at the secretary level in the MEA and the ministers always acted promptly whenever I had the occasion to interact with them.

I would like to narrate an episode that provided me a lot of satisfaction. Towards the end of 1986, I decided to participate in a public auction (conducted by Sotheby's) of certain letters that Mahatma Gandhi had written to his close friend and colleague, Herman Kallenbach, during his South African days. I first obtained the approval of P.V. Narasimha Rao, minister for human resources development, before bidding in the auction to secure these valuable letters for India. I went to Sotheby's along with my senior colleagues in the mission to make sure that the letters did not go to any other bidder. We had received a report that an American university would be participating in the auction and would be willing to pay a very high price for the letters. I realized the veracity of the report when I found on reaching Sotheby's that the bid started with £91,000 though the advertisement mentioned the expected price of the letters as £70,000 to £80,000.

In such auctions decisions have to be made at split-second speed. Consequently, I had told the counsellor, education, who was participating in the auction on behalf of the mission, to keep on bidding as long as I held my right thumb up. Within a couple of minutes the Americans had raised the bid to £135,000 and still I had kept my thumb up. Very quickly, after that, the deal was clinched by us at £140,000. In addition, we had to pay the value-added tax (VAT). However, I felt happy and greatly relieved that we could procure all the letters, though I had far exceeded the limit that I had indicated to Narasimha Rao. I immediately sent these letters to the Ministry of Human Resources Development, New Delhi and was confident that Narasimha Rao would not disagree with my decision to outbid the Americans given the historical importance of the letters.

❖

Indo–British relations took a dip again because of certain adverse developments that took place despite earnest efforts on both sides to improve them. The British were very unhappy at the delay in the Government of India agreeing to their proposal to post drug relations officers to their mission in New Delhi to deal effectively with the increasing traffic in narcotics in the subcontinent and spreading to other parts of the world. New Delhi had legitimate reasons to be unhappy with the British Government on another sensitive issue, namely, discrimination in the new visa policy against India and a few non-white member countries of the Commonwealth. The prime minister had described this policy as 'racist' in character. I had fixed up a meeting with Baroness Young, minister of state in the British Foreign Office, long before the prime minister's statement on the visa policy. Hence, during my meeting with her on 16 October 1986, she said that her government considered Rajiv Gandhi's statement as 'unfortunate'. I asked her what other conclusion could be drawn by us when only non-white Commonwealth countries had been chosen for the proposed visa restrictions. I also explained how the system of issuing visas in the Indian Mission in London had been streamlined over the last one year and now 700 to 800 visas were being granted every day. I also emphasized the fact that most of the applicants were British passport holders. Baroness Young could not explain why such a discriminatory treatment had been extended to countries like India. Meanwhile, the *Telegraph* and a few other newspapers in the UK published reports that I had been summoned to the Foreign Office by Baroness Young to convey the government's displeasure on Rajiv Gandhi's statement on visas. I therefore had to issue a clarification that my meeting with Baroness Young had been fixed *well before* Rajiv Gandhi made his statement.

Critical comments appeared in the UK press about the unfortunate incident of removing A.P. Venkateswaran, the foreign secretary, from his post. On 20 January 1987, Rajiv Gandhi, in the course of a press conference in Delhi, was asked by a Pakistani journalist whether the foreign secretary's statement that the PM would be visiting Pakistan later that year was correct. Since no final decision had yet been taken by the PM about this visit, he was probably annoyed with the foreign secretary for 'jumping the gun'. He replied to that question with a somewhat acerbic remark: 'You will talk to a new foreign secretary soon.' The large gathering of journalists and government officials at the press conference were taken aback by the prime minister's reply and the obvious discourtesy that had been shown to the foreign secretary. The prime minister, no doubt, had every right to change any secretary in the Government of India if he wanted to, but the manner in which he announced his intention to remove Venkateswaran was quite unfortunate. This move came in for a lot of criticism from not only the civil servants but also almost all sections of public opinion in India. Venkateswaran felt humiliated by this statement and submitted his resignation, which was promptly accepted.

During the course of a lunch with the senior editors of the *Financial Times* (London) on 21 January (an engagement that had been fixed long before Rajiv's press conference), they raised the question of the foreign secretary's somewhat abrupt removal and about the propriety of the announcement during the press conference. The question was very embarrassing for me but I evaded giving a reply, claiming that I did not, at that stage, have full facts of what had happened the previous day.

Another awkward incident, though in a totally different context, occurred on 1 February 1987, when I was on a visit to Glasgow, essentially to participate in the Republic Day celebrations organized (a few days later) by the Indian community there. I had received information that demonstrations would be held against the Government of India (and against me as its representative) by certain pro-Khalistani elements. Nevertheless, I was determined to go ahead with the programme. When I arrived at the hall where the celebrations were to take place, I observed two groups of Sikhs standing near the two main entrances to the hall wearing black turbans and shouting slogans against India, Rajiv Gandhi and me. As the British police had made elaborate arrangements for ensuring security, I did not face any difficulty in reaching the dais to begin the proceedings. According to the programme printed and distributed earlier, the celebrations were to start with the Indian national anthem. However, when I stood up and called for the tune to be played and the singing to start, I noticed that the music group from Birmingham, which had been hired for the function, deliberately remained seated without giving the lead. This group was entirely made up of Sikhs and obviously they had been instructed by the extremists not to participate in any activity. After watching the heated exchange between the organizers of the meeting and the music group for a few seconds, I announced that we would all sing the national anthem together. I myself begun the singing. Fortunately, the entire audience, except the demonstrators outside the hall and the music group from Birmingham, joined me. After that, I could proceed with the rest of the items on the agenda smoothly. The demonstrators kept up their slogan shouting while I was leaving the hall at the conclusion of the function.

Traditionally, the Indian high commissioner to the UK used to host what came to be called the 'curry lunch' once a month. This nomenclature owed its origin to the main item served on this occasion, which was a dish of chicken or mutton curry. This dish was particularly relished by the British. Members of Parliament of both the Houses used to be invited turn by turn. For a long time curry lunches had been abandoned. I decided to revive this tradition. The informal atmosphere provided a good opportunity for the high commissioner to cogently explain the Government of India's stand on various topics of interest to the British parliamentarians. A lively question-and-answer session (for about twenty minutes) was another feature.

A major change I introduced in the curry lunch programme was to invite leaders from other professions (say, journalism and academics) as well by turn. During one occasion, the guest list included quite a few prominent intellectuals from the Indian community, such as Amartya Sen, I.G. Patel, Bhikku Parekh and Anil Seal. I recall that all of them chipped in with useful suggestions for not only improving the services of the Indian Mission to the Indian community but also enhancing the mission's interaction with the British academic fraternity.

An important decision that the government took during my period as high commissioner was to purchase the British aircraft carrier *Hermes*, which the British Government had decided to decommission. The ship needed extensive repairs and refitting, a task which the Indian Navy was well qualified to undertake. A team of over 900 sailors and their senior officers had been deputed to undertake this work at the dockyard at Plymouth. Captain Vinod Pasricha (later vice-admiral and commanding-in-chief Western

Command), who was in overall charge of this assignment, had been in close contact with me through the Naval Wing of the High Commission. I had also undertaken a few trips to Plymouth to ascertain progress of the repair work and to meet the sailors there. I commissioned the ship at a very impressive function on 12 May 1987. The British secretary of state for defence, Archie Hamilton, invited me to sign the documents of transfer. My wife Ackama formally named the ship INS *Virat* by unveiling the new signboard.

✧

As 1987 rolled by, turbulent political developments took place in India. I had to meet the press or appear on the TV very often to explain India's position or to provide the full facts on some of these developments. It was during 1987 that controversies relating to the Fairfax deal, the HDW submarine purchase, the Bofors scandal and the resignation of V.P. Singh from his position as defence minister arose. Also, many reports appeared in the media about the growing estrangement between President Zail Singh and Prime Minister Rajiv Gandhi over the question of whether the prime minister was keeping the president adequately informed about all important issues. The opposition parties had mounted a strong attack on the prime minister, openly alleging that he had been a party to the corruption in various defence purchases, particularly the Bofors gun deals. V.P. Singh and some of his previous close confidants such as Arun Nehru and Arun Singh had either been expelled or had resigned from the positions they held in Rajiv's government. V.P. Singh had set up a new political outfit called Jan Morcha, which launched a countrywide campaign accusing Rajiv Gandhi of accepting kickbacks. Meanwhile, in July 1987, R. Venkataraman, the vice-president, had been elected as president to succeed Zail Singh, who had completed his five-year term. Strong rumours and speculations were rife that Zail Singh had been planning a coup of sorts to dismiss Rajiv Gandhi as prime minister and instal a new government, which may be generous enough to provide him a second term as president. However, these rumours remained rumours and the transition in Rashtrapati Bhavan took place smoothly and without any controversy.

✧

In 1987, India's southern island neighbour, Sri Lanka, was going through a volatile phase. Consequently, the relations between New Delhi and Colombo underwent major changes. Sri Lanka witnessed regular clashes between its security forces and the cadres of the Liberation Tigers of Tamil Eelam (LTTE), who wanted a separate state for the Tamils in the northern part of the island-nation. President Junius Jayawardene of Sri Lanka had entered into an agreement with the Tamil groups, which conceded a large measure of autonomy to the northern and north-eastern regions of Sri Lanka. He did so on the basis of active support from Rajiv Gandhi, who had agreed to send Indian soldiers to Sri Lanka (in the form of the Indian Peace-keeping Force or IPKF) to oversee the surrender of arms by the LTTE militants. In a dramatic move, Rajiv had visited Colombo along with some of his senior cabinet colleagues on 29 July 1987 and signed a formal accord with Jayawardene to this effect. However, this accord could not bring peace to that country and, ironically, made both the Sinhalese and the Tamils turn hostile towards India. There was a large-scale outbreak of violence in Sri Lanka and many people lost their lives as a result of either rioting or police firing. On the day of Rajiv's departure from Colombo, while inspecting the guard of honour, a Sri Lankan sailor suddenly attacked him with his rifle butt. Rajiv ducked quickly and escaped the blow, which was aimed at his head. The sailor was arrested and Rajiv was escorted to a safer area.

The Sri Lankan accord was doomed to fail from the very beginning because none of the major parties to the accord were fully committed to it. Jayawardene was mainly interested in shifting the burden of maintaining order and peace in his country to the Indian troops as he had realized that his own military and police forces were grossly inadequate to handle this task. The opposition parties in Sri Lanka saw in the accord an opportunity to discredit the government, accusing it of having surrendered Sri Lankan sovereignty to India. The LTTE was dissatisfied as it believed that the accord did not provide the substance of power it had hoped for. The LTTE chief, V. Prabhakaran, felt that he had been pressurized by the Government of India to sign the accord. He went through the charade of accepting the accord without any intention of abiding by it and was of the view that the accord benefited the Sinhalese more than the Tamils and was bent upon subverting it right from day one. The LTTE's immediate concern was to grab total power in its region of influence and liquidate political rivals in the Tamil areas rather than honestly attempt to make the autonomy scheme a success. The IPKF found, to its great dismay, that the Tamils, whom it was supposed to protect, had become its worst enemies.

One of the provisions of the accord was that the LTTE would surrender arms, but Prabhakaran, far from asking his cadres to do so, gave a clarion call to them to wage a vicious guerrilla war against the IPKF. The hostility between the LTTE and the Sri Lankan Government reached a flash point in October 1987, when one of its prominent militants went on an indefinite hunger strike. He died within eleven days of beginning his fast. Another incident that contributed to the escalation of the tension was the capture of a boat carrying LTTE activists along with large cache of arms, which they were smuggling into their strongholds in Sri Lanka from India. Some of the culprits caught were important leaders of the LTTE and the Sri Lankan authorities wanted to send them to Colombo for interrogation. The LTTE vehemently objected to this proposal on the ground that they would be subjected to torture and violence by the Sri Lankan police. All the arrested men carried cyanide pills, and eleven of them consumed the poison and died before they could be interrogated. When the news about the suicides spread, the LTTE cadres went berserk and unleashed a reign of terror against the Sinhalese population in the north of the island. Prabhakaran publicly repudiated the accord and announced that he would resume the fight for an independent *eelam* (state). Within a few days, the LTTE attacked a rival group of Tamils and killed more than 100 people in a ghastly operation. They then turned against the Sinhalese in the eastern region and massacred over 150 of them. Such heinous acts led to revenge killing of Tamils by the Sinhalese in other places.

The IPKF personnel in Sri Lanka found themselves in the most unenviable position of remaining spectators to the open violation of the accord, which they were expected to enforce. The IPKF, at this stage, decided to act and began operations by mid-October 1987 against all those elements indulging in violence and terror. Such operations pushed the IPKF into direct confrontation with the LTTE.

The IPKF was, however, in no position to deal effectively with the guerrilla tactics used against them by the LTTE militants, who were on 'home ground' and could play 'hide-and-seek' games at will. Consequently, the causalties suffered by the Indian forces started increasing day by day. Rajiv was castigated by not only the opposition parties but also the media and several sections of the people in India, who, till then, had not objected to the despatch of Indian troops to Sri Lanka. Most of his detractors felt that India had been caught in a Vietnam-like situation where a highly professional and disciplined army trained for regular military operations found itself enmeshed in a guerrilla war, in which the LTTE distinctly had the upper hand. The LTTE proclaimed that it would never surrender its weapons, but would 'fight till the very last'. Large-scale demonstrations (to express sympathy for the Sri Lankan Tamils) in Tamil Nadu against the Central Government were organized by both the rival parties, i.e., the DMK and the AIADMK. The Government of India found itself in the embarrassing position of having to justify its action to its own people. Mrs Sirimao Bhandarnaike, the leader of the opposition in Sri Lanka, challenged the legality of the accord in the Supreme Court. Even the prime minister of Sri Lanka, R. Premadasa, did not disguise his strong dislike, if not hatred, for India and for the 'peace-keeping role' it had taken on under the accord.

Various sections of the media in the UK sought me out for interviews on the developing situation in Sri Lanka. I tried my best to put in proper perspective the circumstances that led to India's intervention in the Sri Lankan dispute. In most of these interviews, I found that my main task was to rebut the allegation that India had rushed into the island-nation with the ulterior motive of asserting its position as the dominant power in South Asia. When I appeared on the Channel 4 'News' on 27 October 1987, I was pointedly asked the question: 'Where do you go from here?' I replied that India stood firmly committed to a political settlement in Sri Lanka through negotiations with all parties involved. I elucidated that the military operations against the LTTE were *temporary* in nature and were forced upon India. I also declared that talks would be resumed very soon to find a peaceful solution to the imbroglio. In my appearance on the BBC 'Today' programme on 29 October, I was questioned as to how long India would keep fighting the LTTE. By this time the casualties suffered by the IPKF had become uncomfortably high. I tried to explain in this interview, as on all other such occasions, that India's sole objective was to help in bringing about a settlement through negotiations, and that, though we had been forced to resort to a military operation, it would be only a temporary phase. Very soon it became obvious that there had been a gross miscalculation on the part of the Government of India in general and on the part of the senior officers of the Indian Army (who planned the operation) in particular about the capacity of the LTTE forces for fighting a guerrilla war, especially about their commitment to keep on fighting 'till the very last'. Many months later (when I was governor in Tamil Nadu and the state was placed under president's rule), Rajiv Gandhi, during one of his several visits to the state on his election campaign, had (in a *tête-à-tête* with me) broached on his own the subject of the decision to send the IPKF to Sri Lanka. He went on to the aspect of authorizing them to launch military operations against the LTTE. He disclosed that the senior military officers in charge of the IPKF operations, in particular General K. Sundarji, had assured him categorically that the Indian forces would be able to bring the conflict in Sri Lanka under full control in a matter of four to five days. He pointed out that he had acted according to the advice given by the Army top brass, as he had no reason to disbelieve their assessment at that time. Obviously, General Sundarji, at that point of time, had no clue about the sophisticated weapons that the LTTE possessed. Moreover, he was probably unaware of their special skills and expertise in fighting a guerrilla war. Of course, the ultimate responsibility for deploying the IPKF rested with the prime minister, irrespective of the advice given to him by the senior Army officers or by anyone else. Eventually, in late 1989, the IPKF had to withdraw from Sri Lanka with its mission unaccomplished.

Towards the end of 1987, reports started appearing in the Indian media that Rajiv Gandhi was considering appointing me as the governor of Maharashtra after my three-year tenure in London. I myself had mentioned to him during one of my meetings that I would not like to continue in London beyond the requisite period of three years and that I longed for a period of rest and relaxation. Rajiv did not believe that I could quit serving the government but assured me that he would think of a change to a job, which may not prove too hectic. Obviously, he was seriously thinking of the post of governor for me. However, the transition happened much sooner than expected and, when it did, the new assignment demanded much more arduous effort and much higher inputs. I was appointed the governor of Tamil Nadu, which had just been placed under president's rule.

I had requested for leave to visit Kerala for a family function (scheduled for early January 1988) and the PM had approved my request. According to the travel plan I had submitted to the PM, I was to go from London direct to Kerala without visiting Delhi. However, on 23 December 1987, I received a phone call from V. George (in the PMO) inquiring whether I could briefly stop over at Delhi (en route to Kerala) to meet the prime minister on 8 January 1988. I had no inkling as to why Rajiv wished to meet me and started speculating about various possibilities. Gopi Arora, special secretary to the prime minister, referred to the talk that Rajiv had had with him a few days earlier whether I would be willing to return as principal secretary. When Gopi mentioned this talk to me I informed him that a job like that would mean too much strain on me and I jokingly reminded him that I had grown three years older since I left that post. Gopi informed the PM about my reaction. Rajiv obviously appreciated the validity of my reasons and did not broach this subject at all when I called on him. Instead, he told me that he was thinking of appointing me as the governor of Maharashtra. He asked me how much time I would need for winding up in London. I replied that a month would be adequate. He paid handsome compliments for my work in London during a particularly difficult period for India and I thanked him for his continued support.

After spending ten days in Kerala, I returned to London on 19 January 1988, quietly preparing for the impending transfer to Mumbai. However, destiny was to lead me elsewhere. Highly unexpected developments had taken place in a South Indian state, which changed the course of events in my life. M.G. Ramachandran, the charismatic chief minister of Tamil Nadu, passed away on 23 December 1987. Even though he had been in a bad shape for quite some time, his sudden death created a serious problem of succession within his party, the AIADMK. V.R. Nedunchezhian, the seniormost minister in MGR's cabinet, had been sworn in as acting chief minister, but the tussle for succession started even before the funeral of MGR was over. R.M. Veerappan, another senior minister in MGR's cabinet, was supporting Janaki Ramachandran (MGR's widow), for the post of chief minister, whereas another faction, owing loyalty to J. Jayalalithaa* was supporting Nedunchezhian. Eventually, Janaki emerged as the party's candidate for the chief ministership even though she was hardly qualified or experienced to occupy that high post. Obviously, a powerful clique within the party, which supported her, believed that it could wield real power, behind the scenes, with Janaki up front as chief minister. As a result of this tug of war, the AIADMK split vertically, with Janaki holding the office of chief minister and the rival group controlling the party organization. The Janaki Government could not survive very long because of internal squabbles as well as her own inability to cope with the heavy responsibilities imposed on her. Her government fell in a few days time, leaving no other alternative for the Central Government but to proclaim president's rule in the state. The prime minister obviously did not want to retain S.L. Khurana, who had been the governor over five years at that point of time.

On 4 February 1988, I was woken up by a phone call (at about 3.30 a.m.) from Rajiv to inform me that he would like to appoint me as governor of Tamil Nadu. He briefly told me about the situation there and his wish that I should take up the post as governor in Madras during the period of the president's rule. I accepted the post most willingly. He was happy to hear my response and asked whether

---

* Jayalalithaa has acted as MGR's heroine in several Tamil films. She later became the chief minister of Tamil Nadu, a post that she has held on and off.

I could join in about a week's time, as the situation there needed my presence urgently. I needed a little more time as there were certain inescapable formalities such as making farewell calls on the Queen, the prime minister and the foreign minister. He agreed with my reasons and hoped that I would be able to take up the new assignment latest by the middle of February.

✧

The next morning, I asked my office to inform the Buckingham Palace, the British Prime Minister's Office and the Foreign Office about my new posting and put in requests for making farewell calls. Despite the rather short notice, I was fortunate enough to get an audience with the Queen, besides being able to call on the British prime minister and foreign secretary.

Because of the shortage of time, I could not make farewell calls on all the senior ministers and officials in the British Government with whom I had developed friendly relations. Therefore, I invited them as well as my friends and acquaintances in the UK to a farewell reception that I hosted at the India House. I left for Delhi on 14 February.

Before I end this chapter, I would like to mention the fact that my wife Ackama had prepared and left behind a small but informative brochure on the elegant residence of which we were the occupants for nearly three years.

Ackama had also prepared a complete inventory of all the household items in the building such as furniture, cutlery, crockery and paintings for the information of the future occupants. When we occupied the house no such record existed. We felt that since all these items belonged to the Government of India, there should be a reliable list for reference by future occupants.

THIRTEEN

In Tamil Nadu

On arrival in Delhi on 14 February 1988, I found that I had been invited for lunch hosted by Rajiv Gandhi on the same day at his residence in honour of the delegates to the Lawyers' Conference. I attended the lunch, where I got an opportunity to talk to Rajiv very briefly. I met him again for a more leisurely exchange of views on 15 February morning.

During the second session, I made three requests for Rajiv's consideration. First: the MPs and ministers from Tamil Nadu, particularly those belonging to the Congress, should be asked *not* to interfere in any way with my work as governor. Second: nobody should be able to tell me that PM wants this or that to be done. Since I knew Rajiv so well I felt that I should be accorded the privilege of hearing from the PM directly whenever he wished to convey any message to me. Third: I needed a third adviser.

I was somewhat unhappy when I heard that two advisers had already been appointed at the initiative of the minister for home affairs, Buta Singh, without ascertaining my views even though the minister was well aware of the fact that I would be joining duty on

17 February. One of the advisers was A. Padmanabhan who, before this appointment, was the chief secretary of the state, and the other was S.S. Sidhu, who at the time of his appointment was secretary, civil aviation. I came to know that a few other officers were also considered but their names had not been approved on the ground that they belonged to the Brahmin community and their appointment may not be easily accepted by the people of Tamil Nadu. I, nevertheless, requested the prime minister to appoint G.V. Ramakrishna, secretary in the Ministry of Petroleum, as the third adviser. I had known him closely for several years and I had high regard for his competence and integrity. I pointed out to Rajiv that the 'Brahmin' factor about him need not be taken seriously because the governor, two of his advisers and the chief secretary (M.M. Rajendran) were all non-Brahmins. In fact, my view was that people would gladly welcome Ramakrishna's appointment, which would be seen by them as one made solely on the basis of merit. With regard to the first two requests, the PM enquired whether I harboured apprehensions that the Congress MPs and ministers would interfere in the day-to-day administration. My reply was that on the basis of my experience of having dealt with the states under president's rule in the past, I knew that MPs and ministers from such states assumed that they had a 'management' role to play. Consequently, I told the PM that I did not want my discretion to be fettered by their intervention. I, nevertheless, assured him that I would gladly listen to their suggestions and recommendations carefully, but they should realize that it would not be possible for me to always accept their viewpoints. The prime minister had no hesitation in assuring me that nobody would interfere with my working and that if he wanted anything to be communicated to me he would do it directly. He also told me that I could telephone him at any time or write to him or convey any message through the director, Intelligence Bureau, as I considered appropriate in each case.

With regard to the third request, the PM straightaway agreed with my suggestion to bring in Ramakrishna as the third adviser and told me that he would convey the message to Buta Singh. Rajiv assured me again that he had full confidence in me and I had a free hand to do whatever I considered appropriate for improving the administration in Tamil Nadu.

I arrived in Madras on 16 February to a grand reception at the airport. As soon as I reached the Raj Bhavan, I began studying the arrangements for the swearing in ceremony, scheduled for the next day. I noticed that a ceremonial procession had been planned from the Raj Bhavan to the Rajaji Hall, the venue of the swearing in ceremony, along Anna Salai (formerly known as Mount Road), one of the busiest thoroughfares in the city. I was informed that some portion of Anna Salai had to be closed for regular traffic during the governor's ceremonial procession (in a horse-drawn coach). Obviously, this closure would have caused tremendous inconvenience to the public. I immediately telephoned the commissioner of police asking him to cancel all instructions to block the traffic and that the ceremonial escort by the mounted police would start only from the outer gate of the Rajaji Hall so that there was no stoppage of traffic. He announced my decision to the press. This announcement had an electrifying effect on the public, who warmly appreciated my decision. The press welcomed my move as 'the signal for a new style of administration'. This was indeed a good start for me.

The swearing in ceremony at the Rajaji Hall was of special satisfaction for me for a personal reason. K. Subrahmanyam, my old colleague in the IAS, had telephoned me to inform that this was the first time that a person who had started his career as an assistant lecturer in a university (Annamalai University) had returned as its chancellor and a person who had started his career as an assistant collector in the state had returned as its governor. These were the thoughts that went through my mind as I was walking from the entrance of the Rajaji Hall towards the dais to take the oath of office.

The oath-taking ceremony was followed by a well-attended press conference in the room adjacent to the Rajaji Hall. In answer to a question from one of the journalists, I replied that my main priorities would be to provide a clean administration and to tone up its efficiency and pace of working at all levels. In response to a tongue-in-cheek question from another journalist whether people should address me as 'His Excellency' or as the 'Hon'ble Governor', I stated that I could not guarantee that I would be 'excellent' in all my functions, but I certainly would try to be 'honourable' in whatever I did. I announced that I would be attending office at Fort St George (where the Secretariat was situated) every working day and that I would be interacting with the officers as also with the public who wished to meet me there.

For a governor to attend office every day at the Secretariat was rather unusual. The practice had been for the governor of a state under president's rule to delegate the main administrative functions to the advisers, who would keep him informed about the important decisions taken by them or seek his guidance on special issues. However, I went in for a different style of working as I wanted to be an active and functioning governor. I met my three advisers and the chief secretary every morning and kept myself fully informed on all important items of work. I disposed of most of the pending files at the Secretariat itself and called in the secretaries for discussion on the files sent by them as and when necessary. I met the members of the public at the Secretariat by prior appointment every forenoon and also set apart almost an hour every day to meet those individuals who did not have an appointment but had come to the Secretariat in the hope of meeting me to present their grievances. On the basis of my attending office on every working day, I could gain an overall perspective of the administration and make the officers feel that I was *directly involved* in their activities and guide them whenever needed.

I convened my first meeting of all the senior officers in the cabinet room of the Secretariat on 26 February and spoke to them for nearly an hour, spelling out my priorities and my methods of work. I told them that I had issued orders delegating to secretaries, heads of departments and senior district-level officers full powers as they existed in the past when Tamil Nadu used to be one of the best administered states in the country and told them that all cases relating to matters such as transfers, postings and recruitments, except those relating to senior officers of, and above, the rank of district collectors and the superintendents of police, would in future be handled at the level of secretaries and heads of departments. I decided that all secretaries should dispose of such cases at their levels except those which, under Standing Orders, had to be seen by the ministers or the chief minister. Such cases would now be submitted to the advisers or to me as per the new instructions on delegation of powers.

Even though Standing Orders existed, regarding delegating powers on certain specified lines, the practice in the past had been to send almost all files to the top level, with the result that over 4000 files had been pending in the office of the previous chief minister. I asked the officers to list them out immediately, priority-wise, and dispose them of under the powers now delegated to them. A target of three weeks for the clearance of all such pending files was set, with directions that I be kept informed of the progress every week. The aim was to create a sense of urgency among the senior officers and also to instil the necessary confidence while taking decisions, which they seemed to have lost over the past few years. In fact, even senior officers used to function merely as post offices for the movement of files from the bureaucratic to the political level. They were assured that if they committed any bona fide mistake I would stand by them but I would not tolerate dishonesty in any form and that if I had to choose between an inefficient but honest officer and an efficient but dishonest officer, my preference would be for the former. I added that such a choice did not mean that I would condone inefficiency.

My first week as a 'functioning governor' produced the desired effect. The message went around loud and clear to all strata of the administration that Tamil Nadu would have a new culture of functioning whose hallmarks would be efficiency and honesty.

One of the first things that struck me while driving through the streets of Madras was that it had degenerated into a city overwhelmed by filth and muck. Even basic services such as sweeping the streets, collecting the garbage, desilting the drains or providing streetlights were not being attended to regularly by the Municipal Corporation. I decided to straightaway introduce a 'cleaning-up operation' throughout the city. In order to emphasize the seriousness attached to this work, I personally went to the Ripon Building, the headquarters of the Madras Corporation, and summoned all the senior officers of the corporation for a meeting. My visit to this place made some sort of history, which I realized only later, when informed that I was the first governor *in about 150 years* to visit the corporation building, not to preside over any ceremonial function, but to talk to the officers on matters concerning the service that they had to provide to the people. I asked the commissioner, the special officer and their senior colleagues to come up with a plan of action for the clean-up operation within a week, assuring them that they would be provided with all the funds required for such an operation. I later found that the entire exercise would cost about Rs 15 crore, which was sanctioned immediately. I did not want to give the officers any excuse for delaying the operation on the pretext of shortage of funds. I told them that I would be monitoring the progress of the work by visiting various areas of the city personally and that they should send me regular reports in this context.

My visit to the corporation, a straight talk with the officials and, more importantly, the promptness with which I sanctioned the funds requested by them indeed had a definite impact. The corporation swung into action and one could see the effect of the new clean-up drive within a fortnight or so. The media and the public heartily cooperated in this massive exercise. 'Clean Madras' became a very popular slogan and appeared to ring true, given the campaign for cleanliness in administration, which was well underway and to which I was paying equal attention.

My next destination was the Police Headquarters, again a place that no governor before me had ever visited. I felt that I should meet the director general of police (DGP) and the senior inspectors general in the DGP's office itself in order to convey the message that I would treat them with trust and dignity and impress upon them the highest priority I attached to corruption-free administration. I explained to them why I had transferred to the senior police officers the powers that they had once enjoyed with respect to posting and transfer of the officers and the men under their charge. Over a period of time, the police officers had not been exercising such powers. Even transfers of subinspectors used to be handled by the ministers. I asked them to exercise their new powers with strict impartiality and fairness and assured them that they could always depend on my backing as long as they tried to discharge their duties without being influenced by extraneous recommendations or favouritism.

Within a short time I realized that a sizeable chunk of officers occupying senior posts in the Secretariat and in some departments had been handpicked by the previous administration on considerations other than merit. In this process, some very efficient and honest officers had been sidelined to relatively unimportant posts such as heads of corporations and autonomous bodies controlled by the state.

At the district level a large number of collectors and superintendents of police had been specially selected for their respective posts solely on the criterion of 'dependability'. As a result, some bright officers from outside the state had been kept out of the collector's post. I decided to go in for a thorough shake-up both at the Secretariat and district levels. After discussing individual cases with my advisers and the chief secretary, a series of transfers and new postings was set in motion. The entire exercise was done in two or three instalments and, on the whole, the impact was very good.

I did not want to replace the advocate general, R. Krishnamurty, who had submitted his resignation to me and was willing to quit. The general practice had been to appoint a new advocate general when a new government came into office. Some of the Congress leaders were particularly insistent that their nominees be considered for this post. I strongly believed that it would be wrong to replace the existing incumbent merely because he was appointed by the AIADMK Government at the behest of the Congress Party. I therefore decided to let Krishnamurty continue along with other officers such as the public prosecutors and government pleaders, much to the chagrin of some Congressmen in the state.

My refusal to replace the advocate general became the starting point for a campaign launched against me by some Congress leaders, who obviously expected that I would take decisions on such matters on their recommendations. They wanted to exploit even small incidents in their campaign against me. One such instance was the police commissioner's decision to strictly enforce traffic regulations, in the city, which I had fully endorsed. Some sections of the Congress started complaining that the administration was too rigid in its dealings with the public. At a public function attended by me, Vyjayanthimala Bali (a famous classical danseuse and actress), a

Member of Parliament, mentioned in her speech that the enforcement of traffic rules had become too harsh for the ordinary people. In my speech I referred to her observations and pointed out that every rule, when first enforced, would create some discontentment initially but law-abiding citizens should cooperate by following the rules and not circumventing them. I casually mentioned the fact that my daughter Mariam had been fined Rs 50 the previous week for the offence of crossing a red traffic light. She had promptly paid the fine but later the police officer found out that she was my daughter and rushed to the Raj Bhavan to meet my ADC and explain to him that he had fined her without knowing her identity. I sent for the police officer and told him that I appreciated his prompt action in imposing the fine on the person who violated the traffic rules but I heartily disliked his attitude of apologizing for it and wanting to make amends. My stand was extensively reported in the newspapers the next day. For many days after that, there was a spate of readers' letters to the newspapers congratulating the governor for his exemplary behaviour.

When some Tamil Nadu MPs found that they could not make me 'pliable', they rushed to meet the PM at Delhi and grumbled about the governor's 'unhelpful' attitude. When the PM asked them to specify matters, they complained about my instructions to the police chief to enforce traffic rules strictly, which, they felt, was hurting the ordinary people. They also brought to the PM's attention my refusal to replace the advocate general. In their opinion, they would appear 'small' in the eyes of the public if they did not have their way. After listening to them, Rajiv gave them a piece of his mind. He affirmed that he had full confidence in my abilities as an administrator and that no one should attempt to teach me how to run a government or force my hand. The MPs were taken aback at the PM's reaction. (I got a full account of what transpired during the meeting from C.K. Kuppuswamy, the MP from Coimbatore, who had come straight to the Raj Bhavan from the airport.) After this chastisement, the Congress leaders stopped interfering in my work.

❖

One of the most important achievements during president's rule was the introduction of two packages of assistance measures to stimulate industrial development in Tamil Nadu. Over a period of time, industrialization in the state had been stagnating. The bold industrialization policy, which had been introduced (in the 1960s) by former chief minister K. Kamaraj and former industries minister R. Venkataraman, had created a fairly solid industrial base in the state, particularly for small-scale industries. However, in subsequent years, factors such as an unimaginative tax structure, neglected infrastructure and lack of special incentives had led to industrial stagnation. (Because of the need for a wide range of welfare measures introduced by the previous governments, the state administration had resorted to indiscriminate levy of commercial taxes unmindful of its impact on economic development. Commercial taxes at high rates, ranging from 8 to 15 per cent, had reduced many industrial units to sickness.) Some industrialists were surviving by indulging in all sorts of malpractices with the connivance of the government officials, leading to large-scale leakage of revenues. The incentives given by Tamil Nadu were found to be grossly inadequate compared with those in other advanced states such as Gujarat and Maharashtra. Hence, positive steps were needed to stimulate industrial growth in the state. In this context, several meetings were held with representatives of trade and industry to understand their problems firsthand. I then explained to all my senior officers that I would like to introduce a slew of measures, such as: (1) a considerable reduction in commercial taxes; (2) provision of increased incentives; and (3) liberalization of the procedures for industrial approvals. After that, I asked for their specific suggestions. Many useful suggestions emerged, on which I focused again at various levels, namely, heads of departments, secretaries and, finally, the advisers.

At the end of this elaborate exercise, a package of measures was evolved, which were announced at a press conference on 8 May 1988 at the Raj Bhavan. This news was widely disseminated by the media in the state, and all sections of people enthusiastically supported these measures. Normally, such major changes are not made during president's rule but I was determined to create conditions for the healthy revival of industries in the state. The prime minister too told me to go ahead with whatever I thought was good for the state. While the media and the industrial and business communities welcomed the package, the DMK-led opposition opposed it vigorously. The DMK members created uproarious scenes in both Houses of Parliament by questioning the propriety of a governor announcing such changes in policy while the state was under president's rule. They contended that I was not authorized to reduce commercial taxes. However, on all the points raised by the DMK and its allies, I was on safe ground. I was fully within my rights to take these measures and the government spokesmen in both Houses strongly defended my action. The DMK went to the extent of alleging that I was introducing all these measures to promote the chances of the Congress winning in the forthcoming state elections and that I was acting as an 'agent' of the party in the state.

The DMK's opposition to me was mainly motivated by political factors. Within a fortnight of my assuming office, practically all senior leaders of political parties had made courtesy calls on me. Some of the earliest were Janaki Ramachandran and Jayalalithaa. However, the only exception was M. Karunanidhi, the DMK chief. He had been nursing a grievance against me that I had played an active role in bringing about political reconciliation between Indira Gandhi and his rival MGR when I was her principal secretary. However, my role then should not have prevented him from showing the courtesy due to a new governor. Other senior members of his party had met me with petitions and representations on various occasions, but Karunanidhi and his party publications, particularly the *Murasoli*, hurled accusations at me continuously for various 'acts of commission or omission'. Sometimes, Karunanidhi levelled totally baseless allegations against me: for example, that I had asked senior police officers to campaign against the DMK in the forthcoming elections! The charge that I was acting as an agent of the Congress was repeated *ad nauseam*, but I had chosen to ignore it altogether. On quite a few occasions, journalists sought my reaction to some of these allegations but I maintained the stand that I would not be dragged into such controversies by any political leader.

However, Karunanidhi changed his opinion about me within a few weeks of his assuming office as chief minister after his party's success in the Assembly elections in early 1989. Consequently, I withdrew to playing the role of a constitutional governor. Being a shrewd and experienced administrator, Karunanidhi soon realized that I was not the type of individual who would function as an agent of any party or leader. Further, he also knew that the people of Tamil Nadu, who had appreciated my efforts tremendously, would never believe his party's allegations against me. As he got an increasing number of opportunities to study some of the important decisions I had taken and to analyse the reasons I had recorded on the files, he began to realize how much he had misunderstood my motivations. He soon got over the initial prejudices he had about me and we worked harmoniously during the eighteen-month period after the president's rule came to an end. Our relations remained cordial and warm even after I relinquished my post as governor.

I announced the second instalment of the package on 7 October 1988 at a packed press conference at Fort St George. Again, I had gone through an elaborate exercise of consultations at different levels. The second package was much more comprehensive than the first. Further cuts in sales tax were announced, the green channel clearance for small-scale industries was introduced and new measures of assistance for certain thrust areas such as electronics, drugs and pharmaceuticals, leather and ancillary industries were drawn up. The second package was welcomed by the industrialists with the same enthusiasm as the first. Taken together, they provided the necessary climate and conditions for the revival of industry in Tamil Nadu and for the stimulation of new investment. A virtual cascade of telegrams and letters poured in from all over the state widely appreciating these measures and hailing me as 'one who saved the industries from total ruin'. The criticism from the opposition parties was quite subdued this time as the critics had realized that the packages had become very popular with the people at large and it would be imprudent to find fault with them.

The two packages cost the government an additional Rs 30 crore per annum. The finances of the state were in a bad shape and I just could not levy new taxes during the period of president's rule. I started scouting around for other sources of revenue and, much to my surprise, soon found that substantial sums of money were being siphoned off by certain politicians from the liquor trade. During the previous regimes the seven breweries in the state had been given the monopoly for the supply of liquor to the Tamil Nadu State Marketing Corporation. The prices at which they were supplying their brands of liquor were much higher than those for other purchasers, including the state governments of Karnataka and Kerala and the defence establishment. I discovered that a large part of the difference in prices was going into the coffers of certain powerful individuals every month. When I asked my officers to negotiate for a substantial reduction in price, they were informed by the liquor suppliers, point-blank, that they could not do so as they had incurred huge losses in the past. Those losses were the result of massive 'donations' they had to make to various politicians and political parties.

I decided to confront the liquor barons head-on. I informed my officers that if the brewers failed to reduce the prices we would go in for purchase from outside the state on a tender basis. The leader of the suppliers, Ramaswami Udayar, a wealthy businessman of South India, tried to exert pressure on me and my officers by threatening us with dire consequences if we bought liquor from outside Tamil Nadu.

When the local brewers refused to reduce the prices, I invited open tenders from all over India, which showed that the government could procure supplies at considerably lower prices. Meanwhile, some higher-ups in the Central Government were trying to garner support for Udayar and the local brewers on the ostensible pretext of favouring state-based brewers. I thought it prudent to report all the facts to the prime minister who was horrified by the information I placed before him and asked me to take whatever action I considered appropriate without bothering about the pressures from any quarters. Udayar and the other local brewers soon found that I could not be prevented from going in for tenders, which was in the best interests of the state. They immediately brought the price level down to that offered by the outsiders. I did not want to reduce the price for the consumers because my main intention was to mop up the difference to fill the state coffers. This move brought in an extra revenue of Rs 25 to Rs 30 crore.

I intervened strongly in another project, which had been approved by the previous government for starting a medical college but had run into rough weather. Here again the 'protagonist' involved was the very same Ramaswami Udayar, who had been given permission to start Ramachandra Medical College (named after MGR). Over 120 acres of land in Chingpet district, very close to Madras city, had been allotted to him for this purpose and MGR had laid the foundation stone before formally fixing the price of the land or the conditions for its lease or sale. Udayar himself was reported to have acquired about 150 acres of private land near this site, knowing fully well that the price of land in the neighbourhood of the college would increase manifold once the project came up there. He, however, took care to ensure that the buildings for the college were constructed entirely on the land that the government had allotted to him. A ridiculously low price had been fixed for the land by the collector, obviously under pressure from the higher-ups. I appointed a committee of senior officials to determine the exact amount of land that would be needed for the college and the reasonable price that the government should charge for giving land under its custody for construction purposes. The committee submitted its report on both the variables according to which only about 50 acres of land was necessary for the college project and the price fixed by the committee for the land was 10 to 15 times higher than what the collector had fixed earlier. Udayar was naturally very disappointed by this report, but he realized that my decision would not be overruled by New Delhi. The construction of the college building was undertaken later by Udayar. The medical college has come up well.

Another surprise was when I found that recruitment to fill up vacancies in a wide range of government posts had not been done for years for various reasons. The main recruiting body, the Tamil Nadu Public Service Commission, was sharply divided between the chairman on the one side and the rest of the members on the other about the methods and procedures for recruitment. As the chairman had serious doubts about the integrity of some individuals on the commission, he did not entrust them with any recruitment work. On the question of recruitment to the cadre of *munsifs* and *subjudges*, he was at loggerheads with the high court, which rightly wanted to have its decisive say in the selection process. The situation was absolutely intolerable, given the two irreconcilable stands. I held a series of meetings with the chairman, where I made it amply clear that any further postponement of recruitment would not be acceptable. I had also discussed the matter with Justice S.R. Pandiyan, the officiating chief justice. After that, as a compromise formula, I put across to the chairman that rules could be amended to enable direct recruitment of 50 per cent from the Bar and that the commission should respect the advice of the high court judge who would be present at the interviews for the recruitment to the *munsif*'s cadre. The chairman persisted with his rigid stand. In one of the meetings, he even threatened to resign in protest. He probably thought I would be reluctant to face such a situation. I asked the chief secretary later to convey to him that if he wished to resign, I would accept his resignation without any delay. The chairman realized that he could not pressurize me and immediately fell in line. The selection to the posts of assistant surgeons, subjudges and *munsifs* went on smoothly thereafter.

Over 7000 posts of teachers were also filled up through district committees and the teachers' recruitment boards. In addition, 7800 posts of teachers appointed earlier were regularized.

Six vacancies had been existing in the high court for quite a while, because of differences of opinion between the previous chief justice and the former chief minister, MGR, on certain names. After holding discussions with Chief Justice Pandiyan on the eligibility of some of the candidates recommended by the high court, I sent in my suggestions to the Central Government which met with its approval.

My initiative to ensure that vacancies pending for three to four years were filled up in just two to three months time was widely appreciated by the public. The judiciary also felt happy that its views regarding the recruitment procedure had been accepted.

In keeping with my promise that I would provide a clean administration, I asked the Anti-Corruption Department to organize a series of raids and surprise checks at all suspected areas, i.e., the subregistrar's office, the Regional Transport Office, checkposts (toll gates), the civil supplies and public distribution system as also statewide raids on illicit distillation of liquor. Hundreds of illicit liquor manufacturing units were identified and action taken against their owners while several crores of rupees involved in the illicit liquor trade along with the equipment and vehicles used were taken into custody by the police. These raids and checks were widely seen by the public as proof of the government's earnestness in rooting out corruption.

At a meeting of government secretaries along with the vigilance commissioners, I was disturbed to find a huge backlog as some secretaries were according very low priority in dealing with the pending cases. Immediately targets were set for the disposal of such cases. An enquiry was also ordered into complaints against some senior IAS and Indian Police Service (IPS) officers. The fact that even senior officers were not being spared if complaints that were prima facie true were received against them had a salutary effect on the drive against corruption.

During one year of president's rule, a few major law and order problems also cropped up. The first was the call for a 'Bharat Bandh' on 15 March 1988 by all non-Congress labour unions. In Tamil Nadu, on all such previous occasions, the practice had been to close all schools and colleges and cancel public transport facilities, thereby rendering it easy for the organizers of the bandh to shut down all activities. But this time around, we decided to face the situation squarely and keep all essential services going. A few cases of damage to buses and dislocation of traffic were reported but, by and large, all essential services were maintained satisfactorily and there was not a single case of police firing.

Another major incident was the strike by government servants and teachers, which lasted a whole month, beginning 22 June, thus posing a far more serious challenge. The main demand was for parity with Central Government scales relating to salary and bonus. I had assured the union leaders, even at the very early stages, that a pay commission would be appointed to consider their demands and an interim increment would be announced for all categories of employees. The union leaders, however, wanted a categorical assurance about parity in salary. The two unions controlled by the leftist parties and the union to which the teachers and Tamil Nadu Government officials belonged were wrangling with each other for control over all the labour unions. Such discord helped the administration in dealing with the less aggressive groups in its attempt to dissuade them from going on strike. I had nominated my adviser, G.V. Ramakrishna, to handle the negotiations with the union leaders. Finally, using both firmness and persuasion, the government could reach a settlement with the various labour unions separately. Even though the strike dragged on for a month, the work in government offices was not seriously affected as the officers and the supervisory staff took on the main burden of the work and kept up the tempo of activity. Further, public sympathy for the strikers was nonexistent and they had to come back to work after accepting the face-saving formula we had offered.

A bandh call given by the Vanniyar Sangham under the leadership of Dr S. Ramadoss in the third week of December 1988 was the most serious of all law-and-order problems that I had to handle. The Vanniyar community in Tamil Nadu was economically one of the most backward. Its members had been demanding compartmental reservations for their brethren in government service and in admissions to educational institutions. While one sympathized with the hardship suffered by Vanniyars, I took the stand that we could not allot to them a specified percentage of reservation without verifying their claims regarding numbers through a proper survey. Taking into account the political sensitivity of the demand, the prime minister had deputed Narasimha Rao to assist in the negotiations. We held several rounds of talks with them but, meanwhile, practically every other backward community in the state began claiming the 'most backward status' and wanted compartmental reservation on that basis. Finally, after extensive negotiations in Madras and Delhi, the Central Government decided to accept, in principle, the demand of the Vanniyars for compartmental reservation. But the precondition was that a house-to-house survey was to be completed within nine months to collect reliable data on the claims of different communities, including the Vanniyars, regarding their levels of economic and social backwardness. The Vanniyar Sangham had expected that the government would announce some share of compartmental reservation for them. I held a press conference on 12 December 1988 to announce the government's decision and explained why the government considered the survey very important. Whereas every other community welcomed the government stand, the Vanniyars expressed great disappointment and announced that they had been cheated. The members of the Vanniyar Sangham resorted to many acts of violence, such as attacking buses, felling trees on roads and disrupting traffic in the districts where they were the dominant community. Large bands of rowdy elements were rounded up. The Vanniyar Sangham called for a total bandh on 16 December, for which elaborate arrangements were made all over the state so as to handle it. I addressed the people of the state on TV and radio on 15 December explaining why the government could not go further than what it had already conceded and warned all potential troublemakers that the government would maintain law and order at any cost. On the day of the bandh some unruly incidents took place in the Vanniyar-majority districts of North Arcot and South Arcot, but passed off as almost a normal day in most other parts of the state. Essential services, including road and railway traffic, were maintained without any disruption. By about noon, it was clear that the bandh had fizzled out. Dr Ramadoss admitted, in his press conference the next day, that the bandh had flopped but attributed it to the repression by the state government.

The normal period of president's rule, which was six months, had been extended by another six months and, as per constitutional requirements, elections to the State Assembly had to be held before the expiry of the second six-month period. The mood among the general public was clearly against elections, whatever party may win. People had started appreciating the peaceful and conducive atmosphere and the corruption-free administration for the last almost one year. They also applauded the various measures initiated to improve the efficiency and efficacy of the administration. Many newspapers vigorously pleaded for one more year of president's rule, though it was impossible to do so. Literally hundreds of letters started pouring into the PMO in Delhi, with copies to me, demanding an extension of president's rule. Finally, all speculations were set at rest by the notification announcing that State Assembly elections would be held on 21 January 1989.

During 1988, Prime Minister Rajiv Gandhi had been visiting Tamil Nadu at regular intervals in anticipation of elections. He covered different districts in each visit. During 1988 he made eleven trips to Tamil Nadu and addressed over a dozen meetings on each trip. The Congress Party had very little organizational presence in most districts and it virtually depended on the prime minister's charisma to attract votes, which he did in large numbers. Initially, he was hesitant in referring to my work as head of the administration though, in his private talks with me he was very profuse in his compliments. The first occasion that he publicly mentioned his appreciation was at a speech he made at Coimbatore. I was then camping in that city to attend a meeting of the district officers, which the PM had called to discuss the Panchayati Raj legislation, then under active consideration. On reading the report in the newspapers highlighting the PM's views, I was quite touched by his magnanimity and thanked him for this public expression of appreciation. He told me that he had first mentioned my name at a large public meeting hesitatingly, not being sure as to how the people would react to such a comment, but he said that every time he mentioned my name thereafter, he drew a big applause from the crowd. He later told me jokingly: 'I had to mention your name for getting an applause and therefore I kept on doing it.' Almost all the local newspapers accorded wide publicity to the prime minister's public praise of my administration. The *Dinamani* (a popular Tamil daily belonging to the *Indian Express* group) editorial of 3 April 1988 ran as follows:

A strange situation when the people of democratic India detest the party politics and show support for Governor's rule prevails in Tamil Nadu.... Their view is that since the Governor's rule eradicates corruption and makes government machinery work well, it has gained the wholehearted support of people. They have also made a strange suggestion that in the ballot paper there should be a column for those who support the Governor's rule. The fact that the Governor in his rule during this short period has tried to solve a number of problems, which have not been looked into during people's rule, shows his determination. It is no wonder that people wish that he should be given some more time for achieving the goals of his good work. If people's rule means the rule as per the wishes of the people, the Governor's rule now in Tamil Nadu is the people's rule.

My anxiety, however, was that my senior officers should not be lulled into complacency by such high praise lavished on the governor's rule by the press. Consequently, I had to repeatedly remind them at my staff meetings that they should not feel that what had been done was good enough as much more remained to be done.

Looking back at the one year of direct administration by the governor, I derived a good deal of satisfaction from the fact that I could motivate the officers to give their best without being suspected of having narrow party loyalties. When I had taken over as governor, I had found that almost every senior officer had a party label informally attached to him; he was always referred to as either pro-AIADMK or pro-DMK or pro-Congress and seldom as an impartial or independent civil servant. I had to put in considerable effort to create a feeling among the officers that they had to keep themselves completely free of party affiliations and that efficiency and integrity in performance alone would count in the matter of promotions and postings. My daily attendance at the Secretariat and my repeated insistence on the expeditious disposal of files helped a great deal in creating the image of a government that worked fast. I tried to set an example myself by disposing of every file within twelve hours of reaching my table and took special interest in fields such as education, rural development and the public distribution system, where the complaints from the people had been the largest in the past.

I had travelled extensively in every district of the state during the one year I was in charge of the administration and met literally thousands of people during each visit. I had a fairly good knowledge of Tamil; therefore, I did not need any interpreter for my interaction with the people. I addressed them wherever possible and tried to sort out their day-to-day problems to the best of my abilities. The Tamilians are fiercely proud of their language. And they have every justification for being so because Tamil is one of the oldest and richest languages of not only India, but also of the world. During my years as a research student I had become a great admirer of the Tamil language and I did everything in my power during the one year of president's rule to encourage the development of this ancient and rich language.

✧

I accorded the highest priority to the preparations for the Assembly elections and to conduct them in a free and fair manner. Great care was taken to ensure that the campaign for elections and the involvement of the civil servants in conducting them did not in any way interfere with the tempo of the implementation of the various development programmes such as a crash programme for digging and desilting of drinking water wells and construction of pathways to burial grounds. Nearly 3000 such works were undertaken in a record period of six to eight weeks by the district officers in spite of their preoccupation with election work.

My only disappointment as governor during president's rule was that I was not able to conduct the elections to the cooperative societies, particularly credit societies, which played an important role in giving power to local leaders. I had notified the rules and set the date for the elections but the Congress, which was totally unprepared for the elections, managed to get the elections postponed indefinitely. In fact, the Union home minister Buta Singh was roped in for this cause. He announced the postponement in Parliament during the discussion on the Tamil Nadu budget when the question of elections to cooperative societies was raised by some Congress MPs from the state.

The Congress had no organizational base in the rural areas and therefore it did not want to take the risk of exposing its weakness through participation in the elections to the cooperatives. It could not have the elections to the Assembly postponed because of legal constraints and therefore it contested them in the hope that Rajiv Gandhi's personal charisma and popularity would help in bagging the votes. However, the results of the Assembly elections further served to expose the weakness of the party. The party infighting turned out to be a major cause for the drubbing it received at the polls. Ever since K. Kamaraj left the Indian National Congress to join the Congress (O)* in the late 1960s, the former had ceased to function in the state as the party of the common people. Elections to the party organization at any level had not been held and those who were nominated to various positions by the party high command in Delhi were more interested to undercut each other than to build up the party from the grassroots. Rajiv had nominated G.K. Moopanar, who had been functioning as general secretary of the All India Congress Committee (AICC) for long years, as president of the Tamil Nadu State Congress Committee, but this change was too late to make any visible impact. The Congress Party continued to exist only on paper in most districts.

The elections to the State Assembly on 21 January 1989 were conducted very peacefully and in a free and fair manner. All political parties uniformly appreciated the impartiality with which the polls were held. The DMK, under the leadership of Karunanidhi, secured a convincing majority in the Assembly, winning two-thirds of the total number of seats. The Congress came in third, behind the AIADMK.

I held a meeting with my advisers and the chief secretary on 23 January to finalize the necessary arrangements for the swearing in of the new chief minister. Karunanidhi was formally elected as leader of the DMK legislature party on 25 January and he called on me along with his senior colleagues K. Anbazhagan, Murasoli Maran and T.R. Baalu to hand over the letter informing me of his election as the party leader. This was the first time he was calling on me after my taking over as governor. I extended to him my warm congratulations. The swearing in ceremony was fixed for 27 January 1989.

During the election campaign Karunanidhi had been a severe critic of president's rule and the various measures taken by me for the revival of industries in the state. However, after assuming office as chief minister, his criticism was mainly directed against what he

---

* O stands for organization.

described as the corrupt misrule of the former AIADMK Government
as he soon realized that, throughout one year of president's rule, I
had maintained the highest standards of fairness and impartiality in
all decision-making processes.

After the new government came into power, I quietly withdrew
from the active role of administration, leaving the business of
governance in the hands of those who were the beneficiaries of the
mandate of the people. I continued to take special interest in university
administration, particularly in the selection of vice-chancellors
whenever there was a vacancy to be filled up. I am happy to say that
Karunanidhi never differed with me in any of the choices I had made.

The first budget session of the Tamil Nadu Legislative Assembly on
25 March 1989, after the return of the DMK to power, witnessed
some very ugly and shameful scenes inside the Assembly Hall. When
Karunanidhi, who was also the state finance minister, rose to present
the budget, the leader of the opposition, Jayalalithaa, raised an
objection to his doing so on the grounds that a notice of breach of
privilege against him and an adjournment motion had been tabled
earlier. She wanted these issues to be considered first. The speaker
refused to allow any discussion on these issues and the chief minister
started making his budget speech. When the AIADMK members
insisted that the speaker should hear them first, the DMK MLAs tried
to shout them down, hurling filthy invectives against Jayalalithaa.
There was a virtual shouting match between the members of the
DMK and the AIADMK, with one side trying to outdo the other.
Members from both sides came close to each other and adopted very
menacing postures. According to the account given by the DMK
later, some AIADMK MLAs hit Karunanidhi on his face and his
spectacles were broken in this melee. The AIADMK version was that
the physical attack was started by the DMK members who had gone
very close to Jayalalithaa and were abusing and insulting her. The
AIADMK also alleged that there was an organized attempt by the
DMK MLAs to cause grievous hurt to Jayalalithaa and that they had
even flung chairs and microphones at her head in order to kill her.
According to one version of the AIADMK members, Dorai Murugan,

a minister in Karunanidhi's cabinet not only caught hold of Jayalalithaa's sari and kept tugging at it in order to publicly humiliate her but had even pulled at her hair. She was saved from further attacks by the AIADMK MLAs who quickly formed a protective ring around her. Then a free-for-all followed, with blows being exchanged between two sides. However, Jayalalithaa and her party members quickly withdrew from the House and more serious incidents were averted.

Jayalalithaa immediately sought an appointment with me at Raj Bhavan. Accompanied by all the AIADMK legislators and some senior members of her party, she was in a very agitated and angry mood. I noticed that her hair was dishevelled and the top portion of the back of her blouse was slightly torn. The AIADMK members told me that all this had happened during Dorai Murugan's attack on her. S. Thirunavukkarasar, who was then a senior member of the Legislative Assembly (he later became a member of the BJP and minister of state in the Central Government), pulled up his shirt and showed me his back, which had several fresh red and blue marks. He attributed these marks to the efforts of some DMK MLAs who had punched him hard with their fists.

The AIADMK demanded a high-level enquiry into the events inside the Legislative Assembly and particularly on the attack by Dorai Murgan on Jayalalithaa. They wanted the government to be dismissed, as there had been a breakdown of the constitutional machinery. I pacified the agitated MLAs, promising to have the matter enquired into thoroughly. Later in the day, Karunanidhi had sent his broken spectacles to me through the chief secretary, Rajendran, who had been present in the official gallery when these incidents took place, as proof of the physical attack on him inside the Assembly.

All these opprobrious incidents showed how strained and bitter the relations between the two Dravidian parties in the state had become. The DMK had steadfastly maintained that the attack on Karunanidhi had triggered off violence inside the Assembly. However, the attempted physical attack on Jayalalithaa and, particularly, the endeavour of a minister to pull her sari had shocked not only the people of Tamil Nadu but also people all over the country. This particular crime has neither been forgiven nor forgotten by the rank and file of the AIADMK and has become a major factor in widening the rift between the two parties. From then on, the two political rivals, the DMK and the AIADMK, had become political enemies.

✧

The political climate in India changed radically after the defeat of the Congress Party in the general elections of 1989 and after V.P. Singh became the prime minister. I had known V.P. Singh ever since he was a deputy minister in the Ministry of Commerce, where I was the secretary. Later, he had been promoted as the minister of state in the same ministry. He had high regard and respect for me as a civil servant. Consequently, I never expected that he would treat me as a stranger when he assumed the office of the prime minister of India. I noticed this sudden change in his attitude during his very first visit to Madras a few days after assuming office. I was at the tarmac of the airport along with the chief minister, Karunanidhi, and his cabinet colleagues to receive the prime minister. As V.P. Singh stepped down from the ladder, he shook hands with me formally, but without exchanging a single word, he went straight into the arms of Karunanidhi with exuberant enthusiasm. Even though it was a normal practice for the visiting prime minister to meet the governor first on his arrival in a state he had not included such an item in his programme.

One of the first steps V.P. Singh took after coming to power was to ask for the resignation of the governors appointed by the previous Congress Government. The new home minister, Mufti Mohammad Sayeed, went to the extent of even declaring that with the change of government at the Centre there should also be a change of governors in the states. In other words, the governors were to be treated as political appointees and they should remain loyal to the government that appointed them and not to the Constitution of India to which they had pledged their loyalty through the oath they had taken.

The National Front (consisting of a motley band of political parties from the right-wing BJP to the leftists and led by V.P. Singh) leaders had vociferously proclaimed before they came to power that they were determined to restore the prestige and independence of the institutions of democracy, which, according to them, had suffered great erosion during the previous Congress regimes. But among their first acts on coming to power was to strike at the very root of the independence of the institution of governors. The theoretical justification in support of this mass dismissal of governors was that since the governor was appointed by the president and held office during his pleasure, he could also be relieved of his office by the president, which, in effect, means by the Central Government. The procedure resorted to by the V.P. Singh Government was to request the president to advise the governors to submit their resignations. I soon received a formal letter (dated 14 January 1990) from President R. Venkataraman asking me to send in my letter of resignation as 'the Government desired to change the governor'. No self-respecting governor could even think of asking for reasons or delaying the submission of the resignation. I put in my papers on the same day.

I, however, felt unhappy that a person like me, who had earned the reputation for impartiality and fairness in his dealings with all political parties, should have been treated in this shabby manner and dismissed as an unwanted political appointee. Even a clerk in a government office could not have been removed from service without giving him a chance to know the reasons for such removal. When I came to know that a few other governors, who were also appointees of Rajiv Gandhi, such as Khurshid Alam Khan and Chintamony Panigrahi, had not been 'ejected', I felt more insulted because some of us were being singled out as persons undeserving of the new government's trust and confidence. I was later informed that these governors were allowed to continue in service because V.P. Singh had known them personally as they had worked with him when he was a cabinet minister. V.P. Singh had also known me personally as secretary in the Commerce Ministry and even more closely when I was working as Indira Gandhi's principal secretary. I recall how annoyed Indira Gandhi was when she saw the news on the PTI ticker about V.P. Singh's resignation as chief minister of Uttar Pradesh after a close relation of his was brutally killed by a gang of dacoits. She was livid at the fact that V.P. Singh had not discussed the issue of his resignation with her though she was the president of the Congress Party. For several months after this incident, V.P. Singh had not been able to meet her to explain his conduct. One day he invited me home (in Delhi) for lunch to explain how dejected he felt in not being able to meet her. I honestly felt that Indira Gandhi would understand his state of mind at the time of his sudden resignation if only he got a chance to explain the circumstances to her. I made very sincere efforts to make her agree to V.P. Singh's request for a meeting. I had also played a very important role in making her agree to his induction as commerce minister in her cabinet when a vacancy arose as I was convinced that he was the best choice then available. Probably, he now thought that since I had been the recipient of the esteem and regard of Rajiv Gandhi, who had become his arch-enemy in politics, I should not be allowed to complete my term as governor and I had to be shown the door.

Continuing as governors, even after having submitted the resignations demanded of them, was a very humiliating experience for all of us who had been deprived of our posts. The position of the governor had been reduced to an unwanted one by the Central Government, but carrying on merely because the powers that be had not been able to make up their mind about the substitute was a bit too much.

By mid-May 1990, I came across an item in the newspapers that S.S. Barnala was the nominee of the V.P. Singh Government to replace me as governor of Tamil Nadu. Therefore I informed the chief minister that I would be leaving within a couple of days' time. Karunanidhi was very kind and considerate in expressing his anguish at the manner in which I was being relieved. He organized a grand farewell party and spoke poignantly about the services I had rendered to Tamil Nadu as governor. In an eloquent speech, he remarked with his natural wit: 'This Alexander had conquered the hearts of the people of Tamil Nadu.' He had given instructions to all his ministerial colleagues to be personally present along with him at the railway station to bid me goodbye when I left Madras on 23 May 1990.

A few years later, when V.P. Singh was staying at the Raj Bhavan, Mumbai (when I was the governor of Maharashtra), during his medical treatment, I asked him whether he had any regrets for having treated the governors in the manner he did. I told him that 'command resignations' taken from us through a letter from the president was not a dignified way of relieving a serving governor of his charge and that it surprised and distressed me as well that a person like him could resort to the unusual step of dismissing governors for no other reason than that they had been appointed by the previous regime. He was honest enough to admit that this had been a big mistake on his part. He said that, on looking back, he believed that he should never have acted in the way he did. I left the conversation at that, as I had no intention to embarrass a guest of mine at the Raj Bhavan.

I should refer to an event that occurred towards the end of my tenure as governor, which had caused me a good deal of sadness. The V.P. Singh Government had taken the decision to withdraw the Indian Peace-keeping Force from Sri Lanka. Lieutenant General A.S. Kalkat, who was in overall command of the IPKF, had telephoned me enquiring whether I could be present at the Madras Port to extend a formal welcome to the returning soldiers. I told him straightaway that I would consider it a great honour and a privilege to do so. Later, I felt very sorry to hear that the chief minister, Karunanidhi, and his ministerial colleagues had decided not to participate in the welcome function, which marred the solemnity of the occasion. I sincerely felt that our soldiers deserved better. Even the chief secretary was not present at the function. I made a warm-hearted speech conveying to the brave officers and jawans the deep sense of appreciation and admiration that the people of India had for their devotion to duty, patriotism and discipline.

While I was hurt at the manner in which I was removed from office, I felt extremely grateful that I was leaving Tamil Nadu with the goodwill and affection of the entire people of the state, irrespective of their party affiliations and loyalties. Even though fifteen years have gone by, I continue to get affectionate letters from the ordinary people of the state on occasions such as my birthday or the new year. They make me feel very happy and proud of my close association with the state as its governor.

FOURTEEN

Back in the Thick of Politics

WITHIN A FEW DAYS OF MY LEAVING MADRAS, I WAS APPROACHED BY K.M. Mathew, the chief editor of *Malayala Manorama* group of publications, with the request that I write a weekly column for their recently launched journal *The Week*. I readily agreed as I thought that such a creative endeavour would keep me fully engaged. My book, *My Years with Indira Gandhi*, had been ready for publication even before I left Madras and I had given the proof copy to Rajiv Gandhi for his comments, if any. When I called on him on 29 May 1989 at Delhi, he told me that he had no particular comment to offer on the book and as far he and Sonia Gandhi were concerned, all the facts had been correctly presented. M.J. Akbar (chief editor of the *Asian Age*) arranged for the serialization of some of the chapters of the book in more than fifteen newspapers all over India. These extracts started appearing from early June 1990 onwards.

Life became quite busy and I was not inclined to take on any more responsibilities. I was sounded out by a few business houses about my interest to serve as director on their boards, but I firmly declined to take up any such offer. This type of work had never interested me and I would have declined such an offer even if I had little else to occupy me.

I turned down two other offers also, for specific reasons. Rusy Modi, one of the leading lights of the Tata Iron and Steel Company, wrote to me on 10 October 1990 requesting me to take over as the chairman of a social audit committee, which was to consist of, besides the chairman, an economist and another eminent person. He had already obtained the consent of an eminent economist and told me that I could nominate a suitable person of my choice for the third place. The terms offered were very generous. However, I replied to Modi on 23 October 1990 expressing my inability to accept his offer.

Another invitation I received was from the cabinet secretary, V.C. Pande, on behalf of the prime minister, V.P. Singh, to serve as a member of the National Security Advisory Board. This was a body that the V.P. Singh Government was planning to set up under his chairmanship. In the first place, I was put off by the manner in which my interest in serving on such a board was being ascertained. I thought that for such an important assignment, the prime minister himself should have shown me the courtesy of writing directly, particularly since he had known me personally for several years. Instead, the letter was a routine one, signed by the cabinet secretary. Pande had worked with me as joint secretary in the Ministry of Commerce and later I had appointed him as a consultant with the International Trade Centre at Geneva, when I was its executive director. However, from the casual and impersonal manner in which he wrote to me, it appeared as if he was writing to a stranger. I had to gently chastise him for this lack of courtesy to a person who had always been kind and considerate to him. I felt that it was my duty as his senior in service to remind him of the need for such courtesies. He promptly apologized for this lapse in his letter of 1 October 1990 to me adding, 'I sincerely regret the discourtesy and I apologize for the lapse. I have always had the highest regard for you and you are undoubtedly one of the greatest civil servants of India'. I did not want a compliment from him, but I felt happy that he had the magnanimity to make amends for a lapse.

Even if V.P. Singh himself had offered me the post on the National Security Advisory Board, I would have turned it down for other reasons. I wrote to him on 21 September 1990: 'You had known me ever since you were deputy minister in commerce and I was secretary in the ministry, in 1975. I am sure you would have had no occasion to doubt my impartiality, fairness and integrity as a public servant, but I found that you had lost that confidence in me after you became prime minister. In these circumstances, I do not think I can be very useful as a member of the proposed board.'

V.P. Singh understood the genuineness of my sentiments on this matter. Eventually, nothing came out of the proposal to set up a National Security Advisory Board as political developments took place very fast in Delhi and V.P. Singh himself lost his prime ministership in November 1990 as a result of a no-confidence motion against his government.

A new minority government, with Chandrashekhar* as prime minister and supported by the Congress from outside, was formed on 10 November 1990. It was obvious to all observers of the political situation in India at that time that this government would not last long. Chandrashekhar remained in power only till 6 March 1991, when he had to resign as the Congress withdrew support. The president called for fresh elections in May 1991 as Rajiv Gandhi, the leader of the single largest party in Parliament, did not stake his claim to form a government.

Let me narrate here how another governorship just eluded me. On 12 December 1990, I received a call from Rajiv's office in Delhi to ascertain whether I would be available for appointment as governor of Karnataka. I was later informed that Rajiv had been asked by the prime minister, Chandrashekhar, whether I would be interested in this post. Even though the thought of going back to a governor's post had never crossed my mind after my rather unceremonious removal by the V.P. Singh Government, I replied that since I had already settled down in Bangalore (the capital of Karnataka), I would accept the post. Rajiv conveyed this message to Chandrashekhar and I was informed that an announcement in this context would be made

---

* He was once called a 'Young Turk' and was a general secretary of the Congress in 1967. He quit that party and later became the president of the Janata Party (1977).

in two or three days' time. However, the anticipated announcement did not materialize and I did not bother to check with Rajiv as to what happened to this proposal. On Rajiv's visit to Bangalore on 8 February 1991, he brought up the subject on his own and explained to me the reasons why the offer fell through. When Chandrashekhar met the former president, Giani Zail Singh, who was then living in retirement in Delhi, he had casually mentioned about his intention to appoint me as governor of Karnataka. Zail Singh, on the basis of his long-standing friendship with Chandrashekhar, had strongly advised the latter against any such move. As a result, Chandrashekhar dropped the proposal. I was truly amazed that Zail Singh could allow his resentment against me to fester for such a long time.

During an exchange of views with Rajiv (at Bangalore on 8 February 1991), I got the distinct impression that he was quite confident of staging a big comeback if general elections were to be held that year. In fact, he was sure that general elections would have to be held early because of the continued instability of the government at the Centre.

However, all calculations about Congress' return to power went awry as a result of Rajiv's assassination in a bomb blast at Sriperumbadoor in Chingelpet district near Madras. He was blown to bits at 10.30 p.m. on 21 May 1991, right in the middle of the elections. At about 11.40 p.m., I was woken up by a call from my younger daughter Rajani who was living in Ottawa in Canada. 'Daddy, is the news true?', she kept asking repeatedly and in great anguish. On asking what she was talking about, she replied that she had just seen on TV the news that Rajiv Gandhi had been killed in a bomb blast at Sriperumbadoor. She had checked with my son Ashok, who was then in New York, and he had confirmed having seen the news on TV. I was stunned beyond words. Within a minute I switched on the BBC channel on the radio and I myself heard the incredible news. Rajiv had just arrived at Sriperumbadoor to address an election meeting when the bomb strapped on the body of a female suicide bomber belonging to the LTTE killed him instantly. Obviously, there had been a colossal security failure at the venue. Rajiv had been exposed to grave danger as a result of the withdrawal of the high-level security arrangements that had been provided to him earlier. Still, the elementary precaution, which should have been taken by those in charge of Rajiv's security at Sriperumbadoor, was to frisk those approaching him with garlands and bouquets. This precaution had been overlooked and the result was that the suicide bomber on her sinister mission could carry out her design without any hindrance. Rajiv's body was completely mutilated and could be identified mainly from the special brand of shoes that he used to wear.

Sonia and daughter Priyanka went by an IAF plane to Sriperumbadoor to bring the body to Delhi. After the plane returned, the body was taken to the All India Institute of Medical Sciences and from there to his residence at 10, Janpath. Later, Rajiv's body was taken to Teen Murti House where the scenes from the tragic incident of 31 October 1984 (when Indira Gandhi was assassinated) were to have their sombre rerun.

I reached Delhi on 23 May and rushed to pay my homage to Rajiv's memory at Teen Murti House. Sonia and Priyanka were by the side of the body along with a few other ladies close to the Gandhi family. Coming out I met a large number of Congress leaders who had arrived in Delhi from all parts of the country to pay their respects to the departed leader. I went to the cremation site along with my friend, P. Shivshankar, who had loyally served both Indira Gandhi and Rajiv as cabinet minister. The cremation rites were performed on 24 May. In every detail they were a repetition of the ceremonies performed for Indira Gandhi, about seven years earlier; in the place of Rajiv in 1984, Rahul (his son) was there in 1991 to light the funeral pyre.

I had stated earlier in this chapter that after I left Tamil Nadu in May 1990, I thought I would remain fully occupied with my writing assignments, free from any active involvement in politics. But I was wrong. After the unexpected events of 21 May 1991, I found myself again in the thick of Indian politics, this time mainly because of my proximity to, and friendship with, P.V. Narasimha Rao who had suddenly been catapulted to the centre of political developments in Delhi.

Even when Rajiv's body was lying in state at Teen Murti House on 23 and 24 May, Congress leaders from various parts of the country, in small clusters, had been busy confabulating with each other about who should take over as the Congress president and lead the party in the remaining states where the elections to the Lok Sabha were yet to be held. One group, consisting of Arjun Singh, Makhan Lal Fotedar, Satish Sharma* and others close to the Rajiv family, had decided among themselves that Sonia should succeed Rajiv as Congress president. The Congress Working Committee had met and hurriedly approved her name even without consulting her. Sonia, who was in a state of indescribable grief and shock, was in no mood even to think about such matters. She used the earliest opportunity to issue a statement declining to serve as the president of the party and thus the question of finding a successor to Rajiv remained wide open.

I received a message from Narasimha Rao that I should meet him immediately. Ever since I became Indira Gandhi's principal secretary, I had maintained cordial relations with him and had always admired him as a great scholar and as one of the few towering intellectuals then in Indian politics. A great computer wizard even in the early 1980s, he had a vision about the nation breaking away from the past without losing its pride and anchorage in its heritage. His profound knowledge of Sanskrit and his intricate grasp of the nuances of Indian politics had impressed everyone who knew him. When I reached Bangalore (after quitting as governor of Tamil Nadu in May 1990), one of the first calls I received was from Narasimha Rao: 'Alex we should keep in close touch with each other wherever we are. You are the one person with whom I would like to retain my close contacts.' In fact, we had remained in close touch and I used to spend long hours with him, engrossed in stimulating conversations whenever I had an occasion to visit Delhi.

After visiting the Teen Murti House on 23 May, I called on Narasimha Rao at his residence at 9 p.m. At that time, I found him the usual shy and reserved person unwilling to project himself for any office or to approach any individual or group for support. However, he told me unambiguously that since Sonia was not agreeable

---

* Arjun Singh's claim to fame was his tenure as chief minister of Madhya Pradesh, India's largest state (area-wise). Fotedar, a Kashmiri, had been close to both Indira Gandhi and Rajiv Gandhi while Satish Sharma was Rajiv's friend.

to becoming Congress president, many people had already requested him to state whether or not he would be willing to take on this responsibility. He told me that he would discuss this matter further with me later and that I should stay on in Delhi and remain accessible to him. He asked me whether I had broached the subject of election to the post of Congress president with any important Congress leader. When I replied in the negative, he suggested that I should start doing so discreetly.

Among the Congress leaders in Delhi, I had always maintained friendly relations with Fotedar. We had often discussed personalities and political issues very frankly with each other and Fotedar knew very well the extent to which Narasimha Rao trusted and respected me. Following Narasimha Rao's suggestion I decided to meet Fotedar at his house on 23 May night for a preliminary assessment of the situation on the ground. I deduced from my interaction with him that he had been in touch with Arjun Singh and had already discussed with him and a few other colleagues about proposing Rao's name for the post of party president. I noticed that Fotedar had become very active on the question of choosing a candidate for the post of president; in fact, several prominent Congress leaders had been discussing this issue with him. Although Fotedar these days has been relegated to the periphery of the Congress Party's affairs, at that point of time, he wielded a good deal of influence with regard to decision making within the party.

After our initial review of the situation within the country in general and the Congress Party in particular, Fotedar gradually began revealing some of the details of the plan that seemed to have been approved by Arjun Singh and his supporters. I could discern that the most important component of this plan was that Arjun Singh should be elected as the vice-president of the Congress if Narasimha Rao became the choice of the majority for presidentship. Fotedar next asked me whether or not Rao would agree to Arjun Singh as vice-president. I did not answer immediately as I had not discussed this matter with Narasimha Rao. I asked for a day's time.

I met Rao at his house at 7 a.m. on 24 May. During the course of a *tête-à-tête* on the suggestions made by Fotedar, he underlined the fact that his primary concern was that the Congress Party should remain united and strong. He added that the party rank and file should not get the impression that differences existed among the senior leaders with regard to the election of the party president and affirmed that he would gladly accept Arjun Singh as vice-president provided a consensus could be reached within the party as a whole. I met Fotedar at 8.30 a.m. on the same day and apprised him of Narasimha Rao's stand. Fotedar then raised the question of the likely attitude of President Venkataraman about inviting a Congressman to form a single party government. Fotedar's apprehension was that the president favoured a national government, which, in his view, was the best option for the country. I brought to Fotedar's notice that, in my assessment, the president would go strictly by the Constitution, although he may personally prefer a national government because of the serious financial crisis in which the country was enmeshed. I also pointed out that the president would not impose his preferences on this issue if a consensus could not be reached. Nevertheless, I firmly believed that it would be useful to meet the president and apprise him about the doubts and fears entertained by some leaders of the Congress on this issue.

The president invited me to breakfast on 25 May. I had known him ever since his days as a minister for industries in Tamil Nadu in the early 1960s when I was development commissioner for small-scale industries in the then Ministry of Commerce and Industry. He had high regard for me and I could speak to him candidly on any matter on which I held strong views. My interaction with the president convinced me that he would always strictly follow the provisions of the Constitution. The same day (at 10.15 a.m. to be precise), I reported the gist of my conversation with the president, first to Narasimha Rao, and later to Fotedar. I also informed Narasimha Rao that I had to make a dash to Bangalore for personal reasons, but I would remain in touch with him.

I returned to Delhi within three days to find that the opinion in the Congress was getting crystallized in favour of Narasimha Rao becoming the party president and the idea of Arjun Singh being appointed vice-president had been put on the back burner. However, it was not clear whether Rao would be accepted as the leader of the Congress Parliamentary Party (CPP) too. That could be decided later as the immediate priority for the Congress was winning the elections to Parliament.

Narasimha Rao launched a country-wide campaign from 3 June onwards in those states where the elections were yet to be completed. Considerable sympathy for the Congress had been generated in most states because of the dastardly assassination of Rajiv Gandhi; still, it was doubtful whether the sympathy could be converted into votes. In Tamil Nadu the anti-LTTE sentiment proved to be a favourable factor for the Congress. Karunanidhi and his party came under a cloud because of their past sympathies for the LTTE.

By the first week of June 1991, rumours gained ground in political circles that Sharad Pawar, the powerful chief minister of Maharashtra, would emerge as a contender for the top slot of the CPP. The Congress was expected to win an overwhelming majority of seats in Maharashtra and Pawar knew very well that this factor would provide him a solid base if he decided to stake his claim for the leadership of the CPP. In the 1991 election campaigns, V.P. Singh had ceased to attract the large crowds that he used to in the past. His not very glorious innings as prime minister and his constant manoeuvring against his political potential rivals, sometimes against Devi Lal and sometimes against Chandrashekhar, had not enhanced his reputation as a reliable candidate for the top post again. Overall, the dice seemed to be loaded in Narasimha Rao's favour but the main question was whether he would be willing to accept another leader as president of the Congress Party and relinquish this post according to the time-tested principle of one-man-one-post, opting instead for the prime ministership.

I returned to Delhi on 14 June evening and stayed on till 25 June. During this period, I met Narasimha Rao regularly, sometimes two or three times a day. Our focus was on the strategy to be adopted in the contest for the post of the CPP president.

Meanwhile, Arjun Singh's name cropped up as a likely contestant for the leadership of the CPP along with that of Pawar. Yet another aspirant was N.D. Tewari (who was once close to Sanjay Gandhi), but after the Congress debacle in his home state (UP), he had to withdraw to the background. Narasimha Rao had to tread cautiously. He had to make sure that Arjun Singh and Pawar did not reach an agreement to share the two top posts between them, leaving him in the lurch. The atmosphere in the capital was rife with an incredible array of rumours, though it was quite clear to close observers of the political situation like me that Narasimha Rao was far ahead of the others in terms of getting support from within the party. However, he did not want to take any risk and decided to reach an understanding with Arjun Singh and his supporters.

As suggested by Narasimha Rao, I held several meetings with Fotedar on 14 and 15 June on this knotty problem. At one stage, Narasimha Rao appeared to be prepared to give up the post of Congress president if that would ensure his unanimous election as leader of the CPP, although he personally believed that this move would weaken his position as prime minister. However, he was keen to ensure that if he were to step down as Congress president, the person elected in his place should be acceptable to him. Fotedar, who had again become very active, suggested that Narasimha Rao should make an announcement, as soon as possible, about his willingness to accept the one-man-one-post principle. Fotedar also wanted Rao to make clear that he preferred to be the leader of the CPP rather than Congress president. In response to Fotedar's suggestion, Rao told me that he had no objection to making such an announcement, but that he would himself choose the time for doing so.

However, when the results of the elections to Parliament were declared, the entire scenario underwent a major change, which could be attributed to the fact that the Maharashtra Congress had secured thirty-seven of the total forty-eight seats in the Lok Sabha and had emerged as the largest chunk of votes for the Congress in the country. On the basis of this impressive tally, Pawar's chances of winning, if a contest for the CPP leader became necessary, suddenly looked much brighter. He arrived in Delhi on 17 June evening and straightaway began consultations with various sections within the Congress. Very soon a powerful 'Pawar group' emerged and immediately demanded that the election of the CPP leader should be on the basis of a secret ballot. This group seemed to believe that a secret ballot would boost the chances of Pawar's victory if a contest became necessary.

Narasimha Rao had asked me to ascertain Pawar's views on the election of the CPP leader. He told me that I should convey to Pawar that he (Rao) would like him to occupy a senior position in the Central cabinet when it would be formed. I thought of conveying this message to Pawar through an intermediary than doing it directly. Consequently, on 19 June, I decided to rope in P.C. Chacko, a Congress leader of Kerala and a friend of Pawar, for this cause. I told Chacko that Narasimha Rao was expecting full cooperation from Pawar for his election as leader of the CPP and that it was Rao's intention, if elected as leader, to invite him (Pawar) to join the Central Government in a senior position. My own personal advice to Chacko was that Pawar should accept the assurances given by Narasimha Rao and not contest the post of leader of the CPP as, in my considered assessment, the chances of Pawar winning were not very high.

Chacko called on me on 19 June at 1.30 p.m. after discussions with Pawar and told me that Pawar would not contest for the post of leader of the CPP but expected to be offered the post of deputy prime minister taking into account the fact that he had the support of a sizeable block of MPs from all over the country, though not of a majority. I told Chacko that Narasimha Rao would definitely be against any arrangement that would look like a 'deal' and that Rao expected Pawar to assert and affirm the solidarity and unity within the Congress at a time when the party was trying hard to recover from the trauma it had suffered as a result of the assassination of Rajiv Gandhi. Nevertheless, I informed Chacko that I would convey his suggestion to Narasimha Rao and also let him know Rao's reaction immediately.

On the same day, at 2.15 p.m., I took Chacko with me to Narasimha Rao's house. I met Rao alone while Chacko waited in one of the rooms. Rao was very firm in his stand that the number two slot could be not offered to Pawar or to any other leader in the Congress. Instead, he repeated his earlier assurance, which had already been conveyed by me to Chacko, that Pawar would be inducted into the Central cabinet in a senior post. I conveyed Narasimha Rao's reply to Chacko and came to know later that Pawar was not particularly happy with Rao's reply. He sent a signal through his aides that he was serious about contesting the election to the post of the CPP leader. A veteran Congress leader, N.K.P. Salve, had by now become the focal point for organizing support for Pawar within the party. Almost forty high-ranking Congress leaders, who were ardent supporters of Pawar, had prepared a statement asking for a secret ballot for the election (of the CPP leader). The CPP Board met on 19 June and fixed 21 June as the date for the election. The board had also authorized K. Karunakaran and Siddhartha Shankar Ray (a former chief minister of West Bengal) to ascertain the views of individual MPs about their choice of the CPP leader. By this time, most of the MPs had arrived in Delhi and they had gathered at Rao's house to express their support for him. The 'Pawar group' had by late 19 June night realized that if a contest took place, Narasimha Rao would gain a clear majority.

In the forenoon of 20 June, Sharad Pawar held a press conference where he announced that he would not be a contestant for the post of CPP leader. Pawar, along with the senior leaders supporting him, went to Rao's house at noon on the same day and informed him about this decision. Consequently, Rao emerged as the unanimous choice. The CPP met at 4 p.m. and elected Rao as the leader. The swearing in ceremony was fixed for 12.50 p.m. on 21 June.

Even as the discussions about Sharad Pawar's candidature for the CPP post were going on, Rao had asked me to set in motion the exercise for the formation of the new Council of Ministers, on which I had begun working from 18 June itself. Therefore, I was ready with my first list on 20 June. This list also highlighted various options for the division or grouping of ministries and departments, the names of persons eligible for appointment as ministers and the names of those who could be considered at different levels such as full cabinet rank, minister of state with independent charge and minister of state under a cabinet minister. I had gained some experience in performing such exercises for both Indira Gandhi and Rajiv and Rao knew that I would always keep in mind all relevant factors including regional and community representation, experience, capability and seniority in the party. All said and done, the final decision had to be made by the prime minister and my job was limited to helping him in making the decision.

I met Rao on 20 June immediately after his election as CPP leader and showed him my draft proposals. He spent quite some time with me dissecting them and specified to me the additions and deletions he wished to make. The next step was to match the man with the ministry.

Narasimha Rao had earlier hinted (to me) that he was thinking of choosing a professional economist as the finance minister. During his discussions with me on 20 June he had mentioned the name of Dr Manmohan Singh and that of Dr I.G. Patel, another well-known and experienced economic administrator who had been recommended to him by a few influential individuals. I told him, without any hesitation, that my personal choice would be Dr Manmohan Singh and I briefly explained why. I could see that Rao was very happy at my wholehearted endorsement of Manmohan Singh. He then said that since the finance minister's post was a political one, he hoped that Manmohan Singh would not hesitate to join politics. I asserted that I was confident that Manmohan Singh would accept the offer. Being a good friend, I would be able to persuade him even if he expressed any reservations about acceptance and I would tie up the loose ends, if any, quickly.

On 20 June, when I telephoned Mammohan Singh's house, his butler informed me that he was on a trip to Europe and was expected to reach Delhi only much later that night. I left word that I would call again early in the morning the next day. When I telephoned his house at 5 a.m. on 21 June his butler told me that he was fast asleep and could not be disturbed. However, I insisted that I had to meet him without any delay and told him my name again hoping that my identity would make a difference. But it made no impression on the man. Upon insisting that I had to talk to Dr Manmohan Singh very urgently, he came on the line. I just told him that I had to meet him immediately, without giving any reason, and that I would be reaching his house within a few minutes. When I arrived there, he had gone back to sleep as he was obviously jet-lagged. He could not have possibly guessed that I was on a very important mission – not only to him but also to the nation as a whole. He was hurriedly woken up again and I straightaway conveyed to him my message. His immediate question was: 'What is your reaction?' My response was that, if I had any other view, except to support his appointment as finance minister I would not have met him at that unusual hour. He was happy upon hearing this view, but asked me whether I thought that Rao would stand by him even if some of his own cabinet or party colleagues were to oppose his proposals and plans as finance minister at a later stage. I assured him on behalf of Rao that he would have the latter's full trust and support. Manmohan was delighted at this assurance and gladly accepted the offer and requested me to convey his thanks to Rao. He reminded me with great warmth how he felt especially happy that I was again becoming an instrument in a major change in his official career. I told him that he was Narasimha Rao's choice and my role in this appointment was mainly because I happened to be his friend as well as Rao's.

I went to Rao's house directly after taking Manmohan Singh's leave and informed him about the latter's positive response and that I had conveyed the assurance that Rao would fully back Manmohan Singh in the discharge of his duties as finance minister. Rao felt very happy that he had succeeded in selecting the right man for this vital post when the country's financial position was at its nadir. He then spent an hour with me finalizing the names of different ministers, their rank and their portfolios and asked me to meet him again within a couple of hours with the final draft.

I met Rao again at his office at 12, Willingdon Crescent (Rao's residence was at 9, Motilal Nehru Marg but he had kept a room as his office also at the Willingdon Crescent mansion, which was then in the possession of the Congress Party). At this meeting a few more names were added by the prime minister-designate. I had requested both the cabinet secretary, Naresh Chandna, and the director of the Intelligence Bureau (M.K. Narayanan), to be present at 12, Willingdon Crescent for quick consultations, if necessary.

On 21 June, by about 10.45 a.m., the Congress leaders started arriving at 12, Willingdon Crescent, one by one. Some had come to seek a higher rank in the cabinet than what they had earlier occupied during Rajiv's prime ministership. Others had turned up to canvass support for their colleagues in the Congress for inclusion in the cabinet. I found that Rao was willing to comply with some of these requests even at the proverbial eleventh hour. Those knowledgeable individuals who are familiar with this type of exercise will know how very difficult it is to make last-minute changes without diluting some of the important considerations that had been taken into account in preparing the earlier list. Time was ticking away; we had to send the list without any more delay to the president, who was impatiently waiting for it. The list, which by then had swelled to include fifty-eight ministers as against the original ceiling of forty-five (the figure that Rao had in mind when the exercise was started), as well as the letter to the president was quickly given the final shape and, by 11.30 a.m., it was despatched to Rashtrapati Bhavan.

I reached Rashtrapati Bhavan at noon to attend the swearing in ceremony. On meting the president in his office I explained the circumstances under which the list had been finalized by the prime minister-designate. There was some delay in informing some of the individuals selected for inclusion in the new Council of Ministers that they should reach Rashtrapati Bhavan well in advance of the time fixed for the ceremony. I recall that there was a slip-up in informing Mamata Bannerjee, who was to be sworn in as minister of state. Fortunately, she saw her name on TV as one of the ministers who had to take oath on that day and rushed to Rashtrapati Bhavan; she managed to reach the venue in the nick of time, i.e., when the proceedings had just begun.

On the whole, the list of ministers found favour in the media. Of course, a few were disgruntled that they had been retained only as ministers of state and not elevated to the cabinet rank.

Manmohan Singh was the only minister who knew his portfolio beforehand and therefore could start preparing for his new responsibilities even before the formal allocation of portfolios was done. Two more days were needed to finalize the specific portfolios. Some ministries had to be bifurcated in order to accommodate the last-minute entrants. The prime minister had asked me to work out various permutations and combinations for his consideration and I had carried out this exercise on 21 and 22 June. The prime minister, after discussions with me on 23 June, affixed his stamp of approval around 4.30 p.m. By about 5 p.m., the list was on its way to the president for his formal approval.

After sending the list to Rashtrapati Bhavan, Narasimha Rao and I met at Hyderabad House (located near India Gate in New Delhi – a palatial mansion where banquets for foreign dignitaries are usually held) for about two hours. Here, he spelt out those issues that deserved top priority. He also sought my opinion on the selection of the principal secretary in the PMO. After a meticulous process of elimination, Rao approved A.N. Verma (whose name I had recommended) for this post. He was immediately informed as also the cabinet secretary.

Once the Council of Ministers had been formed, the portfolios allotted and the principal secretary appointed, I felt that I should return to Bangalore. Even though I had tried to perform the duties allotted to me confidentially, I could not escape media attention as I had been meeting Rao several times a day during that hectic period. However, journalists were considerate while referring to my presence in Delhi. *The Times of India* and a few other dailies had referred to me as the 'invisible hand', but all such news reports were friendly in their tone. Speculations arose in the media about my having been offered some important post in the new set-up by the prime minister. I thought if I stayed any longer in Delhi, such a situation would only add fuel to the fire. Consequently, I returned to Bangalore on 25 June after taking leave of the prime minister at his residence.

I had to visit Delhi frequently during 1991 and 1992 to attend meetings called by various committees and organizations with which I was connected and also to meet the prime minister and hold discussions with him on matters crucial to the nation. Our meetings always lasted for an hour to an hour and a half. Rao had always given me the freedom to express my views on men and matters candidly. He had specially asked me to keep him informed of the political developments in Karnataka and Kerala, of which I was a keen observer.

Narasimha Rao had mentioned to me on a couple of occasions that he was considering me for the post of the vice-president of India, which was expected to fall vacant on the elevation of Dr Shankar Dayal Sharma as president (in 1992). However, I had been sceptical about occupying this post because of the emergence of a powerful lobby in New Delhi in favour of an individual belonging to the Dalit (downtrodden) community. The name prominently mentioned in this context was that of K.R. Narayanan, who had the support not only of the left parties but also of some influential leaders. The most powerful of Narayanan's supporters then was V.P. Singh. He had gone to the extent of announcing that a Scheduled Caste candidate should be elected as president and not vice-president. He had even declared that he would resign from Parliament and advise all Scheduled Caste and Scheduled Tribe MPs to follow suit if a candidate from these backward communities was not selected. Hence, V.P. Singh had openly introduced the Dalit factor as the main criterion in the selection of the candidates for the highest posts in the country. Pitted against such odds, I knew that I had little chance of winning a contest, as I did not have the backing of any caste, community or political party. I had, of course, the good wishes and good intentions of Narasimha Rao to support me, but he himself did not have a clear majority in Parliament at that time.

The support for Narayanan for the post of vice-president gathered further momentum when the BJP leaders took the line that if the Congress proposed his name for this post, they would also back him. On 26 July 1992, Natwar Singh, who then had held very strong views against the candidature of Narayanan, informed me of the BJP's decision.

Narasimha Rao sent for me late on the night of 28 July. After the usual analyses on the political situation in the country, he observed that the odds were heavily in favour of a Scheduled Caste candidate for the post of vice-president and therefore he was facing serious difficulties in proposing my name for the post. I told him immediately that I was fully aware of the developments on the matter of choosing a Dalit candidate and that I accepted his judgement as to what was possible or not possible.

Rao then told me that he had some other plans for using my services for the country. He wanted to send me as India's ambassador to Washington, a post that had been lying vacant after the return (to India) of Abid Hussain, the previous occupant of this post. Given the prevailing state of relations between India and the US, Rao felt confident that I could play a productive role. However, I was not interested in any foreign posting and pointed out that I had spent more than thirteen years living abroad in the service of the UN or as high commissioner in London. He was somewhat taken aback by my instant reaction to his thoughtful offer. He told me that instead of saying 'no' straightaway, I should think about it in a tranquil frame of mind and also consult my wife. When I did so, Ackama fully agreed with my decision. The next day I spoke to Narasimha Rao, thanking him for his kind offer but regretting my inability to accept it.

During my meetings with Rao in subsequent months, the impression I got was that he was still seriously considering the possibility of using my services in a suitable position within India. My impression was correct in that he offered me the governorship of Maharashtra in January 1993. I accepted this offer enthusiastically. Factors such as the cosmopolitan traditions of the people, the premier position that the state occupied in business and industry and, above all, its rich cultural heritage had made Maharashtra a preferred destination for me. The state was, however, then going through a catastrophic phase because of the outbreak of Hindu–Muslim communal riots immediately after the incidents of 6 December 1992 at Ayodhya. (On this day, the Babri Masjid was demolished by some Hindu fanatics.) Reports of continuing violence in the city of Mumbai in the form of daily incidents of arson and killings poured in. Narasimha Rao believed that I would be able to help the state administration in its efforts to tide over the crisis quickly. I knew that as a constitutional head of state, my role would be a limited one; still I felt that I should give the highest priority to this task in my new assignment.

FIFTEEN

In Maharashtra: 1

My APPOINTMENT AS THE GOVERNOR OF MAHARASHTRA CAME AT A TIME
when I was least expecting it. C. Subramaniam* had been appointed
as governor of this state in 1990. In the normal course, he would
have completed his tenure in 1995. However, he quit in January
1993 under rather unexpected circumstances.

He had gone to Goa in the first week of January 1993 to attend
the annual session of the Indian Science Congress, which Prime
Minister Narasimha Rao was to inaugurate. At the inaugural session,
Subramaniam's speech was somewhat harsh and critical of the policies
and working of the Central Government. For a governor to publicly
criticize the Central Government, irrespective of the reasons, was
quite unusual, more so at a forum where the prime minister himself
was present. Subramaniam had probably chosen to make such
observations because of his acknowledged position as a respected
elder statesman. However, the august gathering at this function had

---

* Subramaniam (1910–2000) had held ministerial posts during the prime
ministership of Jawaharlal Nehru, Lal Bahadur Shastri and Indira Gandhi.

noticed that Narasimha Rao was feeling visibly unhappy at the tenor and tone of Subramaniam's speech. After the session, a few journalists, some of them personally known to Subramaniam, accompanied him to his room and took the opportunity to ask him a few questions with regard to the observations he had made in his speech. Thinking that his replies would be purely off the record, Subramaniam continued to make some more adverse comments vis-à-vis the Central Government. Unfortunately, one of the journalists published verbatim Subramaniam's remarks in his paper published from Goa. This news item attracted a good deal of public attention and stirred up a hornest's nest. The prime minister returned to Delhi, naturally feeling distressed with the whole episode. Subramaniam too felt embarrassed that the remarks he had made in private had been published without his permission. On his return to Bombay, he sent his letter of resignation. The prime minister promptly recommended to the president that it be accepted. Subramaniam himself had to visit Delhi on 6 and 7 January 1993 in connection with other official work and, in fact, had attended a function at the Rashtrapati Bhavan where he had met both the prime minister and the president. It was only on his return to Mumbai on 7 January night that he learnt that his resignation had been accepted.

At 8.30 p.m. on 7 January I saw a news item on TV in Bangalore mentioning that Subramaniam's resignation had been accepted by the president. I telephoned him to ascertain the veracity of the news item. He admitted that he had sent in his resignation but had not received any information so far about its acceptance by the president. I then informed him that according to the TV report, his resignation had been accepted. Within a few minutes of this conversation, I received the formal message that I had been appointed as the governor of Maharashtra to replace Subramaniam.

The Union home minister, S.B. Chavan, telephoned me at 9.15 p.m. on 7 January offering his congratulations on my appointment. He suggested that I get in touch with Subramaniam to decide on a mutually convenient date for the changeover. By this time, the news of my appointment had spread all over the country through radio and TV and Subramaniam too had come to know about the impending 'change of guard'. I telephoned him again in the night confirming that

I had been informed about my new appointment. He first warmly congratulated me and then told me that he was planning to leave Bombay by the forenoon of 12 January. In view of the critical law and order situation in the state, I decided to take over on 12 January itself.

I reached Bombay by the government plane that had transported Subramaniam to Madras on the morning of 12 January. While travelling by helicopter from the Bombay airport to the Raj Bhavan, I noticed that the city had a ghostly appearance. I could see that most of the shops were closed and the streets of Bombay, which are normally bustling with frenetic activity, were practically deserted. The only occupants of the streets were the police and military personnel on security duty.

Despite the bleak and sombre scenario, I took the oath of office at 5.30 p.m. on 12 January. However, even before being sworn in, I called for a meeting of top officials including the chief secretary and all other senior secretaries as well as police officers concerned with law and order and rehabilitation work. The objectives were to understand the situation on the ground and to resolve the problems facing the government. Senior officers informed me that, ever since the riots broke out in December 1992, the death count had been around thirty daily. They, nevertheless, reassuringly added that the count had come down over the past few days, but intensely palpable tension still gripped the metropolis. In certain areas of the city, ordinary people lived in an atmosphere of fear and uncertainty. Hundreds of riot victims, particularly women and children, had been shifted to temporary camps, which had been set up hurriedly in various parts of the city. Curfew had been imposed in the trouble spots; it was relaxed from early in the morning only up to noon.

Even on the day I took over as governor, five deaths were reported due to stabbing. Mercifully, this figure marked a fairly steep fall from the disturbingly high counts of thirty-eight on 8 January and twenty-eight on 9 January. The most serious problems facing the administration were the prevention of further killings and arson as well as providing basic amenities such as food and drinking water to the various camps. I could see that the officers were trying to do their best to cope with the harrowing situation, but most of them appeared to be overstretched due to the continuously tension-ridden nature of duty. I told them that I proposed to visit the affected areas from the next day onwards and that I wanted to remain in constant touch with them, which would enable me to ascertain the progress of their efforts not only in restoring peace and law and order but also in implementing relief and rehabilitation programmes.

Within an hour of my reaching the Raj Bhavan, several senior retired officers (whom I had known previously) informed me that there was tremendous resentment among the people of the city because neither the chief minister (or his colleagues) nor the governor had visited any of the riot-affected areas or the camps to know the conditions there first-hand. One could not really blame the ministers or the governor because the security personnel would have found it virtually impossible to arrange such visits, given the gravity of the situation prevalent in the city. Nevertheless, I decided to visit the main affected areas and the hospitals where the injured persons were being treated. I also decided to see for myself the conditions in the major camps.

During my rounds the next morning, I found that the camps were indeed in a miserable condition. Hundreds of people had been herded into them without adequate arrangements for sanitation, food and even drinking water having been made. The situation in the J.J. Hospital, where large clusters of injured persons were being treated, was equally depressing. The doctors and paramedical staff there had been working virtually round the clock without proper rest for several days. Even then they found it very difficult to attend promptly to the needs of the new entrants being brought to the hospital with injuries. At different places in the city, I stopped the car to talk to small groups of people. While expressing their hardships due to lack of transport facilities and closure of shops, they emphasized that they were confident that the city would bounce back to normalcy in a week or so. Their confidence was symbolic of the determination of the Mumbaites to face crisis situations courageously, however serious they might be. I felt particularly happy to learn about the valuable services that were being provided by a range of voluntary groups to those in acute distress and in urgent need of essential items such as food, water, shelter and clothing. My wife Ackama too visited several camps, particularly those where women had been accommodated in large numbers. Over the next three to four days, she covered most of the large camps in the city and ascertained from the women their immediate needs. The information my wife and I gathered through our separate visits was promptly passed on to the government officers responsible for relief and rehabilitation work. I was happy to note that prompt action was being taken by these officers to ameliorate the situation.

The prime minister, Narasimha Rao, came to Bombay on 15 January and I accompanied him on his visits to some of the hospitals and the riot-affected areas. Later, at the prime minister's press conference, there were complaints galore about the alleged delay and inaction on the part of the government when the riots first broke out. I noticed that many journalists were ignorant of the vast magnitude of the problems that the government faced. They were also unaware of the measures that the authorities had already taken to provide relief and rehabilitation to the people. Obviously, the government had lagged behind in keeping the people adequately informed about its programmes and measures.

The logistics involved in running the camps were indeed complex. There were more than thirty-three camps in different parts of the city, where over 24,000 persons had been accommodated (in reality, stuffed). Among the camps I visited, those located at Musafirkhana and Crawford Market housed over 4500 Muslims who were highly agitated. In fact, in both these camps, pushing and jostling were the dominant factors as people appeared to be overanxious to present their grievances to me. I also visited the camp at Jogeshwari (a suburb in western Bombay) where many Hindus who were displaced from their residences were given shelter. Some of them wanted to be rehabilitated in a different area.

Even though there was a marked improvement in the overall situation, incidents of violence continued to occur in certain areas of the city. From 6 p.m. on 14 January, fifty-six such incidents were reported and the police had to open fire on eight occasions.

By the last week of January, the city had started attaining a *semblance* of normalcy. The number of incidents of killing and arson had come down sharply; curfew had been lifted in several places;

shops had started reopening; and buses began plying in most areas. However, I could feel the tremendous resentment among both Hindus and Muslims against the alleged failure at senior political levels of the state government in enlisting the support and involvement of the public in the action to control the riots when they first erupted in December 1992. I continued to meet several delegations every day. Almost all such delegations alleged that the government had failed to understand the seriousness of the situation in the first few days of violence and it was this lapse that had led to the large-scale escalation of the riots.

On 17 January I convened a meeting attended by the chief minister, Sudhakar Rao Naik, and some of his senior cabinet colleagues apart from senior secretaries and police officers. The objective was to discuss the steps to be taken for more speedy implementation of the relief and rehabilitation programmes. The outcome of this meeting was that fifteen areas were identified, which urgently needed attention. Consequently, local committees consisting of prominent social workers, non-governmental organizations (NGOs) as well as the government, were formed for each such area. Each local committee was to be presided over by a minister. The meeting also decided to form an Apex Committee consisting of prominent citizens of the city, leaders of political parties and representatives of voluntary organizations as well as business concerns and banking institutions to provide guidance in the work of relief and rehabilitation. The chairmen and vice-chairmen of the local committees were included as members of the Apex Committee. I was to be the chairman and the chief minister the vice-chairman of this committee.

The first meeting of the Apex Committee was held at Raj Bhavan on 21 January. This meeting was attended by the chief minister and several prominent businessmen and industrialists including J.R.D. Tata. A rehabilitation fund with a corpus of Rs 1 crore (received from the prime minister) and Rs 10 lakh (received from the Rajiv Gandhi Foundation) was set up. The chief minister announced a contribution of Rs 10 crore at the meeting to this fund. A variety of charitable organizations and individuals came forward with offers of assistance and generous contributions to the fund. It was decided to increase the number of relief camps to sixty-one. By the end of January, the death toll in the riots had reached 555. The number of injured persons was 1184.

✧

Even though the situation in the city in general had shown a distinct improvement, tension continued to prevail in certain areas. I had an experience of the impact of this tension while I was on a visit to one of the seriously affected areas. On 1 February 1993, violence had suddenly broken out at Behrampada, when twenty-five huts belonging to Muslims were burnt down. The police intervened promptly, but two people had been killed in the firing. On the forenoon of 3 February, I visited a large camp of Muslims in the suburb of Santa Cruz (east). I had to walk through very narrow lanes over a long distance to see for myself the scale of destruction that had taken place there during the riots. Huge mobs had collected near a school building and I found them in a very angry mood. Agitated people were trying to come close to me in spite of the earnest efforts of the police to protect me from the rush of the crowd.

While I was on the verge of leaving the Santa Cruz camp, Sunil Dutt, Member of Parliament and a respected leader of the Congress in Bombay, and a few others present there, requested me to visit Behrampada as well. The police officers were not very happy with the idea of my visiting Behrampada, particularly when they had not made proper arrangements for my security due to lack of time. However, Behrampada was only 2 km away from Santa Cruz and I thought I should accept Sunil Dutt's suggestion and visit this place too. Sunil Dutt accompanied me in my car to Behrampada where a large crowd of Muslims put forward their grievances to me. I tried to calm their feelings and reassure them. As I was returning to the place where my car was parked, I noticed that a gathering of about 500 Hindus, mostly women, had blocked the road on which my car was to proceed. They were gesticulating wildly and virtually screaming with rage. I was later informed that the presence of Sunil Dutt was the main provocation as he had been organizing relief in the neighbouring localities where Muslims had been the main victims of the riots. Sunil Dutt was active in the rehabilitation work in *all* riot-affected areas, irrespective of whether the people were Muslims or

Hindus. But, unfortunately, certain extremist groups in the Hindu community had branded him pro-Muslim. The scene was becoming increasingly ugly as I noticed that Sunil Dutt himself was being roughed up. I also noticed that some of the senior officers who had accompanied me, particularly Satish Tripathi, secretary, Rehabilitation Department (whom I later selected as governor's secretary), were also being physically attacked by some individuals in the crowd. The people assembled there were in no mood to listen to any sane or rational voice and were shouting acrimonious slogans against the government. I thought that the prudent course would be to leave the place without much delay, as the flare-up of violence seemed imminent. If the police were to use force to disperse the crowd, such a move would have led to an ominous situation. I quickly got into my car and asked my driver to move forward though the women were still squatting on the road in front of the vehicle. Fortunately, when the car started moving, the women gave way; thus, I could leave the place without any more unpleasant incidents occurring. The next day, the newspapers published highly exaggerated reports of this incident. Some journalists described it as an attempt to *gherao* the governor. This setback, however, did not deter me from making my rounds of the riot-affected areas as they enabled me to gain a first-hand knowledge of the actual situation in the city and, above all, to understand the problems of the people living in various camps. Even though the mood of the crowds was somewhat hostile to the government in certain places I visited, in all other areas I found the people highly appreciative of the fact that they could directly inform me about what they urgently needed and what more could be done.

✧

I issued an appeal in my capacity as chairman of the Apex Committee for contributions in kind and cash for the massive programme of rehabilitation launched by the government and was indeed overwhelmed by the generous scale of response by the people of Maharashtra in general and the Mumbaites in particular. Items such as foodstuff, soft drinks, clothes, medicines and household utensils reached the government reception centre and sometimes the Raj Bhavan in large quantities. The government also received large sums of money through cheques and in cash for its rehabilitation programmes.

By mid-February, Mumbai had returned to normalcy. The government still came in for some criticism, but as one who was involved in the relief and rehabilitation efforts during those extremely arduous days, I should state that I was quite impressed by the high standards of efficiency and dedication to duty on the part of the government officers in coping with a crisis of such a colossal magnitude.

The year 1993 was an unusually difficult one for Maharashtra. This period was dominated by crises and disasters unprecedented in the history of the state. Just when we thought we had got over the adversities created by the communal riots spread over December 1992 to February 1993, we had to face a totally unexpected calamity in the form of the serial bomb blasts that shook Mumbai on 12 March 1993. These blasts were followed by devastating earthquakes in the Latur and Osmanabad districts on 30 September 1993. Let me first deal with the serial bomb blasts.

Narasimha Rao had, by the first week of March, made up his mind that Maharashtra needed a new chief minister. Some of his senior party colleagues and also prominent non-party leaders in Maharashtra had sent reports to Rao detailing the rather cavalier manner in which Sudhakar Rao Naik had handled the communal riots in the state. Rao was convinced that only Sharad Pawar, who had the requisite calibre and experience, could provide the leadership that would enable trade and industry to recover from the setbacks they had suffered. Rao also believed that only Pawar could restore peace and harmony between the Hindu and Muslim communities in the state. Pawar, quite happy with his portfolio as defence minister in the Central cabinet, was very reluctant to once again occupy the chief minister's post, which he had quit only a couple of years earlier. He had been hoping to play an active role at the national level and did not plan a return to state-level politics. However, Rao succeeded in persuading him to take up the chief ministership at least for a couple of years to help the state regain its lost momentum in development programmes and also to prepare his party for the elections to the State Assembly due to be held in 1995. Rao had assured Pawar that he would be brought back to the Central Government as soon as the State Assembly elections were over. With great reluctance Pawar yielded to the persuasions of the prime minister and took charge as chief minister of Maharashtra on 6 March 1993. Ironically, Pawar's political enemies in Maharashtra launched a whispering campaign against him as soon as he returned to the state that he had deftly manoeuvred to get the post of chief minister for himself. Sudhakar Rao Naik himself believed this theory. He never forgave Pawar for what he considered the latter's plot to oust him. Those of us who knew the reason for Pawar's leaving the Central cabinet and taking over as Maharashtra's chief minister were truly surprised that such false propaganda could be mounted against him. Pawar was a powerful leader with a very large base in the state, but such leaders have also equally powerful enemies. However, the vast majority of the people of Maharashtra wholeheartedly welcomed Pawar's return as chief minister.

Pawar had been in the saddle for hardly a week when the city of Mumbai was rocked by the deadly serial bomb blasts. The immediate repercussion was that it triggered off a new wave of communal riots in the state similar to those it had experienced only a few weeks earlier. In fact, those who planned and executed these blasts essentially wanted to spark off a fresh spate of riots. On 12 March 1993, between 1.20 p.m. and 4.20 p.m., bombs of a very high magnitude were set off at ten different places in the city. Huge explosions occurred in localities as diverse as Fort, Dadar, Worli, Santa Cruz, Bandra, Juhu, Mahim and Masjid Bunder, all very highly crowded. The death toll was 257 and the persons injured were 713. In one area, hand grenades were hurled at some hutments from a passing vehicle. On the same day a vehicle containing weapons such as AK 56 assault rifles and hand grenades was found abandoned on a street. I received the news of the serial bombs from the new chief secretary, N. Raghunathan, who had taken charge of his post only on the forenoon of that day. He had called on me that morning at the Raj Bhavan before proceeding to the Mantralaya to take over his new post, and I was struck by the irony of the fact that his first telephone call to me after joining duty was to convey this terrible news. I visited the main sites of the blasts the next morning. The hub of commercial activity, the Bombay Stock Exchange building, had been badly damaged, bringing all work there to a stop. The prestigious Air India building and the office of a foreign bank nearby had also been damaged in the blast. The danger of people getting into a state of panic was imminent.

Fortunately, the state now had a government that fully understood the seriousness of the incidents and their potential for much greater havoc. Within less than an hour of the bomb blasts, Sharad Pawar succeeded in harnessing the full resources of the government, the Municipal Corporation, the defence establishments located in the state and various public sector undertakings to begin the stupendous task of bringing the city back to normal. The most difficult job was to restore more than 700 telephone lines of the Bombay Stock Exchange building destroyed in the blasts. Pawar gave clear instructions to the the Telephone Department and all other concerned authorities that he wanted to see the Stock Exchange working in a normal manner from the next working day, which was Monday, 15 March. He remained in his office during the next forty-eight hours directing the operations in all the affected areas in the city without going home even for a couple of hours for meals or rest. He had enlisted the services of the officers of the Defence Research and Development Organization (DRDO) and the experts of the Defence Department to help the Mumbai police in tracing the culprits. Over fifteen persons who were actively involved in this dastardly crime were arrested by the police on the night of 12 March itself and huge quantities of fire arms and explosives were also seized from them.

Much to the surprise and relief of the Mumbaites, all essential facilities including the city transport, milk supply, suburban trains, water and electricity had been made available to the people as in normal times from the very next day itself. All the shops were open and it looked as if no serious dislocation in services had taken place in the city. Equally impressive was the fact that all the telephone lines in the Bombay Stock Exchange building were restored and the BSE started functioning normally from 15 March. There was no communal violence of any type in the city and the only evidence of the blast that people could see was the damage caused to a few big buildings.

The problems created by the serial bomb blasts of 12 March 1993 had hardly subsided when a new controversy arose in the state about the continuance of Pawar as chief minister in the state because of an order of the Aurangabad Bench of the Bombay High Court 'naming' him in an election case. The court, in its order of 30 March 1993, set aside the election of Congress candidate Yashwantrao Gadhok from the South Ahmednagar parliamentary constituency and declared Bala Saheb Vikhe Patil, whom Gadhok had defeated in the elections, as having been duly elected from that constituency. The court had also found that some statements made by Pawar in the course of his election campaign in the constituency fell within the provisions of Section 123(4) of the Representation of the People's Act and therefore had 'named' Pawar under Section 99 of this Act. The charge against Pawar was that at certain meetings addressed by him on behalf of Gadhok, he had made some statements on the conduct of Patil calculated to prejudice the prospects of his election. The high court had granted an interim stay on its order without any condition attached to it and allowed six months' time to appeal to the Supreme Court. Despite this stay, the opposition parties in the state started an agitation demanding the resignation of Pawar. They created uproarious scenes in the State Legislature for two days taking the stand that a chief minister against whom 'strictures' had been passed by the high court had no right to continue in office. They claimed that even though the judgement had been stayed by the high court itself, Pawar had lost the moral right to continue as chief minister.

It was quite clear to me that no action was called for from my side in this case. The chief minister called on me on 31 March 1993 to inform me that he was filing an appeal against the judgement before the Supreme Court. All members of the opposition parties in the State Legislature came on deputation to meet me at the Raj Bhavan on 1 April to press the demand for the chief minister's resignation. I had no doubt in my mind that there were no grounds for my asking for the chief minister to quit. I had taken the precaution of obtaining the opinion of the advocate general who had confirmed in his advice to me that no 'strictures' had been passed against Pawar by the high court and that since the court itself had allowed time to file an appeal in the Supreme Court, there was no justification for asking the chief minister to resign. I conveyed my views on this matter to the delegation and soon the agitation on this issue subsided. Pawar filed his appeal in the Supreme Court, which accepted it, and thus the whole issue was resolved without any more acrimony.

✧

After the communal riots and the serial bomb blasts, both of which were man-made calamities, a greater catastrophe engulfed the state and that was the severe earthquake that struck Latur and Osmanabad districts at 3.55 a.m. on 30 September 1993. The epicentre of the earthquake, Killari, in Latur district, was 500 km east of Mumbai, but despite the distance, many people in the state capital experienced the tremor, though mildly. I myself had woken up from my sleep upon feeling the impact of the tremor, but it was only in the morning of the next day that I came to know about the enormity of the damage caused by the earthquake. The gravity of the tragedy can be understood from the fact that 9774 persons had died and 15,565 had been injured. In nineteen villages of Latur and in thirteen villages of Osmanabad, all houses had been totally destroyed. More than 114,000 houses had been damaged in other places. By any reckoning, it was one of the biggest calamities that had hit any place in India in recent times.

This tragedy also revealed how the energetic and prompt action taken by the Government of Maharashtra could help in restoring a fair degree of normalcy in the affected areas within a short period of two months. Within three hours of the earthquake striking, Pawar reached the scene of the calamity. He visited all the affected areas and prepared an estimate of the items needed most urgently. He also specified the quantities required and delineated the categories of speciality whose services were needed immediately and in what numbers to organize relief measures. He himself contacted a number of Central Government departments and heads of business houses in Mumbai to inform them of the priority requirements for relief work. The senior officers of the Government of Maharashtra received clear instructions from the chief minister who was camping in Latur as to what should be done, how it should be done and in what order of priority. A control room had been set up in the Secretariat to take charge of the supply operations from the Mumbai end. The chief minister remained in contact with the control room round the clock. Temporary camps were set up within twenty-four hours to accommodate those people who had lost their houses and possessions. Also, arrangements were made to provide essential items such as food, water and blankets, to the camps. Pawar announced that the construction of regular houses for the affected people would commence on 24 October, which was the Dussehra day. Most people at that time thought that this was too optimistic an announcement, but as subsequent developments proved, this target was met without any hassles.

Several VIPs were keen to visit the affected areas but the chief minister politely conveyed the message to all intending visitors that they should postpone their visits by at least a week. He did not want the relief work to be hampered in any way. No such restrictions were in place for journalists and volunteers who wished to participate in the relief work.

Narasimha Rao visited some of the affected areas on 4 October and I accompanied him along with the chief minister. Some of the villages visited by the prime minister, for example, Killari and Talni, had suffered near-total destruction, but we found that the survivors were gritty and appreciative of the measures taken by the government for their prompt rehabilitation.

The programme of construction of regular houses began on 24 October itself. I reached Latur and Osmanabad early in the morning of 24 October along with the chief minister. We visited the five most seriously affected villages in Latur district. Each village had been adopted by a donor organization, e.g., Oil India, Tatas and the newspaper *Malayala Manorama*. We participated in the *bhoomi puja* (literally, 'earth worship') ceremonies and interacted with the local people. We were heartened to find that they were feeling happy that construction work for new houses had started so promptly. We then visited three more badly affected villages in Osmanabad district. Here too, new houses were being constructed by donor organizations.

Many donors had come forward to undertake the rebuilding of whole villages, complete with roads, houses, community centres and prayer halls.

✦

One of the most gratifying aspects of the relief and rehabilitation work was the generous contributions that the Government of Maharashtra received from various state governments, international organizations, friendly foreign governments, business and industry and, above all, from the ordinary people of India. The US Administration was one of the earliest among foreign governments to send relief materials for Latur and Osmanabad (on 4 October). Jonathan Lynn, called on me at 8 p.m. on that day at the Raj Bhavan to inform me that he had brought two planeloads of relief materials to Mumbai. I conveyed thanks on behalf of the government for the promptness with which aid materials had been despatched. Pakistan too had despatched 24 tonnes of relief materials in two planes. The World Bank came forward with a massive loan of $300 million for which a project had been quickly prepared by the state government with the help of the Government of India. The contribution from the Prime Minister's Relief Fund itself added up to Rs 104 crore (released in instalments). The Government of India also issued a notification granting 100 per cent income tax exemption for contributions to the Earthquake Relief Fund. Several teams of doctors and paramedical staff, along with adequate quantities of drugs and medicines, arrived at the affected areas to provide relief to the injured persons. The Army set up a forty-five-bed field hospital, from where teams of doctors fanned out into the villages affected by the earthquake. The Navy also had sent a sixty-member team of doctors and paramedical staff from Mumbai. On the whole, there were nearly 500 government and private medical personnel operating in the quake-affected areas. I should mention the quick and generous response from the state governments, particularly Gujarat, the immediate neighbour of Maharashtra. By the evening of the second day after the earthquake, Gujarat had despatched 20,000 pairs of *dhotis* (a garment to drape the lower part of the body) and saris and large quantities of drugs, medicines and medical appliances worth over Rs 2 crore. The state had also made a donation of Rs 5 crore to the Earthquake Relief Fund. Many leading business houses of Mumbai also came forward with handsome donations. Many of them had placed their private aeroplanes at the disposal of the state government for transporting essential medicines and personnel required for relief operations.

The ordinary people of Maharashtra, including students of schools and colleges, actively cooperated by contributing to the relief fund and by collecting donations in kind and cash and sending them to the government.

✧

Even though 1993 (my first year as governor) turned out to be a year marked by calamities and disasters for the state, I was not deterred from following my programmes, which I had drawn up for the year. I had decided that I would visit all the districts and also all the universities during the first year itself. I was able to fulfil this target fairly satisfactorily.

I recall with great pleasure and satisfaction one of the trips I had made outside the state in the first year of my tenure. This trip was to pay my respects to the great sage of Kanchi, Jagadguru Chandrasekharendra Saraswathi, on 13 June 1993. I was returning to Madras by car from Pondicherry after receiving an honorary degree of LLD (doctor of laws) from the Central University there. En route, I had informed the Kanchi Math in advance that I would like to call on the Paramacharya. He was in very poor health at that time and had not been meeting visitors for some weeks. I had been informed that it would be difficult for him to talk to me or even to meet me. His disciples, nevertheless, indicated that they would convey my request to him and I may take a chance.

As soon as I arrived at the Kanchi Math, I was informed that the Paramacharya would be glad to meet me and my wife who was also accompanying me. When we were ushered into his presence, we found him alert and gracious, even though he was looking very weak. We had called on him on a few occasions earlier during my term as governor of Tamil Nadu. I had always revered him as one of the greatest sages of modern India and had been deeply impressed by his erudition, particularly by his in-depth understanding of other religions. I knew he would not be able to speak to me as on the previous visits, but I was looking for only a few minutes to offer my *pranams* to him. However, he spent over fifteen minutes with us and raised his hand in blessings on five or six occasions during this meeting.

As we were taking leave of him, his personal staff had brought, as usual, a shawl and a sari in a tray to be presented by the Paramacharya to us. He then motioned to them to take away the shawl. He removed the silk blue shawl that was draped on his shoulders and handed it to me and gave the sari to my wife, blessing us again.

❖

The next year, 1994, was a very important one for me as governor of Maharashtra. It was during this year that the new Maharashtra University Act, which bestowed a wide range of powers and responsibilities on the governor as chancellor, was passed. Again, it was during 1994 that the Central Government and the state government decided to entrust the governor with the special responsibilities described under Article 371(2) of the Constitution for the development of the economically backward regions of the state. Normally, a governor's post is considered as a ceremonial one in most states. But these two enactments had assigned to the Maharashtra governor important responsibilities that his counterparts in other states did not have to shoulder. In fact, I found that more than 50 per cent of my time had to be devoted to discharging duties resulting from these two enactments.

Here, let me digress a bit. I would like to mention an initiative I had taken in September 1994. I placed before Prime Minister Narasimha Rao a proposal for instituting the Gandhi Peace Prize. Rao was then on a visit to Maharashtra and I was travelling with him in the state government aircraft on 29 September from Nagpur to Delhi. The date 2 October 1994 marked the 125th birth anniversary of Mahatma Gandhi and celebrations on this momentous day had been planned on a large scale all over the country. I mentioned to him that it would be befitting if the Central Government could institute a Gandhi Peace Prize on the model of the famous Nobel

Prize for Peace. I suggested that this award should be the highest offered by the Government of India and a high-level committee could be formed to select a suitable person every year for this award. The award could be presented on 2 October every year by the president of India at a public function held in Delhi.

I told Narasimha Rao that the Hindujas (prominent business tycoons) had offered to place with the Government of India a very large amount for instituting the Gandhi Peace Prize. However, the then prime minister, Indira Gandhi, was not in favour of accepting a donation from a private party for this purpose and I had duly informed the Hindujas about her decision. The proposal I was making now was for the government itself to provide the funds for the prize without depending on donations from any private business group.

Within a minute of listening to my proposal, he concurred with it and told me that he would take action immediately in this context. He asked me to send a note on the proposal on the basis of which he could initiate action for instituting the prize. I did so promptly. The Gandhi Peace Prize is now the highest cash award offered by the Government of India and has become a fitting tribute to the memory of the Mahatma by a grateful nation.

Let me return to the main narrative. One of the important features of the Maharashtra University Act 1994 was that it enabled the students councils in various universities and the colleges affiliated to them to function without being influenced by political parties or groups outside the academic institutions. In several universities and affiliated colleges in India, elections to student bodies are fought exactly or the same lines as political parties fight elections to the legislatures or the Parliament. The student bodies in several universities and colleges have become instruments for proxy contests between political parties to whom the students owe allegiance. Huge sums of money are spent on these elections by the political parties, which sponsor the students as their candidates. The students are forced to divert their energies and time for such elections. The Maharashtra University Act provided for the establishment of the University Students' Council and students councils for each college to look after the welfare of the students and to promote and coordinate extracurricular activities. The most important part of this provision was that it *explicitly prohibited* students councils from engaging in political activities. The Act provided that representatives of students in their councils should be those who had shown academic merit in the preceding year or excellent performance in activities such as sports, National Cadet Corps, cultural programmes and National Service Scheme.

Some political parties strongly criticized the ban on students councils engaging in political activities but this opposition died down in due course and all parties in the state came to accept the fact that it was in the students' interest to have their councils' representatives selected on merit and not on votes cast on a party basis.

Another important feature of the Maharashtra University Act 1994 was that it accorded full powers to the chancellor (i.e., the governor) to appoint vice-chancellors, contrary to the practice in most other states. In several states, the selection of vice-chancellors was made by the government and the role of the chancellors was only to formally endorse the proposal sent to them by the government. According to the procedure laid down in the Maharashtra University Act, a selection committee of five members, consisting of the secretary of higher education as ex-officio member and one person each nominated by the University Grants Commission, the management council, the academic council and the chancellor, would prepare a panel of three to five names for the consideration of the chancellor. The chancellor would nominate one of the members of the committee as its chairperson. It had been my practice in most cases to request eminent jurists like retired chief justices or serving judges of the Supreme Court and the high courts to serve as chairmen of these committees. I would then interview all those candidates recommended by the panel, spending over forty-five minutes for each candidate. After making up my mind as to who was the best among the persons interviewed, I would hold consultations with the chief minister before announcing my choice of vice-chancellor. I have worked with five chief ministers in Maharashtra during my nine-and-a-half-year tenure as governor: Sudhakar Rao Naik, Sharad Pawar, Manohar Joshi, Narayan Rane and Vilasrao Deshmukh. I must have appointed more than thirty-four vice-chancellors for the seventeen universities in the state. I should record here with immense satisfaction that in no case had any one of the chief ministers differed from my decision as to who should be offered the post. In the appointment of the pro-vice-chancellor, I adopted the same procedure except that I dispensed with holding consultations with the chief minister. Of course, I cannot claim that every vice-chancellor or pro-vice-chancellor selected by me proved to be the ideal choice for the post, but I can claim without fear of contradiction that all selections were made strictly on merit, as far as I could assess them based on their biodata and my interviews, without being influenced in any way by considerations such as political support, caste, community, region or religion.

I earnestly tried to introduce some much-needed reforms in university administration. There had been persistent complaints about delays in the publication of examination results by several universities. I introduced a system of special reporting to me by the vice-chancellors so that I could review the situation and suggest guidelines to expedite the process.

Among the various reforms I attempted to introduce, the most important were those relating to the granting of autonomy to the affiliated colleges and the reform of the examination system. Some of the universities in Maharashtra such as Mumbai and Pune had each over 300 affiliated colleges and it was obvious that the universities could not exercise any effective supervision over the quality of instruction provided in these colleges. I was convinced that granting of autonomous status to those colleges that had the required facilities for functioning independently would be helpful in improving the standards of higher education in the state. I appointed a committee of senior vice-chancellors to draw up a comprehensive scheme for autonomous colleges. The report of the committee was then discussed in great detail at a series of meetings with the vice-chancellors and the minister and secretaries. A scheme was finally drawn up, which received the concurrence of the University Grants Commission (UGC).

In spite of all the efforts made by me and the full support provided by the government, the autonomy scheme could not be introduced even in a few selected colleges. Some interested groups made up of both college teachers and the management of private colleges tried to block the introduction of the scheme by frequently raising objections. When their objections were satisfactorily resolved, new ones came up and this cycle continued till the academic year 2002–03.

✧

While the efforts for introducing the autonomy scheme were underway, I had been holding discussions simultaneously with the vice-chancellors and other experts on higher education on the equally important issue of examination reforms. The progress in such reforms was fortunately much better than that in the autonomy scheme. A major scam in the Nagpur University with respect to the conducting of public examinations provided the opportunity to expedite the decisions on the reforms.

In view of the rapid increase in the number of affiliated colleges, the universities had been experiencing difficulties in conducting public examinations without giving room for complaints about malpractice or irregularities. All the universities in the state had introduced the system of central valuation of answer papers and also made arrangements for additional invigilators from outside the institutions where students took their examinations. However, there had been many complaints about connivance of some teachers and the administrative staff of certain universities with the students indulging in malpractices in the examinations.

In July 1999 a serious scandal about the conduct of university examinations by the Nagpur University came to light in the media. Some of the foreign employers of university graduates from India had been following the practice of verifying the authenticity of the degree certificates and of the marksheets produced by applicants for jobs. Nagpur University had received, as part of this practice, a few certificates for verification and the university authorities found that the certificates and marksheets were fraudulent. This discovery led to the obvious conclusion that such malpractices were not isolated and must have existed on a large scale. Preliminary investigations by the university authorities and the police in Nagpur showed that the assistant registrar working in the Examination Division of the university had been the kingpin of a racket for issuing of false certificates and marksheets in return for money. This news hit the headlines and I was shocked to know about such a state of affairs. I talked to the vice-chancellor, B.B. Chopane, to ascertain the facts. I could see that such malpractices had been going on for some time and that there had been serious laxity on the part of the higher authorities in the university in supervising the work of the staff in the Examination Division. I visited Nagpur on 26 and 27 July 1999 to assess the situation personally and to take the urgently needed remedial action. After detailed discussions with the vice-chancellor, a few university teachers and police officers investigating the case, I decided to take drastic action against the persons who were prima facie guilty of either neglect in duties or complicity in the crime. Though the vice-chancellor was not trying to shield any of his employees, it was obvious that there had been a failure on his part and some of the senior teachers responsible for the conduct of examinations in exercising proper control and supervision over the staff. The vice-chancellor, Chopane, offered his resignation and I promptly accepted it. Over thirty-five persons suspected to be involved in the scam including the dean of the Facutly of Engineering Technology and the assistant registrar in charge of the Examination Division were arrested by the police. The police also registered cases against some students and their parents suspected to be involved in this scam. A senior professor who had a good reputation for discipline and efficiency was appointed to be in charge of the entire work relating to examinations. The divisional commissioner of Nagpur, J.S. Saharia, a senior IAS officer, was appointed as acting vice-chancellor. I also appointed another IAS officer, Kishore Gajbhiye, who was already working in Nagpur, as officer on special duty (OSD) to perform the functions of the pro-vice-chancellor. In both cases, I obtained the concurrence of the chief minister over the phone.

I instructed the acting vice-chancellor to weed out staff of doubtful reputation from all sections dealing with examination work and to post persons with a sound reputation as assistant registrars and deputy registrars and also instructed him to review the performance of the staff members at lower levels working in the examination section and transfer those who had worked for very long periods of time.

While these steps helped in restoring credibility to the examinations conducted by the university, I was convinced, after a careful study, that the issue of revaluation was the single largest factor that had contributed to the malpractices and therefore had to be immediately changed if the sanctity of the examinations in the university was to be restored fully. Accordingly, I invoked the emergency powers under Section 9(3) of the Maharashtra University Act 1994 and amended the relevant Ordinance of the Nagpur University on revaluation and prescribed restrictions on the number of papers for which a candidate could apply for revaluation and the minimum percentage of marks obtained before which a request for revaluation could be made. I instructed the acting vice-chancellor to implement these directives with effect from the winter examinations of 1999.

While going through the methods used by the chief culprits in manipulating the examination results, I became convinced that radical changes needed to be introduced in the examination system in *all* the universities without any delay. The procedure of revaluation of answer papers at the request of the students had several loopholes that were being exploited by the students for manipulating the results. The Nagpur University, I found, had been unusually liberal in accepting requests for revaluation. In fact, over 60 per cent of the students who took the examinations had been asking for revaluation of the answer books. Such a state of affairs itself proved that the system was being exploited by the students for getting undeserved better results. The university had taken revaluation as a good source of revenue because of the revaluation fees it could collect from the applicants. I appointed a committee of senior vice-chancellors, under the chairmanship of Arun Nigavekar, vice-chancellor of the Pune University (later chairman of the University Grants Commission), to look into the whole issue of examination reforms. The committee, after a comprehensive study of the subject and discussions with other vice-chancellors and several experts, submitted its report to me, which I duly accepted. The state government had also made known its full support to the recommendations of the committee. One of its most important recommendations was to replace revaluation with a system of moderation of marks for which the committee had made several practical suggestions.

Within a few weeks after the new vice-chancellor and the new OSD had taken charge of the administration of the Nagpur University, they were able to streamline the entire system of administration in the university and restore the credibility it had lost because of the examination scam. The academic staff of the university heartily cooperated with the acting vice-chancellor in his efforts to bring about the much-needed changes in the systems and procedures followed in the management of the university in the past.

It was obvious that I could not have succeeded in introducing the reforms I did if I did not have adequate powers as chancellor under the Maharashtra University Act. At the forum of the Conference of Governors, which the president of India used to convene, I had raised the issue of conferring on the governors of all states the powers required to ensure better efficiency in the administration of the universities. In December 1996, the president, Dr Shankar Dayal Sharma, had appointed a Committee of Governors under my chairmanship to submit a report to him on the role of the governors as chancellors of the universities. In our report to the president submitted in April 1997, we had recommended several changes on the basis of the rules followed in the Maharashtra University Act for consideration by other state governments. However, it remained doubtful whether all state governments would accept these changes.

Before I conclude my observations about my role as chancellor of the universities in Maharashtra, I should mention two initiatives I had taken to promote interuniversity cooperation in extracurricular activities. The first was to organize an annual interuniversity sports meet that was named 'Ashwamedha'.* Here, all universities in the state participated. The responsibility for hosting this event was to go by rotation to every university. In order to ensure that this event did not languish in future for lack of funds, we decided to collect from every student a small additional fee for sports. A part of the fees so collected would be retained by the university to meet its expenses for training the participants for the Ashwamedha and for sending the university team to the venue of this event. The rest of the collections would go to the host university to meet the expenses for conducting the Ashwamedha. The theme chosen for the Ashwamedha in the first three years was 'AIDS awareness', a

---

* In Hindu mythology, Ashwamedha refers to a ritual involving horses.

programme that had been introduced in all universities to create awareness among the students about the danger of HIV and allied diseases. The Ashwamedha, which was attended by several thousands of students and spectators, proved to be good occasions to give publicity to the AIDS awareness campaign through cultural events, posters and banners focused on this scourge. It soon became an eagerly awaited event in the calendar of all the universities. Since the financial problem involved in conducting such a big event was also taken care of, every university was keen to host it. The decision as to who should host the Ashwamedha in a particular year was taken at the annual conference of the vice-chancellors convened by the chancellor.

The second initiative to promote interuniversity cooperation taken by me was to institute two competitions in elocution, one in the Marathi language (to be organized every year by the Pune University) and the other in English (to be organized by the Mumbai University); I did not want this activity to impose a burden on the universities finances and therefore I made a personal donation of Rs 1 lakh to each of the two universities to create an endowment. The interest from this endowment would be used to meet the expenses involved in the purchase of prizes and hiring of furniture and other equipment. I am happy to note that these interuniversity elocution competitions have become very popular among the students.

From my long experience as chancellor of the universities of Maharashtra, I am glad to say that the state has some of the best universities in the whole country, which have maintained the highest standards of academic excellence as well as all-round development of the personality of the students.

Looking back to my tenure as governor of Maharashtra, I should emphasize that my role as an active chancellor of the universities has been one of my most satisfying experiences in the state.

✧

Even though Maharashtra was economically the most advanced state in India, certain districts there have always remained at relatively low levels of development. For instance, the Marathwada and Vidarbha regions have been lagging far behind in development compared with the western regions. The districts in Marathwada originally formed part of the Hyderabad state and those in Vidarbha were part of the former Central Provinces, both of which were backward states compared with the then Bombay state.

A brief historical perspective would be in order. A few months before the announcement by the Government of India, in December 1953, of its decision to set up a States Reorganization Commission, a few prominent leaders of Maharashtra convened a meeting at Nagpur. Here, they drew up an agreement (known as the Nagpur Agreement), which constituted the basis for bringing together the Marathi-speaking regions of the then states of Bombay, Central Provinces and Hyderabad into one state. An amendment to the Constitution was made in 1956, making a provision under Article 371(2), enabling the president to assign to the governor special responsibilities for the development of the backward regions in the state. Article 371(2) provided for the establishment of separate development boards for Vidarbha, Marathwada and the rest of Maharashtra. This article bestowed on the governor the responsibilities to ensure equitable allocation of funds for development expenditure among the different regions. The governor was also responsible for making equitable arrangements for technical education and vocational training and for providing employment opportunities in the services under the control of the state government.

Even though Article 371(2) had been included in the Constitution in 1956, its implementation took several years more mainly because of the rethinking on the part of some important political leaders that it would make the governor a supraconstitutional authority and lead to the erosion of the responsibilities of the elected representatives of the people. Successive chief ministers of the state had been reluctant to concede to the governor the powers provided under Article 371(2). Some of the governors themselves were not happy to take on those responsibilities as they thought that exercise of such powers might lead to needless conflicts between them and the chief ministers. Some governors also thought that such responsibilities would impose too much of an additional burden on them. Consequently, the special responsibilities of the governor contemplated under Article 371(2) remained on paper till July 1984, when both Houses of the

Maharashtra State Legislature took an initiative in passing a resolution recommending to the president that the governor exercise his powers. However, neither the state government nor the Centre appeared to be keen to take further action on this resolution.

It was only in 1994 that the Central Government and the state government decided to give Article 371(2) a fair chance. The main initiative in this context was taken by the prime minister, Narasimha Rao, who hailed from the Telangana region of Andhra Pradesh. He had once been elected to Parliament from the Vidarbha region; thus he understood very well the problems of the region arising mainly due to economic backwardness. Sharad Pawar, the chief minister of Maharashtra, was equally enthusiastic. They both agreed to take further action on the resolution passed by the State Legislature in July 1984.

Rao told me that he was confident that I would be able to tactfully manage the implementation of the scheme for exercising the governor's powers under Article 371(2) without coming into conflict with the chief minister or the State Legislature. He was also sure that I would leave behind commendable conventions and procedures, which would enable successive governors in Maharashtra to carry forward the scheme without controversies. I replied that I would do my best to make the scheme work smoothly though I was conscious of the fact that I was taking on a very difficult task. One person who continued to oppose the scheme was S.B. Chavan, a former chief minister of Maharashtra, who was then the Union home minister. He met me at the Raj Bhavan, Mumbai, and explained to me that his opposition was strictly because of the constitutional impropriety of a governor exercising the powers that were legally bestowed on the elected representatives of the people. I told him that I fully agreed with his views, but now that a decision had been taken to implement the scheme, I would try to give it a fair trial.

The president issued a formal notification on 19 March 1994, based on the resolution passed by the Maharashtra State Legislature on 26 July 1984, assigning to the governor the special responsibilities specified in Article 371(2) of the Constitution. The order was to remain in force for a period of five years or up to such date as the president may decide. Following the presidential order, I issued an order on 30 April 1994 constituting separate development boards, for Vidarbha, Marathwada and the rest of Maharashtra. The order also specified the composition and the functions of the boards. Further, the order spelt out the governor's special responsibilities, which (as mentioned earlier) included making equitable allocation of development funds, ensuring arrangements for education, training and employment equitably among all regions, making rules and issuing directions for the proper functioning of the boards.

One of the provisions of the Nagpur Agreement was that the allocation of funds for expenditure over the different regions would be in proportion to their population. Vidarbha accounted for 21.30 per cent of the population, Marathwada 16.11 per cent and the rest of Maharashtra 62.59 per cent. However, allocation merely on the basis of population would not have been adequate as a big backlog of development expenditure had built up over the years in the Vidarbha and Marathwada regions. There was, therefore, an obvious need for special allocation of funds for removal of the backlog.

In order to assess the problem of regional disparity in development, the government had appointed a committee of experts under the chairmanship of the renowned economist V.M. Dandekar. This committee had identified a backlog of Rs 3187 crores in 1984 and the government had been making small allocations every year ranging from Rs 200 to Rs 500 crores for the clearing up of the backlog.

Finding that the backlog had continued to increase in the Vidarbha and Marathwada regions, a committee of experts was appointed in 1995 to identify appropriate indicators for evaluating the relative levels of development and for assessing the backlog in different regions on the basis of these indicators. This committee estimated that the backlog was of the order of more than Rs 14,000 crores, the bulk of which was in Vidarbha and Marathwada regions. I issued directives to hike the allocations for the removal of the backlog in the annual budgets, increasing the provision from Rs 500 crores in 1994–95 to Rs 1720 crores in 2001–02. Still the disparities continued to be very serious and the need for a comprehensive formula that would help in eliminating the disparities and preventing the creation of new backlog started engaging my attention seriously.

The most conspicuous increase in disparity was in the irrigation sector. The proportion of the backlog in this section vis-à-vis the overall backlog of Vidarbha had increased from 42.3 per cent in 1984 to 68.5 per cent in 2000 and that of Marathwada from 42.18 per cent to 61.29 per cent in the same period. On the other hand, the proportion of backlog in the irrigation sector in the rest of Maharashtra region had decreased from 45.56 per cent to 18.42 per cent. It was obvious that very drastic measures were necessary at the policy level to rectify the situation.

When the people of Vidarbha and Marathwada regions became aware of these facts, they started demanding extra allocations for the irrigation schemes. I met many delegations from Vidarbha and Marathwada and held a series of meetings with members of the development boards and the concerned officials of the government apart from experts on these subjects, particularly on irrigation, to try and evolve a more equitable formula for allocation of funds among the different regions.

Before finalizing the formula, I held discussions with the chief minister and the concerned ministers and senior officials. The formula that was finally decided upon was announced on 15 December 2001 as a directive from my side to the government. It was, in my judgement, fair to all the regions and could be practically implemented. I also felt that it could prove adequate in eliminating the backlog within a period of four years. It was widely welcomed by the people of all regions.

I felt unhappy when S.B. Chavan, the Union home minister and an important leader from the Marathwada region, made a statement to the media (during one of his visits to the state in October 1995) that the progress in clearing the backlog in the backward regions was not satisfactory. I promptly wrote to Chavan informing him that I felt hurt at his statement. His reply pointed out that his views had not been correctly reported. When Chavan later found that I had attempted to do full justice to all the regions despite limitations of resources, he was convinced that the directive had been arrived at after careful study of all aspects of the problem and he was gracious enough to send me a letter (dated 17 April 2002) expressing satisfaction that my allocation of funds to eliminate the backlog had justified the provision of special responsibilities to the governor. The following extracts from his letter reflected the general mood of contentment in the state:

I would like to convey my sense of appreciation for deep study and the depth of understanding and responsibility which has been seen in the order. I am happy that the spirit of amendment of the Constitution has been fully justified in your order by directing the state government to remove the backlog in a stipulated period.

Regarding equitable arrangements for education and vocational training I had appointed a committee of the representatives from the three boards to review the existing provisions and recommend changes in admission policies in engineering and medical institutions as necessary. The recommendations of this committee did not prove to be controversial in any way. I accepted these and announced a scheme that would ensure the availability of facilities equitably for technical and vocational education for all regions.

Similarly, I set up a committee with members for the three boards to find out whether or not any special steps would be necessary to ensure that all regions got their fair share vis-à-vis the services under the control of the state government. The report of this committee showed that the existing arrangements were fair and just and no special action was necessary on the part of the governor in this matter.

When I left Maharashtra in 2002, I was fully satisfied of having left behind a policy framework for fulfilling the objectives laid down in Article 371(2).

SIXTEEN

In Maharashtra: 2

Maharashtra has had a long tradition of Congress governments being in power ever since independence. There had been governments led by Congressmen who had left the party for short periods, but the people of Maharashtra had considered such governments too as Congress governments. A sharp break with this tradition occurred in 1995 when the Congress Party lost its majority in the elections held in March that year and a coalition government, whose constituents were the Shiv Sena and the BJP, was installed. Manohar Joshi (Shiv Sena) was appointed as the chief minister. (Joshi later became the Lok Sabha speaker.) The Shiv Sena had earlier won the elections to the Municipal Corporations of Mumbai and some other places. Manohar Joshi himself had been a mayor of Mumbai in the past, but the Shiv Sena got an opportunity to head a government for the first time only in March 1995. During the election campaign, the Congress leaders, including the chief minister, Sharad Pawar, appeared quite confident that their party would bag 140 to 150 seats out of the total 288 seats in the Assembly. But the Congress got only eighty seats, while the Shiv Sena got seventy-four and the BJP sixty-five.

The number of independents who got elected was unexpectedly very high, i.e., forty-five. The Janata Dal and other smaller parties together accounted for twenty-four seats.

The Shiv Sena and the BJP had fought the elections as members of an alliance on the understanding that if they together secured the required majority, they would stake their claim to form the government. The Shiv Sena–BJP alliance with 139 seats was still short of the majority by six, but immediately after the election, the alliance started negotiations with some independents in order to achieve the figure of 145. The Congress emerged as the single largest party in the Assembly. Consequently, speculation was rife in the state that I may be persuaded by the Congress Government at the Centre to give the first chance to the leader of the Congress Party to form the government on the ground that its strength exceeded that of the other parties taken separately. However, the Congress would have needed the support of sixty-five more MLAs to attain the required majority. There were also strong rumours floating in Mumbai city that I might recommend a spell of president's rule since no party or alliance had secured a majority and that the Central Government would readily accept such a recommendation. These speculations were, of course, based on the assumption that the Centre would use all means to prevent a Shiv Sena–BJP government from coming to power in the state and that I would take a decision on the formation of the government only in consultation with the Centre.

I had always held the view that the most important criterion for inviting a party to form the government should be its *ability to provide a stable administration*. Between the Shiv Sena–BJP alliance and the Congress, I was convinced that the alliance had far better credentials for providing a stable government than the Congress. The Congress would have had to rope in all the independent members and almost all members of the smaller parties to reach the required majority. Such an exercise would have involved offering ministerial positions and other incentives to these MLAs. Even if the Congress did succeed in increasing its numbers, it would have faced tremendous difficulties in providing a stable government. I was therefore very clear in my mind that if the Shiv Sena–BJP alliance could convince me that it would get the required number of additional MLAs to support it, I should give it the chance to form the government. I had always maintained that the governors should take such decisions using their own discretion and should not seek the advice of the Centre on such matters.

Even as early as 22 February 1995, a delegation of six senior leaders of the Shiv Sena and the BJP had presented a memorandum to me stating that since they had formed a pre-electoral alliance on a previously agreed minimum programme, they should be treated as one party by me while deciding upon who should be called to form the government.

On the morning of 13 March 1995, at a joint meeting of the Shiv Sena–BJP MLAs, Manohar Joshi was elected as the leader of the alliance and Gopinath Munde of the BJP as its deputy leader. I had agreed to meet a delegation of senior leaders of the Shiv Sena–BJP alliance at Raj Bhavan in the afternoon (of 13 March), to hear what they had to say about their claims to form the government. By about 1.15 p.m. about sixty MLAs and senior party leaders, including L.K. Advani (later deputy prime minister) and Balasaheb Thackeray (president of the Shiv Sena), assembled at the conference hall adjacent to my office in Raj Bhavan. A large number of mediapersons and photographers (belonging to the print and electronic media) also managed to enter the conference hall. I shook hands first with Advani and Thackeray and then with Joshi to whom I offered my congratulations. Immediately, Thackeray humorously remarked: 'That means you have already accepted him as the next chief minister.' I promptly replied that my congratulations were for his election as leader of the Legislature Party.

I had earlier received reports that an atmosphere of tension was prevailing in the city and I could notice this tension on the faces of many of the persons present there.

Thackeray handed me the formal letter informing about Joshi's election as leader of the Joint Legislature Party. The Shiv Sena hoped that Joshi would be invited to form the government. Advani supported him by explaining that Joshi was the leader of the majority party in the Legislature and the Shiv Sena–BJP alliance had been formed before the elections. On asking how they proposed to make up the deficiency of six, I was informed that the required number of MLAs had already given, in writing, their support to the alliance government if formed. I then asked Joshi to give me letters from those MLAs from outside the alliance who had agreed to support the government. There was a quick consultation among the leaders. Soon Joshi said that he would give me signed letter of eight MLAs within a couple of hours. In order to remove any doubt in their mind that those mentioned in the list might be approached by the Congress Party, I told them that the names would be kept confidential by me.

I was now fully satisfied that a stable government could be formed by the Shiv Sena–BJP alliance and I informed them that I would be communicating my decision formally after I got the letters from their supporters among the independents.

The alliance leaders made a request that the swearing in ceremony – in case they were invited to form the government – be held at Shivaji Park, the largest maidan in Mumbai city, as the Raj Bhavan lawns would be too small to accommodate the huge crowd that would gather on this occasion. I was aware of the fact that there was no precedent in Maharashtra for holding a swearing in ceremony outside Raj Bhavan. Nevertheless, I acceded to their request, taking care to add that the function should conform to the norms of protocol and decorum followed by the Raj Bhavan, even though the venue was elsewhere. Thackeray immediately took the hint and replied that he would not sit on the dais, but sit 'wherever you ask me to'. Thus, every important issue was discussed in a relaxed and friendly atmosphere and the Shiv Sena–BJP leaders attending the meeting appeared to be fully satisfied. I took Advani, Joshi and Thackeray inside my office for a few minutes to enable the huge crowd which had already gathered on the lawns outside the conference hall to disperse so that they could leave the Raj Bhavan without being jostled and pushed around. However, the people waited till the three leaders came out of my room. The security personnel had a tough time in escorting them to their cars. Festive celebrations were held in the city throughout the day by the followers of the Shiv Sena and the BJP.

Sharad Pawar came to see me at 7.50 p.m. on 13 March straight from a meeting of the Congress Legislature Party. I briefly told him about the claim of majority made by the alliance and that I was

◄ The author with the .
president of Russia,
Vladimir Putin, and his
wife (among others) at
the Raj Bhavan, Mumbai.

The author and his wife ▶
with Prince Philip at the
Raj Bhavan, Mumbai.

◄ The author with the
chief minister of
Tamil Nadu,
M. Karunanidhi,
at the Raj Bhavan,
Madras (January 1988).

The author receiving Prime Minister Rajiv Gandhi during the latter's visit to Tamil Nadu.

The author with L.K. Advani (*to his right*) and Balasaheb Thackeray (*to his left*) at the Raj Bhavan, Mumbai, discussing ministry formation (March 1995).

The author's wife, Ackama, and Mother Teresa warmly embrace each other
at the Raj Bhavan, Mumbai.

The author receiving the US president, Bill Clinton, at the Mumbai airport (March 2000).

The author with Prime Minister Atal Behari Vajpayee at the Raj Bhavan, Mumbai.

The author sharing a joke with Sharad Pawar at the Raj Bhavan, Mumbai.

inclined to believe the claim to be true. He appeared to be quite relaxed and even happy with my decision. Pawar was feeling relieved apparently because he did not have to undertake the laborious exercise of garnering the support of sixty-five additional MLAs from outside the Congress Party.

After satisfying myself that the alliance actually had the additional support, I telephoned Joshi later in the night to invite him to form the government and also sent him the formal letter. The swearing in ceremony was fixed for 6 p.m. the next day (14 March) at Shivaji Park. I apprised the prime minister (over the telephone) of the decisions I had taken. I also dashed off a message by fax to both the president and the prime minister immediately thereafter. For the people of Maharashtra, this event was not just a change of government, but something like a regime change because two parties, which had an altogether different political ideology from the Congress, were assuming power in the state.

Huge crowds (estimated at over three lakh) had collected in and around Shivaji Park to witness the ceremony. However, despite their mammoth proportions, they cooperated very well in maintaining the protocol and dignity of the function. The actual ceremony lasted just seven minutes as only Manohar Joshi and Gopinath Munde were being sworn in that day as chief minister and deputy chief minister, respectively. Before leaving Shivaji Park, I walked over to the place where some of the prominent guests were seated and shook hands with them. They included, besides Advani and Thackeray, Madan Lal Khurana, the chief minister of Delhi, and Bhairon Singh Shekhawat, the chief minister of Rajasthan (later vice-president of India).

My decision to invite Joshi to form the government, without any loss of time, was widely appreciated by the people at large and the entire media. On 18 March, the second group of ministers, including fourteen at the cabinet level, was sworn in. The venue was the Raj Bhavan lawns.

A very interesting feature of the change of government on 13 March was that some Congressmen themselves appeared to be happy at the fact that Sharad Pawar was not given a chance to stake his claim. In fact, a few senior members of that party, known to belong to the anti-Pawar lobby, congratulated me (over the telephone) on my 'wise decision'. I could perceive how deep the fissures in the Congress Party in the state had become. Out of the forty-five independents who had won the elections, as many as thirty-nine were reported to be Congress rebels. It was a well-known fact that a large number of these rebels had the backing of some of the senior Congress leaders in the state. The latter had encouraged the rebels in order to undercut their opponents in the elections, probably thinking that they could defeat their rivals within their party without damaging the party's prospects of forming the government. But this time the non-Congress votes had been so well consolidated behind the Shiv Sena–BJP alliance that the calculations of these Congress leaders went totally awry. The practice, in the past of bringing back the rebels into the party fold, by offering them ministerial berths, had also encouraged the ambitions of some Congressmen to stand as independent candidates.

Some Congress leaders tried to restore the morale of their rank and file by claiming that even though the party had secured only eighty seats, its share of votes was 30.13 per cent of the total votes polled, while the share of the Shiv Sena–BJP alliance, which won 139 seats, was only 28.40 per cent. However, the 1995 elections to the State Assembly appeared to be a watershed in Maharashtra politics as the Congress, which had dominated the political scene ever since independence, had been relegated to a minority of less than one-third of the strength of the Legislature. The results of the elections also showed that the Shiv Sena–BJP alliance had succeeded in reducing the Congress seats in certain regions of the state to a very insignificant level. For example, in the Konkan region, the Congress could win only three seats as against the twenty-one bagged by the SS–BJP alliance. The Congress position in Mumbai city was even worse; it won only one seat as against the thirty of the alliance.

There were two major changes of government during my tenure as governor of Maharashtra, and I had followed different criteria in choosing the party to form the government because different situations had prevailed on those two occasions. However, on both the occasions the guiding factor in my decision was my assessment as to which party or alliance could provide a stable government. In 1995 I had chosen the pre-election alliance of the Shiv Sena and the BJP, while, in 1999, the post-election alliance of the Congress and the Nationalist Congress Party (NCP) was chosen. In 1999 also I would have preferred a pre-election alliance to a post-election alliance, but the circumstances developed in such a manner that only a post-election alliance proved to be capable of assuring a stable government. I will briefly describe the circumstances leading to the formation of a new government.

Even though the elections to the State Assembly were not due in October 1999, the NDA Government at the Centre took a decision in July that elections would be held simultaneously for the Lok Sabha and the Maharashtra Assembly in October that year. By that time, a change in the chief ministership in Maharashtra had taken place. Manohar Joshi had resigned and Narayan Rane (also of the Shiv Sena) had taken his place. Meanwhile, a very significant change had also taken place in the Congress in Maharashtra in that the party had split vertically over the expulsion of Sharad Pawar.

A new party, the Nationalist Congress Party, with Pawar as its leader was formed. The repercussions were widespread. Forty-five of the seventy-seven Congress MLAs and fifteen of the twenty-eight Congress MLCs (Members of the Legislative Council) broke away to join the NCP, thereby reducing the official Congress to a minority. Since there was hardly any chance of the NCP and the Congress fighting the elections jointly against the Shiv Sena–BJP alliance, most people in Maharashtra had expected that the Assembly polls would result in a clear victory for the alliance. However, the October elections had a few surprises in store. The results again threw up a hung Assembly, with the Congress getting seventy-five seats, the Shiv Sena sixty-nine, the NCP fifty-eight and the BJP fifty-six. The independents and other smaller parties together secured the remaining thirty seats in the 288-member Assembly. The Shiv Sena–BJP alliance, with 125 seats, needed twenty more to form a government. The Congress leaders approached me with the request that their party should be given a chance to form the government as it was the single largest party in the Legislature. I was informed that the Congress had started negotiations with the NCP for forming a coalition government on the basis of an agreed programme even though they had fought against each other in the elections in almost every constituency. A formal letter, I was informed, had been sent by the president of the Maharashtra Pradesh Congress Committee to the president of the NCP, calling him for talks on the formation of a coalition government. Both the Congress and the NCP were expecting support from some independents also and were sure of acquiring the required majority if they could agree between themselves on the terms to form a coalition government.

I came to know that the Shiv Sena–BJP alliance had run into problems on the issue of choosing a leader for their legislature group. It was reported that the state leaders of the BJP were backing the claim of Gopinath Munde as the leader of the Shiv Sena–BJP combine on the ground that since the former had had the opportunity to lead the government in 1995, the baton now should be passed on to the BJP.

As governor, I was obliged to convene the Legislative Assembly latest by 22 October 1999 as the six months' period prescribed by the Constitution, which could intervene between the last sitting of the previous session and the sitting of the next session, would expire by that date. If the Legislative Assembly had to be convened on 22 October, I felt that a government had to be in position at least by 18 October. There were two main reasons: (1) The governor had to address the first joint session of the Legislature at its commencement immediately after the elections to the Assembly. (2) The draft of the address had to be prepared by the government in power as the governor had 'to inform the Legislature of the causes of its summoning', according to Article 176 of the Constitution.

I was determined to do everything possible within my power to get an elected government inducted by 18 October. If I failed in that attempt, the only alternative would have been to go in for a spell of president's rule, which I wanted to avoid as far as possible. I was therefore getting very impatient and unhappy over the time that was being taken by the four major political parties represented in the Assembly to reach a clear-cut decision about forming a coalition and also as to who would lead it. There were rumours that the BJP and the NCP had been engaged in secret confabulations about forming a government with a neutral non-political leader, though I had no direct information from any of the parties in this context. There were also speculations that the Central Government would not be averse to president's rule if a suitable government could not be formed by the stipulated date. I did not try to verify the truth of either of these speculations because it would have been misunderstood as trying to interfere with the normal process of negotiations among the parties for forming a government. Nor did I wish to seek the advice of the Central Government as to what steps I should take on a matter on which I could act according to my own discretion.

Meanwhile, the Congress Party elected Vilasrao Deshmukh as the leader of its Legislature Party, but he was making very little progress in his negotiations for an alliance with the NCP. There were reports that the NCP was insisting on its candidate to be appointed leader of the Congress–NCP alliance, which was, of course, unacceptable to the Congress because it had a larger number of MLAs than the NCP.

I had been waiting for over a week for the leaders of parties to make up their mind. Finding that they were taking too much time, I decided to take the initiative in ministry making into my own hands. I telephoned Rane and Munde to meet me jointly or separately (as they chose) for talks with me at 10.30 a.m. on 15 October to discuss the subject of cabinet formation. Simultaneously, I telephoned Deshmukh and the state Congress Party president, Pratap Rao Bhonsle, to meet me at noon on the same day. By the evening of 14 October I came to know that the Shiv Sena–BJP alliance had reached an agreement that Narayan Rane would be elected leader of the Joint Legislature Party. I also came to know that the Congress and the NCP had come to an agreement on the sharing of the portfolios but were still negotiating as to which party should get the speaker's post.

Rane and Munde met me together at the Raj Bhavan as scheduled. They handed over the letter affirming Rane's elevation as the leader of the JLP. They also formally staked their claim to form the government and informed me that they had obtained the support of 145 MLAs, but they did not produce any letters from the legislators outside their parties who would back them. I gave them time till noon on 16 October for procuring the required letters of support. I left them in no doubt that if such evidence was not furnished by the time fixed by me I would resort to other options. After they left, Deshmukh and Bhonsle jointly met me at noon. They, in turn, informed me that fifteen MLAs from outside their parties had assured them of support, but, like their rivals, they had not produced any letters to confirm their claim. I gave them time till 1 p.m. on 16 October to produce the required letters and also made it clear to them that if I did not get such letters I would resort to other options available to me on 16 October itself. I had given the first chance to the Shiv Sena–BJP combine alliance to convince me of their support, as theirs was a pre-election alliance.

The Shiv Sena–BJP leaders asked for an extension till 2 p.m. on 16 October to furnish the list of additional supporters. When they met me at 2 p.m. along with some other top leaders of their parties, their list contained the names of only 136 MLAs with their signatures, which was still nine short of the required number. I could clearly see that they were just not in a position to rope in more supporters. However, they left my office with the message that they may return with additional names, if possible, before that evening itself.

For their part, the Congress–NCP leaders also requested me for an extension till the next day. I understood that they had not yet resolved the dispute about the speaker's post, but refused their request and insisted that they should produce letters of support latest by 7.30 p.m. that day itself, failing which I would take my own decision. My refusal to accept their request for more time, in fact, forced all parties to reach a settlement within the time fixed by me. By 6.30 p.m. they were ready with their lists.

A large group of MLAs along with senior leaders of the Congress and the NCP accompanied Deshmukh for the meeting with me at the conference room of the Raj Bhavan. A much larger crowd of supporters and mediapersons had gathered at the Durbar Hall of the Raj Bhavan to know what my decision would be. I checked the list of outside supporters given to me to find out whether there was any duplication of names vis-à-vis the list given by the Shiv Sena–BJP leaders. I also verified the authenticity of the letters of support. On being satisfied that the Congress–NCP combine indeed had the support of 151 MLAs, I decided to announce my decision publicly without letting this matter of ministry formation drag on any further. I told Congress–NCP leaders present in the conference room that

I had decided to invite Vilasrao Deshmukh to form the government. I then shook hands with Deshmukh and congratulated him. This announcement came as a pleasant surprise to the Congress and NCP leaders as most of them thought that I would consult the Central Government before formally taking a final decision.

The swearing in ceremony was scheduled for 11 a.m. on 18 October, the date I had already fixed before I met the leaders of the parties. It was held on the Raj Bhavan lawns. Only two leaders were sworn in on that day: Deshmukh of the Congress as chief minister and Chagan Bhujbal of the NCP as deputy chief minister. On 19 October, twelve cabinet ministers and fourteen ministers of state were also sworn in at a function held on the Raj Bhavan lawns.

Every observer had acknowledged that the elections that brought to power new governments in 1995 and 1999 had been fair and peaceful and free from malpractices or incidents of violence. Normally, one would expect that the losers would reconcile themselves to the verdict of the electorate against them and wait for the next trial of strength through the electoral process. However, in Maharashtra, the losers on both the occasions developed a mood of confrontation with the ruling parties. As a result, the political atmosphere continued to be tension ridden. One of the reasons for such antagonism could be attributed to the fact that the ruling parties' majority in the Legislature in both the elections was wafer-thin. Consequently, they could be replaced by the opposition parties if a serious breakdown of law and order occurred or if defections from the ranks of the ruling parties to the opposition took place. Serious developments of this nature continued to occur during the tenure of both the governments and my role as governor on such occasions was to defuse the crises and ensure that peace as well as law and order prevailed in the state. Whenever such developments took place, deputations consisting of legislators and party cadres from both sides would try to convince me how wrong the other side was. On all such occasions, demands would be made for invoking the provisions of Article 356* of the

---

* This Article empowers the Central Government to dismiss any state government in case of failure of the constitutional machinery.

Constitution and imposing president's rule. Whenever defections from the ruling partners of the opposition took place, the governor would come under pressure to direct the government to prove its majority in the Legislature through a vote of confidence. Fortunately for me, both the ruling and the opposition parties reposed full faith in my impartiality and objectivity and whatever decisions or suggestions I had taken on such occasions had been gracefully accepted by them without any remonstration or allegation of partiality against me.

I would like to briefly recount a few crisis situations that threatened to become flashpoints during the tenure of each of the governments.

A serious confrontation between the ruling SS–BJP alliance and the opposition developed in July 1996 after the death of one Ramesh Kini. The opposition alleged this was a case of murder, whereas the government maintained that the cause of death was a cardiac arrest. The seriousness of this incident stemmed from the allegation levelled by the opposition and a powerful section of the media that Raj Thackeray, a nephew of Balasaheb Thackeray, was involved.

A delegation of thirty MLAs and MLCs (belonging to all opposition parties) met me at the Pune Raj Bhavan, where I was staying then and submitted a memorandum on what they described as 'a breakdown of law and order in the state'. The memorandum contained eight specific instances of alleged acts of violence and high-handedness on the part of the Shiv Sena activists, the most important being the murder of Kini. They alleged that a person with close links to the Shiv Sena had purchased the flat in which Kini had been staying for several years and had been pressurizing Kini to vacate it. But Kini had been steadfastly resisting the pressures on him. Eventually, he was found dead at a cinema hall in Pune. Kini's wife had publicly stated that her husband had been murdered by persons who enjoyed the patronage of Raj Thackeray.

The Kini case attracted considerable media attention and the police had been trying their best to ascertain the truth behind the allegations. The police had arrested a close friend of Raj Thackeray for his alleged involvement in this offence. Raj Thackeray himself had been summoned to the police station for interrogation, which lasted for several hours. The Shiv Sena vehemently denied Raj Thackeray's connection with Kini's death and reacted angrily to the action of the police in summoning the former to the police station for interrogation.

Delegations from both sides continued to meet me to give me their respective versions of the Kini case. The government came in for a good deal of criticism from the opposition because of the fact that the chief minister, Manohar Joshi, made a statement in the Assembly denying any complicity on the part of Raj Thackeray in the Kini episode. When the prime suspect in the murder case was released on bail by the court, the opposition raised a hue and cry in the Assembly that the weak defence on the part of the government prosecutor was responsible for this lapse. The State Legislature was prorogued a week in advance as the Kini issue had frequently disrupted proceedings. I tried to defuse the tension, which was mounting very fast, by assuring the opposition leaders that I was satisfied that the investigations were being conducted by the police impartially and that anyone found guilty would be strictly dealt with according to the law, irrespective of his political connection. I had kept myself fully informed about the progress of this case through my talks with the director general of police. Fortunately, the situation eased considerably within a few days when the public in general and the opposition in particular became convinced that the investigations were indeed being conducted with fairness and impartiality.

Another incident, which threatened to snowball into a serious catastrophe in the state, took place on 11 July 1997, when the statue of Dr Bhimrao Ambedkar* was found garlanded with chappals at Ghatkopar, a suburb of Mumbai. The Dalit community was infuriated by this incident and immediately started organizing large-scale protest demonstrations, which caused serious law and order problems. On the same day, the police opened fire on an irate crowd. Ten Dalits were killed and over twenty wounded. A delegation of opposition leaders met me at Raj Bhavan to demand the immediate dismissal of the government on the ground that the constitutional machinery had totally broken down in the state. The atmosphere in the city of Mumbai had become very surcharged and the attempt by the chief

---

* Dr Ambedkar was one of the chief 'architects' of the Constitution of India. He belonged to a backward community.

minister and the deputy chief minister to defend the police action only infuriated the people further. The opposition parties gave a call for a Mumbai bandh on 12 July, which paralysed life in the city. Reports of violent clashes too came in from various parts of Mumbai.

Joshi (the chief minister) and Munde (the deputy chief minister) called on me separately and assured me that they would punish the concerned police officers if they found that excessive force had been used to control the crowd. I told each of them that they should not have rushed so quickly to defend the police as the full facts about the firing were yet to be ascertained. I conveyed to them my deep concern about the law and order situation in Mumbai and the possibility of the trouble spreading to other parts of the state. They assured me that they would do everything possible to restore normalcy.

Tension, however, continued to steadily rise. Again, vehement demands for the dismissal of the government gained ground. The situation in the city worsened when a mob consisting of Shiv Sena activists led by Mohan Rawle (an MP) attacked the official residence of Chagan Bhujbal, then a leader belonging to the Congress, and destroyed furniture and other household items there. They were basically searching for Bhujbal, but fortunately he had locked himself up in his bedroom in the nick of time and managed to escape the wrath of the horde. The mob then moved on to the house of Madhukar Rao Pichad (the leader of the opposition in the Assembly) and shouted angry slogans against him.

The conduct of the Shiv Sena MP in leading an angry mob to attack Bhujbal came in for severe criticism from all sections of the public. It appeared as if the law and order situation in Mumbai would soon spiral out of control. I visited the hospital where the Dalits injured in the firing incident were undergoing treatment. The bodies of the ten Dalits who were killed in police firing were cremated without sparking off any more incidents of violence. Nevertheless, I was seriously concerned about the possible outbreak of more violence in the state.

On 15 July Balasaheb Thackeray, accompanied by his son Udhav and nephew Raj, called on me at the Raj Bhavan at 12.30 p.m. and were closeted with me for an hour and fifteen minutes. Thackeray told me that he was determined to do everything in his power to restore peace in the city. After discussing the happenings at Ghatkopar and Bhujbal's residence, I told Thackeray frankly that he had to rein in his followers immediately in order to avoid further deterioration of the law and order situation. I also told him that I had heard that he did not take advice from anyone regarding what he wanted to do. Nevertheless, I said I wished to make three suggestions. First, the Shiv Sena leaders should refrain from justifying the police action in Ghatkopar and instead wait till the enquiry revealed the full facts about the incident. Second, Thackeray should issue a statement, if possible that day itself, asking his party cadres to desist from indulging in any demonstrations or protests, and, instead, to cooperate with the law and order authorities to restore peace in the city. Third, he should take strong action against those partymen who participated in the destructive activities in Bhujbal's residence, irrespective of the action the government may take according to the law. Much to my surprise he accepted my suggestions fully and said he would take immediate action. I later learnt that he had issued the required statement and had adequately warned his partymen not to indulge in any provocative acts.

The Union home minister, Inderjit Gupta, arrived in Mumbai (on 15 July) and met me at the Raj Bhavan in the afternoon. I briefed him about Thackeray's meeting and also gave him my assessment that the law and order situation would start improving from then on. A series of delegations met Gupta and conveyed their apprehensions about the breakdown of law and order in the state, but he was able to convince them that normalcy would be restored immediately. Indeed, this was what actually happened within a couple of days after Thackeray's meeting with me.

✧

The atmosphere of confrontation between the ruling and opposition parties continued as before, after the Congress–NCP Government came to power in 1999; only now the roles were reversed. Again, several crisis situations arose. Again, both parties sent representations to me seeking my intervention.

The first major conflict between the ruling alliance and the opposition took place on 15 March 2000 when Narayan Rane and a group of opposition leaders allegedly tried to block the entry of the ministers and members of the Legislature at the gate of the compound housing the Legislature. The purpose was to protest against the action taken by the government to scale down the number of personnel deployed for ensuring security for Balasaheb Thackeray. An ugly situation arose, as even the speaker's entry was blocked by the demonstrators. At this stage, a large group of NCP and Congress legislators and partymen led by the deputy chief minister, Chagan Bhujbal, forced their way into the Legislature compound. In the melee that ensued, members from both sides indulged in kicking and pushing each other. Some individuals, including a lady minister, sustained bruises. The Legislature could not transact any business and both the Assembly and the Legislative Council had to be adjourned by the presiding officer.

More than one hundred opposition legislators, led by Rane, Munde and Nitin Gathkari met me at 1.30 p.m. (on 15 March). Their main complaints were that the Shiv Sena–BJP members, who were carrying out a peaceful demonstration outside the gate, had been attacked by the deputy chief minister and other members of the ruling coalition and that the constitutional machinery had broken down in the state. At 3.30 p.m. a delegation of over ninety members belonging to the ruling coalition called on me. They complained about the illegal action of the Shiv Sena–BJP leaders in blocking the entry of the legislators and the speaker at the gate. At 5.30 p.m. the speaker, Arun Gujarathi, and the chairman of the Legislative Council, N.S. Pharande, came to give their version of what had happened earlier in the day. The chief minister (Deshmukh) met me the next morning and briefed me about the events that had taken place outside and inside the Legislature from his perspective. In all these meetings, I counselled the exercise of patience and emphasized the importance of legislators setting an example for others to emulate as far as law and order and decorum were concerned. My basic effort was to defuse the tension and ensure that the confrontation between parties did not continue any further. The reaction of the people at large to these incidents was quite harsh in that they condemned both sides. The media too lambasted both sides for their behaviour on 15 March and expressed the apprehension that the public could lose respect for, and faith in, the institution of the Legislature itself.

✧

The provocation for a new crisis was provided by the Congress–NCP Government in July 2000 when it sanctioned the prosecution of Balasaheb Thackeray for an offence alleged to have been committed by him seven years earlier. A police report against Thackeray had been filed in 1994 for two editorials published in the Shiv Sena mouthpiece, *Samna*, in 1993 seeking permission of the government to initiate prosecution against him on the charge of inciting communal hatred. The previous Congress chief ministers, Sudhakar Rao Naik and Sharad Pawar, had not issued any order either sanctioning or refusing prosecution. Obviously, these two chief ministers did not want to aggravate the tensions prevalent in the city at that time by instituting a criminal case against Thackeray. The succeeding Shiv Sena–BJP Governments under Manohar Joshi and Narayan Rane also did not take any action on the reference from the police. Technically, the case had become time-barred, but there was provision in the law for condoning the delay in filing a charge sheet. Chagan Bhujbal, the new home minister (as well as deputy chief minister) in the Congress–NCP Government, who was a prominent Shiv Sena leader before he switched over to the Congress and then to the NCP, decided, all of a sudden, to take action on the police reference. He sanctioned the prosecution of Thackeray with the approval of the chief minister, Vilasrao Deshmukh. The Shiv Sena and the BJP, more so the Shiv Sena, reacted very sharply to this decision and attributed it to personal vendetta on the part of Bhujbal.

Very soon, reports began appearing in the press that the police would be arresting Thackeray for interrogation regarding the charge against him. In Mumbai, the Shiv Sena activists took to the streets and organized large-scale demonstrations against the proposed arrest of their leader. Government vehicles were set on fire and government offices were stoned. The whole city was plunged into a state of turmoil. Common people were apprehensive that communal riots, which had rocked the city during 1992–93, would again erupt. Some Shiv Sena leaders publicly threatened that, if Thackeray was arrested, they would make it impossible for the government to function. The police was in a quandary whether to arrest Thackeray or not, while the government took the stand that this was a matter for the police to decide on its own. One section of the public held the view that Bhujbal was trying to settle his personal scores with Thackeray and was unnecessarily creating problems for the government. Another section felt that the government had sent out the right message that no one was above the law. Palpable tension prevailed in the city for about a week. During this period representations came in from several concerned citizens that I should intervene in the matter and find an amicable solution that would uphold the dignity of the law and, at the same time not be seen as an attempt to humiliate Thackeray. Eventually, the police reached an understanding with Thackeray. On 25 July, Thackeray went over to the mayor's house where the police arrested him without provoking any anti-government demonstrations. When he was taken to the court, the magistrate was informed by the prosecutor that the police did not require Thackeray's remand to custody for interrogation. In other words, the police were not objecting to granting him bail. However, at this stage, something very unexpected and unusual happened. The magistrate, on his own, raised the question of the limitation in prosecuting Thackeray and abruptly pronounced an order dismissing the case against him. The magistrate's decision stunned both the prosecution and the defence though it helped in defusing the tension that had built up in the city. Critics of the government saw the entire episode as a blow to the prestige of the government and in particular to that of the home minister, Bhujbal. Later, the government went on appeal to the high court, which heard the case on 8 August 2000, and passed the observation that the magistrate's orders were unfounded in law. The case was posted to a later date for further hearing.

Meanwhile (on 25 July), some Shiv Sena MLAs, not aware of the fact that the case against Thackeray had been dismissed by the magistrate, created unprecedented scenes of pandemonium in the Assembly. They smashed the speaker's table and mace and flung chairs and microphones around. They even punched the marshals who were trying to restore order. In the midst of all this pell-mell, the House adopted resolutions suspending twelve Shiv Sena MLAs.

Six of them were suspended for one year each and another six for six months each. (The strength of the Shiv Sena was now reduced to sixty-two.) This was probably the ugliest scene, where disorder and violence dominated, ever witnessed inside the Maharashtra Assembly.

When the news about the dismissal of the case against Thackeray spread, the Shiv Sena–BJP activists started celebrating. They viewed the court's order as a great victory for their parties. Bhujbal offered to resign, but his offer was not accepted by the chief minister. The Assembly, which was prorogued on 25 July after suspending the Shiv Sena MLAs, was scheduled to meet again on 27 November. As a consequence, the suspended Shiv Sena MLAs would lose their rights for the interim period without the Assembly getting an opportunity to review its decision. The opposition members claimed that the suspension was a ruse resorted to by the government to avoid its downfall. They alleged that the coalition government would have collapsed as a result of major splits, which were expected to take place within the ruling parties.

I was staying at Pune when these unedifying developments took place in the Assembly. I returned to Mumbai on 27 July as I was informed that MLAs from both sides wanted to meet me. A 120-strong delegation of Shiv Sena and BJP MLAs led by Rane and Munde met me at the Durbar Hall of Raj Bhavan immediately after my return to Mumbai. They apologized for the misbehaviour of some of their MLAs inside the Assembly but vigorously protested against the suspension of their party MLAs and the proroguing of the Assembly. Their immediate concern was that I should not allow the early proroguing of the Legislative Council as well, which the government was reported to be planning. (The Shiv Sena–BJP alliance had a thin majority of two in the council.) If the Appropriation Bill, which was pending before the council were not passed by it, the Bill would have to be sent back to the Assembly, which had already been prorogued. Such a state of affairs would have created a deadlock for passing the Bill unless the Assembly was reconvened for this purpose.

The chief minister called on me on 28 July and briefed me about the recent developments. The government's stand was that the Bill should be passed through an Ordinance issued by the governor, after proroguing the council.

The passing of the Appropriation Bill thus became the subject of a major controversy in the state. I had been receiving diametrically opposite representations from both the government and the opposition. The former requested me to issue an Ordinance after proroguing the council and the latter insisted that the Bill should be formally introduced in the council. The government's view was that since the Bill was included in the 'list of business' for 28 July but could not be considered for want of time, that was adequate to satisfy the constitutional requirement that it had to be introduced in the council. However, I felt that mere listing of the Bill in the 'order paper' did not amount to the introduction of the Bill. The government was unhappy with my decision, but it ultimately realized that my stand was the right one. On 3 August, the Bill was again listed in the 'order paper' of the council. When it was formally introduced, the council passed it without any reservation much to the surprise of the government. I felt happy that both the government and the opposition had acted on my advice and avoided a constitutional crisis and also because the council members cooperated by not raising any objection to the Bill.

The confrontation between the government and the opposition continued on several other issues, but took a serious turn in June 2002, when the ruling coalition showed signs of cracking under the pressure of defections.

On 3 June the leaders of the Peasants' and Workers' Party (PWP), which had five members in the Assembly, and the CPI (M), which had two members, handed over to me letters withdrawing support to the government. Three of the PWP ministers informed me (in writing) that they were resigning from the government. Eight independent MLAs, who were till then backing the government, also presented themselves before me, and submitted letters withdrawing their support. Despite all these withdrawals, the government still had a majority in the Assembly, admittedly wafer thin.

On 4 June, I was to administer the oath to three new ministers from among the independents at the request of the chief minister in the place of the three PWP ministers who had quit. Rane, Munde and Ghatkari (leaders of the opposition Shiv Sena–BJP coalition) met me just before the swearing in ceremony of the three independents and requested me not to induct any new ministers into the cabinet, as according to them, the chief minister had lost his majority and, therefore, had no right to recommend the expansion of the Council of Ministers. But I rejected their request as I was satisfied that the chief minister still had the requisite majority and I was duty bound to accept his recommendation.

The matter did not end there. Very soon the process of defections and counterdefections was intensified. I was informed that the opposition parties had nearly succeeded in reducing the ruling coalition to a minority. On the same day (4 June) at 4.30 p.m., both Rane and Munde called on me. They were accompanied by three NCP MLAs who presented to me their letters of resignation from that party. A letter sent by fax from a fourth NCP MLA was also presented to me. Apart from these letters, two or three independents also sent letters to the effect that they were not supporting the Congress–NCP coalition any longer. It looked as if the government was fast slipping into a minority status in the Assembly. A rather comic sequence was enacted when one MLA who had quit earlier from the NCP, suddenly withdrew his letter of resignation, but soon changed his mind and sought refuge in the BJP fold. The political drama in Maharashtra seemed to scale new heights!

As the hours rolled by, the crisis deepened further. Five NCP MLAs, along with some independent MLAs, who had withdrawn support to the coalition government, were staying in the guesthouse of a Mumbai sports club. They were being protected by a group of Shiv Sena men. At 5 a.m., on 5 June, some NCP–Congress activists accompanied by about fifty policemen went to this place and demanded that they be allowed to see the 'deserters'. Rane, who was also staying in the guesthouse, immediately intervened and asked the police to withdraw from the scene. Later, a sizeable delegation of Shiv Sena–BJP leaders met me to protest against the alleged use of police force to browbeat those MLAs who had withdrawn support to the government.

The scene next shifted to the speaker's office. On 13 June the speaker of the Legislative Assembly disqualified the seven MLAs belonging to the NCP and its allies under the Anti-Defection Act, thus frustrating all hopes of the opposition to bring down the Congress–NCP government.

As far as I was concerned, this was the last serious confrontation between the government and the opposition that I had to witness, as I myself resigned as governor a month later for the reasons already mentioned in an earlier chapter.

✧

I would like to relate here an important initiative I had taken for combating the serious problem of HIV/AIDS in Maharashtra. What galvanized me was an article in *Time* (29 July 1996) under the caption 'India – AIDS Capital'. I was shocked to know from this article that India had, at that time, over three million HIV-infected people (a dubious distinction indeed) and that Maharashtra was one of the worst affected states. The article had highlighted the high incidence of AIDS in Mumbai city and had stressed the crucial importance of creating awareness among the people about the danger of the disease spreading rapidly and about the steps needed to prevent such a calamity. The state government, with financial assistance from the Centre, had initiated some pilot projects, but very little was being done for creating awareness about the disease among the specially vulnerable sections of the population such as university students, transport workers, police personnel and, most importantly, sex workers. I felt quite alarmed to learn that, besides Mumbai, several large towns in the state such as Thane, Pune and Sangli already had a very large number of HIV-infected persons and that, because of either ignorance or shyness on the part of the affected people, they had not sought medical help or taken precautions to prevent the further spread of the disease among other members of their families. Immediately after reading the *Time* article, I wrote to the chief minister, Manohar Joshi, that I would like to set up an Apex Committee on HIV/AIDS control under my chairmanship in order to launch and coordinate a campaign about AIDS awareness and to serve as a forum for discussing the issues relevant to AIDS control. I suggested to the chief minister that the state health minister could be the vice-chairman of the Apex Committee and that all departments of the government could be asked to lend their support for the awareness programmes to be launched. Joshi wholeheartedly welcomed the proposal and assured me that the state government would give all support, including financial assistance, for the programmes proposed by the Apex Committee. I took prompt action to constitute this committee. Top-level professionals from universities, municipal corporations, non-governmental organizations and medical institutes were inducted. At its first meeting, various subcommittees for different target groups were formed with specific terms of reference. The Apex Committee and its subcommittees soon swung into action and a statewide awareness campaign was launched. I myself participated in several programmes organized as part of this campaign. As stated earlier, HIV/AIDS control was adopted as the main theme for the inter-university sports festival (Ashwamedha), which had been newly instituted in the state. I am happy to state that in a very short time, these efforts proved to be successful in spreading the message about AIDS awareness throughout the state and that all sections of the people extended wholehearted cooperation to the work of the committees.

I must also mention here my active involvement in the work of a Committee of Governors constituted under my chairmanship by President K.R. Narayanan in August 2000 to look into certain aspects related to the welfare and the rights of the Scheduled Castes and Scheduled Tribes. The committee was expected to assess whether or not the various programmes formulated for the welfare of the SCs and STs were being implemented properly in conformity with their objectives. The committee was also expected to make observations and recommendations to help improve the implementation of various programmes. We held several meetings with the representatives of the state government, non-governmental organizations and social activists in the field. We also had useful interactions with the governors and lieutenant-governors of all the states/union territories and undertook regular field visits in order to assess the impact of the development schemes and prepared a comprehensive report for the consideration of the president.

✧

Let me round off this chapter by describing my unforgettable years in Maharashtra. After I left my home town in Kerala (at the age of fifteen) to pursue my college studies, Maharashtra was the state where I have had the longest continuous stay (nine and a half years) of my life. And this period has been also one of the happiest and satisfying phases of my life.

The governor of Maharashtra has three official residences known as Raj Bhavans, one each in Mumbai, Pune and Nagpur, and a mini-Raj Bhavan in the hill resort of Mahabaleshwar in Satara district. All these residences have been inherited from the British and each has a fascinating history of its own. As one who has had the opportunity of staying in most of the Raj Bhavans in India in the past, I can claim without fear of contradiction that the Mumbai Raj Bhavan stands out as the queen. Situated amidst 50 acres of land and surrounded by the Arabian Sea on three sides, the Raj Bhavan complex at Malabar Hill, Mumbai, is a mile-long stretch studded by thick forests, a sandy beach and several lush lawns and exquisite gardens. A special feature of the complex is that it houses independent buildings to serve as guesthouses, banquet halls and conference rooms, besides the governor's residence. A visitor coming from the Malabar Hill road along the lower road of the Raj Bhavan to the main building will be struck by the resplendent beauty of the evergreen forests on either side of the road and the sea, whose waves lash the sands and rocks on the left of the road. The view (in the night) from the Raj Bhavan of the 'Queen's Necklace' (Marine Drive), lighting up the Chowpathi beach and the buildings in Colaba, is indeed a fascinating one.

The Mumbai Raj Bhavan can boast of a valuable collection of beautiful carpets, fabulous paintings, exquisitely carved doors and elegant French-style chairs and sofas with very intricate portraits etched on them. Some of these precious items had been consigned to the Raj Bhavan storeroom as unserviceable or damaged items by some overvigilant comptrollers of the governor's household in the past! My wife retrieved them from the storeroom and had them restored with the help of the director of the Chhatrapati Shivaji Maharaj Vastu Sangrahalaya (CSMVS), previously known as the Prince of Wales Museum. These beautiful items of furniture have been placed in the governor's main office in the Raj Bhavan. We had also secured the valuable assistance of the experts of the museum in restoring the large panel paintings displayed on the eastern and western walls of the Durbar Hall. The large-sized portraits of various Maratha chieftains in their eighteenth-century attires, which were in a faded state due to neglect, have also been restored and placed in the main guesthouse. The newly relaid lawns and gardens (thanks to my wife's efforts) have considerably enhanced the beauty of the complex.

Visitors to the Raj Bhavan, both Indian and foreign, have often been curious to know the history of this building and some of the valuable items kept there. We thought that it would be useful to bring out a brochure giving the necessary information. Such a brochure was published in August 1997 with beautiful photographs of the buildings and the art objects and has been widely appreciated by all lovers of art and history.

Simultaneously, we had sought the help of the Mumbai Natural History Society (MNHS) to identify the plants, trees, birds and mammals in the Raj Bhavan forests and to prepare a booklet providing the relevant information. For instance the baobab tree and the ghost tree (found here) are rarely seen in other gardens and forests. Some graceful and colourful birds, including some forty-five peacocks, had made the Raj Bhavan forests their home. The scientists of the MNHS undertook a painstaking survey of the flora and fauna wealth of the Raj Bhavan area, and a beautifully illustrated book containing valuable information was published in August 1997. The survey showed that the Raj Bhavan forests contained thirty-six species of birds and 108 species of trees and plants. All of us involved in the work of renovation and restoration of the Raj Bhavan building and its precincts felt very happy and gratified when the Indian Heritage Society's prestigious Urban Heritage Award was conferred on the Raj Bhavan in 1998.

The tremendous interest exhibited by the public in the brochure on the Raj Bhavan and the booklet on its flora and fauna encouraged us to undertake the more ambitious project of publishing the detailed history of all the four Raj Bhavans of Maharashtra. Here again, the credit for the initiative and subsequent sustained efforts should go to my wife. We were fortunate in securing the valuable services of Dr Sadashiv Gorakshar, a former director of the CSMVS, to undertake this arduous task. In June 2002, a very informative book with superb photographs and sketches was published.

Every year, the governor moves to Raj Bhavan, Pune, during July–August because of the ferocious intensity of the monsoon in Mumbai. During this period, all the buildings in the Mumbai Raj Bhavan complex are covered with bamboo matting and locked in order to protect them from the high-velocity, salt-laden winds blowing in from the sea on three sides.

The Legislative Assembly of Maharashtra holds its winter session every year at Nagpur and the governor moves his residence for a few days to the Raj Bhavan there. I undertook most of the visits to the districts in the Vidarbha region during this sojourn. Similarly, I used to stay at the mini-Raj Bhavan in Mahabaleshwar for a few days in summer and used this period for visiting Satara and the neighbouring districts.

I can only conclude that no governor could have expected or received more by way of affection and support than what I had from all sections of the people of Maharashtra during my nine-and-a-half-year tenure there. That is why I describe my years in Maharashtra as 'the unforgettable years'.

Index